Common Law
and Feudal Society
in Medieval Scotland

T0386661

The **Edinburgh Classic Editions** series publishes influential works from the archive in context for a contemporary audience. These works shifted boundaries on first publication and are considered essential groundings in their disciplines. New introductions from contemporary scholars explain the cultural and intellectual heritage of these classic editions to a new generation of readers.

The Democratic Intellect: Scotland and her Universities in the Nineteenth Century
George Elder Davie
with an introduction by Murdo Macdonald and Richard Gunn
and a foreword by Lindsay Paterson
2013 (first published 1961)

Robert Bruce and the Community of the Realm of Scotland
G. W. S. Barrow
with an introduction by Michael Brown
2013 (first published 1965; fourth edition first published 2005)

Kingship and Unity: Scotland 1000–1306
G. W. S. Barrow
2015 (first published 1981; second edition first published 2003)

Historic New Lanark: The Dale and Owen Industrial Community since 1785
Ian Donnachie and George Hewitt
2015 (first published 1993)

Church and University in the Scottish Enlightenment: The Moderate Literati of Edinburgh
Richard B. Sher
2015 (first published 1985)

Common Law and Feudal Society in Medieval Scotland
Hector L. MacQueen
2016 (first published 1993)

www.edinburghuniversitypress.com

Common Law and Feudal Society in Medieval Scotland

HECTOR L. MACQUEEN

Edinburgh Classic Editions

EDINBURGH
University Press

Edinburgh University Press is one of the leading university presses in the UK. We publish academic books and journals in our selected subject areas across the humanities and social sciences, combining cutting-edge scholarship with high editorial and production values to produce academic works of lasting importance. For more information visit our website: www.edinburghuniversitypress.com

First published in 1993
Classic edition published 2016

Edinburgh University Press Ltd
The Tun – Holyrood Road
12 (2f) Jackson's Entry
Edinburgh EH8 8PJ

Printed and bound in Great Britain by
CRI Group (UK) Ltd, Croydon CR0 4YY

A CIP record for this book is available from the British Library

ISBN 978 1 4744 0746 5 (paperback)
ISBN 978 1 4744 0747 2 (webready PDF)
ISBN 978 1 4744 0748 9 (epub)

Corrigenda

Three places mentioned in the text in 1993 that could not then be identified were 'Coschogill' (p. 178), 'Derchestyr' (p. 39) and 'Rausburn' (p. 120). They have since been located. Coshogle is a farm between Drumlanrig and Sanquhar in Upper Nithsdale, Dumfriesshire (Ordnance Survey grid reference NS 863050). Darnchester, which is also a farm, sits near The Hirsel in Berwickshire (OS, NT 815428). Rawburn, yet another farm, lies to the west of Longformacus in Berwickshire (OS, NT 673561).

For Frances

Contents

Acknowledgements

Authors' spouses seem often to be left to last place in acknowledgements such as this. But as Frances has lived with this present work since its inception in doctoral research before we were married, it seems right to start by thanking her for all the tolerance, support and encouragement which she has given over the last fourteen years. The dedication can only begin to indicate how much I owe to her. I am also grateful to Sarah, Patrick and Jamie for at least seeming to enjoy excursions to locations which had been the subject of medieval legal battles; I hope that other holidays compensated for the paternal obsessions. The supervisors of the thesis on which this book is based were David Sellar and Geoffrey Barrow, and my debts to them are almost as long-standing as those to my wife. David not only put up with seven years of supervision but agreed in effect to relive the experience by reading the whole of a first draft of the book, while Geoffrey offered invaluable help with one particular chapter, and answered many other questions. Alan Borthwick and John Cairns were two other long-suffering friends who read the whole work in draft, while others undertook chapters or groups of chapters: Paul Brand, Archie Duncan, Sandy Grant and Keith Stringer have all earned my thanks in this respect. The comments which I received were uniformly helpful, and have improved the book beyond measure. Those named have also been endlessly generous in giving me access to the fruits of their research, published and unpublished, answering questions, talking over problems of legal history with me, and being willing to listen as well; this has also been true not only of my parents, John and Winifred MacQueen, but also of John Bannerman, Trevor Chalmers, David Fergus, Angelo Forte, George Gretton, John Hudson, Paul Hyams, Athol Murray and William Windram. The regular conferences of the Scottish Legal History Group and the Scottish Medievalists, and the biennial British Legal History Conference, have enabled me to meet many others, too numerous to name individually, from whom I have learned much over the years. I am grateful to them all, but accept that only I can be held responsible for what is here set down. I wish also to mention the institutions from which I have received assistance, in particular the Faculty of Law and Law Libraries at Edinburgh, which have provided a supportive and encouraging daily working environment. Some of the ideas expressed in this book were first formed in legal history classes at Edinburgh, others in a legal history course taught at the Cornell Law School in the spring semester 1991 (and I give my thanks to the Dean of the Law School, Russell Osgood, for making that possible). In addition, Edinburgh's Department of Scottish History has always been welcoming to a stray lawyer. In Edinburgh the legal historian is also lucky in having access to the magnificent collections of the University Library, the National Library of Scotland and the Scottish Record Office, from the staff of which I have received much help and kindness over the years. Any failings in this work cannot be attributed to difficulties in obtaining material with which to work.

Some of the material published here has appeared previously elsewhere, although all of it has been carefully reconsidered and much rewritten. I am pleased to acknowledge these previous publications as follows:

'Dissasine and Mortancestor in Scots Law', *Journal of Legal History*, iv (1983), p. 21.

'The Brieve of Right Revisited', in *The Political Context of Law: Proceedings of the Seventh British Legal History Conference Canterbury 1985*, ed. R. Eales and D. Sullivan (Hambledon Press, London, 1987).

(with W. J. Windram), 'Laws and Courts in the Burghs', in *The Scottish Medieval Town*, ed. M. Lynch, G. Stell and M. Spearman (Edinburgh, 1988).

I am also grateful to Judith Cripps of the Aberdeen City Archives for assistance with providing the illustration on the dustjacket.

Finally I must acknowledge the cheerful forbearance of Edinburgh University Press in dealing with a dilatory author. I hope that their patience will be rewarded in this book.

Hector L. MacQueen
Old College, Edinburgh

Note on Editions of Texts

It is necessary to say a few words about the editions of the main medieval treatises of Scots law which have been used in this book. The two principal works are *Regiam Majestatem and Quoniam Attachiamenta*. Until recently, there was no satisfactory critical edition of either text. Sir John Skene published versions in Latin and Scots in 1609, both of which have been subjected to severe criticism (some of it perhaps a little unfair) ever since. In the nineteenth century, Cosmo Innes and Thomas Thomson published another edition of the Latin texts in the first volume of the *Acts of the Parliaments of Scotland*. Subsequent scholarship has shown these editions also to be defective in various ways. In 1947, the Stair Society published further texts under the editorship of Lord Cooper. Unfortunately, these were based on the work of Skene, although Lord Cooper provided cross-references to the *APS* edition along with translations. Very recently, an authoritative critical edition of *Quoniam* was at last produced, by Dr David Fergus of Glasgow University in his doctoral thesis, but this has not yet been published (it is hoped, however, that the work will become a Stair Society publication in due course).

Accordingly, in citing and discussing *Quoniam*, Dr Fergus' text has been used; it is cited as *QA* (*Fergus*). Because it is not yet published, I have decided to give references also to the *APS* and Cooper editions, citing them as *QA* (*APS*) and *QA* (*Cooper*) respectively. In the absence of an authoritative version of *Regiam*, I have chosen again to use and cite both the *APS* and Cooper texts, citing them as *RM* (*APS*) and *RM* (*Cooper*) respectively. As a result, the interested reader who consults the relevant footnote references will quickly perceive some of the basic problems which have bedevilled the use of the texts of medieval Scots law. *Regiam* is cited by book and chapter numbers, *Quoniam* by chapter numbers alone.

It is at present generally accepted that the English works known as *Glanvill* and *Bracton* were not written by their eponyms, but I have nonetheless continued to speak as though they had been, indicating that this is not the case by italicising the names. It may also be worth mentioning that Bracton is now thought to be mainly a work of the 1220s. *Glanvill* is cited by book and chapter number in the most recent edition by G. D. G. Hall, and *Bracton* by foliation, although references to the volume and page numbers of the most recent (four volume) edition by S. E. Thorne have been added for convenience.

Preface

This book began life in 1978 in research towards a Ph.D. in the Faculty of Law at the University of Edinburgh.[1] Two years before, David Sellar's Honours course on the History of Scots Law, and the sense that a whole field of study lay out there awaiting further research, had begun to inspire my interest in the subject. David highlighted the medieval more than the early-modern aspects of Scottish legal history, while also emphasising a theme of continuity in the development of the law and legal system down to the present.[2] He presented a direct challenge to the orthodoxy established in the mid-twentieth century by the scholar-judge Lord Cooper of Culross (1892–1955).[3] Cooper's line had been that the story of Scots law was one of 'false starts and rejected experiments',[4] ending only with the 1681 publication of the seminal *Institutions* of James Dalrymple, Viscount Stair. The book came in the nick of time to rescue at least Scots private law from the fate of absorption into English law after the Anglo-Scottish Union of 1707. Borrowing from England had been the false start and the rejected experiment of the 'Scoto-Norman' period before 1300; there had then followed a 'Dark Age' for the system.[5] From this it began to be rescued by the development of a central court in the sixteenth century, the emergence of a legal profession around that court, and (resulting in part from the education of many members of that profession in the law schools of continental Europe) a reception of the learned Roman and Canon laws. The end result, systematised by Stair, was something quite distinct from English law, and it was expressly preserved by the Treaty and Acts of Union along with the separate legal system within the newly united kingdom of Great Britain.

My initial thesis topic was the action or remedy of spuilzie. This seemed an excellent candidate with which to test the argument about rejected experiments and continuity in the development of Scots law. Spuilzie had undoubtedly formed part of Scots law since at the latest the early fifteenth century, but had survived down to the twentieth, the latest reported case when I began my research having been decided only seven years before.[6] The action was thought to be one for the recovery of possession of goods by a person who had been dispossessed of them. The claim was one that the ex-possessor could make even against the owner of the goods. In earlier times, however, and under the name ejection, it seemed to have allowed recovery of possession of land as well as of goods.[7] The name of the action, it was suggested, derived from the *actio spolii* of the medieval Canon law, whence also the maxim often used to summarise its fundamental principle: *spoliatus ante omnia restituendus est.*[8] In continental European jurisdictions, the *actio spolii* had been received into their developing systems, displacing the Roman possessory interdict *unde vi*.[9] But it was also suggested in Scotland that, at least in relation to the possession of land, the spuilzie action had taken over from the earlier brieve of novel dissasine, itself a thirteenth-century borrowing from English law's assize of novel disseisin.[10]

It was this last point that would ultimately take my focus away from spuilzie, although I did not abandon the subject altogether.[11] In a major challenge to Cooper's 'Scoto-Norman' analysis of the twelfth and thirteenth centuries, Geoffrey Barrow (who became the second supervisor of my thesis in 1981) had shown (among many other things about the secular legal system of the period) clear evidence for the use of the brieve of novel dissasine in the justiciar's court in the 1260s.[12] My own realisation that this same brieve was certainly still in use in the 1430s, referred to in a practical treatise of the mid-1450s, and probably still known at the beginning of the sixteenth century[13] made it difficult to see spuilzie as a lineal descendant or replacement of that particular form of action, especially when there was reference to the wrong of 'spoliation' in the fourteenth century as well.[14]

This survival of novel dissasine well into the fifteenth century matched other evidence that Sheriff Hector McKechnie had set out in a lecture at Glasgow University in 1956. The brieve of right, another form of action for the recovery of land for which there was also pre-1300 evidence of borrowing from England, had continued in use until at least the beginning of the sixteenth century.[15] My own researches confirmed this observation and provided further evidence to support it.[16]

McKechnie's lecture, viewed as a whole, further demonstrated that the procedural system of brieves in general had not only lasted long after 1300, indeed down to the twentieth century, but had also been developed and innovated upon until at least 1500. However courteously expressed, the lecture delivered what was very much a knockout blow to Cooper's overall thesis of discontinuous legal development after 1300.[17]

McKechnie did not draw attention to the fifteenth-century evidence for novel dissasine already mentioned, but he did point out a confusion about the brieve of mortancestor or mortancestry into which writers on

Scots law had fallen from the late sixteenth century onwards. That was to give the name 'mortancestor' to the process for service of heirs to land instituted by the brieve known in pre-1500 sources as the brieve of inquest.[18] What my ongoing researches revealed was that the brieve of mortancestry itself, a process by which an heir could recover land being wrongfully occupied by some third party, was also introduced into Scotland before 1300 on the model of the English assize of *mort d'ancestor*, and continued to enjoy its own separate existence beyond 1500 (although perhaps not very long beyond).[19]

What we therefore seemed to have in Scotland up to 1500 was a scheme of actions for the recovery of land: (1) the possessory novel dissaine; (2) the protection of close heirs against intruders under mortancestry; and (3) the brieve of right for all other claims based upon heritable entitlements to land. Moreover, the evidence for the brieves in action showed clear consistency across time with the accounts and styles provided by the treatises and formularies of medieval Scots law. The brieve of right pertained to the jurisdiction of the sheriff and burgh courts, and the other two brieves to the justiciary court; the actions were decided by juries or assizes held in these courts. The brieves were 'pleadable' in that the issue to be determined by the jury was defined by the parties exchanging allegations of fact along with admissions and denials, and the decision of the jury on that issue, once defined, was put into immediate effect. This contrasted with the 'retourable' brieves exemplified by the brieve of inquest, where the jury had to answer questions set out in the brieve and return ('retour') their answers to the royal office that had issued the brieve so that it could order the further action then required: for example, to give the identified heir sasine of the lands in question.[20]

A final point about brieves with which McKechnie had dealt only in passing was the existence in Scots law before 1300 and after 1400 of a jurisdictional rule that said that no person could be made to answer for his freeholding except by the king's pleadable brieve[21] – that is, as it now seemed in the light of my other researches, one or other of novel dissaine, mortancestry and right. Once again there was a parallel rule in England. Much more evidence for the existence of this rule in Scotland was in print than had been the case when McKechnie wrote,[22] while in 1966 Alan Harding had published a fundamentally important study of the king's peace and protection in Scotland in which he identified what I now called 'the brieves rule' as an aspect of his subject.[23] Put in simple terms, the king offered protection to stability of tenure by insisting on the use of certain procedures if the sitting tenant was to be removed. At the same time, these procedures enabled external parties to make claims based upon either their prior possession or their rights of inheritance. Although

Harding took no particular notice of novel dissasine or mortancestry in this regard, he suggested that originally the brieve of right had been simply the king exercising his powers of protection by ordering that right be done, implying later elaboration from this base.[24] Taking all together, then, these pleadable brieves and the brieves rule did indeed amount to a system for the protection of rights to land, which had endured from at the latest 1250 until, at the earliest, 1500. The idea that the development of Scots law in this area on English lines had been rejected after 1300 was clearly no longer tenable; continuity of development appeared, in this regard at least, to characterise the whole medieval period.

There was, nonetheless, an apparent discontinuity in the story that needed further investigation. The whole edifice of pleadable brieves in relation to land disputes seemed to disappear after 1500. The most obvious possible explanation for this, as McKechnie had hinted,[25] was the rise within the king's council in that period of a central court based mainly in Edinburgh – the court that became known as the Court of Session, and succeeded in establishing its superiority in non-criminal matters over the local sheriff, burgh and justiciary courts. In 1532 the court was reconstituted as a College of Justice with jurisdiction in all civil actions.[26] While this development too had its elements of continuity stretching back well before 1500, as Archie Duncan had shown in another major contribution published in 1958,[27] a key fact, as it seemed to me, was that the court's medieval forerunners had no jurisdiction in cases dealing with disputes about 'fee and heritage' – that is, about heritable entitlements to land. But by 1543 at the latest the position had been reversed: the court claimed, not just jurisdiction in heritage cases, but an exclusive jurisdiction.[28]

That the earlier restriction on council related in some way to, or was even to be explained by, the 'brieves rule' seemed to gain support from a mid-fifteenth-century document in which William, Richard and Henry Graham invoked both it and the exclusion of the king's council from cases of fee and heritage in defending an action brought against them in the latter body in respect of the lands of Hutton in Dumfriesshire.[29] But the document shows that there were two separate jurisdictional rules by its date, each having its distinct effect, and I argued that any link between these rules must be indirect, rather than immediate or causal. My proposal was that council and, indeed, the Scottish parliament originally enjoyed a jurisdiction that supplemented ordinary legal processes as necessary: for example, in the regulation of possession of land prior to any dispute about the actual entitlements of the parties.[30] I carefully avoided any suggestion that there was here a latent jurisdictional division between law and equity, bearing in mind that the formal English division of labour between the courts of common law and the courts of equity was a relatively late development in that system. But it may be that Scotland did not go down that route only because from the supplementary processes in the king's council there emerged a court that eventually assumed authority over all other courts (including the ecclesiastical tribunals), thereby establishing and maintaining a unity of judicial administration in which law and equity could be treated together rather than separately from each other. The Scottish legal system changed significantly in the sixteenth century, therefore; but the change was not brought about by any sense that the preceding three centuries had led into an unlit blind alley from which contemporaries recognised a need to make escape. Rather, the process was much more organic or evolutionary, in which part of the established system took on new functions, while the need for some of the other parts gradually reduced to zero. In S. F. C. Milsom's striking phrases about legal development in England:

> Lawyers have always been preoccupied with today's details, and have worked with their eyes down. The historian, if he is lucky, can see why a rule came into existence, what change left it working injustice, how it came to be evaded, how the evasion produced a new rule, and sometimes how that new rule in its turn came to be overtaken by change. But he misunderstands it all if he endows the lawyers who took part with vision on any comparable scale, or attributes to them any intention beyond getting today's client out of his difficulty.[31]

No doubt in this process there was at least implicit criticism of the parts of the law not used, for no longer serving the purposes of users of the system as well as did the now developing parts. But change came about within the system rather than being a reaction to a perception of its having already fallen apart more or less completely.

The significance of the relationship between medieval Scots and English law underpinned at least three other points that I tried to make in my thesis and elaborated on much more in the book that followed some eight years after completion of the former.

First, the development of the writ of right, the assizes of novel disseisin and *mort d'ancestor*, and the rule requiring writs in cases about freeholdings had long been seen as crucial in the development of a Common Law in England in the twelfth century, in the sense that royal justice alone could create a law and legal system that was indeed common to the whole kingdom. The same could be said of Scotland, albeit at a somewhat later time. But what triggered these developments? Milsom had transformed thinking on the subject in England by suggesting that the royal aim in the twelfth century had been, not to create a common law superseding non-royal forms of secular justice, but rather to make what he called 'the legal framework of English feudalism' work according to its own norms; that is, to compel the lords of whom land was held by tenants to do justice to them in accordance with the customary forms of tenure, or else the king would.[32] When I was writing my thesis, Milsom's views had only just begun to receive critical analysis from others, notably Robert C Palmer;[33] but, by the time I came to convert the thesis into a book, many more had waded in, and I therefore sought to make a Scottish contribution to the debate.[34] This linked the subject much more firmly to another, even wider, discussion launched by an article published in 1974 by Elizabeth A. R. Brown.[35] In it she challenged the notion of feudalism as a distortion of the realities of medieval Europe as a whole. In Scotland the major contributors had been Geoffrey Barrow (who had articulated most effectively the concept of a feudal Scotland, albeit principally as a system of government) and Archie Duncan (who had memorably doubted whether the 'tired structure' of land tenure in the thirteenth century had any significance beyond legal formality).[36] In the book I was accordingly led into a much fuller account of, in particular, lordship courts and their role in regulating land tenure, and the relationship that had to royal justice.[37] The view that I took, and continued to elaborate in subsequent publications, was that tenurial relationships remained significant in Scotland from the twelfth to the end of the fifteenth centuries.[38] Even if we accept, with Duncan, that tenurial relationships were by no means invariably indicators of significant social relationships in the Middle Ages, legal form was always critical to the ownership, transfer and inheritance of land; while the landed society of the period can scarcely be understood at all without an appreciation of the forms in which their relationships and transactions were put into effect. Lordship courts played an ongoing role of some importance in their administration throughout, and a key theme still to be fully worked out is the interplay between royal and other jurisdictions, such as those of barony and regality and also burghs, throughout the medieval period.[39] I have continued to find the distinguished work of Keith Stringer and Alexander Grant of particular help in this regard.[40]

The second point is that medieval Scots law was by no means a carbon copy of its English counterpart.[41] The judicial system in existence in Scotland by 1250 was much simpler, much more localised and much less professionally based than royal justice in England. It grew alongside the reach and control of the kings themselves, as I attempted to show in a series of maps published in the *Atlas of Scottish History to 1707* in 1996,[42] and even in the fourteenth and fifteenth centuries that was challenged by English occupation along the border from Berwick to Lochmaben.[43] But otherwise it changed very little before 1500 apart from the growth of judicial business in parliament and the king's council.

The brieve system too remained relatively simple. Novel dissasine may have spawned a brieve *de aqueductu* in the fifteenth century to deal with dispossession of watercourses,[44] but the brieve of right in the mature form it had probably achieved before 1300 looks like a consolidation of the writ of right and the writ *precipe* in England, and needed no development like the multiplication of the writs of entry that occurred south of the border after Magna Carta in 1215.[45] Mortancestry was adjusted by statute in 1318, as was novel dissasine, with the legislation in both cases implicitly bringing Scots law into line with developments that had taken place in England after the first introduction of the brieves in Scotland;[46] but there is no other evidence thereafter to suggest further Scottish developments to take account of anything happening in England.

All this tends to suggest that the legal borrowing, or transplanting, from English into Scots law in the medieval period was not uncritical or simply a by-product of the fact that before the Wars of Independence a substantial number of Scotland's leading landholders also held land in England and therefore looked to have the same legal regime applying in each country. It may well be that the different political and social conditions applying in the two kingdoms, especially after the wars, led to the establishment and then the preservation of a simpler system in Scotland; it was certainly important that there was no parallel to the emergence of the professional lay judiciary or the organised secular legal practitioners pleading in the royal courts in England well before the end of the thirteenth century.[47] Notaries public, on the other hand, began to proliferate in the fourteenth century in Scotland, clearly playing an increasingly important role in legal practice in and out of court;[48] while, as shown in some detail in the book and other articles published since it came out, laymen who were skilled and knowledgeable in matters of law also become more and more visible after 1300, with some at least in the fifteenth century being also graduates.[49] These were perhaps the forerunners of the class of men who in later centuries would become members of the Faculty of Advocates in Edinburgh.

My final point on the relevance of English to Scottish legal history is that I never intended to suggest that the rising Common law was the only influence on the making of Scots law in the medieval period up to 1500. Lord Cooper was surely correct to discern the importance of the Canon law and the church courts as at least equal and even greater than that of the common law.[50] This book confirms that insight at least incidentally,[51] and I have sought elsewhere to demonstrate the point in greater detail, highlighting the way in which the secular and the ecclesiastical interacted in the administration and development of the law, including on the criminal as well as on the civil side.[52] Peter Stein and the late Bill Gordon have demonstrated in as much depth and detail as the sources may allow the role played by Roman law (mainly via the Canon law) from the twelfth

century on.[53] My own work has also sought to show the importance of
what may for convenience be called customary law: not just Celtic or
Gaelic custom, as perhaps exemplified in particular by the laws of
Galloway,[54] but also the possibly Anglo-Saxon *wrang and unlaw*, *bloodwite*,
twertnay and *burthensak* as jurisdictional and procedural terms that
continued to feature in Scots law into the fifteenth century in at least
some cases.[55] *Regiam Majestatem*, the key Scottish legal text of the later
Middle Ages and beyond, may have been largely based upon the late-
twelfth-century English text *Glanvill*; but it was not a slavish copy, and it
also contained significant material drawn from Canon and Roman law as
well as the more native and customary sources.[56] In other words, many
elements went into the mix of law in medieval Scotland, and the Common
law was but one of them.

In conclusion, it has been surprisingly pleasant to return to research
done many years ago and to find that, despite much additional and
important corrective work by others in the same or adjacent fields since
it was published,[57] its basic arguments as just outlined seem still to hold
water. Perhaps a last observation can be made, building on the earlier
discussion of the concept of feudalism and the connection between legal
and social relationships. One of the most important articles to be
published during the time of my Ph.D. research was Jenny Wormald's
justly celebrated piece on the bloodfeud in medieval and early modern
Scotland, with its emphasis on 'informal' justice and dispute resolution
over the more 'formal' processes of the law.[58] Mark Godfrey has produced
a perceptive discussion of this seeming contrast in the Festschrift for
Dr Wormald published in 2014.[59] In the context of my own project as
described in this Preface, the 'justice of the feud' at first looked like a
refreshingly different take on the period Lord Cooper had characterised
as the 'Dark Age of Scottish legal history', albeit one that underplayed the
strength of the legal system in the fourteenth and fifteenth centuries. The
arguments of Dr Wormald (and also Alexander Grant[60]) that the period
was not one of constant violent conflict between crown and an over-
mighty nobility, or between members of the nobility themselves, but
rather one where there was at base a common agenda in the pursuit of
peace, stability and the preservation of the kingdom's independence,
chimed well (as it seemed to me) with my own perception of an operative
law and legal system in the period. Indeed, the law was a crucial dimension
of the kingdom's sense of its own identity among other kingdoms.[61] If
parties more often negotiated than litigated the way to the solution of
their disputes, it could be said that they did so 'in the shadow of the law',[62]
which not only set out the parties' respective legal entitlements but also
often actually provided the means (arbitration procedures, formally
written binding agreements of various kinds, royal orders upholding

agreed arrangements) by which settlement was achieved and enforced.[63] More recent scholarship has, however, tended to emphasise politics, patronage and relative power (including the power to wreak violence against other people and property without any apparent concern about redress) as the keys to understanding the nature of society and events in our period. The significance of law, legal rights and legal processes is downplayed in this perspective if not actually altogether bypassed. My response would still be that at least sometimes, and probably much more often than that, these are always factors in understanding the activities, events and institutions we are researching.[64] Law was (and is) a crucial part of the fabric of society, determining personal status, entitlements to property and inheritance, and (where needed) disputes about things that had gone wrong. So elemental is it to social and indeed to political relationships, in fact, that, if we do not at least attempt to comprehend it, we may actually miss it altogether.

Hector L. MacQueen
Edinburgh
30 May 2015

NOTES

1. The finished version is Hector L. MacQueen, 'Pleadable brieves and jurisdiction in heritage in later medieval Scotland', Edinburgh University Ph.D., 1985 (accessible online at <https://www.era.lib.ed.ac.uk/handle/1842/6861>). It is cited below as 'MacQueen, "Pleadable brieves"'. This book is cited below as 'MacQueen, *CLFS*'.

2. Much of the flavour and content of David Sellar's Honours course is epitomised in his contribution, 'A historical perspective', in M. C. Meston, W. D. H. Sellar and Lord Cooper, *The Scottish Legal Tradition* (Saltire Society and Stair Society; Edinburgh, 1991), 29–64.

3. On Cooper's contribution see now my papers: 'Legal nationalism: Lord Cooper, legal history and comparative law', *Edinburgh Law Review*, 9 (2005), 395–406; 'Two Toms and an ideology for Scots law: T. B. Smith and Lord Cooper of Culross', in Elspeth Christie Reid and David Carey Miller (eds), *A Mixed Legal System in Transition: T. B. Smith and the Progress of Scots Law* (Edinburgh, 2005), 44–72; 'Legal nationalism: The case of Lord Cooper', in N. M. Dawson (ed.), *Reflections on Law and History* (Dublin, 2006), 83–98; and '"A picture of what will be some day the law of the civilised nations": Comparative law and the destiny of Scots law', in A. Brzozowski, W. Kocot and K. Michalowska (eds), *Towards Europeanization of Private Law: Essays in Honour of Professor Jerzy Rajski* (Warsaw, 2007), 521–38.

4. Lord Cooper, 'The Scottish legal tradition', in Meston et al., *Scottish Legal Tradition*, 65–89 at 70.

5. This 'Dark Age' theory was strangely accepted by Cooper's distinguished medievalist contemporary, William Croft Dickinson, despite the latter's invaluable work on the medieval and early modern sheriff, barony and burgh courts: see his 'The administration of justice in medieval Scotland', *Aberdeen University Review*, 34 (1951–2), 338–51.

6. *Mercantile Credit Co. Ltd* v. *Townsley* 1971 SLT (Sh Ct) 37; and see further A. F. Rodger, 'Spuilzie in the modern world', *Scots Law Times*, news section (1970), 33–6.

7. When I began my research, most writing on spuilzie, historical or current in intent, was by David M. Walker: see his 'The development of reparation', *Juridical Review*, 64 (1952), 101–34 at 112–18; *Civil Remedies in Scotland* (Edinburgh, 1974), 1039–40; *The Law of Delict in Scotland* (Edinburgh, 1966), i. 23; ii. 1001–10; 2nd edn (1981), 23–4, 1002–11. For more recent writing on the modern law of spuilzie, see Kenneth G. C. Reid, *The Law of Property in Scotland* (Edinburgh, 1996), paras 161–6; D. L. Carey Miller with David Irvine, *Corporeal Moveables in Scots Law* (Edinburgh, 2005), paras 10.24–10.31; Raffaele Caterina, 'Concepts and remedies in the law of possession', *Edinburgh Law Review*, 8 (2004), 267–72; D. L. Carey Miller, 'Spuilzie: Dead, dormant or manna from heaven?': Issues concerning protection of possessory interests in Scots law', in M. de Waal and H. Mostert (eds), *Essays in Honour of C. G. van der Merwe* (Cape Town, 2011), 129–50; John Townsend, 'Raising Lazarus: Why spuilzie should be resurrected', *Aberdeen Student Law Review*, 2 (2011), 22–51. The latest case to discuss spuilzie is *Calor Gas Ltd* v. *Express Fuels (Scotland) Ltd* [2008] CSOH 13, 2008 SLT 123, paras 51–4. On the historical side, see A. M. Godfrey, *Civil Justice in Renaissance Scotland: The Origins of a Central Court* (Leiden and Boston, 2009), 239–49. Dr Andrew Simpson is now pursuing detailed historical research on the subject.

8. On the *actio spolii*, see still Francesco Ruffini, *L'actio spolii: Studio storico-giuridico* (Turin, 1889).

9. James Gordley and Ugo Mattei, 'Protecting possession', *American Journal of Comparative Law*, 44 (1996), 293–334 at 306 ff.

10. See Walker, 'Development of reparation', 107–12.

11. See MacQueen, 'Pleadable brieves', 268, 269, 287–92, 304; MacQueen, *CLFS*, 224–8, 233–5.

12. G. W. S. Barrow, 'The Scottish justiciar in the twelfth and thirteenth centuries', *Juridical Review*, NS 16 (1971), 97–148 at 126–8, republished in *The Kingdom of the Scots* (London, 1973), 83–138 at 114–16; 2nd edn (Edinburgh, 2003), 68–11 at 92–3. The article originated as 'Judges and judiciaries', the Stair Society Annual Lecture for 1966.

13. See MacQueen, 'Pleadable brieves', 180–200; MacQueen, *CLFS*, ch. 5.

14. MacQueen, 'Pleadable brieves', 90, 142; MacQueen, *CLFS*, 111, 129, 243 n. 47.

15. Hector McKechnie, *Judicial Process upon Brieves, 1219–1532* (23rd David Murray Lecture, University of Glasgow, 1956), 10, 17, 19, 21, 24–5, 29. McKechnie noted only in passing early evidence for novel dissasine: pp. 10, 17.
16. See MacQueen, 'Pleadable brieves', 215–33; MacQueen, *CLFS*, ch. 7.
17. See, e.g., McKechnie, *Brieves*, 16 ('Naturally, I tread softly in such footsteps').
18. McKechnie, *Brieves*, 11.
19. See MacQueen, 'Pleadable brieves', 200–14; MacQueen, *CLFS*, ch. 6.
20. See further MacQueen, 'Pleadable brieves',153–77; MacQueen, *CLFS*, 122–9, chs 5–7; A. A. M. Duncan (ed.), *Scottish Formularies* (Stair Society, vol. 58; Edinburgh, 2011), A18–21; B91, 106–7; TCa17–18; La21–3.
21. McKechnie, *Brieves*, 15, 18.
22. See MacQueen, 'Pleadable brieves', 125–76; MacQueen, *CLFS*, 105–13.
23. Alan Harding, 'The medieval brieves of protection and the development of the common law', *Juridical Review*, NS 11 (1966), 115–49 at 128–9. Professor Harding was later the external examiner of my thesis.
24. Harding, 'Brieves of protection', 125–8.
25. McKechnie, *Brieves*, 17, 21, 25, 29.
26. See Godfrey, *Civil Justice in Renaissance Scotland*, especially ch. 3.
27. A. A. M. Duncan, 'The central courts before 1532', in G. C. H. Paton (ed.), *Introduction to Scottish Legal History* (Stair Society, vol. 20; Edinburgh, 1958), 321–40.
28. My first detailed analysis of this development was published as 'Jurisdiction in heritage and the Lords of Council and Session after 1532', in W. D. H. Sellar (ed.) *Miscellany II* (Stair Society, vol. 35; Edinburgh, 1984), 61–85. See now Godfrey, *Civil Justice in Renaissance Scotland*, ch. 7.
29. *HMC, Various Collections*, v. 77. The original can now be found at National Records of Scotland GD1/1430/1. See MacQueen, 'Pleadable brieves', 14–16, 150–1, 310; MacQueen, *CLFS*, 112, 215; and further R. C. Reid, 'The border Grahams, their origin and distribution', *Transactions of the Dumfriesshire and Galloway Natural History Society*, 38 (1959–60), 85–113 at 89–91, dating the document to 1460.
30. See MacQueen, 'Pleadable brieves', 249–64; MacQueen, *CLFS*, ch. 8.
31. S. F. C. Milsom, *Historical Foundations of the Common Law*, 2nd edn (London, 1981), 7.
32. See in particular two works by S. F. C. Milsom: *Historical Foundations of the Common Law*, 2nd edn (London, 1981) (1st edn 1969); *The Legal Framework of English Feudalism* (Cambridge, 1976).
33. See especially Robert C Palmer, 'The feudal framework of English law', *Michigan Law Review*, 79 (1981), 1130–64.

34. MacQueen, *CLFS*, ch. 1. For my earlier thoughts, see MacQueen, 'Pleadable brieves', 234–48.
35. E. A. R. Brown, 'The tyranny of a construct: Feudalism and the historians of medieval Europe', *American Historical Review*, 79 (1974), 1063–88.
36. On Barrow, see Hector L. MacQueen, 'Geoffrey Wallis Steuart Barrow, 1924–2013: A memoir', *Innes Review*, 65 (2014), 1–12; and see, on the other side, A. A. M. Duncan, *Scotland: The Making of the Kingdom* (Edinburgh, 1975), 368–409.
37. MacQueen, *CLFS*, ch. 2. See now also Cynthia J. Neville, *Land, Law and People in Medieval Scotland* (Edinburgh, 2010), ch. 1.
38. See Hector L. MacQueen, 'Tears of a legal historian: Scottish feudalism and the ius commune', *Juridical Review*, NS 48 (2003), 1–28, responding to Susan Reynolds, *Fiefs and Vassals: The Medieval Evidence Reinterpreted* (Oxford, 1994), and the same author's 'Fiefs and vassals in Scotland: A view from outside', *Scottish Historical Review*, 82 (2003), 176–93. See also, for a different perspective on the whole topic, Alice Taylor, '*Homo ligius* and unfreedom in medieval Scotland', in Matthew Hammond (ed.), *New Perspectives on Medieval Scotland 1093–1286* (Woodbridge, 2013), 85–116.
39 A preliminary investigation is to be found in Hector L. MacQueen, 'Some notes on wrang and unlaw', in Hector L. MacQueen (ed.), *Miscellany Five* (Stair Society, vol. 52; Edinburgh, 2006), 13–26.
40. In addition to works cited in MacQueen, *CLFS*, for Stringer, see 'Acts of lordship: The records of the lords of Galloway to 1234', in Terry Brotherstone and David Ditchburn (eds), *Freedom and Authority: Historical and Historiographical Essays Presented to Grant G Simpson* (East Linton, 2000), 203–34; 'States, liberties and communities in medieval Britain and Ireland (*c.* 1100–1400)', in Michael Prestwich (ed.), *Liberties and Identities in the Medieval British Isles* (Woodbridge, 2008), 5–36; 'Aspects of the Norman diaspora in northern England and southern Scotland', in Keith Stringer and Andrew Jotischky (eds), *Norman Expansion: Connections, Continuities and Contrasts* (Farnham, 2013), 9–47; and, for Grant, see 'Acts of lordship: The records of Archibald, fourth Earl of Douglas', in Brotherstone and Ditchburn (eds), *Freedom and Authority*, 235–74; 'Service and tenure in late medieval Scotland, 1314–1475', in Anne Curry and Elizabeth Matthew (eds), *Concepts and Patterns of Service in the Later Middle Ages* (Woodbridge, 2003), 145–79; 'Lordship and society in twelfth-century Clydesdale', in Huw Pryce and John Watts (eds), *Power and Identity in the Middle Ages: Essays in Memory of Rees Davies* (Oxford, 2007), 98–124; 'Franchises north of the border: Baronies and regalities in medieval Scotland', in Prestwich (ed.), *Liberties and Identities*, 155–99; and 'At the northern edge: Alba and its Normans', in Stringer and Jotischky (eds), *Norman Expansion*, 49–85.
41. Possibly in the twenty-first century one should say 'copy and paste' rather than 'carbon copy'.

42. Peter G. B. McNeill and Hector L. MacQueen (eds), *Atlas of Scottish History to 1707* (Edinburgh, 1996), 192–5, 208–11.
43. See MacQueen, 'Pleadable brieves', 70–1, 88–9; also Alan Borthwick and Hector MacQueen, 'Law, lordship and tenure: A fifteenth-century case study', in Stephen Boardman and David Ditchburn (eds), *Studies in Honour of Alexander Grant*, forthcoming.
44. See MacQueen, 'Pleadable brieves', 197–8; MacQueen, *CLFS*, 158–61.
45. See MacQueen, 'Pleadable brieves', 243–8; MacQueen, *CLFS*, 207–9.
46. See MacQueen, 'Pleadable brieves', 187–96, 202–3; MacQueen, *CLFS*, 146–53, 169–70, 177–8.
47. See further, however, Hector L. MacQueen, 'Legal afterword', in Duncan (ed.), *Scottish Formularies*, 361–74 at 363–4. On the medieval development of the legal profession elsewhere than Scotland, see James A. Brundage, *The Medieval Origins of the Legal Profession: Canonists, Civilians and Courts* (Chicago and London, 2008).
48. See W. W. Scott, 'William Cranston, notary public *c.* 1395 to 1425, and some contemporaries', *Miscellany VII* (Stair Society, vol. 62; Edinburgh, 2015), 125–32 (with references to previous literature on notaries in Scotland).
49. MacQueen, *CLFS*, 74–84; (with A. R. Borthwick), '"Rare creatures for their age": Royal servants and graduate lairds', in Barbara E. Crawford (ed.), *Church, Chronicle and Learning in Medieval and Early Renaissance Scotland* (Edinburgh, 1999), 227–39; Hector L. MacQueen, 'Tame magnates? The justiciars of later medieval Scotland', in Steve Boardman and Julian Goodare (eds), *Kings, Lords and Men in Scotland and Britain, 1300–1625: Essays in Honour of Jenny Wormald* (Edinburgh, 2014), 93–120.
50 Cooper, 'Scottish legal tradition', 68; see further Hector L. MacQueen, 'Mixture or muddle? Teaching and research in Scottish legal history', *Zeitschrift für Europäisches Privatrecht*, 5 (1997), 369–84 at 370–1, 378–9; 'Legal nationalism: Lord Cooper, legal history and comparative law', 399–401.
51. See MacQueen, *CLFS*, 53, 76–7, 78–9, 83, 87–8, 91, 93, 97, 116–18, 156–8, 171, 181–3, 204–7, 228–34, 243 (n. 47), 251, 264, 265.
52. See my articles: 'The foundation of law teaching at the university of Aberdeen', in David L. Carey Miller and Reinhard Zimmermann (eds), *The Civilian Tradition and Scots Law: Aberdeen Quincentenary Essays* (Berlin, 1997), 53–71; 'Girth: Society and the law of sanctuary in medieval Scotland', in O. F. Robinson and J. W. Cairns (eds), *Studies in Ancient Law, Comparative Law and Legal History in Honour of Alan Watson* (Oxford, 2001), 333–52; 'Canon law, custom and legislation: Law in the reign of Alexander II', in Richard Oram (ed.), *The Reign of Alexander II 1214–49* (Leiden and Boston, 2005), 221–51; 'The king's council and church courts in later medieval

Scotland', in Harry Dondorp, Jan Hallebeek, Tammo Wallinga and Laurens Winkel (eds), *Ius Romanum – Ius Commune – Ius Hodiernum: Studies in Honour of Eltjo Schrage on the Occasion of his 65th Birthday* (Amsterdam and Aalen, 2010), 277–87; (with Alan Borthwick), 'Another fifteenth-century case', *Miscellany VII* (Stair Society, vol. 62; Edinburgh, 2015), 133–62.

53. Peter Stein, *The Character and Influence of the Roman Civil Law: Historical Essays* (London and Ronceverte, 1988), chs 18 and 19 (reprints of essays first published in 1968 and 1963 respectively); W. M. Gordon, 'Roman law in Scotland', in Robin Evans-Jones (ed.), *The Civil Law Tradition in Scotland* (Stair Society, Supplementary Series, vol. 2; Edinburgh, 1995), 13–40 at 15–23.

54. See Hector L. MacQueen, 'Scots law under Alexander III', in N. H. Reid (ed.), *Scotland in the Reign of Alexander III* (Edinburgh, 1990), 74–102; 'The laws of Galloway: A preliminary survey', in R. D. Oram and G. P. Stell (eds), *Galloway: Land and Lordship* (Edinburgh, 1991), 131–43; 'The kin of Kennedy, "kenkynnol" and the common law', in A. Grant and K. J. Stringer (eds), *Medieval Scotland: Crown, Lordship and Community: Essays Presented to G. W. S. Barrow* (Edinburgh, 1993), 274–96; 'Survival and success: The Kennedys of Dunure', in S. Boardman and A. Ross (eds), *The Exercise of Power in Medieval Scotland* c. *1200–1500* (Dublin, 2003), 67–94.

55. See MacQueen, 'Some notes on wrang and unlaw'; also 'Laws and languages: Some historical notes from Scotland', *Electronic Journal of Comparative Law*, 6/2 (2002), accessible at <http://www.ejcl.org/62/art62-2.html>.

56. See MacQueen, *CLFS*, 84–98; also *'Regiam Majestatem*, Scots law and national identity', *Scottish Historical Review*, 74 (1995), 1–25; '*Glanvill* resarcinate: Sir John Skene and *Regiam Majestatem*', in A. A. MacDonald, M. Lynch and I. B. Cowan (eds), *The Renaissance in Scotland: Studies in Literature, Religion, History and Culture offered to John Durkan* (Leiden, New York and Cologne, 1994) 385–403; 'Canon law, custom and legislation'. Alice Taylor has since done important work on the authenticity and development of the pre-*Regiam* native written material: see her '*Leges Scocie* and the lawcodes of David I, William the Lion and Alexander II', *Scottish Historical Review*, 88 (2009), 207–88; 'The Assizes of David I, king of Scots, 1124–53', *Scottish Historical Review*, 91 (2012), 197–238. There is still valuable insight in the late Patrick Wormald's 2001 paper, posthumously published as 'Anglo-Saxon law and Scots law', *Scottish Historical Review*, 88 (2009), 192–206.

57. Discussed by Dr Andrew Simpson in the Foreword to this edition.

58. J. M. Wormald, 'Bloodfeud, kindred and government in early modern Scotland', *Past and Present*, 54 (1980), 54–97.

59. A. Mark Godfrey, 'Rethinking the justice of the feud', in Boardman and Goodare (eds), *Kings, Lords and Men*, 136–54.

60. See Alexander Grant, *Independence and Nationhood: Scotland 1306–*

1469 (London, 1984) and other work cited in the bibliography to MacQueen, *CLFS*, 281. Note, too, the debate between Grant and Norman Macdougall in *Scottish Historical Review*, 73 (1994), 4–29.

61. See MacQueen, '*Regiam Majestatem*, Scots law, and national identity'.

62. For this phrase, see Robert Mnookin and Lewis Kornhauser, 'Bargaining in the shadow of the law: The case of divorce', *Yale Law Journal*, 88 (1979), 950–97; Robert Cooter and Stephen Marks with Robert Mnookin, 'Bargaining in the shadow of the law: A testable model of strategic behaviour', *Journal of Legal Studies*, 11 (1982), 225–51; also Ben Depoorter, 'Law in the shadow of bargaining: The feedback effect of civil settlements', *Cornell Law Review*, 95 (2010), 957–87. Note too Hazel Genn, *Hard Bargaining: Out of Court Settlement in Personal Injury Actions* (Oxford, 1988).

63. For royal orders, see MacQueen, 'Legal afterword', 369–70.

64. See also Hector L. MacQueen, 'Scotland: Politics, government and law', in S. H. Rigby (ed.), *A Companion to Britain in the Later Middle Ages* (Oxford, 2003), 283–308. Work on the diplomatic of charters and other formal documents is crucial after as well as before 1300: meantime, see further Dauvit Broun, *The Charters of Gaelic Scotland and Ireland in the Early and Central Middle Ages* (Cambridge, 1995); Dauvit Broun, 'The adoption of brieves in Scotland', in M. T. Flanagan and J. A. Green (eds), *Charters and Charter Scholarship in Britain and Ireland* (Basingstoke, 2005), 164–83; John Hudson, 'Legal aspects of Scottish charter diplomatic in the twelfth century: A comparative approach', in John Gillingham (ed.), *Anglo-Norman Studies XXV: Proceedings of the Battle Conference 2002* (Woodbridge, 2003), 121–38; Dauvit Broun (ed.) *The Reality behind Charter Diplomatic in Anglo-Norman Britain* (Glasgow, 2011), accessible at <http://paradox.poms.ac.uk/ebook/index.html>.

Foreword:
Common Law and Feudal Society in Scholarship since 1993

Andrew R. C. Simpson*

INTRODUCTION

In 1995, Alan Harding described Hector MacQueen's *Common Law and Feudal Society* as 'one of [the] most penetrating studies yet produced of any period of Scottish legal history'.[1] In the twenty years since then that claim has been vindicated by countless studies that have relied heavily upon MacQueen's work, and several substantial contributions to scholarship that have directly engaged with it.[2] While those contributions have certainly contested, developed and refined elements of his arguments in significant ways, they have left largely untouched many of his central claims. So it is no longer doubted that there emerged in medieval Scotland a complex and broadly coherent common law that furnished litigants with a sophisticated framework of actions designed to remedy a wide range of feudal disputes.[3] Nor is it doubted that both the English common law and the canon law strongly influenced this Scottish legal culture.[4] Subsequent work has also confirmed MacQueen's insightful argument that the law which emerged from that culture 'took on a life of its own which did dictate the pattern of change to a large

* Lecturer in Law, University of Aberdeen. I would like to thank Professor Jørn Øyrehagen Sunde and the Centre for Legal Culture at the University of Bergen for the invitation to be a guest researcher in Bergen during November 2014. While in Bergen I spent a great deal of time researching the history of medieval Scots law for the purposes of writing a textbook on Scottish Legal History, which I am co-authoring with Dr Adelyn Wilson. The research carried out in Bergen also forms the basis of the arguments presented here. I am also grateful to Professor Hector MacQueen, Professor Mark Godfrey, Professor John Ford and Mr Eddie Simpson for their comments on this Foreword. Any errors remain my own.

degree'.[5] Put another way, while political, social and economic factors all performed roles in causing legal changes, the nature of the changes in question were strongly informed by the existing tradition.[6] Furthermore, it seems clear that there was broad continuity in these developments. The strong influence of the Scottish common law in shaping the nature of legal change can be traced throughout the medieval period.[7] Only in relation to certain particular matters – such as the development of new forms of centralised justice and jurisdiction at the end of this period, and the foundation of the College of Justice in 1532 – has new research superseded MacQueen's analysis.[8]

As MacQueen himself has explained in his Preface to this edition, all of his arguments mentioned above represented challenges to orthodox views of Scottish legal history at the time.[9] Indeed, his arguments also made a significant contribution to contemporary debates concerning Scottish history more generally. For example, Jenny Wormald and Alexander Grant had attacked the older view that Scottish politics of the fourteenth and fifteenth centuries were dominated by violent power struggles between a weak crown and an over-mighty nobility. They had sought to show that the period was more generally characterised by the pursuit of stability and peace, and the maintenance of Scottish independence. MacQueen's argument that there was indeed a functioning legal system during this period that was effective in the resolution of disputes complemented these claims.[10] Furthermore, given the origins of much of the Scottish common law in English feudalism, MacQueen's work retains a broader relevance for students of English legal history. Indeed, MacQueen demonstrated this to be so by considering the emergence of the Scottish legal system in the light of debates concerning the development of the English common law.[11]

Yet it is not the purpose of this Foreword to discuss these matters. Rather, the aim here is to explore how various scholars have engaged critically with some of the claims advanced in *Common Law and Feudal Society* since its publication. In order to do this, the elements of MacQueen's thesis that have proven contestable will be examined. Reference will first be made to recent research concerning the reconstruction and interpretation of medieval Scottish legal texts dating from the thirteenth and fourteenth centuries. Subsequently, one significant attempt to challenge MacQueen's account of the thirteenth-century Scottish common law will be examined. Finally, reference will be made to important research concerning the development of the Scottish courts and the common law during the late fifteenth and early sixteenth centuries. In the process, it will be suggested that some of the challenges to MacQueen's work are perhaps less robust than one might think.

RECONSTRUCTING AND REINTERPRETING THE SOURCES

The articles published by Alice Taylor over the past few years are among the most significant recent contributions to the study of medieval Scottish legal history.[12] Taylor has reconstructed the textual traditions emanating from a variety of legal compilations dating from the thirteenth and fourteenth centuries, such as the *Leges Scocie* and the *Statuta Regis Alexandri*. She has also underlined the point that the editions of those compilations printed in the nineteenth-century *Acts of the Parliaments of Scotland* (hereafter *APS*) are not wholly reliable.[13] Taylor has already taken considerable steps towards remedying the problem with her critical edition of the *Leges Scocie* (*LS*).[14] Her forthcoming Stair Society publication, *The Auld Lawes of Scotland: Law and Legal Culture in Medieval Scotland*, together with David Fergus's edition of the fourteenth-century text *Quoniam Attachiamenta*,[15] will enable historians to work confidently with the sources. In addition, Taylor is demonstrating that her research into the textual traditions underpinning the legal compilations has significant consequences for how medieval Scots law is to be understood. The full implications of this will be made clear with the publication of her forthcoming book, *The Shape of the State in Medieval Scotland*.[16]

From Taylor's published articles, it seems likely that she will offer some critical comments on the argument pursued in *Common Law and Feudal Society*. For example, that book used versions of texts published in *APS* that cannot now be said to be entirely reliable in the light of her research.[17] It is to be hoped that she will explore the consequences of this in detail in *The Shape of the State*. For the purposes of this Foreword it seems appropriate to make reference to one way in which she has already enriched the reconstruction of the medieval Scottish common law presented in *Common Law and Feudal Society*. This relates to the statutes enacted in 1318 by Robert I (r. 1306–29) and the extent to which that legislation can shed light on the origins and purposes of one contemporary legal text.[18]

MacQueen's Research Concerning the 1318 Legislation

In *Common Law and Feudal Society*, MacQueen examined the acts promulgated in 1318, and several features of that legislation have been explored in more detail since by Taylor. The first is the declaration of the brieves rule. This provided that

> no one is to be ejected from his free holding [*liberum tenementum suum*] of which he claims to be vest and saised as of fee without the king's pleadable brieve or some similar brieve nor without being

first reasonably summoned to a certain day and place for his free holding.[19]

(Hereafter this will be referred to as the 'brieves rule'.) MacQueen argued that a 'free holding' (*liberum tenementum*) was 'in effect any life interest in land, whether or not that interest was heritable, a common example from the fourteenth century onwards being the liferent which fathers often reserved to themselves when granting the fee of their lands to their sons in order to minimise inheritance formalities'.[20]

Alongside the brieves rule, the 1318 legislation also reformed the brieve of novel dissasine. What was a dissasine? To explain, to have 'sasine' was 'to have been put into possession of land by the grantor, typically although not invariably the lord of whom the lands were to be held'. Consequently, 'dissasine' arose where one with sasine was ejected from his possession. The remedy that the brieve of novel dissasine promised was the restoration of the 'relationship of sasine between [the dissaised] and the land's lord'.[21] MacQueen argued that there was thought to be a problem with this form of action during the early fourteenth century, and that this was addressed in 1318. Prior to that date the brieve of novel dissasine was frequently brought not against the actual dissaisors, but rather against those they had put into the disputed lands as their feudal tenants. That meant that an innocent third party, and not the actual wrongdoers, could be made to answer the brieve. Thus in 1318 the procedure used in disputes concerning novel dissasine was reformed to give added protection to the tenant. Thereafter the dissaised was required to name the original dissaisors – if still living – in his brieve, as well as the tenant. As MacQueen put it, '[a] crucial consequence was the spreading of the pains of losing the action'.[22]

MacQueen also attempted to explain these reforms of the procedures used to protect landholdings in terms of the political situation in 1318. During the previous decades the Wars of Independence had resulted in the dispossession of many of the political enemies of Robert I (r. 1306–29). Robert I now offered the 'disinherited' the opportunity to enter his allegiance, and to recover their lands. But he knew that would result in some upheaval, particularly where his supporters had simply seized the lands of the disinherited, and perhaps then granted sasine of those lands to innocent third parties. Consequently he sought to maintain control of the situation by underlining the point that the 'disinherited' should rely upon due legal process when attempting to recover their lands. He also developed the law to deal with the possibility that some of his supporters might have committed dissasines during the war, and then put innocent tenants into the lands they had seized. The king made it clear that the dissaisors were to answer for the wrong, as well as the individual tenants.[23] Elsewhere MacQueen also suggested that Robert I had broader purposes in enacting this legislation in the wake of the Wars of Independence. As he puts it, 'the wide-ranging legislation enacted at the symbolically significant location of Scone in 1318 was perhaps an assertion by Robert I of the regal authority to make law which Edward I [of England] had sought to exercise in 1305'.[24]

The 1318 Legislation and the Medieval Compilations of Scots Law in Taylor's Work

MacQueen's account of the 1318 legislation has now been revisited, enriched and refined by Taylor's work concerning what would seem to be a near-contemporary treatise known as the *Capitula Assisarum et Statutorum Domini Dauid Regis Scotie (CD)*.[25] Having reconstructed this text, Taylor has sought to explore its origins and purposes by comparing its provisions in detail with both the 1318 legislation and also her critical editions of other texts that were in circulation during the thirteenth and early fourteenth centuries. Among those works are the compilations known as the *Leges Scocie (LS)* – the contents of which can largely be dated to the reign of William I (r. 1165–1214)[26] – and the *Statuta Regis Alexandri (SA)*, which contains laws attributed to Alexander II (r. 1214–49).[27] When comparing these works, Taylor notes that *SA* c.7 and *CD* c.41 preserve different versions of the statute that is said to have introduced a remedy for novel dissasine into Scots law. *CD* c.41 declares that the successful claimant in a case of novel dissasine should receive '"damages or arrears" (*dampnis seu arreragiis*)'. This provision is absent in *SA* c.7. Might that help scholars to date *CD*? Taylor states that the 1318 act that reformed the procedure of novel dissasine contains the earliest known reference to the payment of *dampnum* for the wrong. Indeed, *CD* c.41 and the 1318 legislation both emphasise the need for an immediate award of damages to a successful pursuer. Drawing on these and other similar arguments Taylor suggests that *CD* c.41 'fits the context of its earliest manuscript – the reign of Robert I'.[28] Yet Taylor's work also draws attention back to the question of exactly which party benefited from the reforms of 1318 to the procedures designed to remedy novel dissasine. It will be recalled that MacQueen suggested that the primary beneficiary of these reforms was the sitting tenant, because as a result of the promulgation of the 1318 statute he could only be sued for dissasine alongside the original dissaisor, assuming that individual was still alive. But Taylor, noting MacQueen's arguments in this regard, also suggests in passing that under the 1318 act and the rules outlined in *CD* c.41 'there were also significant benefits for the dissaised'.[29] Presumably she has in mind the points that the dissaised could definitely seek damages under the statute, and the evidence does not reveal whether or not he could do so prior to 1318. If the act of 1318 at least confirmed his rights to damages, then this may have conferred a significant benefit upon him. Indeed, the rule that he had to sue the actual dissaisors, if still living, might have made this development more palatable. Innocent sitting tenants would not now be left to face alone both the loss of land and *also* a claim for damages for a wrong they did not perpetrate. Consequently, it may be that the legislation was not designed to change the law so as to benefit only the sitting tenant.

Furthermore, it should be noted here that Taylor's published articles, and those of others citing her unpublished work, indicate that she will attempt to revise MacQueen's account of the brieves rule, and in particular the extent to which it was in operation prior to 1318. Again it is clear that she will draw on her knowledge of the texts mentioned above and the surviving formularies containing the older forms of action. More will be said about this below while discussing the work of David Carpenter; he has also re-examined MacQueen's work on the brieves rule and challenged his conclusions.[30]

Taylor also advances other arguments that serve to enrich MacQueen's account of the purposes underlying the enactment of the 1318 legislation, and the law-making activities of Robert I more generally. Again, her argument begins by reflecting on what can be said about the fact that *CD* and the statutes of 1318 resemble one another quite closely in various respects. Reference has already been made to the similarities between *CD* c.41 and the legislation of 1318 concerning the brieve of novel dissasine. Taylor also shows that the rules regarding repledging of men from one court to another changed between 1230 and 1318, and that *CD* c.38 reflects the later position. Yet, while one might conclude that *CD* c.38 must have been enacted after 1318, Taylor goes to some lengths to point out that this is not so. This is because the rules enacted in 1318 may have reflected the existing common law, at least to some extent. But what her research does prove is that *CD* – which is first attested in a manuscript of 1318 × 1329 known as the Ayr Manuscript – fits the legal context of the early fourteenth century better than that of the first half of the thirteenth century. Taylor then goes on to point out that there is further evidence that may serve to date the original compilation of *CD* to the years immediately following 1318.[31]

Having made these points, Taylor then poses the question of how one is to explain this extensive interest in the law and in law-making during the reign of Robert I. In so doing, she develops MacQueen's arguments.[32] It will be recalled that in *Common Law and Feudal Society* he explained the 1318 legislation in terms of the need to accommodate the returning disinherited. In a later article he also hinted that this might have served to underline very publicly Robert I's own assertion of regal authority over his realm. Taylor develops these themes by drawing attention to just how insecure Robert I's kingship still was in 1318, both within the Scottish polity and outside it. She notes Robert I's own attempts to establish the legitimacy of his rule, and makes reference to Harding's arguments concerning the possibility that the king used the composition of the text *Regiam Majestatem* to demonstrate his role as the preserver and enforcer of the old laws of the Scots around which the whole nation could unite.[33] *CD* may have served a similar purpose. It placed legislation of Robert I alongside that attributed to his ancestor, David I (r. 1124–53), who was remembered as a great and just law-giver. It attributed the whole work to King David, presenting Robert I's own contribution as a seamless extension of the tradition of law-making initiated by his predecessors.[34]

Thus Taylor's work on *CD* serves to shed further light on the 1318 legislation and also law-making more generally in Robert I's reign. As shown by the examples given here, it promises to enrich – and also to some extent challenge – the understanding of medieval Scots law presented in *Common Law and Feudal Society*. It is hoped that the debate that will undoubtedly result will be studied very carefully by all other scholars in the fields of Scottish legal history and Scottish medieval history more generally.

HOW COMMON WAS THE COMMON LAW IN THE THIRTEENTH CENTURY? PROFESSOR CARPENTER'S ARGUMENTS

Taylor is not the only scholar to have engaged critically with the account of the medieval Scottish common law that is presented in *Common Law and Feudal Society*. Recently David Carpenter has published an important article-length study of Scottish royal government in the thirteenth century. In so doing, he has directly challenged several elements of MacQueen's thesis, and so it is appropriate to say something about his arguments here.

Carpenter's approach is comparative. He considers Scottish royal government in the thirteenth century from an English perspective. Consequently he begins with the observation that 'English identity in the thirteenth century was shaped by both the burdens and the benefits of royal government'. Obvious examples of the 'burdens' were the various devices used to raise royal revenue. By contrast, among the 'benefits' in England was the 'common law'. It has long been thought that the burdens of royal government in Scotland were lighter, as Carpenter notes; but he also notes that '[w]hen . . . it comes to the benefits of royal government in the shape of the common law, the contrast between England and Scotland, according to the usual view, is far less marked'. He continues by stating that 'the belief that, in the thirteenth century, a common law on the English model developed in Scotland has become almost axiomatic amongst historians'. In the introduction to his essay Carpenter promises to mount 'a direct attack on this view'.[35] He suggests that, if the burdens of Scottish royal government were light, the benefits of the common law in particular were quite limited. He suggests that the nobility in Scotland may have resisted any change to this situation. It is obvious that burdensome government was not in their interests; and furthermore a strong common law would have weakened their own jurisdictional powers – as it had in England. In fact, Carpenter suggests this may help to explain why the Scottish nobility were so prepared to defend the autonomy of their realm during the Wars of Independence. Government along English lines would have served to weaken their power. As Scottish noblemen generally held lands in both kingdoms, they would have been well aware of their privileged position in the north.[36]

Critical engagement with this broad line of argument is beyond the scope of this Foreword, but it merits serious attention. What is relevant here is that Carpenter directly challenges elements of MacQueen's thesis in *Common Law and Feudal Society* when suggesting that the benefits of royal government were significantly more limited in thirteenth-century Scotland than they were in contemporary England. His starting point is that 'no one doubts that, in the thirteenth century, equivalents emerged [in Scotland] of two of the most popular of the English common law actions'. These were the brieves of novel dissasine, and mortancestor, which were modelled on the English writs of novel disseisin and mort d'ancestor.[37] In passing it may be noted that the brieve of mortancestor enabled a litigant to make a 'claim to succeed to an immediate ancestor who had died vest and saised in lands which were now being unjustly withheld by some unentitled person'.[38] Carpenter disputes not the existence of these procedures but rather 'the extent of their use'.[39] His argument in this regard is grounded in the work of Alexander Grant concerning the geographical range of the activities of those royal judges and officials who presumably administered the common law – the sheriffs and the justiciars.[40] Drawing on Grant's work, Carpenter suggests that the sheriffs and the justiciars were largely inactive in the central highlands and in much of north-west Scotland, regions dominated by 'great provincial earldoms and lordships' that 'covered 425 (46%) of [the country's] 925 parishes'.[41] He argues that within those earldoms and lordships much of the administration of justice, and its associated profits, was simply left to the great lords.[42] Those lords who held their lands in regality could even hear pleas normally reserved for the king and his justiciar, such as the crown pleas of murder, robbery, rape and arson.[43] Having argued these points, Carpenter then turns his attention to what all this may reveal about the administration of the brieves. The argument runs that the brieves were administered by the justiciars and the sheriffs; but there were large tracts of Scotland where the justiciars and the sheriffs were inactive; therefore the brieves were not in use commonly across the whole realm. As Carpenter puts it, '[i]n terms of its geographical range . . . the Scottish common law was not common at all'.[44]

The Geographical Limits of the Scottish Common Law

Of course MacQueen considered this matter in *Common Law and Feudal Society*, as Carpenter acknowledges.[45] MacQueen recognised that much of the administration of justice occurred in the courts of the great earls and lords, but nonetheless maintained that '[r]oyal justice was nevertheless always ready to interfere with lords' autonomy, although this could only be made a reality where the instruments of royal authority – justices, sheriffs and others – were in place'.[46] This would seem to be no response, *prima facie*, to Carpenter's argument about what happened in the regions where those officers were inactive. However MacQueen goes on to show that, under the terms of several grants of jurisdiction to lords from the twelfth century onwards, the grants were subject to a rule that a royal officer should – or at least *could* – be present to ensure that justice was done.[47] It should also be noted here that the sheriffs and the justiciars were not the only royal officers with apparent authority to monitor the justice dispensed by the lords. Royal sergeands and the king's *judices* in different provinces also seem to have had such roles, at least in some cases.[48] Consequently, while a royal officer might have had no authority to interfere in the exercise of jurisdiction within a lordship *qua* royal officer, he may have been able to do so by virtue of the original grant that created the lordship in question. That point does not seem to be factored into Carpenter's assessment of the geographical extent of the activities of royal officers. Yet it might be objected in response to this criticism that no evidence has been led here to show that the sheriffs, sergeands or *judices* actually *did* interfere in the administration of justice in the lordships or the earldoms.[49] Furthermore, even if these royal officers were actively monitoring the ways in which the lords adjudicated in disputes, it is not clear what powers or legal machinery they had at their disposal to 'correct' judicial errors. Admittedly *LS* c.15,[50] promulgated during the reign of William I, indicates that from 1197 lords who failed to do justice could lose their courts 'in perpetuity', but the act does not link this with any role of the sheriffs, their sergeands and the royal *judices* to monitor the administration of justice. Nonetheless, the theoretical possibility that such officers *could* interfere in the exercise of power within the earldoms and lordships is surely significant. This is because, on the evidence of *LS* c.15, one cannot assume that thirteenth-century royal officers were powerless to ensure the observance of common legal standards outwith the sheriffdoms and the routes followed by the justice ayres.

Regardless, even if these arguments were to find support through the further study of contemporary records, they would not fully address Carpenter's real point. This is that there is no evidence to suggest that the *brieves* were used commonly across the realm in the administration of justice during the thirteenth century. In this regard, Carpenter notes that the 'forms of the novel dissasine and mortancestry brieves in the early fourteenth-century Ayr Register, the best guide to contemporary practice, are quite specifically for land within the sheriffdoms'. Furthermore, Carpenter points out that the surviving evidence for the operation of the brieves of novel dissasine and mortancestry during the thirteenth century comes exclusively from the sheriffdoms.[51] The point is that it is difficult to show those brieves in operation in the great earldoms and lordships that lay outwith the sheriffdoms. Note, in passing, that the question under consideration here is not concerned with whether or not the king was generally able to use the brieves to interfere in the feudal relationship between a lord and his tenants. *SA* c.7 makes it clear that the brieve of novel dissasine was in principle available where a man's lord dissaised him.[52] The problems relate to whether or not the brieves could be used to regulate such legal issues *within* the great earldoms and provincial lordships.

When considering this question, there are various points one should note. MacQueen did cite some evidence to the effect that the brieves could be used to enforce rights in courts other than those of the sheriffs and the justiciars. This was drawn from a series of mid-thirteenth-century cases where innominate brieves of the king were pled in the courts of the prior of Coldingham, and a further case of 1270 where another such royal brieve was pled in the court of the earl of Lennox. In the latter case the dispute did not raise questions of dissasine or mortancestry, but it was nonetheless concerned with rights in land.[53] On this basis MacQueen suggested that the brieve in question may have been something like the later brieve of right, which came to be available in disputes over title that did not fall within the ambit of the brieves of novel dissasine or mortancestry.[54] The case of 1270 is potentially important because it does suggest that royal brieves *could* find their way into the courts of the earls. Carpenter notes this, commenting that 'MacQueen argues, on the basis of several cases, that in the thirteenth century there was also a form [of the brieve of right] addressed to the lord'. But he then immediately states that if there was a form of the brieve of right 'addressed to the lord . . . it made no lasting impact for there is no sign of it in the Ayr Register'.[55] Regardless of whether or not the form of the brieve had any 'lasting impact', its existence does indicate that there is more to be said about the ability of the royal brieves to interfere with the administration of justice in the greater lords' courts by the second half of the thirteenth century. MacQueen also pointed out that the evidence concerning the use of brieves in the court of the prior of Coldingham is intriguing because on two occasions the sheriff of Berwick was present. As MacQueen put it, 'was he there to do right had the prior refused to do so?'[56] This brings to mind the point mentioned above concerning the authority of royal officers to exercise supervisory roles in the courts of at least some of the great lords, and indeed MacQueen suggested that this role may have extended to the supervision of disputes over land.[57] This point will be considered again in more detail shortly.

While the use of a royal brieve in the court of the earl of Lennox in 1270 is intriguing, Carpenter is undoubtedly correct to express puzzlement as to why there is no evidence of a form of brieve of right addressed to a lord in the Ayr Manuscript (which, it will be recalled, can be dated approximately to 1318 × 1329). The puzzle cannot be resolved by suggesting that the Ayr Manuscript simply focused on practice in the courts of the sheriffs and the justiciars; it also contains, to name an example, a form of the brieve of right addressed to the provost and bailies of a burgh.[58] One possible explanation might be that, by the time the Ayr Manuscript was produced, questions concerning the enforcement of the common law in the regalities and the great lordships had become less relevant owing to developments in practice. MacQueen pointed out that Robert I's grant of land in regality to Thomas Randolph came 'with the four complaints belonging to our royal crown and with all pleas and complaints both in common indictments and in pleadable brieves'. MacQueen then commented: 'It seems highly probable that this meant that the lord of regality was empowered to issue pleadable brieves within his regality wherever the king would have done so elsewhere.' He cites fifteenth-century evidence to show that lords of regality did indeed issue their own brieves by that period. The brieves used in the regality chancery of St Andrews during the sixteenth century ran 'in the name of the archbishop but [were] otherwise exactly similar to those issued by the king'.[59]

Given that this is so, a tentative solution might be suggested to the problem Carpenter perceptively raises concerning the use of royal brieves in the courts of the great earldoms and lordships. Perhaps if it was *possible* to use such brieves in those courts, it may also have been becoming possible to purchase brieves from 'chanceries'[60] or chapels maintained by local lords of regality. Interestingly, the surviving evidence of a later period suggests that such brieves offered procedures and remedies that closely resembled those that were outlined in the royal brieves. Indeed, it would hardly be surprising to discover that the courts of the great earls and lords sought to mirror royal mechanisms for the administration of justice, at least to some extent. One of Taylor's recent articles has pointed to the seemingly curious fact that, while several of the acts that can probably be attributed to William I in *LS* outlined how crimes such as theft were to be dealt with procedurally, they did not define the crimes themselves. Taylor suggests that the determination of what did and what did not constitute the wrong itself was left to 'local communities'. William I seems to have been less interested in establishing a unitary definition of theft across his realm than he was in 'claiming a monopoly over best practice to inform others dealing with a crime'. Indeed, Taylor's conclusion is that he was more interested in this than in establishing 'a monopoly of jurisdiction and punishment over theft'[61] – even though it would seem that William I's son, Alexander II, was keen to present the right to exercise jurisdiction in such cases as proceeding from royal grants.[62] While obviously much more research needs to be carried out on the point before any firm conclusions can be drawn, it is conceivable that statutes like *SA* c.7, which established a procedure to remedy novel dissasine, were conceptualised in the same way. Perhaps what did and did not constitute a dissasine would have been approached slightly differently in different communities. But what *SA* c.7 did was to lay down the procedural framework to be used by the justiciars when called upon to address the problems. It may also have served to provide a template for how the earls and the great lords were to deal – or came to deal – with dissasines within their own jurisdictions too. In a later period they certainly followed that template, and the templates of the other procedures outlined in the brieves, and the evidence MacQueen cites suggests that they may conceivably have done so from the early fourteenth century onwards. One element of the brieves rule may in fact serve to support this – a man could not be put out of his *liberum tenementum* of which he claimed to be vest and saised as of fee 'without the king's pleadable brieve *or such a kind of brieve as is similar* [emphasis added]'. What was meant by 'such a kind of brieve as is similar'?[63] Was this a direct reference to a royal policy that gave the great lords freedom to administer their own justice, so long as they adhered to royal procedural standards in so doing? Furthermore – to continue in this admittedly rather speculative vein – one might consider the possibility that all this reveals something about the supervisory role of the royal officers who were apparently entitled to oversee the administration of justice in the provincial courts of the lords and the earls. Perhaps their purpose was to ensure – or to try to ensure – that the basic royal procedural standards for handling problems like novel dissasine were observed when reaching judgement.[64]

Thus arguably there could have been a degree of 'commonality' in the administration of the legal standards expressed in the brieves across the thirteenth-century Scottish kingdom, even though much of the realm lay outwith the sheriffdoms. The geographical limits of the sheriffdoms are significant, but they do not take into account the apparent right of royal officers to exercise supervisory jurisdiction in several of the great lordships. Furthermore, there is some evidence to suggest that brieves purchased from the king's chapel could have been pled in the courts of the great earldoms and lordships. In addition, the fact that this evidence is limited might conceivably be explicable. Perhaps the great earls and lords who were active during the thirteenth century were beginning to issue commands to do justice to their baillies that were modelled on the royal brieves. It is possible that the lords of regality were actually doing just that in the early 1300s, as they undoubtedly were during the fifteenth century. Those lords' brieves ran in their own names, but the evidence – such as it is – suggests that the procedures they adopted imitated those outlined in the royal brieves. Such an approach would have shown due deference to a Scottish royal policy of creating a monopoly over 'best practice'[65] in dealing with various legal disputes. Furthermore, it would have at least helped to ensure that broadly common procedural standards were observed in dispute resolution across the kingdom. In a later period similar common legal standards could sometimes be enforced in the regalities by royal officers – at least in theory.[66]

That last point is obviously relevant to Carpenter's argument that '[i]n terms of its geographical range . . . the [thirteenth-century] Scottish common law was not common at all'. The evidence cited here suggests that Carpenter's powerful critique does not necessarily disturb MacQueen's analysis as much as might be thought, but it does require careful consideration and further debate.

Was the Law Common in its Use within the Ayres and the Sheriffdoms?

Carpenter's argument continues by asking whether or not the Scottish common law 'was common in its use even within the compass of the ayres and sheriffdoms'.[67] In this context he turns his attention to the legislation of 1318 that was discussed above. He examines in particular MacQueen's conclusion that the brieves rule compelled the use of the brieves of novel dissasine and mortancestry in certain circumstances. It will be recalled that the brieves rule was that a man could not be put out of his *liberum tenementum* of which he claimed to be vest and saised as of fee without the king's pleadable brieve or a similar brieve. MacQueen argued that the brieves rule existed in Scots law prior to 1318, and cited various pieces of evidence to support his claim. First he cited a provision in the text known as the *Leges Burgorum* – which is attested in a manuscript of *c.* 1270 – which provided that '[i]f anyone is challenged for his lands or tenement in a burgh, he need not answer his adversary without the lord king's letters unless he freely wishes it'. Alongside this MacQueen referred to a case decided in the burgh court of Aberdeen in 1317, in which William Duncan sued Philip Gaydon, 'alleging *wrang et unlaw* in Philip's retention of a house against parties to whom William had leased it'. With justification Philip argued that 'his possession was based on a heritable title derived from the tenure of his parents, and that accordingly he did not have to answer William's complaint unless it was made by a letter of the king's chapel'. The burgh court admitted this defence and dismissed the case.[68] Commenting on the version of the brieves rule observed in the burgh courts prior to 1318, Carpenter places some reliance on the point that no one had to answer for his lands without a brieve *unless he wished it*. Carpenter argues that the fact '[t]hat the king advertised the possibility of litigating without his brieve, hardly suggests he was very confident in spreading its use, let alone seeking to compel it'.[69] However, the evidence can be interpreted in a different way. Admittedly the rule in question was clearly not concerned with compelling a litigant to use a particular royal protection from which he might have benefited when the litigant in question definitely did not wish to do so. But the evidence also indicates that, as soon as the litigant *did* want the protection of the brieves rule, then it was absolute, and the king stood ready to compel its observance. Furthermore, the fact that the litigant was left with the choice may tell us little – or possibly nothing – about whether or not the king 'was very confident in spreading [the] use' of the brieves. Even today litigants might wish to be able to waive rights afforded to them in law during the course of civil litigation for a variety of practical reasons, such as ensuring a speedy outcome to the dispute, or securing other rights.[70]

Carpenter also argues that 'outside the burghs, there is virtually no evidence for the [brieves] rule'.[71] MacQueen pointed out that in 1296 Alexander MacDonald of Islay claimed 'many people say that according to the laws of England and Scotland no-one ought to lose his heritage unless he has been impleaded by brieve and named in the brieve by his own name'.[72] Carpenter's response to this evidence is that it is 'a remarkably tentative statement if the rule had long been compulsory' – and this is of course worth emphasising. MacQueen tried to explain this doubt by admitting that there was probably no enactment declaring the existence of a brieves rule outwith the burghs prior to 1318. And yet, as MacQueen argued, one does still have to explain why 'many people' believed a brieves rule did apply across the realm. MacQueen's explanation of this does still seem at the very least plausible. He suggested that it was widely known that the Scottish brieves originated in the

English writs. He then pointed out that there was an English rule that provided that 'no man could be made to answer for his freeholding without a royal writ'. On this basis 'many people' may have concluded that the Scottish brieves were to be interpreted as conferring the same basic protection.[73]

Carpenter's next argument seeks to challenge the idea that there was any direct association between the act of 1318 that declared the brieves rule and the act that reformed procedures in cases of novel dissasine. He points out that '[t]he 1318 rule applied quite specifically to land held "in fee"', and he suggests that 'in fee' here probably meant 'with some degree of hereditary right'. He then notes that the text of *SA* c.7 'refers simply to dissasine unjustly and without judgement without specifying the subject of the dissaine at all'. He also states that the brieves rule as formulated in 1318 'does not match up with the developed brieve of novel dissasine found in the Ayr Register which refers to a tenement of which the plaintiff had been "*vestitus et saisitus*" not just "*ut de feudo*" but also "*de dote vel firma ad terminum qui* [*non*] *dum preteriit*"'.[74] Note that the last phrase means 'as of terce (*dote*) or by a rent (*firma*) whose term has not yet expired'[75] (terce being a 'widow's liferent of part of her estate'[76]). Put another way, novel dissasine as presented in the Ayr Register could be used not only where one was '*vestitus et saisitus*' 'as of fee', but also where one held lands on the basis of a liferent or fixed-term tenure. So it does not 'match up' well with the brieves rule of 1318, which was simply concerned with lands held 'in fee'. Carpenter's argument does also raise a point that should be borne in mind when assessing the impact of the brieves rule. This is that after 1318 litigants might only have been compelled to use a brieve – whether a brieve of novel dissasine, mortancestry or right – where the defender alleged he held his lands 'as of fee'. Perhaps a defender who did not advance that argument – such as one who held his lands simply '*in liberum tenementum*' but not 'as of fee' – could not invoke the protection of the brieves rule. If Carpenter's interpretation of the extent of the protection offered by the pleadable brieves rule is correct, then it would seem to imply a common law concerned primarily with protection of heritable rights, leaving a greater ambit to other jurisdictions and remedies than MacQueen's account allowed.

One further argument advanced by Carpenter against MacQueen's general thesis will be considered here. Having argued that there is 'some evidence suggesting a low level for the purchase of the common law brieves',[77] he then turns his attention to another piece of evidence 'arguing against the widespread use of the common law'. He suggests that it 'might seem to have devastating consequences for hypotheses of that kind'.[78] Broadly the argument is that the costs of using the brieve of novel dissasine were potentially so prohibitive as to prevent all but the richest in society from making any use of them. This claim rests upon an interpretation of *SA* c.7. This provided that, once convicted, a dissaisor was to be 'at the mercy of the lord king for £10'. But *SA* c.7 went on to provide that if it was 'understood that the complainer said an untruth, he shall give the forfeiture over the matter'.[79] Commenting on this, Carpenter argues that '[t]he text of the assize does not specify the nature of the forfeiture but almost certainly like the penalty faced by the disseisor, it was £10'. He continues by noting that the phrase '"Upon pain of the king's full forfeiture of £10" appears twenty-one times in the PoMS material' – a reference to the People of Medieval Scotland database, which is 'a database of all known people of Scotland between 1093 and 1314'.[80] The suggestion that the forfeiture for failing to sustain an allegation of novel dissasine was £10 is also attested in *CD* c.41.[81] Given that in 'thirteenth-century Scotland a knight's fee could be thought to yield £20 a year', it seems to follow that '[a]nyone seeking to bring a novel dissasine action . . . faced a very heavy penalty in the event of failure'.[82] Carpenter then goes on to show that there is evidence to demonstrate that at least one litigant – John Scot of Reston – who failed to sustain his allegation of novel dissasine did indeed forfeit £10 as a result in 1261.[83]

This is a very serious challenge to any argument that defends the 'widespread use of the common law' in thirteenth-century Scotland. Nonetheless, it may be possible to qualify the force of the challenge, at least to some extent. First it should be noted that the actual act that introduced novel dissasine did not, it would seem, specify the nature of the forfeiture that would result from failure to sustain a claim of novel dissasine. Nothing was said in *SA* c.7 about whether a full forfeiture was automatic or not. *CD* c.41 does, admittedly, make reference to a forfeiture of £10. Yet arguably all that *CD* c.41 and the case of John Scot of Reston unquestionably demonstrate is that full forfeiture *could* result from failure to demonstrate that a novel dissasine had occurred. Admittedly *CD* c.41 indicates that full forfeiture was also a *necessary* consequence of such failure by the early fourteenth century. But it is worth noting that *CD* c.41 was not, it would seem, representative of the work of a law-making body in the way that *SA* c.7 was. Rather, *CD* 'reflects fourteenth-century conceptions of legal practice and procedure to the point of updating earlier laws enacted by past kings of Scots'.[84] Consequently, while *CD* c.41 constitutes extremely strong evidence concerning what actually happened in practice in cases of novel dissasine, it may be worth pausing to consider whether or not the text in itself demonstrates that full forfeiture was always a *necessary* consequence of failure to sustain a claim.

This is not merely pedantic. I have argued elsewhere that other acts promulgated in 1230 may have privileged the position of certain classes of litigants. Arguably *SA* c.6 reveals that most people who made allegations of theft or robbery risked falling into the mercy of the king if they failed to sustain their accusations. *SA* c.5, by contrast, did not compel widows, clergymen and those who were unable to fight more generally to take this risk when seeking redress for theft.[85] While the context of this development is complex, part of the reason for the special protection offered may lie in what MacQueen described as the duty of the king and his council 'to protect the specially vulnerable and needy' and in particular clergymen, widows, orphans and foreigners.[86] Is it possible, then, that the vague 'forfeiture' referred to in *SA* c.7 could have varied depending upon the identity of the litigant?

No firm evidence has been found to answer that question in the affirmative. Consequently the assumption must remain that one forfeiture applied to all litigants. Furthermore, the best evidence that historians currently possess indicates that the forfeiture in question was the full forfeiture of £10. But it is suggested that the claim that failure to vindicate a claim of novel dissasine *necessarily* resulted in full forfeiture does rest primarily on the evidence of *CD* c.41. Those who believe that the rest of the surviving evidence of the period indicates that the common law *was* widely used in the thirteenth century may wish to explore that observation further. In particular, they may wish to examine in detail what is known about forfeiture, and the question of whether or not different levels of forfeiture were applied in practice. In this regard it is worth mentioning that Carpenter does note three other examples of the uses of brieves in practice, and concludes that the claimants involved 'were all women of some substance'. The implication, presumably, is that they could afford to take the risk of losing their cases. Yet Carpenter admits that one of the women in question, Emma of Smeaton, was 'self-confessedly "poor"' but he suggests that '[t]his poverty . . . was evidently relative since she was able to achieve a settlement which brought her 20 marks a year for life'. Yet Emma of Smeaton was not just poor; she was a widow, and this may be of some significance.[87] Likewise the two other litigants mentioned by Carpenter were also widows who used the brieve of novel dissasine.[88] So one possible conclusion is that these women were all 'of some substance', and could afford to risk losing an action begun by brieve – even though one might reasonably doubt that in the case of Emma of Smeaton. The other possibility – which, it must be strongly emphasised, is nothing more than a possibility – is that these litigants took no risk, or a very small risk, when they brought actions by brieve, because, as widows, they were protected litigants. On my reading of *SA* c.5–6, widows did not risk falling into the king's mercy when they initiated proceedings in cases of theft. Perhaps the same was true when they sought to initiate actions through the brieves. However, even if this were to be proven, it might be objected that, if the king 'needed to waive the rules' of forfeiture for certain ligitants, 'then the brieves were . . . more brieves of grace than brieves of course'.[89] In response to that argument it could be noted that it depends on the view that 'full forfeiture' was the normal rule in such cases, which rests on the evidence of *CD* c.41.

How widely, then, was the Scottish common law used in practice? The arguments advanced above do not conclusively answer that question one way or the other. Nor do they prove that MacQueen's reading of the evidence on the subject is to be preferred to that of Carpenter. What they do perhaps show is that there may be more to be said concerning the validity of many of Carpenter's objections to MacQueen's broad thesis. It is also hoped that the outline of the debate between the two scholars offered here may help to stimulate further research into the topics discussed.

THE 'FEE AND HERITAGE' RULE AND THE ORIGINS OF THE COLLEGE OF JUSTICE: PROFESSOR GODFREY'S ANALYSIS

In the case of *Weems* v. *Forbes* (1542), the supreme Scottish court in civil matters declared that 'the breif of rycht is nor hes nocht yit bene mony yeiris usit in this realme'.[90] Similarly MacQueen concluded that the brieves of mortancestry and novel dissasine had fallen out of use by the early sixteenth century, and indeed perhaps earlier than that in the case of the latter form of action.[91] Given the significance of the brieves in the thirteenth and fourteenth centuries as discussed above, and, given their continuing importance during much of the fifteenth century,[92] this calls for some explanation, and in *Common Law and Feudal Society* MacQueen attempted to tackle the problem. In so doing he developed a sophisticated thesis that linked the decline of the brieves system, on the one hand, with reforms in the administration of justice and the Scottish courts more generally, on the other.[93] On the basis of rigorous and scholarly engagement with that thesis, supported by original and extensive archival research, Mark Godfrey has since produced a new study of the decline of the brieves system and the development of the Session, the court that he has argued came to enjoy *de facto* supreme jurisdiction in Scottish civil matters at some point prior to 1532.[94] This does demonstrate that elements of MacQueen's argument are no longer tenable in relation to the acquisition of jurisdiction over fee and heritage by the Session, and are no longer convincing in relation to the significance of the foundation of the College of Justice. Nonetheless, Godfrey's conclusions sit well with much else of MacQueen's research concerning the decline of the brieves and the work of the Session, especially for scholars exploring doctrinal legal developments in the fifteenth century.[95]

Here the aims will simply be to explain MacQueen's original thesis, and to explore the ways in which Godfrey has engaged critically with it.

MacQueen's Thesis

MacQueen introduced his thesis by examining the extent to which the brieves rule originally limited the jurisdiction of certain courts to hear disputes over title to land. Given that no one could be ejected from his free tenement of which he claimed to be vest and saised as of fee without the king's pleadable brieve, it followed that only those courts to which the brieves were addressed could deal with such matters. While brieves might be addressed to the courts of the sheriff, the justiciar and also to the burgh courts, they were never addressed to Parliament or to the King's Council. It should be noted that the the King's Council was 'a smaller, less formal and more flexible body' than Parliament, which 'had always exercised a residual jurisdiction outside the normal course of the common law'.[96] The reasons why the brieves were never addressed to Parliament or the King's Council were simple. As Godfrey puts it, '[b]eing in the King's name and requiring local process in a particular area of the country, no "coursable" brieve (i.e. those in standard form relating to established forms of remedy) could be addressed to King and Council directly, in Parliament or otherwise'. He continues by explaining that '[t]he very structure of the procedure presupposed the direction of a brieve to a local (albeit royal) judge who could carry out the royal instructions on the ground'. Of course, the resulting judgment or 'doom' might be falsed by a higher court, and ultimately by Parliament.[97]

Consequently, when sitting in its judicial capacity, the King's Council could not hear actions concerning matters protected by the brieves rule. MacQueen also argued that there was a further limitation on the jurisdiction of the King's Council; it could not hear disputes concerning matters that touched 'fee and heritage'. Given what has been said above concerning the significance of the requirement that one had to hold lands '*ut de feudo*' in order to claim the protection of the brieves rule, it might be thought that Carpenter's research implies a fundamental similarity between the two rules. And yet, regardless, MacQueen's work continues to demonstrate that the two rules were distinct. This can be seen from the case of *Forbes* v. *Wemyss* (1479). There the claimants sought a remedy for spuilzie of oxen and corns out of lands before the King's Council. A '[s]puilzie was in essence an action to recover possession of goods'.[98] During the 1540s a spuilzie was said to arise where a man had been in possession of a thing and had then been violently dispossessed of it, and the remedy was restitution.[99] While the King's Council did have jurisdiction over spuilzies under an Act of Parliament of 1458,[100]

MacQueen noted that sometimes 'the defender's justification for seizing the goods was his assertion of some right in land'.[101] In the action of spuilzie brought in *Forbes* v. *Wemyss* (1479), the King's Council declined to exercise jurisdiction 'because the landis that the said gudis was takin of is clamyt fee and heretage be baith the said parties and the questioun of the richt dependis apoun heretage'. Importantly this 'fee and heritage' rule was not simply the brieves rule in operation, because the defenders 'could show no ex facie valid title to justify any possession of Rires [the disputed lands] they may have had' and so 'they could not have claimed the protection of the 1318 act'.[102] On this basis MacQueen argued that the 'fee and heritage' rule operated *alongside* the brieves rule to exclude the jurisdiction of the King's Council in disputes over questions of right in land. He argued that the 'true origin' of the fee and heritage rule lay 'in the exclusion of the jurisdiction of parliament and council where there was an ordinary common-law remedy'.[103] In the process, he put many fifteenth-century statutes into their proper context, facilitating their interpretation. A very good example is the act of 1450 'concerning defenders contumaciously not compearing in answer to summonses before council'.[104] MacQueen's work therefore remains essential reading for anyone wishing to engage in detailed research concerning Scottish doctrinal legal history.

In *Common Law and Feudal Society*, MacQueen also observed that the King's Council, through its judicial 'Sessions', eventually acquired jurisdiction over matters touching fee and heritage, in spite of the older rules that limited its authority in relation to such disputes.[105] In the past scholars have suggested that this might have had something to do with the fact that the Session was placed on a new institutional footing as a College of Justice in 1532.[106] This will be discussed in more detail shortly. In an article published in 1984 MacQueen argued there was no direct, causative link between this institutional change and the acquisition of jurisdiction over fee and heritage.[107] He examined several cases decided in the Session after 1532, and argued that '[t]he jurisdiction in heritage of the lords of council and session seems . . . to have been developed over a period of years, rather than in any one particular case'.[108] Nonetheless, he also argued that the acts of the Scottish parliament that reconstituted the Session as a College of Justice 'could be used to give legal authority to what clearly appears as an expansionist attitude of the court to its jurisdiction in the 1530s and 1540s'.[109] He outlined essentially the same position in 1993, in *Common Law and Feudal Society*.[110] MacQueen also offered several explanations for the success of the Session in asserting jurisdiction over matters of fee and heritage. He noted that procedure on brieve had become fraught with delay by the beginning of the fifteenth century. This was particularly true of the form of process known as 'falsing the doom', whereby the decision reached by procedure on brieve could be challenged. Furthermore, the local judges, and in particular the sheriffs, who administered the common law, often lacked the legal training required to make sense of the complex legal disputes that came before them. For such reasons, litigants put pressure on the King's Council to accept jurisdiction in an increasing number of cases, in the hope of finding speedier justice administered by more professional judges.[111]

Godfrey's Qualifications of MacQueen's Thesis

Godfrey's work qualifies various elements of this thesis and rejects substantial parts of it.[112] In so doing, he draws on his own ground-breaking archival research into the Acts of the Lords of Council surviving from the late fifteenth century and the early sixteenth century. In fact, Godfrey is the first scholar to attempt to reconstruct the practice of litigation in the Session on the basis of systematic scrutiny of the extensive archive of original manuscript records of the court, and it is this methodology that has allowed him to build on, develop and in some places depart from the earlier analysis put forward by MacQueen.

Godfrey considers the cases cited by MacQueen as evidence for the proposition that the judges or Lords in the Session were consciously expanding their jurisdiction during the 1530s and 1540s so that they could deal with matters of fee and heritage. He argues that the cases do not, in fact, reveal that the Lords were attempting to assert a new authority to adjudicate in relation to such disputes.[113] Rather, they are simply examples of a jurisdiction that the Lords had been asserting throughout the 1530s and indeed before the reconstitution of the Session as a College of Justice in 1532.[114]

How, then, are historians to explain the development of the jurisdiction of the Lords of Session, and the consequences this had for both the brieves rule and the fee and heritage rule? Godfrey explores these matters through a detailed examination of the relevant evidence. He concludes that the fee and heritage rule only ever limited the jurisdiction of the Session where there was 'more than one competing claim to a disputed title, backed up by showing lawful interest in the title'; and even then the authority of the Lords was only limited if 'the decision would involve a final determination of right'.[115] Godfrey then shows that from 1513 onwards the Lords ceased declining jurisdiction on the basis of the operation of the fee and heritage rule. However, rather than directly confronting either the fee and heritage rule or the related brieves rule, he argues that they did something subtler. While they did not have jurisdiction to determine the outcome of disputes where there was 'more than one competing claim to a disputed title', it would seem that they always had enjoyed authority to 'examine the intrinsic validity of title and reduce such titles when some cause of invalidity was shown such as fault in transfer or incidental legal process'.[116] Godfrey thus reconceptualises the fee and heritage rule and interprets its scope more narrowly than MacQueen. On this basis, Godfrey argues that the Lords were able to adjudicate in disputes that involved *some* element of fee and heritage. During the late 1400s and the early 1500s this seems to have enabled them to exercise jurisdiction in an increasing number of cases that previously would have fallen foul of the fee and heritage rule (or indeed the brieves rule). A good example is the case of *Spittal* v. *Spittal* (1531). In that case there was an underlying dispute over title to lands between two parties – Archibald Spittal and Finlay Spittal. But that was not how the matter was approached in court. Archibald Spittal argued that Finlay Spittal acquired sasine of his lands 'by sinister information circumnevand the kinges grace', even though Archibald himself had been 'heretably infeft' in the lands. Consequently Archibald sought reduction of Finlay's title. This remedy was granted, and Finlay was left in the lands, but without any lawful basis to remain there. Archibald then raised a subsequent action of removing in February 1532 against Finlay to recover possession of his property.[117]

Godfrey suggests that, through exercising its jurisdiction to reduce infeftments in this way, the Session had already acquired *de facto* supreme jurisdiction in civil matters prior to its reconstitution as a College of Justice in 1532. This is actually just one example of how the court developed a whole framework of actions and remedies that operated *alongside* that provided by the brieves. It was within the latter framework of the brieves that the administration of justice locally according to the common law – and so the fee and heritage rule – made sense. Godfrey argues that there was no single moment in which the framework of remedies offered by the Session replaced that which operated through the brieves. Rather, as he puts it, '[i]t seems that both the remedial frameworks applicable to heritage disputes were simultaneously valid over an extensive transitional period which was thereby marked by legal ambiguity'. But '[b]y 1532 . . . the undoubted competence of the Session to approach heritage disputes in terms of reduction seems to have left the older framework with no useful application'.[118] It was for this reason, too, that by 1542 the Lords in *Weems* v. *Forbes* could hold that 'the breif of rycht is nor hes nocht yit bene mony yeiris usit in this realme' without making any departure from their past practice.

There is one final way in which Godfrey rejects an element of MacQueen's argument. This concerns the significance or otherwise of the creation of the College of Justice at the time of its foundation in 1532. The older established view of Richard Hannay and Archibald Duncan was that this was no more than an excuse to tax the church with papal blessing, and that it made little difference to the operation of the Session in practice.[119] In the light of this, MacQueen took the view that 'the erection of the College [of Justice] effected no change in the structure, personnel or record-keeping of the court'.[120] Godfrey challenges this claim during the course of a broader argument concerning the reconstitution of the Session in 1532.[121] In very brief terms, Godfrey argues that the developing jurisdiction of the Session arose in part as a result of pressure from litigants who wanted the Lords to hear an increasing range of disputes. They were dissatisfied with the quality of justice offered by untrained judges in the localities. Gradually the jurisdiction of the Lords developed in response. Ultimately it seems to have been recognised during the 1520s that one of the great advantages of the justice administered in the Session was that many of its judges were experienced adjudicators who were learned in the law, and specifically in the learned laws, the legal traditions structured around the texts of Roman law and canon law. At the same time, the personal rule of James V from 1528 seems to have given impetus to attempts to remodel the Session, enhance its effectiveness as a law court, and liberate it from the influence of the noblemen who were in attendance at the King's Council. To explain, while the Session remained nothing more than a sitting of Council in its judicial capacity, any member of the King's Council could participate in reaching its judgments, and many members of the King's Council were not legally trained. Drawing also on the work of John Cairns on the intentions behind the idea of establishing such a College,[122] Godfrey argues that the reconstitution of the Session as a College of Justice was intended to remedy this problem, and that it represented a coherent final step in a process of institutional reform that had been in train since the 1520s. Now that the Session existed on a separate institutional footing from Council, it would be possible to control more easily who could and could not sit in a court that was, after all, exercising supreme civil jurisdiction.[123] Thus, departing from MacQueen's analysis, Godfrey argues that the formal institutional changes were highly significant in establishing the Session as a supreme court in 1532. Furthermore, the supreme character of the court is reinforced if he is correct in arguing that it was already exercising an unrestricted civil jurisdiction before this time as a result of longer-term development of its remedies and jurisdiction.[124]

CONCLUSION

Harding's assessment of *Common Law and Feudal Society* as 'one of [the] most penetrating studies yet produced of any period of Scottish legal history'[125] is vindicated by the ways in which scholars have engaged with the work since its publication in 1993. Time and again MacQueen's detailed reconstruction of the framework of the medieval Scottish common law has inspired and enabled researchers to explore its development further. Where historians have departed from his views, they have often done so in such a way as to show that this would not have been possible without the foundation laid by MacQueen's scholarship. Even in areas of his argument that have been undermined or superseded – such as that advanced in the eighth chapter of his book concerning the fee and heritage rule – readers who are aware of how the discipline has developed since 1993 can still hope to learn a great deal through studying his work. The book undoubtedly merits the status of being a 'classic' text among works on Scottish legal history.

The arguments advanced above also show that historians interested in the study of medieval Scots law have a great deal to look forward to as regards the development of research into the field. It should be noted that, while the focus of this introduction has been on *Common Law and Feudal Society*, MacQueen's more recent contributions to the discipline have shed considerable light on a variety of other areas of medieval Scots law, and continue to explore intriguing lines of enquiry.[126] Furthermore, based on the work she has already produced, Taylor's book *The Shape of the State* promises to be perhaps the most significant contribution to the study of medieval Scots law since *Common Law and Feudal Society* was published in 1993. Carpenter's article has done much to challenge orthodox views of the Scottish legal past, and his debate with MacQueen's work will undoubtedly prove fruitful. Godfrey's work has convincingly shown how the use of the brieves in the administration of justice gradually gave way to the framework of remedies administered by the College of Justice. This makes it possible now to examine how – and why – the medieval heritage of the Scottish common law came to embrace so extensively the learning of Roman law and canon law during the medieval period.[127] It may also facilitate the study of the important jurisdictional shifts that took place during the mid-sixteenth century.[128]

What is very clear is that all these contributions to the discipline of Scottish legal history will derive much of their force from the rigorous research contained in *Common Law and Feudal Society*. That is surely a very great tribute to the book, and also to its author.

June 2015

NOTES

1. A. Harding, 'Review of Hector L. MacQueen, *Common Law and Feudal Society in Medieval Scotland*', *Scottish Historical Review*, 74 (1995), 115–17 at 115.
2. To name a few important examples, see J. W. Cairns, 'Historical introduction', in K. C. G. Reid and R. Zimmermann (eds), *A History of Private Law in Scotland, Volume 1: Introduction and Property* (Oxford, 2000), 14–183, in particular at 27–50; A. M. Godfrey, *Civil Justice in Renaissance Scotland: The Origins of a Central Court* (Leiden, 2009); C. Neville, *Land, Law and People in Medieval Scotland* (Edinburgh, 2010), at 19 and 42, A. Taylor, 'The assizes of David I, king of Scots, 1124–53', *Scottish Historical Review*, 91 (2012), 197–238, in particular at 216–21; D. Carpenter, 'Scottish royal government in the thirteenth century from an English perspective', in M. Hammond (ed.), *New Perspectives on Medieval Scotland 1093–1286* (Woodbridge, 2013), 117–59; A. Taylor, *The Shape of the State in Medieval Scotland* (Oxford, forthcoming).
3. See H. L. MacQueen, *Common Law and Feudal Society* (Edinburgh, 1993), 105–214. Admittedly Carpenter, 'Scottish royal government', 138–54, challenges the extent to which this law was truly 'common' during the thirteenth century; more will be said about this below.
4. As regards the significant role performed by both legal systems in the development of a Scottish legal culture, see MacQueen, *Common Law and Feudal Society*, and also H. L. MacQueen, 'Canon law, custom and legislation: Law in the reign of Alexander II', in R. Oram (ed.), *The Reign of Alexander II, 1214–49* (Leiden and Boston, 2005), 221–51 at 242–3.
5. MacQueen, *Common Law and Feudal Society*, 266; see also A. R. C. Simpson, 'Procedures for dealing with robbery in Scotland before 1400', in A. R. C. Simpson, S. C. Styles, E. West and A. L. M. Wilson (eds), *Continuity, Change and Pragmatism in the Law: Essays in Memory of Professor Angelo Forte* (Aberdeen, 2016). A similar, but not identical, idea can be traced in Barrow's statement that the office of the Scottish justiciar 'began as an exotic innovation yet within a few generations took on the protective colouring of a thoroughly native species'. See G. W. S. Barrow, *The Kingdom of the Scots* (Edinburgh, 2003), 98. I am grateful to Mark Godfrey for drawing this to my attention.
6. MacQueen, *Common Law and Feudal Society*, 264–7; the point was also argued convincingly in W. D. H. Sellar, 'The resilience of the Scottish common law', in David L. Carey Miller and Reinhard Zimmermann (eds), *The Civilian Tradition and Scots Law: Aberdeen Quincentenary Essays* (Berlin, 1997), 149–64 at 164.
7. The theme of continuity in the development of the common law was first developed by Sellar, and can be traced in a number of his articles, perhaps most obviously in W. D. H. Sellar, 'Scots law: Mixed from the very beginning? A tale of two receptions',

Edinburgh Law Review, 4 (2000), 3–18. For a more recent study
defending this view, see Simpson, 'Procedures for dealing with
robbery'.

8. See, e.g., Godfrey, *Civil Justice*, 94–160; this point is discussed in
more detail below.

9. See above at xiii–xxi.

10. See above at xx–xxi; see also, e.g., J. Wormald, 'Scotland: 1406–
1513', in C. Allmand (ed.), *The New Cambridge Medieval History,
Volume VII: c.1415–c.1500* (Cambridge, 1998), 514–31; A. Grant,
Independence and Nationhood: Scotland 1306–1469 (Edinburgh, 1984;
reprinted 1991).

11. See, e.g., MacQueen, *Common Law and Feudal Society*, 1–26, 35–50,
115–22, 247–54.

12. To name a few important examples, see A. Taylor, '*Leges Scocie*
and the lawcodes of David I, William the Lion and Alexander II',
Scottish Historical Review, 88 (2009), 207–88; A Taylor, 'The assizes
of David I, king of Scots, 1124–53', *Scottish Historical Review*, 91
(2012), 197–238; A Taylor, 'Crime without punishment:
Medieval Scotland in comparative perspective', in D. Bates (ed.),
*Anglo-Norman Studies: Proceedings of the Battle Conference 2012,
35* (Woodbridge, 2013), 287–304; A Taylor, '*Homo ligius* and
unfreedom in medieval Scotland', in M. Hammond (ed.), *New
Perspectives on Medieval Scotland, 1093–1286* (Woodbridge, 2013),
85–116.

13. This is explained in Taylor, 'Assizes of David I', 199–200.

14. Taylor, '*Leges Scocie*', 250–88.

15. T. D. Fergus, *Quoniam Attachiamenta* (Stair Society, vol. 44;
Edinburgh, 1996).

16. I should mention here that in May 2014 Alice Taylor very kindly
let me read a draft of chapter 5 of *The Shape of the State*
concerning the thirteenth-century law. I have not made reference
to this draft when preparing this Foreword, nor have I made any
conscious use of the arguments presented there, because it
seems best to wait until Taylor's work is in print before comparing
it with that of MacQueen in detail. Nonetheless, it is worth
emphasising that elements of the arguments presented here may
have to be refined or qualified in the light of *The Shape of the
State*. Note that in a recent article Dauvit Broun has made
reference to a draft of Taylor's book as a whole. He states that a
'key feature' of her work 'is that, time and again, her innovative
understanding of statehood hinges on an overlooked word or
phrase, or on seeing sense in the untidy arrangement of a text or
in an apparent contradiction'. While sociological accounts of
statehood can, of course, be illuminating, Broun points out that,
in Taylor's analysis of what it might mean to speak of medieval
Scottish 'statehood', '[t]he starting point is a textual puzzle, not
an explanatory construct'. See D. Broun, 'Statehood and
lordship in "Scotland" before the mid-twelfth century', *Innes
Review*, 66 (2015), 1–71 at 8–11; the passages quoted are to be
found at pp. 8 and 9. I am grateful to Hector MacQueen for
drawing the significance of this article to my attention. Taylor

employs this approach to great effect – as indeed does Broun. It is worth noting that MacQueen also treated the rigorous exploration of textual puzzles generated by the brieves as the 'starting point' in his research, and it was on that basis that he engaged critically with the 'explanatory construct' of the 'legal transplant' that was developed by Alan Watson. See MacQueen, *Common Law and Feudal Society*, 5, 264–7. For Watson's account of legal transplants, see A. Watson, *Legal Transplants: An Approach to Comparative Law* (2nd edn, Athens, GA, and London, 1993). Watson's own explanatory construct was derived from rigorous historical textual scholarship; see, e.g., Watson, *Legal Transplants*, 1–9, 21–30.

17. Taylor, 'Assizes of David I', 216–18.

18. Taylor, 'Assizes of David I'. The statues themselves can be found in A. A. M. Duncan, *The Acts of Robert I, King of Scots, Regesta Regum Scottorum*, vol. 5 (Edinburgh, 1988), no. 139, and 414–15; see also *The Records of the Parliaments of Scotland to 1707*, ed. K. M. Brown et al. (St Andrews, 2007–15) (hereafter *RPS*) 1318/ 1–29, available at <http://rps.ac.uk/> (accessed 26 May 2015).

19. MacQueen, *Common Law and Feudal Society*, 106 (the rule is discussed in detail at pp. 105–22); see also Taylor, 'Assizes of David I', 228, and *RPS* 1318/27. The extent to which this rule simply confirmed existing common law rules in 1318 is controversial; see Carpenter, 'Scottish royal government', 143–5.

20 MacQueen, *Common Law and Feudal Society*, 157, summarising the more detailed argument outlined at pp. 113–14. Note that MacQueen's account of the operation of the 1318 act is challenged in Carpenter, 'Scottish royal government', 144–5. More will be said about this below. Note that the rule that one could not be ejected from a free holding of which one claimed to be vested and saised as of fee without the king's pleadable brieve or some similar brieve was not without qualification. MacQueen discusses in some detail the point that lords could exercise disciplinary jurisdiction over their tenants through a procedure known as 'recognition'. They could do this without a brieve, and this could result in the temporary loss of the tenant's lands. Disciplinary jurisdiction was available where the tenant failed to render services owed to the lord, and on the basis of the following particular causes of action: the tenant's unlicensed alienation of his lands to a third party (possibly rendering the tenant unable to perform services due to the lord), purpresture or purprision ('defined as encroachment by a tenant upon the demesne of his lord') and showing the holding. 'Showing the holding' was 'an action by which, in its developed form, a lord compelled his tenant to display the charters on which he held his lands . . . the aim of the process was not so much to challenge tenants' titles as to enable a lord to take stock of his tenants and the services which they owed him . . . If the services had not been provided, the lord could recognosce, and the brieves rule was inapplicable to cases of this type.' For this sort of disciplinary jurisdiction, which could be exercised regardless of the brieves

rule, see MacQueen, *Common Law and Feudal Society*, 115–22; the passages quoted are at pp. 118, 120 and 121.

21. MacQueen, *Common Law and Feudal Society*, 140.
22. For these points, see MacQueen, *Common Law and Feudal Society*, 146–53; the passage quoted is at p. 151; see also *RPS* 1318/15.
23. MacQueen, *Common Law and Feudal Society*, 106–7, 152–3.
24. H. L. MacQueen, '*Regiam Majestatem*, Scots Law and National Identity', *Scottish Historical Review*, 74 (1995), 1–25 at 5.
25. Taylor, 'Assizes of David I'.
26. Taylor, '*Leges Scocie*'; Taylor's nuanced conclusion that '*LS* must be seen to contain legislative information primarily relating to the twelfth and early thirteenth centuries' is at p. 243.
27. This is discussed in Taylor, 'Assizes of David I', 197–201, 214–21, 226–8.
28. See Taylor, 'Assizes of David I', 220–1.
29. Taylor, 'Assizes of David I', 220.
30. See Taylor, 'Assizes of David I', 221–3; Carpenter, 'Scottish royal government', 143–4. For MacQueen's views concerning the origins, development and roles of the brieve of right, see MacQueen, *Common Law and Feudal Society*, 188–214.
31. Taylor, 'Assizes of David I', 226–31. The date of the Ayr Manuscript is given at pp. 201–2; a digitised copy of the manuscript itself is also available online at <http://stairsociety.org/resources/manuscript/the_ayr_manuscript> (accessed 26 May 2015). The act of 1318 to which she refers here can be found at *RPS* 1318/12.
32. Taylor, 'Assizes of David I', 231–5.
33. A. Harding, '*Regiam Majestatem* amongst medieval law books', *Juridical Review*, NS 29 (1984), 97–111.
34. Taylor, 'Assizes of David I', 235.
35. See Carpenter, 'Scottish royal government', 117–18.
36. Carpenter, 'Scottish royal government', 117–18, 154–5.
37. Carpenter, 'Scottish royal government', 140.
38. MacQueen, *Common Law and Feudal Society*, 167.
39. In so doing Carpenter expressly engages in an existing debate among Scottish historians; as he notes in 'Scottish royal government' at p. 140, Lord Cooper in particular thought that 'the common law procedures had very limited currency in the thirteenth century' and that 'most civil disputes were settled by agreement, arbitration, and litigation in ecclesiastical courts'. Carpenter cites, for example, T. M. Cooper, *Select Scottish Cases of the Thirteenth Century* (Edinburgh, 1944), pp. xxi–lxviii. Of course, Cooper's view was subjected to criticism in *Common Law and Feudal Society*, as is explained in MacQueen's Preface to this edition.
40. See A. Grant, 'Franchises north of the border', in M. Prestwich (ed.), *Liberties and Identities in the Medieval British Isles* (Woodbridge, 2008), 155–99. For the work of the sheriff, see W. Croft Dickinson, *Sheriff Court Book of Fife* (Scottish History Society, Third Series, vol. 12; Edinburgh, 1928), particularly at pp. xi–cv and 309–88. On the justiciar, see G. W. S. Barrow, *The*

Kingdom of the Scots: Government, Church and Society from the Eleventh to the Fourteenth Century (2nd edn., Edinburgh, 2003), 68–111; see also MacQueen, *Common Law and Feudal Society*, 58–65, and H. L. MacQueen, 'Tame magnates? The justiciars of later medieval Scotland', in S. Boardman and J. Goodare (eds), *Kings, Lords and Men in Scotland and Britain, 1300–1625: Essays in Honour of Jenny Wormald* (Edinburgh, 2014), 93–120.

41. Carpenter, 'Scottish royal government', 118–19, 129. Carpenter acknowledges (at p. 119) that the evidence for this pattern is drawn from the late fourteenth and early fifteenth centuries, but follows Grant in suggesting (at n. 8) that 'most of the earldoms and provincial lordships dated back much earlier'.

42. Carpenter, 'Scottish royal government', 118–38.

43   Carpenter, 'Scottish royal government', 132, citing Grant, 'Franchises', 167, 172.

44. Carpenter, 'Scottish royal government', 141–3.

45. See, e.g., MacQueen, *Common Law and Feudal Society*, 33–54.

46. MacQueen, *Common Law and Feudal Society*, 42.

47. See MacQueen, *Common Law and Feudal Society*, 42–7; note also the provisions of *LS* c.7, in Taylor, '*Leges Scocie*', 282–3, and G. W. S. Barrow (ed.), *The Charters of King David I: The Written Acts of David I King of Scots, 1124–53 and of his Son Henry Earl of Northumberland, 1139–52* (Woodbridge, 1999), 147 (no. 190). Grant, 'Franchises', 191, suggests that the final clause of *LS* c.7 was a 'dead letter', but the only contemporary evidence he cites to show this is the precise wording of the 'restatement' of this rule found in *Regiam Majestatem*, and the textual authority of the printed version of *Regiam* is questionable.

48. Again, see *LS* c.7 and Barrow, *Charters of David I*, 147 (no. 190). See also (possibly) the role of the sergeands in *LS* c.1, in Taylor, '*Leges Scocie*', 280–1. For the *judices*, see Barrow, *Kingdom*, 57–67, and also now D. Broun, 'The king's "brithem" (Gaelic for "judge") and the recording of dispute-resolutions', Feature of the Month: No. 11, April 2010, available at <http://paradox.poms.ac.uk/feature/april10.html> (accessed 27 May 2015). For the sergeands, see, e.g., W. Croft Dickinston, 'Surdit de sergeant', *Scottish Historical Review*, 39 (1960), 170–5; H. L. MacQueen, 'The laws of Galloway: A preliminary survey', in R. D. Oram and G. P. Stell (eds), *Galloway: Land and Lordship* (Edinburgh, 1991), 131–43.

49. I am grateful to Greg Gordon of Aberdeen University for discussing this point with me.

50. See Taylor, '*Leges Scocie*', 285.

51. Carpenter, 'Scottish royal government', 142.

52. See Taylor, 'Assizes of David I', 218, for the text of *SA* c.7; see also MacQueen, *Common Law and Feudal Society*, 140, and more generally the argument advanced at pp. 136–44.

53. MacQueen, *Common Law and Feudal Society*, 193–4.

54. MacQueen, *Common Law and Feudal Society*, 204–7 (discussing evidence drawn primarily from periods later than the thirteenth century).

55. Carpenter, 'Scottish royal government', 142.
56. MacQueen, *Common Law and Feudal Society*, 193.
57. MacQueen, *Common Law and Feudal Society*, 194–6.
58. T. M. Cooper (ed.), *The Register of Brieves as Contained in the Ayr MS, the Bute MS and Quoniam Attachiamenta* (Stair Society, vol. 10; Edinburgh, 1946), 40; A. A. M. Duncan (ed.), *Scottish Formularies* (Stair Society, vol. 58; Edinburgh, 2011), 17 (item A19).
59. MacQueen, *Common Law and Feudal Society*, 112–13. For the use of brieves similar to royal brieves in the regality courts, see also W. Croft Dickinson, *The Court Book of the Barony of Carnwath 1523–1542* (Scottish History Society, Third Series, vol. 29; Edinburgh, 1937), pp. xl–xlii; J. M. Webster and A. A. M. Duncan (eds), *Regality of Dunfermline Court Book 1531–1538* (Alva, 1953), 8–9, 30–1. I am grateful to Mark Godfrey for referring me to these works.
60. The word 'chancery' does not seem to have been used in thirteenth-century Scottish sources; brieves were issued by the king's 'chapel'. See Carpenter, 'Scottish royal government', 121, citing A. L. Murray, 'The Scottish Chancery in the fourteenth and fifteenth centuries', in K. Fianu and D. J. Guth (eds), *Écrit et pouvoir dans les chancelleries médiévales: Espace français, espace anglais* (Louvain-la- Neuve, 1997), 143–9.
61. Taylor, 'Crime without punishment', 293–4.
62. Taylor, 'Crime without punishment', 300.
63. *RPS* 1318/27.
64. Obviously this argument owes a great deal to that advanced in Taylor, 'Crime without punishment'.
65. Taylor, 'Crime without punishment', 294.
66. By the fifteenth century such lords were frequently ordered to administer essentially the legal standards that were observed in the rest of the kingdom within their own regalities. Failing this, they could theoretically face direct interference in their jurisdiction by the sheriff, who was empowered to see that right was done in the case in question. See, e.g., *RPS* 1372/3/6, 1404/9, 1425/3/25, 1434/5; A1438/12/1, 1450/1/9/–10.
67. Carpenter, 'Scottish royal government', 143.
68. MacQueen, *Common Law and Feudal Society*, 105–6.
69. Carpenter, 'Scottish royal government', 143–4.
70. An obvious example in the modern law can be found in the rules of legitim, which entitle a child to inherit a portion of moveable goods from a deceased parent. Claiming legitim bars a child from inheriting under the parent's will. The child is thus left with a choice. Obviously in this case the fact that the law does not compel a child to claim legitim does not imply any lack of commitment to the enforcement of the right if it is invoked. For legitim, see, e.g., Lord Eassie and H. L. MacQueen (eds), *The Law of Scotland by The Late W. M. Gloag, KC, LLD and The Late R. Candlish Henderson, QC, LLD* (13th edn, Edinburgh, 2012), paras 38.08–38.15.
71. Carpenter, 'Scottish royal government', 144.

72. MacQueen, *Common Law and Feudal Society*, 105.
73. MacQueen, *Common Law and Feudal Society*, 105–9.
74. Carpenter, 'Scottish royal government', 144–5.
75. MacQueen, *Common Law and Feudal Society*, 156; see also Duncan, *Scottish Formularies*, 18–19 (item A21).
76. MacQueen, *Common Law and Feudal Society*, 157.
77. Carpenter, 'Scottish royal government', 145–8.
78. Carpenter, 'Scottish royal government', 148.
79. Taylor, 'Assizes of David I', 218.
80. See the PoMS website at <http://www.poms.ac.uk/> (accessed 28 May 2015).
81. Taylor, 'Assizes of David I', 219.
82. Carpenter, 'Scottish royal government', 148.
83. Carpenter, 'Scottish royal government', 148–50.
84. Taylor, 'Assizes of David I', 230.
85. See Simpson, 'Procedures for dealing with robbery'. I am very grateful to Alice Taylor for sharing with me a draft of her critical edition of *SA* c.5–6. I am not certain that she agrees with the interpretation I place upon those acts as outlined here, and of course any errors in this regard remain entirely my own.
86. MacQueen, *Common Law and Feudal Society*, 220 (I am grateful to Hector MacQueen for initially drawing this point to my attention). The point is discussed at more length in Simpson, 'Procedures for dealing with robbery'.
87. See PoMS, H1/8/20, available at <http://db.poms.ac.uk/record/ source/979/#> (accessed 28 May 2015).
88. Carpenter, 'Scottish royal government', 152–3.
89. Carpenter, 'Scottish royal government', 152.
90. The case is discussed in MacQueen, *Common Law and Feudal Society*, 239–42; the contemporary note of the decision itself can be found in A. L. Murray and G. Dolezalek (eds), *Sinclair's Practicks*, available at <*http://home.uni-leipzig.de/jurarom/scotland/dat/sinclair.htm*> (accessed 28 May 2015), case-note 308.
91. MacQueen, *Common Law and Feudal Society*, 161–2, 183.
92. See MacQueen, *Common Law and Feudal Society*, 153–61, 177–83, 200–9.
93. MacQueen, *Common Law and Feudal Society*, 215–42.
94. Godfrey, *Civil Justice*.
95. That work is largely contained in chapter 8 of MacQueen, *Common Law and Feudal Society* (at pp. 215–42).
96. Godfrey, *Civil Justice*, 11. Of course the 'sessions' later became the Session, the predecessor of the modern Court of Session (of which more will be said below).
97. Godfrey, *Civil Justice*, 21.
98. MacQueen, *Common Law and Feudal Society*, 224.
99. Dolezalek and Murray (eds), *Sinclair's Practicks*, case-note 389, *Laird of Lochinvar* v. *Earl of Cassillis* (1546). MacQueen's work on fifteenth-century spuilzie remains the most authoritative, in part because it is rooted in the important context of disputes over rights in land. See MacQueen,

Common Law and Feudal Society, 224–8, which is now
admirably complemented by Godfrey's work on spuilzie in the
late fifteenth and early sixteenth centuries; see Godfrey, *Civil
Justice*, 239–47. Note Godfrey's point that violence did not always
have to be libelled in an action for spuilzie. For a masterly discussion
of the later history of spuilzie, with a view to sketching the structure
of the modern action, see D. L. Carey Miller, 'Spuilzie: Dead,
dormant or manna from heaven?: Issues concerning protection of
possessory interests in Scots law', in M. de Waal and H. Mostert
(eds), *Essays in Honour of C. G. van der Merwe* (Cape Town, 2011),
129–50.

100. *RPS* 1458/3/3.
101. MacQueen, *Common Law and Feudal Society*, 224–5.
102. MacQueen, *Common Law and Feudal Society*, 227.
103. MacQueen, *Common Law and Feudal Society*, 228–8; the passage
     quoted is at p. 228.
104. MacQueen, *Common Law and Feudal Society*, 234; see *RPS*
     1450/1/30.
105. On the link between the King's Council and its Sessions, see
     Godfrey, *Civil Justice*, 11–12, 40–93.
106. For the most authoritative modern treatment of the foundation of
     the College of Justice, see Godfrey, *Civil Justice*, 94–160.
107. H. L. MacQueen, 'Jurisdiction in heritage and the Lords of
     Council and Session after 1532', in D. Sellar (ed.), *Stair Society
     Miscellany Two* (Stair Society, vol. 35; Edinburgh, 1984), 61–85 at
     84–5.
108. MacQueen, 'Jurisdiction in heritage', 82.
109. MacQueen, 'Jurisdiction in heritage', 85.
110. MacQueen, *Common Law and Feudal Society*, 239–42.
111. MacQueen, *Common Law and Feudal Society*, 240–1, 257–9.
112. See Godfrey, *Civil Justice*, particularly at 150, 155–6, 315–28,
     450.
113. See A. M. Godfrey, 'Jurisdiction in heritage and the foundation of
     the College of Justice in 1532', in H. L. MacQueen (ed.), *Stair
     Society Miscellany Four* (Stair Society, vol. 49; Edinburgh, 2002),
     9–36. Note that Godfrey demonstrates that *Cunningham* v.
     Glengarnock (1535), cited in MacQueen, *Common Law and Feudal
     Society*, 241 at n. 137, does not show – as MacQueen thought – that
     the Lords were prepared to hold that they 'could not reduce "old"
     infeftments' as late as 1535. See Godfrey, 'Jurisdiction in heritage',
     21–3.
114. Godfrey, 'Jurisdiction in heritage'; Godfrey, *Civil Justice*, 268–354,
     particularly at 310–12.
115. Godfrey, *Civil Justice*, 310.
116. Godfrey, *Civil Justice*, 310.
117. Godfrey, *Civil Justice*, 338–40.
118. Godfrey, *Civil Justice*, 452.
119. See MacQueen, 'Jurisdiction in heritage', 61–2, citing R. K.
     Hannay, *The College of Justice* (Edinburgh and Glasgow, 1933),
     37, and A. A. M. Duncan, 'The Central Courts before 1532', in
     An Introduction to Scottish Legal History (Stair Society, vol. 20;

Edinburgh, 1958), 321–40 at 336. Note that Hannay's work was reprinted by the Stair Society in *The College of Justice: Essays by R. K Hannay. Introduction by Hector L. MacQueen* (Stair Society, Supplementary Series, vol. 1; Edinburgh, 1990).

120. MacQueen, *Common Law and Feudal Society*, 242; see also MacQueen, 'Jurisdiction in heritage', 61–2.

121. Godfrey, *Civil Justice*, 150.

122. J. W. Cairns, 'Revisiting the foundation of the College of Justice', in H. L. MacQueen (ed.), *Stair Society Miscellany Five* (Stair Society, vol. 52; Edinburgh, 2006), 27–50.

123. Godfrey, *Civil Justice*, 94–160.

124. A. M. Godfrey, 'Royal councils, law courts and governance: The role of litigation in early modern Scotland', in N. Jansen and P. Oestmann (eds), *Rechtsgeschicte Heute. Religion und Politik in der Geschichte des Rechts Schlaglichter einer Ringvorlesung* (Tübingen, 2014), 77–94. I am grateful to Mark Godfrey for this last reference.

125. Harding, 'Review of *Common Law and Feudal Society*', 115.

126. See, to name two examples, H. L. MacQueen, 'Some notes on wrang and unlaw', in H. L. MacQueen (ed.), *Stair Society Miscellany Five* (Stair Society, vol. 52; Edinburgh, 2006), 13–26; H. L. MacQueen, 'Legal afterword', in Duncan, *Scottish Formularies*, 361–76.

127. See my article 'Legislation and authority in early modern Scotland', in A. M. Godfrey (ed.), *Law and Authority in British Legal History, 1200–1900* (Cambridge, forthcoming).

128. For highly significant work being carried out concerning jurisdictional shifts in Scotland during the mid-sixteenth century, see T. M. Green, *The Consistorial Decisions of the Commissaries of Edinburgh* (Stair Society, vol. 61; Edinburgh, 2014).

1

Introduction

In or just after 1254, the English chronicler Matthew Paris inserted in his *Chronica Majora* the supposed text of a papal bull issued by Innocent IV which referred to Scotland as a land where, like France, England, Wales, Spain and Hungary, the causes of the laity were decided by lay customs and those of the church by the canons of the holy fathers. Accordingly, unless the kings of those realms would have it otherwise, the imperial laws, i.e. the Roman law, should not be taught there.[1] The bull has been dubbed a forgery, concocted by Matthew or others as part of a propaganda war against instruction in, and use of, Roman law.[2] Nonetheless, Matthew's text reflects something of what was thought to be the law of the kingdom of the Scots in the middle of the thirteenth century. Its statements may at first surprise those accustomed to thinking of Scots law as a system which, unlike that of England, was built on Roman or civilian foundations. Contact with the learned laws in Scotland is, according to Matthew, through the canon law of the church rather than Roman law. The law used by the laity in Scotland is, however, customary in nature, comparable in this not only with English but also with Welsh law and the northern French '*droit du pays coutumier*'. Finally, given that the highly-developed English law is also referred to as a law of customs, it seems that a customary system is not necessarily to be seen as a primitive and backward one.

The passage in Matthew's chronicle is yet further evidence of a thirteenth-century perception of Scotland as a kingdom which enjoyed its own native system of laws and customs. It is a perception which emerges through treaties between Scotland and other nations, such as those of Perth in 1266 and Birgham in 1290, both of which refer to the 'laws and customs of the realm of Scotland',[3] and through comments like those made in 1277 by Llywelwyn ap Gruffydd, prince of Wales, to justify the continued survival of the Welsh laws in a land conquered by the English, that every province under the dominion of the English crown – England, Gascony, Ireland and Scotland – had its own laws and customs without prejudice to English suzerainty.[4] Even when in the 1290s Scotland was

indeed brought under the dominion of Llywelwyn's conqueror, Edward
I, the English king continued to recognise its laws and customs, even
where he did not especially like them.[5] The Scots themselves referred to
the 'laws and customs of the realm' frequently in the thirteenth century,
as well as to the 'common law' of the realm.[6] Although this latter phrase
is more readily associated with the law of England, it was used first by
medieval canon lawyers seeking 'to distinguish the general and ordinary
law of the universal church both from any rules peculiar to this or that
provincial church, and from those papal *privilegia* which were always
giving rise to ecclesiastical litigation'.[7] The *jus commune* was the law of all
Christendom, the law of the Holy Roman Empire, distinct from local
specialities or the *jus proprium*. Thirteenth-century English lawyers spoke
not so much of the *jus commune* as of *communis lex*, translating the French
commune lei, but they nonetheless appropriated the idea of common law
in this sense of the general as opposed to the particular to describe the
law of their royal courts, and to distinguish it from the several rules and
customs which might be applied locally within the kingdom.[8] This
meaning also appears to have been used in Scotland, for example in a
brieve of King Alexander III (1249–86) in 1264, which refers to 'the
usage throughout our kingdom of Scotland according to ancient approved
custom and by the common law [*jus commune*]'. Again a statute of King
Robert I (1306–29) in 1318 speaks of the king's desire that 'common law
[*communis lex*] and common justice should be done to both rich and poor
according to the old laws and liberties used before this time'.[9]

   It was once thought that this thirteenth-century common law of
Scotland dissolved in the later Middle Ages. According to the late Lord
Cooper of Culross and William Croft Dickinson, the period after the
reign of Robert I was one of retrogression in law and its administration,
brought about by the failure to develop a centralised court structure and,
instead, the deployment of a multiplicity of courts based in the localities
and administered by resident landowners rather than lawyers.[10] This
'Cooper/Dickinson view' has come under increasing challenge. Social
and political historians have argued that the structure of Scottish central
government, revolving round the figure of the king, was much more
powerful than would have been acknowledged when Cooper and
Dickinson were writing. They have also argued that one source of this
power was the effective partnership which existed between central and
local administration, and that, at least in the Scottish context, local
peacekeeping was likely to be more effective than any centrally-directed
effort with the same goal.[11] For their part, legal historians have been
challenging the thesis that the common law of the thirteenth century
gradually disappeared in the fourteenth and fifteenth centuries, stressing
instead the considerable degree of continuity of earlier institutions, forms

and rules into the later period.[12] There is plenty of evidence that contemporaries still believed in the existence of a common law of Scotland, and that they associated this with the existing decentralised court structure. Where there was 'default of the kepyng of the common law', it was the responsibility of the king and his officers in the localities.[13] The common law was the king's law, and it was to prevail over 'particulare lawis . . . speciale privilegis . . . [and the] lawis of uther cuntries and realmis'.[14] Rather than dissolving in the face of divisive elements, the common law was increasingly used in the fifteenth century and later to challenge 'particular' laws such as the laws of Galloway and the laws of the Lordship of the Isles. Thus, for example, in 1490 the local custom of 'cawp taking' in Galloway and Carrick was abolished by parliament,[15] and in 1504 it was asserted that Scotland was to be 'reulit be our soverane lordis ane lawis and commone lawis of the realme and be nain other lawis', a provision seemingly directed at the laws of the Lordship.[16]

This book is a study of some aspects of the medieval Scottish common law. Its principal focus is the use of certain pleadable brieves – those of right, mortancestry and novel dissasine. Brieves were documents in which one person, typically the king, commanded another (a court-holder in the case of pleadable brieves) to do something. With our three brieves, the command was to determine through the court process certain types of dispute concerning land. The study of these brieves shows the validity of the criticism of the Cooper/Dickinson view of later medieval legal development. All three had appeared on the Scottish legal scene before 1300, and all three continued in use until well into the fifteenth century or later. Although the brieves were issued by central government – that is, in the king's name and from the king's chapel (chancery or writing office) – the litigations which they initiated took place in local courts held by local royal officers. The law which underlay each form of action was complex and significant. Land was the most important single source of wealth and economic activity in medieval Scotland, and the law which developed in this period relating to its ownership, transfer, exploitation and recovery from intruders needed to be sophisticated to deal adequately with the requirements placed upon it. It can be seen, therefore, that complex rules of law could develop and be administered through the decentralised court structure of the period: a central court staffed by professional lawyers was not a prerequisite of a Scottish common law.

At this level, of course, the study of these brieves is mainly technical and even antiquarian in character. However, a number of other, more general, issues are also raised. From the point of view of the social historian, for example, there arises the question of the significance of law and courts in medieval Scottish society. Partly as a result of the Cooper/Dickinson view that the courts were either unused or ineffective, there has been a tendency to stress instead the importance of extralegal and extracurial techniques for settling disputes and guiding social conduct. Thus there have been invaluable studies of the interacting factors of lordship, kinship and community as the principal means whereby peace was achieved and maintained, feuds settled and social dislocation avoided.[17] Yet it does not follow from the existence and undoubted importance of these peacekeeping devices that law and the courts either were no longer involved in the maintenance of good order or had never really been involved at all. Powell's studies of arbitration in fifteenth-century England have shown that, while such methods of dispute-resolution were indeed an alternative to legal procedures, there was also a complex interaction between them. As he puts it, 'the two went hand-in-hand, and far from precluding negotiation, the bringing of legal action, with its formalised court encounters and protracted procedure, allowed ample opportunity for it'.[18] This view makes good sense to the modern court lawyer, much of whose activity is directed not towards advocacy and pressing home points of law before a judge but towards the achievement of agreement and settlement between the parties and towards the avoidance of a court appearance. In this process of negotiation, the law is merely a bargaining counter, albeit a very important one. The lawyer who appears to have the law on his side can drive a harder bargain for his client, while making some discount in recognition of the fact that the open-textured nature of many legal rules makes few things wholly certain once a case is before a judge or, even worse, a jury. Actual court cases represent only a very small percentage of the disputes with which the modern lawyer will deal in the course of his profession, although he may get to the point of formally raising the action or even starting in court before settlement is reached. The unpredictability inherent in litigation was clearly recognised early in the twelfth century by the author of the English *Leges Henrici Primi* of c.1118 when he wrote of the 'utterly uncertain dice of pleas' while also commenting on how it was better to settle by agreement and love than to press for adjudication by law.[19] Many of the cases which will be examined in this book were settled rather than being pressed to the point of decision by the court, and, as Powell argues, it seems likely that, as in modern practice, the threat of law and litigation was part of the background to the resolution of disputes where possible by agreement rather than judgment.

  The legal historian will also want to know the answers to questions about change in the law and about the forces which generate that change in a phenomenon, the basic concept of which is a set of rules that are constant unless acted upon by external forces, ranging from legislation to revolution. Why did the brieves of right, mortancestry and novel dissasine enter Scottish legal history, and why, some three centuries later, did they disappear? The questions become even more sharply focused by the observation that each brieve is clearly modelled on an equivalent writ of medieval English law, respectively the writ of right, the writ of *mort d''ancestor* and the writ of novel disseisin, each of which was established in England before 1200. The development of the brieves was therefore linked in some way with the early development of English law. Further, it was a rule of Scots law (henceforth the brieve rule) that no man could be made to answer for his free holding in a court unless he was impleaded by one of the king's pleadable brieves. This rule was also part of the early English common law (herein called the writ rule). The earliest account of all these matters in Scots law, found in the treatise *Regiam Majestatem*, was derived from *Glanvill*, the late twelfth-century work which is one of the prime pieces of evidence for the early history of English law. It seems clear from all this that we have here an example of what Alan Watson has called a legal transplant[20] – that is, where one legal system develops by imitating institutions and rules found in another.

That there was a close relationship between the laws of medieval Scotland and England has long been widely accepted.[21] This is usually explained on the basis of the similarity between the two societies, at least at the level of the landowning classes, the protection of whose legitimate interests was the main concern of each kingdom's legal system. This similarity arose from the penetration of the British Isles by the Normans, who first arrived in 1066 with William the Conqueror and whose descendants spread not only through England but also through Scotland, Ireland and Wales, often holding land in two or more of these territories as well perhaps as in Normandy itself. The idea of a twelfth-century 'Norman Empire' has recently come under challenge, but it still seems that a common core of institutions and customs relating to justice and landholding is identifiable among the aristocracy of the British Isles and Normandy.[22] However, even though writs of right, *mort d'ancestor* and novel disseisin are found not only in England but also in Normandy, Ireland and Wales, they were not products of purely Norman custom. We will turn to precisely what did produce them in a moment. Their appearance in all the countries just mentioned is explicable as a result not merely of common custom but also of subjugation to a single sovereign power, the king of England. Scotland was different. However much it might be claimed that the king of Scots held his kingdom of the king of England, however much it was the case that individuals held lands in both kingdoms and owed allegiance to both kings, the practical reality (with the possible exception of the period 1174–89) was that Scotland was a sovereign state with control over the shape of its own laws. The brieves of right, mortancestry and novel dissasine ran in the name of the king of Scots, not of the king of England in any of his guises as, for example, duke of Normandy or lord of Ireland. The development of the Scottish brieves in imitation of the English writs was therefore not absolutely inevitable. An element of choice was involved; part of the problem is to explain that choice.

We can nevertheless begin to understand some of the factors which may have underlain the decisions of Scottish government in these matters by examining the history of the English writs for the recovery of land and the rule requiring their use. This has been the subject of much investigation lately, the outcome of which has been to illuminate the nature of the society in which the English writs took shape and effect in the twelfth century, as well as the forces driving legal and social change thereafter. If, as has just been argued, Scotland and England had strong political links at this period, and landed society in both kingdoms held its property by broadly similar customs, then it seems clear that the detailed studies which have been carried out in England must be considered in an investigation of the Scottish situation, if only to help us to identify some of the questions which may be asked of the Scottish sources. Unfortunately, the English discussion has been complex and contentious, and it is necessary to set out the elements of the debate in some detail. The starting point is the work of F. W. Maitland, mainly published at the end of the nineteenth century; then we will turn to the powerful critique and revision of Maitland proposed by S. F. C. Milsom; and finally a summary of the main points of debate provoked by Milsom's work will be offered.

In Maitland's interpretation, writs and rule were developed during the reign of Henry II (1154–89), in more or less deliberate opposition to the local feudal courts in which lords held sway and actions relating to land held of them were begun.[23] While the writ of right was merely a command to the lord to do right in cases of competing claims to land, it also enabled a transfer to the king's courts if the lord failed to do justice. Further, in 1179, trial by the grand assize or jury was made available, an option much more attractive to litigants than trial by the duel which was otherwise the mode of proof of right in land.[24] In the 1160s, the assize of novel disseisin was enacted. This was a possessory rather than a proprietary remedy, unlike the writ of right – that is to say, it allowed a former seisin or possession to be recovered, but did not preclude the possibility of the defendant later claiming ownership in another action. The writ commanded the immediate restoration of one ejected, or disseised, by another unjustly and without a judgment, with the issue always to be tried by a petty assize in the king's court. As a speedy remedy using rational modes of trial, it was immediately taken up by great numbers of litigants. The assize of *mort d'ancestor* was the result of the Assize of Northampton in 1176. It enabled a claim to possession of land to be made by one within certain close degrees of relationship to a deceased holder who had not been a mere life-tenant. Again, the issue was to be determined by an assize in a royal court. Since both novel disseisin and *mort d'ancestor* actions would succeed if the relevant facts were established, even if there was a party who could show a better right than the claimant, each was a blow at the proprietary jurisdiction exercised in the lord's court. The same was true of the rule requiring writs in freehold cases, also the result of legislation by Henry II in Maitland's view even though it was stated to be a custom of the realm by *Glanvill*.[25] The writ rule meant that the lord's court was allowed to use its jurisdiction in such matters only at the king's command. The whole edifice of writs and writ rule was thus part of a grand design by which the king's more rational justice, founded on possessory remedies, began to supplant that of the feudal lords.

Milsom opposed Maitland's view with a new model for the origins of the English common law in *The Legal Framework of English Feudalism*, published in 1976.[26] Where Maitland saw royal initiatives in deliberate opposition to the world of feudal courts, Milsom proposed royal acceptance of the feudal world and a series of attempts to make it function according to its own norms but which had the wholly unintended and accidental effect of destroying it. Basing his argument on close consideration of *Glanvill* and the earliest plea rolls, Milsom gave a different emphasis to the significance of the feudal context in which writs and rule took shape. Lordship and its exercise through the courts of private lords lay at the heart of rights to land. A tenant held land only if he was seised of it by its lord, and, within the lord's own court, that seisin was the only right to the land which could exist. The tenant held the land in return for payment of relief on entry and the rendering of service and rightful aids; for failure of service or his other obligations, duly adjudged by the lord's court, the tenant could be put out or disseised of the land. A customary process of seizing first the tenant's chattels and then the land by means of distraint preceded final forfeiture. The intimate relation between the holding of land and the rendering of feudal services meant that the tenant could not transfer his land outright to another (substitution) without the lord's consent, but it was legitimate for the tenant to grant at least part of it to be held of him by a subtenant (subinfeudation) so long as it enabled the tenant to continue the performance of the services due to the lord. When land fell vacant, typically as the result of the sitting tenant's death, the lord had a choice as to who should next have seisin; until that choice was made, no-one other than the lord had any right to the land. The only right of inheritance, therefore, was the one recognised by the lord and his court. However, the lord's exercise of his discretion was hedged around with customary expectations – for example, that the tenant's eldest son would inherit. Although regularly followed, these customs were not absolutely binding: 'a custom is something that happens before it becomes a rule'.[27] Instead, they provided the lord and his court with criteria for selecting a successor to a dead tenant; once that choice was made, there was no mechanism for undoing it on the grounds that the custom had been broken.[28]

The customs started to become laws with an existence independent of the lord and his court when the king's courts began to intervene regularly in their affairs. A significant degree of intervention came in the aftermath of the 'Anarchy' of King Stephen's reign (1135–53), when settlements had to be made between the descendants of those who had held 'in the time of peace' before the Anarchy – that is, in the reign of Henry I (1100–35) – and those who now held in their place having gained title, or simply intruded themselves, during Stephen's reign. The restoration of the descendants of the dispossessed – the disinherited – was the job for which the writ of right was initially designed, as shown by the fact that claimants had to trace their titles back to the time of Henry I. On this view, the writ was not so much an abstract protection of rights of inheritance in general. Its link with inheritance arose because a generation had passed since the dispossessions of the Anarchy had begun, meaning very often that it was necessary for claimants to start from the seisin of a now-deceased ancestor who had been holding the land when Henry I died.

The classical writ of right addressed to the lord commanding him to do right to a named demandant in respect of lands held by another obviously reflected a feudal world in Milsom's sense, in that the action was begun in the lord's court, and the claim was to hold lands of the lord – in Milsom's phrase, it was upward-looking. However, the writ also provided that if the lord did not act, the sheriff would. It was, argued Milsom, an order to act in which disobedience was expected. The lord's court had already taken its decision in the matter by permitting the enfeoffment of the tenant, and, bound by the homage which he had performed to the lord and the lord's obligation of warranty, it could do none other than refuse the demandant's claim. Accordingly, the case would be transferred to the king's court; unburdened by any obligation to the tenant, the royal court could decide the issue of whether the demandant had a better right to the land.

The lord's commitment to the tenant whose homage he had received and whom he had enfeoffed also explained the rule that no man need answer for his free tenement without the king's writ. The lord could not question the holding of his accepted tenant so long as the tenant per-formed his services. Only the king's writ – the writ of right – could even succeed in having the matter raised in the lord's court, whence it would have to proceed elsewhere. Thus the writ rule was in origin not a rule but a statement of fact – that is to say, in Milsom's own terms, a custom – about the steps needed to obtain a hearing for a claim against a sitting tenant. Milsom further argued that, to begin with, both novel disseisin and *mort d'ancestor* actions were conceived as means to curtail abuse by lords of their powers of control over their tenants and the lands which those tenants held of them. Thus a tenant was enabled to sue the lord who put him out without cause or due process of distraint – unjustly and without a judgment – by bringing novel disseisin in the king's court. The lord whose tenant died had to put in that tenant's heir or else be liable to an action of *mort d'ancestor*. While therefore the assize protected freeholders, they were not necessarily among the greater magnates of the realm. If anything, the purpose of the assizes was to curb the power of such magnates over their tenants, and to compel compliance with certain norms: if tenants were to be disseised, it had to be for just reasons and by judgment of the lord's court, while a tenant's heir had a right to be enfeoffed.

The effect of all this upon the feudal world embodied in the lord's court was drastic. The lord's disciplinary powers ceased to be operable in his court, squeezed partly by novel disseisin and partly by the rule about writs. If the lord and his court erred in following the due process of distraint, the tenant could bring the assize. When the tenant denied that he owed the service claimed by the lord, the writ rule hampered the lord's ability to take action in his own court against the tenant's lands. So, instead of taking risks in his own court, the lord turned to royal justice, which provided the writ of customs and services; actions of replevin in the county court, under which the tenant reclaimed distrained chattels from the lord (chattels were not protected by the writ rule and were indeed distrainable without any prior judicial authorisation), also became a vehicle for litigation about services. Similarly, the lord's power to choose the successor to a dead tenant was removed by the compulsitor to enfeoff particular heirs imposed by *mort d'ancestor*. The tenant, and the tenant's heirs, were coming to have rights that were stronger than those found under the old feudal customs, and which were coming to approximate to ownership burdened by the claims of the lord.

Even the lord's power to control the tenant's alienations was affected by the new controls of royal justice: substitutions became rare because the lord would not give his consent for fear that the former tenant's heir would later seek recovery by means of the royal protection of inheritance. The lord was indeed forced to seek the protection of royal justice against alienation, where in the past he might have been able to take action under his own authority. This explained the writs of entry, which were in origin the means by which lords challenged the rights of their tenant's alienees to hold. Because the typical alienation was by subinfeudation, the lord's court had no jurisdiction over the subtenant, and the classical writ of right addressed to him of whom the lord claimed to hold was inappropriate and of no use in this situation. Instead, the lord turned to the king's court, starting his action with the writ *precipe* under which the subtenant's right could be tested against that of the lord. The lord's right was really irrelevant, however; the issue was whether the subtenant was entitled to hold of the tenant. So, increasingly, *precipe* writs spelt out the flaw in the way in which the subtenant had come by the land – the tenant was out of his mind at the time of the grant, for example – and, as these became standardised, the writs of entry emerged. A particularly important event in this development was clause 34 of Magna Carta in 1215, which provided that *precipe* writs should not be issued to deprive lords of their jurisdiction. Writs of entry were *precipe* writs, but their use multiplied after 1215; therefore, argued Milsom, the entry clause in the writ showed that no lord was being deprived of jurisdiction in this case.

In a characteristic passage, Milsom remarked that we should not 'see Henry II and his advisers as cutting across the grain, as meaning to depart from the framework of their world'.[29] The debate on Milsom's work has come to centre on the nature of that world. Was it a world of powerful lords operating through their autonomous courts, with a discretion fettered only by the norms of feudal custom, or was it a world of active and interventionist royal justice in which lords could exercise only limited control over their tenants? Were the Henrician reforms designed only to make the feudal world operate according to its own norms; or did the reforms create those norms before destroying them; or is a third interpretation, that the reforms were not particularly connected to feudal ideas, a possibility? Hyams has written of Henry's 'persistent conscious legislative experimentation',[30] and Brand of 'careful and deliberate change',[31] but were the effects of change part of what was intended? Indeed, were there changes at all as a result of the Henrician reforms, other than the expansion and regularisation of royal justice?

It is clear that the origins of the English writ system must be set in the context of the pre-existing structures of royal and seigneurial justice, but on virtually every other central point in Milsom's thesis there is dispute and dissension. The principal protagonists have been historians of medieval law such as Donald Sutherland, Robert Palmer, Paul Hyams, Stephen White, Joseph Biancalana, John Hudson and Paul Brand.[32] Not all of what they and others have said can be relevant to Scotland – for example, issues as to the chronology of events and the precise political factors stimulating particular developments – but many of their more general points plainly require consideration. Equally, as the discussion about England has taken little, if any, account of Scottish developments, it may be that consideration of these will throw fresh light on the matters at issue. The value of such comparative work in coming to grips with Scottish and English problems should be obvious in the context of the world of common Anglo-Norman customs discussed earlier, and has been well demonstrated in White's thought-provoking work on lordship and land tenure in western France.[33] The case for looking at Scotland, where society and law were even more closely connected with England, needs no special justification.

We may start with the observation that Milsom's feudal world is an essentially legalistic one in which society seems almost solely dependent upon fairly precisely-defined tenurial relationships to define the exercise of power and authority. Elizabeth Brown's memorable attack on the whole concept of feudalism as giving 'a distorted, simplistic picture' of medieval society[34] certainly provides a challenge to Milsom, whose vision of how lords' courts functioned is primarily dependent not on an investigation of their actual operation but on legal sources coming from the period immediately after that in which he says that they were most powerful. These naturally tend to emphasise the court as a taker of decisions on disputed matters. However, as Hyams has commented, to what extent do these sources reflect 'an Angevin lawyers' ideal of how lordships ought to have been run in the old days [rather] than any memory of how they actually were run'?[35] What evidence there is of seigneurial courts in operation before Henry II tends most often to suggest, not bodies invariably acting according to certain criteria but participants in the processes of discussion and negotiation by which disputes were settled. Only occasionally were courts forced into imposing decisions on the disputing parties. Moreover, disputes were not always settled in the forum which tenurial relationships might have suggested was appropriate; politics and the facts of local power had a role to play alongside jurisdictional rules.[36]

Milsom's feudal world is also rather reminiscent of the traditional picture of feudal western Europe, where public authority represented by the king was either weak or undeveloped, and where responsibility for the administration of justice and the maintenance of order lay predominantly in private hands.[37] Yet medieval England is the land usually contrasted with contemporary Europe, where kingship was exceptionally strong, both pre-and post-Conquest, and there was an established system of public justice exercised through the county and hundred courts and operating alongside the courts of private lords.[38] Milsom derived his picture of a highly autonomous lord's court from the analysis of 'the honour' – a lordship composed of numerous fees held of the lord – in Sir Frank Stenton's *First Century of English Feudalism*, which dealt with the period between 1066 and 1166.[39] Stenton saw the honorial court as a 'feudal order . . . independent of the king's direction or control' and as a 'self-contained feudal community in action'.[40] He summarised the matter thus, in his *Anglo-Saxon England*:[41]

Every important honour was a state in miniature governed, as was
the kingdom, by its lord with the help of tenants whom he convened
to form a court . . . In the honorial court . . . the lord's baronial
tenants played a leading part. They shaped its decisions and
became the keeper of its precedents. They preserved a collective
memory of transactions within the honour, and thereby gave the
character of an institution to what had been, in origin, an
accumulation of separate estates.

Just how far Stenton's model should be taken is, however, uncertain. In
many of his examples of the honorial court in action, it is acting to
confirm a negotiated settlement rather than adjudicating.[42] Further,
some of the cases may be exceptional, or at least not capable of being a
basis for generalisation, because they occurred during Stephen's reign
or were located in northern England, where royal authority was less
strong than elsewhere. In terms of time and place, therefore, Stenton's
honours may have been unusually autonomous.[43] Stenton also acknowledged that the practice of the king's court in feudal matters 'must have
governed the whole of English feudal practice', and that the king 'could
legislate on matters of feudal interest', although 'even the Angevin kings
. . . were slow to legislate on matters within the province of the honorial
court'.[44] An example of legislation on feudal matters from before 1153
to which Stenton referred was a '*statutum decretum*', as it is described in
a charter, which provided that 'where there is no son the daughters
divide their father's land by the spindles'.[45] More recently, Hudson has
pointed to a '*statutum regni*' before 1166 dealing with distraint, another
matter which might be thought to be primarily the province of the
honorial court. Stenton had also noted this reference, with the slightly
puzzling comment that '*statutum regni* does not give the definite
impression of an enactment which is conveyed by *statutum decretum*'.[46]

External constraints other than the practice and statements of the
king's court also certainly existed before the Henrician reforms. Milsom
himself refers to the limitations imposed by the general norms of feudal
custom as to when a lord could disinherit a sitting tenant or refuse to
recognise a claim of inheritance. His point was that no regular mechanism
existed by which lords and their courts could be made to follow these
norms. Diverse arguments have been made to in response to this, to show
that the lord's court 'was not an enclosed and self-sufficient world'.[47]
Many tenants held lands in more than one honour, or were themselves
also lords with tenants, or engaged in the business of the world outside
the honour, which exposed the court to the generally-understood norms
of honorial society.[48] The fees which made up an honour were typically
widely scattered and did not form a compact territorial unit;[49] accordingly,
when a tenant fell into dispute with his neighbour, it was very likely that

each would hold of a different lord. In that situation, as both the *Leges Henrici Primi* and *Glanvill* make clear, it would be necessary for them both to seek some external forum – the court of a common overlord, the county court or the king's court – for the resolution of their differences.[50] Most importantly, royal intervention was by no means unknown and may have been common even before the accession of Henry II. The king could come in where there was default of justice (*defectus justicie*) in the lord's court, a principle of jurisdiction stated in the *Leges Henrici Primi*.[51] There is evidence that such interventions took place both to permit and to prevent the raising of actions in the lord's court in the reign of Henry I.[52] Accordingly, the lord's court lacked full independence even before the Anarchy. A general point which has been made most forcefully by Biancalana is that the lord's court with which Milsom is concerned was still a relatively novel feature of the English legal landscape in the twelfth century. He suggests that the problem lay in coordinating the existing structure of royal government with these new courts so that their place in the system became relatively clear.[53] Brand also argues that the primary aim of many of Henry's changes was 'integrating the various pre-existing local courts into a single nationwide legal system', although he goes further by showing how the administration of royal justice was itself deliberately transformed as part of this process.[54]

While lords' courts in England exercised proprietary and disciplinary jurisdiction, Milsom's conception of the scope and limitation of these jurisdictions has been criticised. Where he sees the reforms of Henry II being shaped by an understood framework of feudal custom, Biancalana argues that instead they 'imposed royal conceptions of lordship and of tenurial relationships upon the actual relationships of lords to their men'.[55] There is evidence that not all courts were equally able to impose discipline upon the lord's feudal tenants. The *Carte Baronum* of 1166 was a royal inquiry into the number of subtenants holding of tenants-in-chief for knight service, conducted at a date well before the Henrician reforms had taken full effect or even been fully established. It shows that many lords already had great difficulty in ejecting tenants who had failed to render their due services.[56] Biancalana has noted pre-Conquest laws providing for distraint only if preceded by a claim in the hundred or county court, and mid-twelfth-century cases where lords obtained royal writs to authorise distraint of their tenants by the fee; he argues that, in the early part of Henry II's reign, 'it was not altogether clear to lords that they could exercise disciplinary jurisdiction without royal authorization'.[57] It was the assize of novel disseisin which introduced regularity into the procedures by which lords distrained their tenants, by enabling analysis of what constituted a 'just judgment' by a court in such matters.[58] Hudson, too, draws a picture of procedures of distraint in the first half of the twelfth century which were flexible rather than governed by precise rules such as Milsom suggests were then customary, and he accepts that the assize of novel disseisin was 'at least in part aimed at unjust distress by lords'. But, supporting Brand, he casts doubt on whether a preliminary judgment was always necessary for distraint, at least of chattels. Indeed, it was often a violent process of self-help, and controls were necessary to keep the peace.[59]

By the early thirteenth century, however, 'and probably for half a century prior to that', distraint of lands needed judicial authorisation.[60] That judicial authorisation came increasingly rarely from the lord's own court, which was indeed squeezed by the rule requiring the use of a royal writ to make the tenant answer for his free tenement.[61] Outright forfeiture of the lands, which Hudson shows did occur (albeit rarely) before the Henrician reforms,[62] also disappeared in the thirteenth century, so that the lord's power of distraint could not deprive the tenant permanently of his lands. Only action in the king's court under the Statutes of Gloucester (1278) and Westminster II (1285) enabled the lord to recover a defaulting tenant's lands in full in the later medieval common law.[63]

With respect to proprietary jurisdiction, Milsom's suggestion that the standardisation of the writ of right by Henry II was the result of a general tenurial settlement in 1153 following the 'Anarchy of Stephen' has been elaborated by Palmer but disputed by Biancalana. In the latter's view, the concept of royal jurisdiction over *defectus justicie* provided a background to royal commands to do right in the twelfth century, but, before Henry's reign, these commands operated not only in favour of tenants claiming to hold of lords but also in favour of lords reclaiming lands from occupiers. The limitation of the writ to upward-looking claims was the conscious imposition of a tenurial framework compelling disputants over land to use the court of the lord of whom the land was held. This was a reaction to a tendency towards territorial as opposed to tenurial lordship;[64] the writ recognised the claims of lordship but only within a framework which it defined on tenurial principles.

Milsom's idea that the lord's obligation of warranty bound his court to reject any challenge to the accepted and sitting tenant has not gained support.[65] Warranty was known in eleventh-century Norman law as an obligation owed by a lord to a tenant, whether or not it was expressed in a charter, to defend him in his lands and to compensate him with lands of equivalent value in the event of a successful third-party claim.[66] Similarly, in Lombard feudalism, warranty seems to be an obligation to replace lands in which the superior is unable to maintain the vassal against an outsider.[67] It would seem, therefore, that Palmer's comment that 'no feudal logic absolutely required the rejection of a claimant' is correct.[68] As Palmer observes, if Milsom is right, then all concerned must have known that the writ of right in the lord's court was a mere fiction to get a case into the king's court. Palmer also notes that *Glanvill* includes a style for a writ of peace prohibiting a lord from continuing further a case over land in his court between a claimant and the tenant, suggesting that such a situation could and did occur.[69] The most detailed critique of Milsom's position is by Hyams,[70] who remarks that:[71]

> Talk of an absolute bind on lords will seem very strange to most historians of English society . . . Believers in a seignorial world, not just in England but all over medieval Europe, have taken it as normal to submit land disputes to resolution by a duel before the lord of whom the claimants wished to hold. The right to hold such duels was a mark of baronial status. Nowhere in the previous literature has there been any hint that duels might only be held where the disputed holding was vacant, by the tenant's death or otherwise. The supposed iron logic of warranty would surely have been recognised somewhere in Europe by a writer whose thoughts survive. To believe that men felt themselves irrevocably bound by every grant once made is to believe in a world without sin. It makes warranty too mechanical an obligation for the tough society of the early twelfth century with its largely oral memory. The hard politics of the seignorial world unquestionably accepted the ousting of once-accepted tenants for all kinds of reasons, not excluding the making of fresh grants of lands previously given to men now out of favour . . . Certainly the rivalries and local politics of the honorial community were as often behind the ousters and regrants as any national allegiance.

Hyams also shows that the concept of warranty developed first in the context of transfer of goods and was therefore not something inherent to the seigneurial world of landholding.[72] He argues that it was established in England as an implied obligation before 1100, and that the slow rise of express warranty clauses in charters is to be explained by grantees' concerns over anticipated trouble from outside.[73] Such concern would only arise if there was a danger that the grant just made would turn out not to be definitive. One source of potential trouble from Henry II's time onward was the developing common law itself; but, as Hyams hints and others have suggested subsequently, the upheavals and tenurial uncertainties of Stephen's reign may also have prompted a greater desire for the better-defined protection offered by a written warranty clause.[74]

If warranty did not compel the lord's court to default on the writ of right, commentators have nonetheless accepted the probability that it was biased in favour of the sitting tenant, so it remains possible to explain the rule requiring a royal writ to initiate an action against such a defendant within a feudal framework.[75] Warranty was not the only device by which grantees were secured against outside interference in the twelfth century, and some of these techniques, such as statements of the grantor's 'firm will', promises of maintenance and protection of peaceful possession, pledges of faith and the *laudatio parentum*, survived into the thirteenth century.[76] As a matter of fact, therefore, the lord was not likely to look favourably on a challenger against one to whom he had made such commitments. There is also acceptance of Milsom's contention that the writs rule therefore began as a statement of fact rather than in consequence of royal legislation. This is consistent with *Glanvill's* statement that the requirement was a custom;[77] as van Caenegem points out, 'when [*Glanvill*] expounds a rule that is of legislative origin he says so clearly enough'.[78] However, it may be further observed that, long before *Glanvill's* time, pleas in lords' courts were regularly, if not invariably, begun by royal writ, and that the rule may reflect not the bias of these courts but the interventionism of the king and his officers, facilitated by the strength of English royal administration inherited from the Anglo-Saxons and developed by the Norman conquerors. It is certainly striking that there was no equivalent rule in Normandy, even though one might expect to find there lords' courts with the same values and just as biased as those in England.[79]

Milsom's argument, that before the Henrician reforms took effect the only right to land was that acknowledged by the lord – in other words, seisin – and that there was no contrast between seisin and right, has gained both qualified support and criticism. The critics point to a case in the 1150s where a plaintiff failed in a suit for seisin for want of proof but the judgment of the court expressly reserved the question of the right.[80] Palmer has argued, however, that the distinction between seisin and right had only arisen very recently, as the result of the general tenurial settlement in 1153 following the 'Anarchy of Stephen'. Those who had gained seisin during the Anarchy might continue to hold it, but there also existed other claimants who would take on the death of the current holder. Accordingly, the early distinction between right and seisin was based not on legal concepts of property rights distinct from the lord-tenant relationship but on a political compromise between two factions.[81] The evidence for such a settlement has been challenged by both Hyams and Biancalana,[82] and, while it is generally acknowledged that the tenurial dislocation which resulted from the Anarchy is important background to the Henrician reforms,[83] it is not clear that previously a distinction between seisin and right was unthinkable. By the end of the twelfth century, the distinction between seisin and right had been further conceptualised as one between the right of possession and the right of property.[84] This was a distinction drawn from the Roman and the canon laws; it had become well developed in the law of the church during the mid-twelfth century.

In Milsom's view, as we have seen, the application of these concepts to
the developing writ system was late, but it is at least possible, given the
state of the canon law in Henry II's time, that the concepts were in fact
among the elements which went into the fashioning of the system at the
beginning.[85]

Milsom's argument that the assizes of novel disseisin and *mort
d'ancestor* were conceived as remedies for tenants or would-be tenants
against wrongdoing lords has been questioned and modified. Van
Caenegem's argument, largely bypassed by Milsom, that the assize began
as a criminal measure requiring presentments of violent disseisins and
was later extended to individual plaintiffs, has recently gained some
support from Biancalana and Hudson, who see antecedents in general
peacekeeping measures.[86] In his study of novel disseisin, Sutherland,
while acknowledging that lords were often disseisors against whom the
assize was regularly brought, argued against Milsom that the main aim of
Henry II and his advisers when introducing the petty assizes in England
was to give better legal protection to all freeholders against dispossession
from whatever source, lordly or otherwise.[87] Brand pointed out that the
writ of novel disseisin contained no reference to the tenement in issue
being held of the lord, unlike the writs of right and of warranty of
charter,[88] while Palmer suggested that the assize was for the enforcement
of the 1153 tenurial settlement, to protect the sitting tenants from
dispossession by the waiting outsiders who had a better right derived
from the time of Henry I.[89] On the other hand, Sir James Holt has
observed that novel disseisin was generally not used by tenants-in-chief
until after Magna Carta in 1215, a fact 'congruous' with Milsom's thesis
about the origin of the assize. Holt also argues that in the period before
1215 'the assize of *mort d'ancestor*, generally in great demand, was used
only occasionally [by tenants-in-chief], sometimes in very unusual
circumstances'. However, Holt's support for Milsom should not be
pressed too far, for, while he finds the origins of the writ of right to lie
'certainly' in the supervisory jurisdiction exercised by the king's court
over lesser ones, this is only 'most probably' the case with *mort d'ancestor*,
and only 'in some degree' true of novel disseisin.[90]

Another dimension was added in an important article by Mary
Cheney.[91] Drawing attention to the canon law rules against alienation of
church property and imposing upon bishops the duty of recovering
property from alienees, Cheney discussed a case before the king in 1164,
in which John Marshal sued Thomas Becket, Archbishop of Canterbury,
to recover lands from which he had been ejected by the archiepiscopal
court applying the canon law rules. The king's court, 'as the law then
stood', according to a source written some ten years later, was unable to
assist Marshal. Cheney went on to suggest that the relevant change in the

king's law was the introduction of novel disseisin, and that one reason why the assize might have been enacted was to protect freeholders against the canonical claims of the church. Milsom omitted consideration of ecclesiastical lordship over land, but, as Hudson points out, 'to ignore ecclesiastical lordship is not only to ignore one quarter of the lands in England, but to leave aside the great majority of twelfth-century evidence'.[92]

The fullest discussion of both novel disseisin and *mort d'ancestor* since Milsom first published his work is by Biancalana, who argues that the guiding principle lying behind the introduction of both remedies was the king's long-established right to correct defaults of justice in the seigneurial courts. This principle, which was overt in the writ of right's command to do right or the sheriff would, lay behind the formula 'unjustly and without a judgment' in the writ of novel disseisin, while the limitation of *mort d'ancestor* to inheritance claims derived from particularly close relatives was because 'within the close range of family ties covered by the assize, the criteria of inheritance were sufficiently clear that, if the ancestor had died seised, there was no good reason for a lord to have denied the heir his ancestor's seisin'. Accordingly, it was appropriate in such cases to presume a failure of seigneurial justice.[93] Biancalana dissents from Palmer's arguments, first, that novel disseisin was for the protection of the sitting tenant in 1153, and, second, that the introduction of *mort d'ancestor* in 1176 followed the baronial revolt in 1173–4.[94] As already noted, Biancalana does not accept Palmer's interpretation of the 1153 settlement,[95] and he suggests that the immediate occasion for the introduction of *mort d'ancestor* was a canon adopted at the Council of Westminster in 1175 that the son of a priest was not to be instituted in his father's church.[96] He also notes that many cases of disseisin before 1166 were downward-looking in nature, that is, brought by lords (including monasteries and churches) to recover lands from tenants. It is therefore difficult to accept that the assize was solely directed against wrongdoing lords.[97]

The place of the writs of entry in Milsom's story has been challenged by Palmer, who argues that their development reflected a conception of property separated from the lord-tenant relationship. He effectively disproves Milsom's contention that before 1215 writs of entry were solely used in cases where there were difficulties in using an ordinary *precipe*, by demonstrating that the four earliest writs of entry had origins in 'assize' writs. The clearest example is entry *sur disseisin*, which was introduced to solve problems arising from the limitations of the assize of novel disseisin.[98] Palmer has also argued that many entry writs had an upward-downward' orientation, where the claimant had first to show deprivation by the lord of whom the lands were held, and then a grant away ultimately reaching the defendant. In later developments, the need to show the role played by the lord disappeared, demonstrating his loss of control over his tenants' lands, and the rise of 'property right' in the tenant.[99] Palmer minimises the importance of Magna Carta for the increasing use of writs of entry in the thirteenth century, suggesting that it was a subsidiary development.[100] Nevertheless, casting the writs of entry in *precipe* form so that cases went before the king's justices avoided difficult questions for the lord in his court or his lord's court.[101]

Enough has now been said to indicate the difficult problems which surround the issue of the origins of the English writs of right, novel disseisin and *mort d'ancestor*. The debate provoked by Milsom's work raises a whole series of questions about why these remedies were adopted for use in Scotland. However, the value of the English comparison does not end with consideration of origins. Barrow has remarked of another medieval institutional transplant from England into Scotland, the justiciar, that it 'began as an exotic innovation yet within a few generations took on the protective colouring of a thoroughly native species'.[102] Whatever the origins of a transplant, it has a life of its own in its new environment. This study is also concerned with the story of the brieves of right, mortancestry and novel dissasine as part of the living law of Scotland from the thirteenth century to the fifteenth, the forces at work developing their application during that period, and the impact which they had in turn on legal development generally. The last question arises particularly because the equivalent English writs are generally reckoned to have played a crucial role in the emergence of the common law itself by drawing into the king's courts business which would otherwise have been determined in the courts of local lords; in consequence, their jurisdiction was gradually destroyed. As was noted in a thirteenth-century treatise, lords did not resist the transfer of cases to the king's court because there was no profit in doing so.[103] Only the king's courts could administer a law common to the whole kingdom, and, so long as the norm was that disputes over land were determined according to the individual customs of the courts of the lords of whom the land was held, there could be no common law of property in land. When the king's courts enjoyed a monopoly in such cases, there was indeed a law common to all the king's subjects.

Conventional wisdom has it that the introduction of the Scottish brieves of right, novel dissasine and mortancestry did not have the effect which the equivalent writs did in England, by accident or design. No-one would deny that courts held by virtue of landownership and grants of franchisal jurisdiction in barony and regality continued to be a most important part of the Scottish legal world until the end of the medieval period. The general assumption has been that these courts continued to enjoy a proprietary jurisdiction, and that royal justice failed to deprive them of it. But assumption it is, rather than proven fact. It is difficult to find many cases where a later medieval lord's court is clearly exercising a proprietary jurisdiction. The assumption that it was so is based on another one, that the brieves and the rule requiring them in freehold cases had either gone out of use or were ineffective. However, when we find that the opposite was the case, then questions are raised about the absence of instances of proprietary jurisdiction in lords' courts and about the overall effect of the brieves.

A further point which can be made here is that, despite the loss of jurisdiction to the king's courts in proprietary matters, lordship in later medieval England continued to play an important sociolegal role in this area. Recent studies have stressed the importance of the great lord and his council in the widespread practice of settling disputes by arbitration rather than through litigation, which continued to be important throughout the period. Such arbitrations often dealt with property disputes which would otherwise have been the preserve of the royal courts.[104] Lordship thus retained much social and political significance as a possible factor in struggles over property at the local level in England, albeit with hardly any reference to the connection between the services and other duties claimed by the lord and the land held by the tenant. Some clear parallels can be drawn here with the situation in contemporary Scotland, where lords also played a key role in dispute settlement, including cases over land, not so much through their courts but as arbiters and mediators.[105] Although these arbitrations did not arise out of the purely feudal relationship of lord and tenant as such, they nonetheless suggest that the contrast between a Scotland where lordship retained considerable importance in disputes over land, and an England where it did not, should not be drawn too starkly on either side of the comparison. The phenomenon of arbitration and other less formal ways of resolving disputes also underlines the point already made, that law was only one aspect, however important, of the ways in which claims to property were worked out in the Middle Ages, and that a picture which focuses exclusively on legal rules and court decisions will be necessarily incomplete. If, in other words, we say that royal justice deprived lords' courts of their jurisdiction, it does not follow that lordship thereby lost significance or influence in the areas where their courts would otherwise once have had jurisdiction.

Two other effects of the English common-law writs have been discussed in recent writing and seem worth exploring in the Scottish context. The first is the relationship between the suggested destruction of feudal lordship by the rise of the common-law writs and the emergence of so-called 'bastard feudalism', where relationships between lord and man were based not so much on land tenure for service but on clientage and money fees. Twelfth- and thirteenth-century inflation undermined the value of renders such as services which were fixed in amount, and the chief significance of tenurial relationships became the feudal incidents, payments due from the tenant to the lord on certain events.[106] The tenant was liable for a payment called relief when he took up the tenancy; while he was under age, he was also subject to the lord's wardship, that is, custody of his person and control of his lands. During this period, the lord would uplift the benefits of the land in ward. The lord also had the right to control the tenant's marriage, to ensure that suitable alliances were made. Already in the twelfth century, there was a market in which these wardship and marriage rights were bought and sold, so that they were losing any connection with the social reality of lordship over tenants, and were merely means of raising income for both seller and buyer.[107] The argument is that as the exercise of lordship over land held for services became increasingly difficult in England thanks not only to economic circumstances but also to the controls imposed by the king's courts on the lord's ability to enforce his rights, so attention switched increasingly to the rights attached to lordship which could be converted into cash. This found its ultimate expression in the great statute of 1290, *Quia Emptores*, which prohibited alienation by subinfeudation to protect the lord's right to incidents, the mischief having been that, when a tenant subinfeudated for a lesser return than the land was worth, his lord's incidents were also devalued. The statute compelled alienation by substitution, previously rare, in Milsom's argument, because the lord would not give his consent in case of a claim founded on hereditary right being made later by the grantor's heirs. Now, under the statute, the need for the lord's consent was removed – a sign, in Milsom's view, of his loss of control and of the limitation of his interest to the incidents of tenure.[108]

In Scotland also, services lost a good deal of their importance to the casualties of relief, wardship and marriage, so much so that, for example, tenure by knight service became known as tenure by ward and relief; and blench tenure, under which a merely nominal service was rendered, or tenure by unspecified service 'as used and wont' (*debita et consueta*), developed into the most common form of honourable tenure.[109] It has been said that 'the principles of feudalism were retained but were modified to accommodate the growing influence of money'.[110] Although there was no *Quia Emptores*, substitution was common in later medieval Scotland; but the lord's consent was still required, and subinfeudation was also regularly used.[111] Feudal services by no means lost their significance completely: scutage, the conversion of military service to a fiscal render, never arose in Scotland, and grants for knight and other military services could still be made in the fourteenth century.[112] A question, therefore, is the extent to which the world in which service was the raison d'etre of the feudal grant was affected by the operation of the brieves of right, novel dissasine and mortancestry; and a further one, if there was little or no effect, may be what that implies either about Milsom's thesis or about the impact of Scottish royal justice in general.

A more strictly legal question is the extent to which the brieves affected the conceptualisation of ownership of land in Scots law. In a feudal or tenurial structure, this is always a difficult issue because in any piece of land there will always be more than one right. The feudal jurists of the medieval and early modern period resolved this dilemma by proposing a division of rights or *dominium* in the land – the lord's *dominium directum* and the tenant's *dominium utile* – and this theory has been the basis of Scots law since at least the writings of Thomas Craig in c. 1600.[113] Today, however, inasmuch as the feudal structure of land law has any content at all, the *dominium directum* is merely a burden on the ownership of the *dominium utile*. At the beginning of the period with which this book is concerned, however, the position might well have been reversed, with the tenant's right being the burden on the lord's right, which would therefore look much more like ownership. Only as the tenancy acquired the characteristics of heritability and alienability, and the lord lost the ability to determine who the tenant should be, did the tenant's right begin to evolve towards ownership. In England, it has been argued, the effect of the writs of right and *mort d'ancestor* was to ensure that a claim based on heritable right was regularly enforced so that, while such inheritance was a customary expectation before their introduction, only afterwards is it possible to say that these rights had become sufficiently detached from lordly control to become recognisable as the beginnings of ownership.[114] Similarly, novel disseisin facilitated alienation, because if the lord took action to prevent the transfer of the tenancy he might find himself liable under the assize. So the writs were a vital step in the creation of tenant, as opposed to lordly, ownership of land. Yet the point should not be overstated; as Brand has commented, the thirteenth-century English lord continued to play an important part in the transmission of land and to have an interest in land held of him going beyond the mere exaction of the feudal incidents.[115] The tenant's right did not wholly exclude the lord's, even after the writs had taken full effect.

Before 1300, however, English land law had come to be structured around the doctrine of 'estates'.[116] Even in this world, though, the holding of land was rarely so simple and undivided as to be termed absolute ownership. An estate, according to a neat sixteenth-century definition, was 'a time in the land, or land for a time'.[117] The tenant who had land for his life which would pass to his heirs on his death, but which he could freely alienate forever during his life, was said to have a fee simple, and this is as near as English law seems to come to the concept of outright landownership. Examples of tenants with a lifetime interest only included the widow's right to dower and the widower's right to curtesy of the deceased spouse's land, which lasted until death, when the lands reverted to the heir in fee simple. Another example was an alienation for the alienee's lifetime only; while such an alienee might in turn alienate, he could only give away as much as he had, namely an estate determined by his own lifetime. The new holder was said to have an estate *pur auter vie*. The original alienor retained a reversionary estate, still known as the fee simple, but limited by the estate *pur auter vie*. Another possibility was an alienation which granted a heritable title to the alienee but restricted by whom the land might be inherited. The classic example in the thirteenth century was the entail restricting succession to defined heirs, whom failing the land would revert to the grantor or his heirs. The grantor was a reversioner, while the defined line of heirs were called 'heirs in tail'. The current holder under the entail, being possessed of a fee less than the fee simple, was said to have a fee tail; the fee simple was in the reversioner. If the grantor provided that on failure of the issue defined by the entail the land was to go to a third party, either in fee tail or fee simple, there was a 'remainder', and the third party was a 'remainderman'. This was from the Latin *remanere*, to stay away; the idea was that the land stayed away from the grantor as long as the remainder lasted.

Although inheritance was restricted by entails, the holder's right to alienate was generally unaffected until a statute in 1285, *De Donis Conditionalibus*.[118] This gave the heirs in tail, the reversioner and the remainderman writs of 'formedon' (from *forma doni*, the form of the gift) to enforce the terms of the grant against the holder who alienated in prejudice of their interests under the entail. These were respectively formedon in the descender, formedon in the reverter, and formedon in the remainder. The protection of such future interests in land led to further recognition of them as estates in land.

It was against this complex background – and only the barest outline of some of the more readily-grasped points has been given here – that the writs of right, *mort d'ancestor* and novel disseisin functioned in the thirteenth and later centuries. Although conceptualised early as proprietary (the writ of right) and possessory (*mort d'ancestor* and novel disseisin),[119] the root idea of all was the recovery of seisin, either the plaintiffs own former seisin or a right to it flowing from the former seisin of another person.[120] Seisin was originally possession of land, but the existence of various forms of action for its recovery led to doctrines of the 'relativity' of seisin. Thus, one who recovered seisin through novel disseisin might find himself in turn displaced by another who, because he could claim through an earlier seisin of another person, had an older, and therefore better, right to the land made good through one of the other forms of action. The picture was complicated further because the forms of action began to be supplemented by the writs of entry, creating new and specific forms of claim. Even the writ of right, which might be seen as the ultimate proprietary action, sought no more than to determine who had the better right (*maius ius*) as between the litigants; at least in theory, it remained possible that the victor in the action would in turn be put out by one who could point to an older and therefore better title, provided that he had made his claim before the judgment in the previous case.[121] And, as Sutherland has noted, when the writ of right went out of use in England, it was as if proprietary rights had vanished from English law, leaving behind a melange – or, in Maitland's phrase, 'that wonderful calculus' – of estates and seisins protected only by actions of varying degrees of possessoriness.[122]

The forms of action interacted with the developing doctrine of estates in a complex manner. Life holdings came to be protected by novel disseisin, but not leases for a period of years or villein holdings (because the two latter were not regarded as free holdings to which alone the writ extended, according to its terms); this was important in establishing that the former was an estate in land and that the others were not. Remainder-men, not being necessarily heirs under the common-law doctrines of inheritance, were unable to claim through *mort d'ancestor* or writs of right; hence the need for the writs of formedon in their favour. Claims when made had to be sustained, and it was necessary to develop categories and classifications with some definitional content to distinguish between them and to determine which one would prevail against another.[123]

Scots land law knew – and to some extent still knows – many of the elements which went into the doctrines of seisin and estates in England: tenure, sasine, lifetime grants, the rights of widow and widower to terce and courtesy respectively (directly comparable to English dower and curtesy), and entails (rendered in Scots and in the remainder of this book as 'tailzies' until the Entail Act 1685). It is also true that neither the doctrine of estates nor the writs of entry are found in Scotland. However, the interaction between the forms of landholding and the brieves of right, mortancestry and novel dissasine has never been discussed, if only because there has not been any awareness that they continued to function until the end of the fifteenth century. Investigation is hampered by the fact that existing histories of Scottish land law tend to take as their starting point Craig's work at the turn of the sixteenth century, leaving the medieval period unexplored.[124] A full account of the law in that period would require as a minimum a thorough survey of the rich charter evidence, and that lies beyond the scope of this work. However, if the matter is approached through the evidence for the use of the brieves, some answers to the question of how that influenced the conceptualisation and structuring of the medieval land law may at least be suggested.

A final point where the existence and use of the brieves throughout the medieval period may have had a significant effect on the development of Scots law – with important consequences for government and society in Scotland – concerns the rule which restricted the jurisdiction of the king's council as its judicial sessions gradually became regularised in the later fifteenth century. The significance of this regularisation was that from it there emerged a central court which in the sixteenth century became (and, as the Court of Session, remains) the principal Scottish court. Anyone reading the printed records of the council's judicial activities in the fifteenth century will quickly become familiar with its practice of remitting matters of 'fee and heritage' – speaking very broadly, the ownership of land – to the 'judge ordinary'. Historians studying the developing institution in the belief that it was conceived as some sort of supreme court to bring good order to the administration of justice have been puzzled by this restricted jurisdiction. The assumption that the Scottish feudal courts continued to enjoy proprietary jurisdiction under-lies most explanations of the rule.[125] The general view was expressed thus by Dickinson:[126]

> The exclusion from the jurisdiction of the 'Lords of Council and Session' of actions relating to 'fee and heritage' was the only feudal victory; only the one basic feudal concept still survived – that a plea relating to the holding of land must be heard in the court of the lord of whom the land is held.

With the understanding that throughout the later medieval period Scots law held that no man could be made to answer for his land except through action begun by brieve of right, novel dissasine or mortancestry, however, the restriction of council's jurisdiction in such cases looks wholly different – the consequence not of jealously-guarded feudal jurisdiction but rather of a common-law rule which, as applied in England, has been seen as fundamentally anti-feudal, either in aim or in effect. Equally, council's eventual assumption of this jurisdiction sometime in the first half of the sixteenth century helps to explain why the brieves went out of use (and may even be the complete explanation). Finally, this may be another area in which Scottish developments can throw light on English ones, for the jurisdiction of the English conciliar courts, including the later medieval chancery, was similarly excluded in cases concerning freeholds, a limitation usually attributed, somewhat unsatisfactorily, to fourteenth-century statutory provision.[127]

This introduction has raised numerous issues which the rest of this book will seek to address, more fully in some cases than in others. The book is divided into two parts. The second part deals with the three brieves of right, novel dissasine and mortancestry, concentrating on the evidence for their origins, development and demise, and exploring the questions of their impact on law and society raised above. The first part is concerned with the framework within which the brieves worked – that is, the structure of courts – and the sources which were used in the period of our concern and from which we can glean our knowledge of the brieves in theory and the brieves in action. In this part, there is also some examination of the men who used these materials, argued cases and decided them. This is not just to provide a context legal, social and political for the brieves. It also challenges the long-established view of the weakness and inadequacy of law in later medieval Scotland, proposing instead a legal system which was integral to landholding society, and which played a crucial role in the settlement of its disputes, whether as a bargaining counter in negotiated settlements or as a means of adjudication where the forces of love failed to conquer and a decision was needed.

NOTES

1. *Chron Majora*, vi, p. 295.
2. P & M, i, p. 123. There is no discussion of this bull in R. Vaughan, *Matthew Paris* (Cambridge, 1958).
3. G. W. S. Barrow, *Kingdom*, p. 89 and note.
4. *The Welsh Assize Roll 1277–1284*, ed. J. Conway Davies (Cardiff, 1940), p. 266.
5. H. L. MacQueen, 'Alexander III', pp. 82–4.
6. G. W. S. Barrow, *Kingdom*, p. 89 and note; W. D. H. Sellar, 'Common law', pp. 86–7.
7. P&M, i, p. 176.
8. P&M, i, pp. 176–8.
9. *Melr Lib*, i, no 309; *RRS*, v, p. 406 (c. 2) see also *APS*, i, 467 (c. 2). The use of *communis lex* in the 1318 statute is unusual in Scotland, and suggests both that the original text may have been in French (a point for which I am indebted to Professor A. A. M. Duncan) and that the legislators may have been influenced by English usage.
10. See Cooper, *Papers*, pp. 219–36; W. C. Dickinson, 'Administration of justice', pp. 338–51.
11. See e.g. J. M. Brown, 'The exercise of power', in *Scottish Society in the Fifteenth Century*, ed. J. M. Brown (London, 1977), p. 33; J. Wormald, 'Taming the magnates?', in *Nobility Essays*, p. 270; A. Grant, 'Crown and nobility in late medieval Britain', in *Scotland and England 1286–1815* ed. R. Mason (Edinburgh, 1987), p. 34; idem, *Independence and Nationhood: Scotland 1306–1469* (London, 1984), pp. 147–99.
12. See W. D. H. Sellar, 'Celtic law' and 'Common law', both passim.
13. *APS*, i,p. 572 (1399).
14. *APS*, ii, 9 (c. 3) (1426).
15. *See APS*, ii, pp. 214 (c. 5), and 222 (cc. 19 and 20).
16. *APS*, ii, p. 252 (c. 24). On this act, see G. Donaldson, 'Problems of sovereignty and law in Orkney and Shetland', in *Stair Misc II*, p. 26.
17. The classic study is J. M. Wormald, 'Bloodfeud, kindred and government in early modern Scotland', *Past and Present* lxxxvii

(1980), p. 54. See also her *Court, Kirk and Community: Scotland 1470–1625* (London, 1981) pp. 24–5, 36–9; *Lords and Men in Scotland: Bonds of Manrent 1442–1603* (Edinburgh, 1985); and 'The Sandlaw dispute', in *The Settlement of Disputes in Early Medieval Europe*, ed. W. Davies and P. Fouracre (Cambridge, 1986), pp. 191–205. See further A. Grant, 'Crown and nobility', pp. 43–6; *Independence and Nationhood*, pp. 156–62.

18. E. Powell, 'Settlement of disputes by arbitration in fifteenth-century England', *LHR*, ii (1984), p. 21 (quotation on p. 39). See also his 'Arbitration and the law in England in the later Middle Ages', *TRHS*, xxxiii (1983), p. 49.
19. *Leges Henrici Primi*, pp. 98 (6, 6) (*incerta alea placitorum*), and 168 (49, 5 a) (*pactum enim legem vincit et amor iudicium*).
20. A. Watson, *Legal Transplants* (Edinburgh, 1974).
21. For general discussion, see W. D. H. Sellar, 'Common law'; H. L. MacQueen, 'Alexander III', pp. 79–82; R. Frame, *The British Isles 1100–1400* (Oxford, 1990), pp. 94–6. See most recently, on specific points of similarity, A. D. M. Forte, 'The horse that kills', *TvR*, lviii (1990), p. 95; W. D. H. Sellar, 'Forethocht felony, malice aforethought and the classification of homicide', in *Legal History in the Making*, ed. W. M. Gordon and T. D. Fergus (London and Ronceverte, 1991), p. 43.
22. See P. R. Hyams, 'The common law and the French connection', *Anglo-Norman Studies*, iv (1981), p. 77; R. Frame, *British Isles*, pp. 50–71. The phrase 'Norman Empire' is derived from the title of J. Le Patourel's book, *The Norman Empire* (Oxford, 1976). For the challenge to this idea, see D. Bates, 'Normandy and England after 1066', *EHR*, civ (1989), p. 851, especially p. 874.
23. For this account of Maitland's views, see primarily P & M, i, pp. 136–8, 144–8, 149–51; ii, pp. 44–62. It should be noted, in fairness to Maitland, that the sketch in his posthumously-published *Forms of Action at Common Law* (Cambridge, 1936), which is often used for a summary of his position, was a set of lectures simplifying matters for undergraduates and not intended by him for publication.
24. For the date of 1179, see J. H. Round, 'The date of the grand assize', *EHR*, xxxi (1916), p. 268.
25. *Glanvill*, XII, 2 and 25.
26. See also S. F. C. Milsom, *HFCL*, pp. 99–151, and his introduction to the 1968 reprint of P & M, i, pp. xxvii–xlix; also his collected papers, Milsom, *Studies*, pp. 210–11, 231–60, 272–6.
27. S. F. C. Milsom, *LFEF*, p. 120.
28. Milsom here drew on S. E. Thorne, 'English feudalism and estates in land', *Cambridge Law Journal*, xvii (1959), p. 193.
29. Milsom, LFEF, p. 186.
30. P. R. Hyams, 'Warranty', p. 481 note.
31. P. A. Brand, 'Henry II', p. 221.
32. D. W. Sutherland, *Novel Disseisin*, responding to versions of Milsom's thesis preceding *LFEF;* P. A. Brand, Review I, *Irish Jurist, x* (1975) p. 363; Review II, *LHR*, vi (1988), p. 197; 'Lordship and distraint'; 'Henry II'; R. C. Palmer, 'Feudal framework', and 'Origins of property'; S. D. White, 'Inheritances'; J. Biancalana,

'Want of justice'; and J. Hudson, 'Milsom's legal structure'; *Land, Law and Lordship*. Other less frequently-cited studies are mentioned later.

33. S. D. White, 'Inheritances', especially pp. 63–4 and 96–103.
34. E. A. R. Brown, 'The tyranny of a construct: feudalism and historians of medieval Europe', *American Historical Review*, lxxix (1974), p. 1063. The quotation is on p. 1077. Cf. J. C. Holt, *Magna Carta*, 2nd ed. (Cambridge, 1992), p. 127 and note.
35. P. R. Hyams, Review, p. 858.
36. S. D. White, 'Inheritances', pp. 64–70, 98–9; M. T. Clanchy, 'Law and love in the Middle Ages', in *Disputes and Settlements* ed. J. Bossy (Cambridge, 1983) p. 47; P. R. Hyams, 'Henry II and Ganelon', *Syracuse Scholar*, iv (1983) p. 24; J. Hudson, 'Milsom's legal structure', p. 61; P. A. Brand, 'Henry II', p. 211.
37. See e.g. M. Bloch, *Feudal Society* (London, 1962), pp. 359–74; F. L. Ganshof, *Feudalism* (London, 1964), pp. 156–67; Robinson et al., *IELH*, pp. 54–8.
38. The classic accounts are James Campbell's articles, 'Observations on English government from the tenth to the twelfth century' and 'The significance of the Anglo-Norman state in the administrative history of western Europe', both reprinted in his *Essays in Anglo-Saxon History* (London and Ronceverte, 1986), pp. 155 and 171. See also W. L. Warren, *The Governance of Norman and Angevin England 1086–1272* (London, 1987), pp. 25–63.
39. Second edition (Oxford, 1961), especially pp. 42–69.
40. F. M. Stenton, *English Feudalism*, pp. 42–57 (quotations on pp. 51 and 55).
41. Third edition (Oxford, 1971), pp. 636–7.
42. F. M. Stenton, *English Feudalism*, pp. 47–9, 52–3, 54–5; cf. S. D. White, 'Inheritances', p. 102.
43. J. Hudson, 'Milsom's legal structure', p. 53 note. But cf. D. Crouch, *The Beaumont Twins* (Cambridge, 1986), pp. 158–62, for powerful and lively honorial courts in the twelfth century.
44. F. M. Stenton, *English Feudalism*, pp. 31–8 (quotations on pp. 33 and 37).
45. F. M. Stenton, *English Feudalism*, pp. 38–41. On this statute, see also S. F. C. Milsom, *Studies*, pp. 248–9, and J. C. Holt, 'The heiress and the alien', *TRHS*, xxxv (1985), pp. 9–19.
46. J. Hudson, *Land, Law and Lordship*, p. 28, citing *Registrum Antiquissimum of Lincoln Cathedral*, no 313; F. M. Stenton, *English Feudalism*, p. 40 and note.
47. For the quotation, see M. Chibnall, *Anglo-Norman England 1066–1166* (Oxford, 1986) 173.
48. M. Chibnall, *Anglo-Norman England*, pp. 173–4; also P. R. Hyams and P. A. Brand, 'Seigneurial control of women's marriage', *Past and Present*, ic (1983), pp. 125–6; R. Mortimer, 'Land and service: the tenants of the Honour of Clare', *Anglo-Norman Studies*, viii (1985) p. 195; K. J. Stringer, *Earl David*, pp. 131–2; D. Crouch, *Beaumont Twins*, pp. 128–32.
49. F. M. Stenton, *English Feudalism*, pp. 65–6.
50. See for references and discussion N. D. Hurnard, 'Magna Carta, clause 34', in *Studies in Medieval History presented to F. M. Powicke,*

ed. R. W. Hunt, W. A. Pantin and R. W. Southern (Oxford, 1948), pp. 157–60.

51. See M. Cheney, 'A decree of Henry II on defect of justice', in *Tradition and Change*, ed. D. Greenway et al. (Cambridge, 1985), pp.189–91, and J. Biancalana, 'Want of justice', pp. 453–8, for the relevant passages.

52. J. A. Green, *The Government of England under Henry I* (Cambridge, 1986), pp. 102–5; J. Biancalana, 'Want of justice', passim; J. Hudson, 'Life grants of land and the development of inheritance in Anglo-Norman England', *Anglo-Norman Studies* xii (1989), pp. 77–9.

53. J. Biancalana, 'Want of justice', p. 452.

54. P. A. Brand, 'Henry II', pp. 217–22.

55. J. Biancalana, 'Want of justice', p. 439.

56. P. A. Brand, Review II, p. 202; J. Biancalana, 'Want of justice', p. 467; J. Hudson, 'Life grants', p. 79, and 'Milsom's legal structure', pp. 64–5. For the *Carte Baronum*, see W. L. Warren, *Governance*, p. 100.

57. J. Biancalana, 'Want of justice', p. 452. Note however the scepticism of P. A. Brand, 'Lordship and distraint', p. 5, as to the continued force of the Anglo-Saxon laws, and see *Leges Henrici Primi*, pp. 359–60.

58. J. Biancalana, 'Want of justice', pp. 452, 467, 476–7, 483–4.

59. J. Hudson, *Land, Law and Lordship*, pp. 22–51; P. A. Brand, 'Lordship and distraint', pp. 5–8.

60. P. A. Brand, 'Lordship and distraint', pp. 6–7.

61. P. A. Brand, 'Lordship and distraint', pp. 14–15.

62. J. Hudson, *Land, Law and Lordship*, pp. 43–4.

63. P & M, i, p. 353; D. W. Sutherland, *Novel Disseisin*, pp. 82–6.

64. For this tendency, see E. King, 'The Anarchy of Stephen's reign', *TRHS*, xxxiv (1984), p. 133.

65. See in addition to the references discussed below, S. D. White, 'Inheritances', pp. 100–1; J. Biancalana, 'Want of justice', p. 454; J. Hudson, 'Milsom's legal structure', p. 57.

66. E. Z. Tabuteau, *Transfers of Property in Eleventh-Century Norman Law* (Chapel Hill, 1988), pp. 196–204.

67. *Libri Feudorum*, II, 25.

68. R. C. Palmer, 'Feudal framework', p. 1162.

69. Ibid.

70. P. R. Hyams, 'Warranty', especially pp. 460–5.

71. Ibid., pp. 464–5.

72. Ibid., pp. 443–7.

73. Ibid., pp. 456–9, 474–81. See also on these themes his '"No register of title": the Domesday inquest and land adjudication', *Anglo-Norman Studies*, ix (1986), p. 127; and 'The charter as a source for the early common law', *JLH*, xii (1991), pp. 177–83.

74. P. R. Hyams, 'Warranty', pp. 450, 476; see J. Hudson, *Land, Law and Lordship*, pp. 51–8 and D. Postles, 'Gifts in frankalmoign, warranty of land, and feudal society', *Cambridge Law Journal*, 1 (1991), p. 330.

75. R. C. Palmer, 'Origins of property', pp. 19–24; J. Biancalana, 'Want of justice', p. 440.

76. See D. Postles, 'Gifts', pp. 335–42; note also his 'Securing the gift in Oxfordshire charters in the twelfth and early thirteenth centuries', *Archives*, lxxxiv (1990), p. 1; P. R. Hyams, 'Warranty', pp. 447–53; and J. Hudson, *Land, Law and Lordship*, p. 53. On the *laudatio parentum*, see also S. D. White, *Custom, Kinship, and Gifts to Saints: The Laudatio Parentum in Western France 1050–1150* (Chapel Hill, 1988).
77. *Glanvill*, XII, 2 and 25.
78. R. C. van Caenegem, *Birth*, p. 27.
79. On Normandy, see J. Yver, 'Le bref Anglo-Normand', *TvR*, xxix (1961), p. 319; R. C. Van Caenegem, *Birth*, p. 59; D. Bates, 'The earliest Norman writs', *EHR*, c (1985), p. 282.
80. The case is now printed and translated in *English Lawsuits from William I to Richard I*, ed. R. C. van Caenegem, 2 vols (Selden Society, 1990–1), ii, no 393. See also no 395. For comment on no 393, see D. M. Stenton, *English Justice*, p. 34; D. W. Sutherland, *Novel Disseisin*, pp. 40–1; R. C. van Caenegem, *Birth*, pp. 44–5; P. A. Brand, Review I, p. 366; R. C. Palmer, 'Feudal framework', pp. 1148–9; J. Biancalana, 'Want of justice', pp. 500–1.
81. R. C. Palmer, 'Feudal framework', pp. 1142–9; 'Origins of property', pp. 8–13. See also, in support of a general settlement founded on the protection of seisin and hereditary right, R. H. C. Davis, *King Stephen 1135–1154*, 3rd ed. (London, 1990) pp. 118–23.
82. P. R. Hyams, 'Warranty', pp. 497–503; J. Biancalana, 'Want of justice', pp. 468–70. See also J. C. Holt, 'Magna Carta 1215–1217: the legal and social context', in *Law in Medieval Life and Thought*, ed. E. B. King and S. Ridyard (Press of the University of the South, USA, 1990), pp. 11–13.
83. Although note M. T. Clanchy, *England and its Rulers 1066–1272* (London, 1983), p. 150: 'the difficulty with this [i.e. connecting the post-1160 reforms with the pre-1154 Anarchy] is the chronological gap'.
84. See *Glanvill*, I, 3; XIII, 1.
85. D. W. Sutherland, *Novel Disseisin*, pp. 20–6, 40–2; J. Hackney, Review, *JLH*, v (1984), pp. 82–3; R. C. van Caenegem, *Birth*, p. 44; J. Biancalana, 'Want of justice', pp. 475–6, 500–2, 505–6; J. Hudson, 'Milsom's legal structure', pp. 61–4.
86. R. C. van Caenegem, *Birth*, pp. 39–47; J. Biancalana, 'Want of justice', p. 475; J. Hudson, 'Milsom's legal structure', p. 56.
87. D. W. Sutherland, *Novel Disseisin*, pp. 30–1.
88. P. A. Brand, Review I, p. 366.
89. R. C. Palmer, 'Feudal framework', pp. 1145–53.
90. See J. C. Holt, *Magna Carta*, pp. 126–39.
91. M. Cheney, 'The litigation between John Marshal and Archbishop Thomas Becket in 1164: a pointer to the origins of novel disseisin?', in *Law and Social Change in British History*, ed. J. A. Guy and H. G. Beale (Royal Historical Society, 1984), p. 9.
92. J. Hudson, 'Milsom's legal structure', p. 65.
93. J. Biancalana, 'Want of justice', passim (quotation on p. 441). The argument of this important but complex article is clearly summarised on pp. 438–41.

94. See R. C. Palmer, 'Feudal framework', pp. 1145–9; 'Origins of property', pp. 13–18.
95. See above, p. 14; J. Biancalana, 'Want of justice', pp. 468–70, 504–6.
96. J. Biancalana, 'Want of justice', pp. 505–6. I find this suggestion unconvincing.
97. Ibid., pp. 471–3.
98. See R. C. Palmer, 'Origins of property', pp. 39–43; 'Feudal framework', pp. 1154–9. On entry *sur disseisin*, see G. D. G. Hall, 'The early history of entry *sur disseisin*', *Tulane Law Review*, xlii (1968), p. 584.
99. R. C. Palmer, 'Origins of property', pp. 24–39; 'Feudal framework', pp. 1156–61.
100. 'Origins of property', p. 39 note; 'Feudal framework', pp. 1154–6.
101. 'Origins of property', pp. 41–6.
102. G. W. S. Barrow, *Kingdom*, p. 122.
103. *Radulphi de Hengham Summae*, ed. W. H. Dunham (Cambridge, 1932), p. 7; J. Biancalana, 'Want of justice', p. 454 note, pp. 535– 6. For the date and authorship of the treatise, see P. A. Brand, '*Hengham Magna:* a thirteenth-century English common law treatise and its composition', *Irish Jurist*, xi (1976), p. 147.
104. See J. B. Post, 'Courts, councils and arbitrators in the Ladbroke manor dispute', in *Medieval Legal Records in Memory of C. A. F. Meekings*, ed. R. F. Hunnisett and J. B. Post (London, 1978), p. 289; and C. Rawcliffe, 'The great lord as peacekeeper: arbitration by English noblemen and their councils in the later Middle Ages', in *Law and Social Change in British History*, ed. J. A. Guy and H. G. Beale (Royal Historical Society, 1984), pp. 45–8.
105. J. M. Wormald, 'Bloodfeud', pp. 72–3, 86–7; 'The Sandlaw dispute', pp. 194–205; *Lords and Men*, pp. 17, 38, 40, 122–8; also A. Grant, 'Crown and nobility', pp. 44–5.
106. R. C. Palmer, 'The economic and cultural impact of the origins of property: 1180–1220', *LHR*, iii (1985), p. 375, argues that the inflation was one consequence of the development of the common law, which had created a market in land.
107. See e.g. J. C. Holt, 'The heiress and the alien', pp. 21–4.
108. S. F. C. Milsom, *LFEF*, pp. 110–12; *HFCL*, pp. 113–16.
109. See, for this by no means steady decline of military service and increasing emphasis on casualties in the thirteenth and fourteenth centuries, G. W. W. Barrow, *Kingdom*, p. 301, *ANE*, pp. 129–44, and *Bruce*, pp. 286–9; Duncan, *Kingdom*, pp. 385–91, 398–405; *RRS*, v, pp. 48–61; A. Grant, 'Thesis', pp. 187–90, and *Independence and Nationhood*, p. 135.
110. R. Nicholson, 'Feudal developments', p. 3. See also C. Madden, 'Royal treatment of feudal casualties in late medieval Scotland', *SHR*, lv (1976), p. 172.
111. For contrasting views on how 'free' the market in land in medieval Scotland was, see A. A. M. Duncan, *Kingdom*, pp. 397–8; R. Burgess, *Perpetuities in Scots Law* (Stair Society, 1979), pp. 51–61, especially p. 56; A. Grant, 'Thesis', pp. 197–211.
112. A. Grant, 'Thesis', pp. 187–90; but note that (p. 190) 'when land was held by military service, the most significant aspect of

the tenure from the lord's point of view seems to have been . . . suit of court'.

113. For a recent, thoroughly-referenced contribution on this subject from a Scottish point of view, see J. W. Cairns, 'Craig, Cujas, and the definition of *feudum:* is a feu a usufruct?', in *New Perspectives in the Roman Law of Property*, ed. P. Birks (Oxford, 1989), p. 75. See also G. L. Gretton, 'The feudal system', *Stair Memorial Encyclopedia of the Laws of Scotland*, forthcoming.

114. S. F. C. Milsom, *HFCL*, pp. 100, 149–51; R. C. Palmer, 'Origins of property', pp. 4–24.

115. P. A. Brand, Review II, p. 202.

116. For what follows, see P & M, ii, pp. 1–29; A. W. B. Simpson, *Land Law*, pp. 81–95; S. F. C. Milsom, *HFCL*, pp. 166–77, 192–4; J. H. Baker, *IELH*, pp. 296–314.

117. *Walsingham's Case* (1573) 2 Plowd. p. 555.

118. But note S. F. C. Milsom, *Studies*, pp. 223–9, and P. A. Brand, 'Formedon in the remainder before *De Donis*', *Irish Jurist*, x (1975), p. 318.

119. See *Glanvill*, I, 3; XIII, 1.

120. P&M, ii, p. 80.

121. On all this, see P&M, ii, pp. 74–9; A. W. B. Simpson, *Land Law*, pp. 37–44; S. E. Thorne, 'Livery of seisin', *LQR*, lii (1936), p. 345.

122. D. W. Sutherland, *Novel Disseisin*, p. 42; P & M, ii, p. 11.

123. P & M, ii, pp. 78–9.

124. See in particular C. D'O. Farran, *Land Law;* also C. F. Kolbert and N. M. Mackay, *History of Scots and English Land Law* (Berkhamsted, 1977); H. H. Monteath, 'Heritable rights', in *ISLH*, p. 156. But note I. A. Milne, 'Heritable rights: the early feudal tenures', *ISLH*, p. 147.

125. See e.g. *ADC*, ii, introduction, p. xlv; *ADC (Stair)*, introduction, p. xxxvii.

126. W. C. Dickinson, 'Administration of justice', p. 350.

127. See e.g. J. F. Baldwin, *The King's Council in England during the Middle Ages* (Oxford, 1913), p. 279; *Select Cases before the King's Council 1243–1482*, ed. I. S. Leadam and J. F. Baldwin (Selden Society, 1918), p. xxvi; T. F. T. Plucknett, *A Concise History of the Common Law*, 5th ed. (London, 1956), pp. 176–7; W. S. Holdsworth, *History of English Law* (London, 1966 reprint), i, pp. 487–9; A. Harding, *The Law Courts of Medieval England* (London, 1973), pp. 102 and 105; E. G. Henderson, 'Legal rights to land in the early chancery', *AJLH*, xxvi (1982), p. 97; A. L. Brown, *The Governance of Later Medieval England 1272–1461* (London, 1989), p. 133.

2

Lords' Courts and Royal Justice

Since the time of Maitland, the historiography of English medieval law has been dominated by the idea of a conflict, either deliberately sought or, more recently following Milsom, unintended but no less real, between royal and feudal justice, with the former expanding at the expense of the latter to create the common law of England. In medieval Scotland, by contrast, the story has traditionally been seen as going precisely the opposite way. Feudal courts retain power while royal justice fails, with generally disastrous consequences both for social order and stability and for the intellectual development of the law. As suggested in the first chapter, however, it may be that the antithesis between royal and feudal justice has been overdrawn, at least so far as it affected Scotland. Certainly, no medieval Scottish king sought conflict with the private courts of his magnates; rather it is clear that their courts were seen as instrumental in the achievement of good governance alongside the royal courts. A fresh analysis of the relationship between the feudal courts and royal justice in Scotland is obviously a necessary preliminary to any discussion of the king's brieves of novel dissaine, mortancestry and right, and of the rule requiring the use of these brieves when it was sought to eject a tenant from his free holding. Before the effect of this rule and the relevant brieves can be assessed, it is necessary to understand the world in which they operated. To what extent were disputes about landholding matters only for the lord of whom the land was held? Did the king's courts have the capacity to compel the use of the remedies which they provided, and to enforce their judgments against recalcitrant lords?

This chapter has three main themes. First, it examines the existence and operation of the courts of private lords in the twelfth and thirteenth centuries, with special reference to their proprietary and disciplinary jurisdictions. Second, it discusses the development of royal justice, stressing the clear pattern of regularisation and its assertion of ultimate control, although not of a monopoly, over justice in the feudal courts. The third theme is the interaction between royal and lordship courts, which came to rest in the later Middle Ages on a theory of the jurisdictional superiority of the king's courts, while still leaving a substantial role for private justice, not only through arbitration and informal dispute-settlement mechanisms, but also in the formal arena of the lord's court. However, this should not be seen either as the product of the weakness of the royal courts, or as meaning that there were competing or alternative systems of justice each playing according to its own rules. Royal justice was regularly administered and was capable of exercising considerable authority; moreover, it was also needed when the feudal courts reached the limits of their jurisdiction and authority.

THE TWELFTH-CENTURY BACKGROUND

The twelfth century was a period of major change in Scottish society: it witnessed the coming of the reformed monastic orders, the establishment of burghs and the settlement of Anglo-Norman knights on lands throughout much of the country. All of these innovations involved the grant of lands to incomers, by the king and others, usually recorded in charters which were expressed in tenurial form, whereby the grantee was to hold the lands of (*tenere de*) the grantor in return for some service. It is the grants made to the Anglo-Norman knights which we think of as most characteristically feudal, in that the service specified was primarily military, and the lord had, or came to have, rights of wardship, marriage and relief over a deceased tenant's heir. However, it would be artificial to leave the other groups of settlers out of account in thinking our way into the legal world of twelfth-century Scotland, as indeed it would be to neglect the native structures which continued to exist during and after the main period of settlement. Certainly later on, many Scottish lords exercised jurisdiction over their tenants in ways which owed nothing to Anglo-Norman feudalism – for example, the rights of *kenkynnol* and *surdit de sergaunt* which were used in Galloway and Carrick into the fifteenth century.[1] The changes of the twelfth century did not occur all at once all over the kingdom. The creation of burghs and the establishment of land-holding monastic houses were processes which went on throughout the twelfth and thirteenth centuries, while Geoffrey Barrow has traced the feudal settlement in a series of magisterial studies, showing that it began south of Forth, in Fife and in Moray under David I (1124–53), and was followed in the second half of the twelfth century by an intensification of existing settlement and 'a steady feudalisation' beyond the Forth and Tay as well as in Clydesdale.[2]

Royal government also began to be transformed in the twelfth century. For our purposes, the most important innovations were the introduction of the offices of the sheriff and the justice or justiciar, to look after the king's interests in the various parts of his kingdom. Largely following the progress of the feudal settlement, the country began to be divided into sheriffdoms. Although this division was not to be complete until the fourteenth century,[3] the sheriffdom was certainly the normal unit of local royal government in most of the kingdom by the mid-thirteenth century, having largely usurped many of the functions of the ancient earldoms, shires and manages, and added others to deal with the new world brought about by the social and political changes of the previous century and a half. Before 1165, however, the sheriff was found only in the south and east, and not at all in the great south-western lordships or north of Forfar; only in the reign of William I (1165–1214) were sheriffdoms established for the first time in Ayr, the Mearns, Moray and (probably) Aberdeen and Banff.[4] The function of the early justice, which office is documented from the reign of David I on, is very obscure; but in the second half of the twelfth century he was clearly linked with, albeit superior to, the sheriff. A justiciar of Scotia, that is, Scotland north of Forth, is found in Malcolm IV's time (1153–65), and it seems probable that there were justiciars of Lothian and, perhaps, Galloway, before the end of the twelfth century.[5] It would be wrong to underestimate the governmental roles played on behalf of the king by the earls, thanes and royal *judices* before and during the feudal settlement, but it is apparent that the twelfth century witnessed the beginnings of an intensification of royal government alongside the other innovations of the period. However, this should also be seen as a gradual process operating for a long time beside and with the older forms of the king's authority.

LORDS AND THEIR COURTS BEFORE 1300

To what extent, then, was Milsom's feudal world of the twelfth century, in particular his world of lords and tenants expressing their relationship in the forum of the lord's court, to be found in contemporary Scotland? We can expect it to be most strongly represented in Scotland among the Anglo-Norman settlers, since they came from that world and brought with them its norms and expectations.[6] This can be most clearly seen in David I's grant of Annandale to the first Robert Bruce in c. 1124, probably for the service of ten knights, under which Bruce was to hold 'with all the customs Ranulf Meschin had in Carlisle'.[7] Carlisle was a great English honour established for Ranulf at the end of the eleventh century;[8] David's employment of the comparison to define Robert's holding suggests that he neither saw nor wanted any difference between the rights and duties of his lords and those of Henry I. Bruce and his knightly tenants would have put their relationship into effect in a court at which the tenants were the suitors and peers. A similar situation would have arisen wherever the king granted a fee for more than one knight's service, within which, it has been said, 'there seems to have been a fairly systematic process of sub-infeudation'.[9] Such royal grants became much less common as the twelfth century progressed, and the typical service came to be that of one knight, or some fraction of a knight's service. Yet even within these relatively small fees there could be subinfeudation by fractionalisation, or further fractionalisation, of the knight's service, and as a result there could be a lord holding a court of tenants with some claim to be described as feudal in the sense given at the outset of this chapter. Moreover, it is clear that many tenants held lands for services which were military but not knightly, or which were wholly unmilitary; yet, whatever the earlier position may have been, in all probability at least some of these were also required to pay suit at the lord's court.[10]

Virtually nothing survives from the twelfth century which tells us directly of these courts and their workings. Express grants of jurisdiction by the king to lay landowners appear only in the reign of William I, and are not confined to lands held for military service or, indeed, to Anglo-Norman grantees.[11] These grants are generally in formulaic terms, the meaning of which is difficult to interpret. However, they seem to relate primarily to what we would think of as criminal jurisdiction, and there is little express reference to the civil jurisdiction of the lord's court over the tenants who held land of him, with which Milsom is most concerned. The obligation of suit of court, owed by such tenants three times yearly at the lord's head courts, was clearly well established by the beginning of the thirteenth century when it is referred to in charters. At much the same time, we can begin to catch sight of lord and tenant giving effect to their tenurial relationship in the lord's court. An example is the resignation and quitclaim of his lands in Annandale which Dunegal, son of Udard, made in the full court of his lord William Bruce between 1194 and 1214.[12] Many other such transactions recorded in twelfth-century documents, which make no express mention of the lord's court but which are witnessed by his other tenants, are almost certainly the product of sessions of the court.

King William's grants of jurisdiction were made to native landowners as well as to Anglo-Norman settlers and families, and it is an intriguing question to what extent the jurisdiction thus obtained had continuity with existing customary rights.[13] Equally, however, it is evident that the new custom of the Anglo-Norman courts might influence the development of these rights. There are a number of references to the pleas and courts of the earls or mormaers;[14] whatever rights these may reflect (and almost certainly within these courts the provincial *judex* or dempster performed his function),[15] it is clear that by the beginning of the thirteenth century a feudal pattern had become established. The earldom of Fife was held feudally of the king from about 1136, and during the twelfth century the earls infeft a number of Anglo-Norman tenants.[16] Almost certainly, their courts were transformed into gatherings of suitors as a result, at least when the affairs of the tenants formed the business of the court. By c.1212, Fergus, the last earl of Buchan of wholly Gaelic stock, was demanding from a tenant suit of court at his three head courts at Ellon,[17] along with payment of relief and the service of one bowman. One of the sons of the Celtic earl of Strathearn was demanding suit at his court of Meikleour in c.1225,[18] and it is likely that suitors made up the courts of the earls themselves, which are relatively well recorded from the beginning of the thirteenth century.[19]

Explicit grants of jurisdiction and the right to hold courts were also made to the ecclesiastical foundations of the twelfth century, and survive in numbers from the reign of David I on.[20] Again, these seem more concerned with criminal than with civil jurisdiction. For our purposes, no real distinction needs to be made between these courts and the courts of lay landowners; both arose from the right of landholders to exercise jurisdiction over all their tenants, whether those tenants held on free or unfree tenures. Moreover, the right to hold courts was enjoyed not only by greater landowners. According to a late fourteenth-century source, only three or four suitors were needed to make up a court.[21] Thus, at the end of the twelfth century, we read of the court of Adam of Lour and that of his tenant in Lour, David Ruffus of Forfar.[22] Throughout the medieval period, we find references to courts which can only have enjoyed an extremely slight jurisdiction, both territorially and in respect of subject matter – for example, the courts at Lesmahagow which in the twelfth and thirteenth century enjoyed a jurisdiction of 'birthinsake' (over as much in goods as might be carried on a man's back),[23] or the court 'called *Couthal*' held on certain lands in Angus, to which the abbot of Arbroath referred somewhat scornfully in 1329 as being for the men residing within the said lands, to deal with the countless acts concerning only themselves'.[24]

From the thirteenth century on, the evidence for the courts of lords, ecclesiastical and lay, becomes much more extensive. Most of what then becomes visible was probably also present in the twelfth century. Those holding land of their lord have obligations of suit at his court, and put their tenurial relationship with the lord into effect there. Tenants receive grants of land from the lord, or resign land, in his court;[25] there they show the charters by which they hold the lands;[26] there the heirs of deceased tenants bargain with the lord over the relief payable for the inheritance, and give him their homage;[27] and there we catch the occasional glimpse of disputes between lord and tenant, or between those who would be tenants, being resolved, although usually by quitclaim and settlement rather than by judgment of the court. Late in the twelfth century, for example, Liulf and his heirs abjured their rights in Reston Parva and quitclaimed them to Adam, son of Cospatric, in the court of the prior of Coldingham, lord of the lands.[28] In the court of his lord, Philip de

Moubray, Patrick of Nawton renounced all his rights to the lands of Moncreiffe in the late 1220s, and quitclaimed them to David de Munehtes and his heir in perpetuity.[29] Another quitclaim of 1266 shows a dispute over lands between Inchaffray abbey and its neighbour Tristram of Gorthy which Tristram initiated 'in the lay forum', seemingly a reference to the court of the earl of Strathearn, of whom both parties were tenants.[30] The court of the priory of Coldingham is unusually well documented for the thirteenth century, and there are a number of examples of the court witnessing tenants quitclaiming the prior or another tenant in respect of lands held of the priory. David of Quixwood quitclaimed the prior of the wood of Aldcambus in his full court,[31] while in 1246, before the lord prior and many of his faithful in his court held at Ayton, Alan de Candela quitclaimed half a carucate of land in Renton to Bertram, son of Robert the cook of Coldingham.[32] In another case, Robert, son of Reginald of Magna Reston, understood that he and his ancestors had unjustly occupied certain lands in Reston, and resigned them in the court of his lord, the prior of Coldingham.[33]

These cases have a proprietorial look to them, although it is worthy of note that all were settled rather than adjudged. The evidence does not disclose how far these settlements were the product of genuinely negotiated consensus between the parties, achieved perhaps with the assistance of the lord and his court, or were the result of coercion by a lord determined to have the tenant he wanted, or to have the lands back in his hands, or even whether they disguise a truly adjudicative process. Certainly, in these lords' courts, there might be trial by battle. The duel is explicitly referred to along with the ordeal as one of the liberties of the courts of the priory of Scone and the abbeys of Holyrood and Arbroath in twelfth-century royal charters.[34] If ecclesiastical courtholders could stage judicial duels, there can be no doubt that their secular equivalents could also do so. An assize of King William, dateable by internal evidence to 1180, refers to the courts of earls, barons and freeholders holding duels as well as those of bishops and abbots.[35] The duel lived on in the lord's court in the thirteenth century; there are references to it as part of the jurisdiction of Melrose abbey in the lands in Kyle which it held of Alexander Stewart of Dundonald,[36] while a little earlier John, the swineherd of Coldingham, had successfully undertaken a duel for the son of Adam of Reston, probably in the court of the prior of Coldingham.[37] Most of our other evidence about the judicial duel in lords' courts ties it to their criminal jurisdiction, but, if the English parallels may be relied on here, at the back of many of the settlements of land disputes discussed in the previous paragraph must have been the possibility of a duel. However, we should not take it that ultimately the only way of resolving such disputes was by the duel. The duel, like the ordeal, was for use where all other methods of proof failed.[38] In many proprietorial cases, the first resort would be the recollection of the suitors of the court, before whom tenants had been infeft and dispossessed in the past. The duel would come in when the memory of the court failed, or there was unresolvable uncertainty. No doubt the possibility of resort to a duel was also used to bully recalcitrant disputants into a settlement, but it should not be assumed that, because the proof of last resort was an irrational one, courts were not required to confront legal issues in such cases.

Examples of tenants losing lands in court as a result of failure to fulfil obligations to their lords can also be found in the thirteenth century, although again typically they are recorded as resulting from agreements or quitclaims rather than outright judgments. An early example may be a resignation of lands in Annan by William, son of Ralph the lardener, and his brother David to Robert Bruce of Annandale in his court, which resulted from their failure to fulfil an obligation owed to Robert.[39] There are a number of clear examples in documents recording the activities of the court of the priory of Coldingham. Thus, in 1246, Sybil and Mariota, daughters of Maurice of Ayton, each acknowledged herself unable to perform her services to the priory for her lands in Ayton, and the prior in his full court adjudged that they should revert to the prior,[40] while in 1239, again in the prior's court, Roger, son of Radulph, resigned his lands in Coldingham *pro defectu servicie*.[41] In yet another, slightly later case, we see the same process between a tenant of the priory and his subtenant, again occurring *pro defectu servicie* with the resignation being made in the prior's court (presumably because the tenant had either an insufficiently powerful court to bring his tenant to heel, or no court at all).[42] In 1258, Helyas Chaimcun of Ayton also acknowledged default of service which she owed and did not do for her lands in the *villa* of upper Ayton which she held of the prior for homage. She quitclaimed her hereditary right to the prior in his full court (at which Hugh Barclay, justiciar of Lothian, was present).[43] For an example of a secular court exercising disciplinary jurisdiction, we can take the earl of Dunbar's court which, in or around 1273, witnessed a resignation to the earl by Sir Patrick Edgar of the lands of Lennel in Berwickshire '*pro defectu servicii de eadem terra*'.[44] Probably at about the same time, Walter, called the chaplain, son of Walter son of Thomas the knight of Derchestyr, resigned the lands of the Hirsel in Berwickshire in the earl's full court, for defect of service due from the lands to the earl.[45] In both cases, the earl regranted the lands to be held of him by the nunnery at Coldstream.

The involvement of the lord's court in these cases probably betokens some antecedent disciplinary process there by which the tenant had been compelled to recognise his failure and to accept its consequences. Our knowledge of such processes is scanty and of uncertain quality, especially

for the twelfth and thirteenth centuries. The later evidence of the 1318
legislation of Robert I shows the familiarity of the idea of a lord seizing
or poinding his tenant's goods to enforce obligations of service. One of
the 1318 acts restricts the lord's right to poind *pro servicio* to goods within
the tenant's fee unless he has authority from a royal officer or the officer
of the other fee; it further instructs the retention in a pound of the goods
taken. No more than will cover what is owed is to be taken. Breach of the
act will lead to the king's grave forfeiture.[46] Other texts also emphasise the
need for leave to poind outside the fee, and provide that unauthorised
poinding is a breach of the king's peace.[47] This may suggest that the lord
needed no authority inside his lordship. It also seems that poinding could
be a violent process, and this may explain why from the twelfth century
grants of royal protection commonly provided against poinding for
another's debts, something which might happen when the lord sought to
poind outside the tenant's fee.[48]

Still later material shows that the lord could also 'recognosce' – that is,
take into his own hands as security – the lands for which the service was
owed.[49] Again according to these later sources, this procedure of distress
(which was not confined to the lord-tenant relationship, but was generally
available to creditors in respect of debts) began with the seizure of the
debtor's moveable property before moving on to his lands.[50] *Regiam
Majestatem*, the principal treatise of medieval Scots law, also incorporated
passages in *Glanvill* providing for the distraint and, ultimately, the
forfeiture of a tenant's lands to the lord for default of service and other
feudal obligations.[51] This last underlines the difficulty in assessing the
clear parallels in the Scottish material with feudal disciplinary procedures
in England: were the later rules also found in the twelfth century, or were
they shaped by subsequent developments; and can the sources for the
later law be trusted? No doubt it was as true of Scottish lords as of English
that they would normally have had no desire to chase tenants out of their
lands by means of disciplinary processes, at least so long as there was no-
one else around to fill the gap. Even then, it would be preferable to use
the processes to achieve results by some sort of agreement, however
coercive, in order to minimise the grievance felt by the ejected tenant.

In his studies of Earl David of Huntingdon, Dr Stringer has argued for
the relative freedom of that twelfth-century Scottish lord in choosing his
tenants, unhampered by hereditary claims and regular royal controls.[52]
The example which he gives of Earl David exercising such lordship is an
interesting illustration of some peculiarities of the Scottish situation
which may have given some lords in some situations a relatively free hand.
Dr Stringer develops his discussion from a grant of the lands of Monorgan
in Perthshire by Earl David to Gillebrigde in fee and heritage in 1172.
The lands had been held by Gillebrigde's father, but there is no suggestion

in Earl David's charter that the grant is anything other than a completely fresh start or that Gillebrigde had any sort of prior claim. Later on, and despite Gillebrigde's written, entirely feudal title, which included a royal confirmation, Earl David's illegitimate son Henry of Stirling held the same lands; we do not know whether this was because Gillebrigde had died without heirs – or at any rate without heirs that Earl David was prepared to recognise – or had simply been ejected in favour of Henry, or whether there had been some rearrangement, perhaps through a sale or exchange under licence of the earl, of which no evidence survives. The example also illustrates some distinctive features of the twelfth-century situation in Scotland which may have conferred even greater discretion upon a lord choosing tenants, in that Anglo-French lordship was being superimposed upon a pre-existing pattern of landholding which it did not need to recognise as giving rise to any particular claim. Such displacements of native landholders by incoming settlers may explain the statement in the *Holyrood Chronicle* that Malcolm IV '*transtulit*' the men of Moray in the 1160s,[53] and something similar may have been involved in the same king's 'deliberate and forcible stroke of royal policy',[54] the feudal settlement of Clydesdale at the expense of the bishop of Glasgow.

Another factor which may have tended to differentiate at least some Scottish feudal lordships from English ones was their territorial character. Where most English honours were not compact geographical units but consisted rather of isolated fees dispersed among the fees of other honours (a classic example being the honour of Huntingdon[55]), the opposite was true in Scotland. The Bruce lordship of Annandale has already been mentioned; other examples would include the de Moreville lordships of Cunningham and Lauderdale, the Stewart lordships of North Kyle, Strathgryfe and Mearns, the de Soules lordship of Liddesdale, and, slightly later in the twelfth century, Earl David's lordship of Garioch.[56] Where lordships were dispersed, it has been argued, royal authority was strong and the lord's power limited; conversely, compact lordships were a sign of relatively slight royal power and of a more self-contained community under each lord, at least where royal administration was no more than tenuous and irregular.[57] Thus all the lordships mentioned were, with the exception of Lauderdale, in 'frontier zones' so far as twelfth-century royal government was concerned, in that they lay beyond the reach of sheriffdoms, burghs and justices. Within these lordships, then, a fairly high degree of de facto autonomy must have existed, at least at the time of their creation. By contrast, in Lothian and on the eastern littoral north of the Tay, the fiefs were smaller and the instruments of royal control were closer to hand. Even here, however, although there were exceptions, as a general rule 'the knight's fee of the twelfth century seems to have consisted of a compact inhabited locality',[58] which may have helped establish some autonomy and sense of community focused on the lord's court. Finally, within compact lordships in general, and by contrast with the typical dispersed English honour, it may have been less common to find tenants who also held land elsewhere of other lords, or for the tenants to be in a position where they came into conflict with neighbours who held their property of a different lord. Thus the conditions in which a dispute would need outside settlement for want of an appropriate lord's court were inherently less likely to arise in Scotland.

ROYAL JUSTICE AND LORDS' COURTS TO *c.*1230

Royal justice was nevertheless always ready to interfere with lords' autonomy, although this could only be made a reality where the instruments of royal authority – justices, sheriffs and others – were in place. Several of David I's grants of franchisal jurisdiction speak of the availability of royal justice should the owner of the court neglect or fail to do justice,[59] while under Malcolm IV and William I the king's justices were often charged with ensuring that sheriffs acted in certain matters to avoid complaints of defects of justice. Malcolm IV commanded his justices to ensure that sheriffs did not connive at the detention of teinds, '*ne pro defectu iusticie querela ad me perveniat*',[60] and William I twice commanded his justices to ensure that sheriffs compelled the payment of teind in the diocese of Glasgow, in order to avoid complaints of defects of justice.[61] This gives us hints of the embryonic structure of justice which was to lead to the later medieval hierarchy of courts, beginning at the bottom with the baron court, and proceeding upward through the sheriff court to that of the justiciar by means of falsing the doom.[62] However, the twelfth-century situation was by no means cognate with the later system. Glimpses of it may be provided by an assize of King William, under which it included the presence of the king's sheriff in the lord's court when a duel was held there, although it is not clear exactly what his function would have been.[63] Perhaps it was something like the special privilege with which the king vested Robert Bruce of Annandale, allowing one of the men of his fief to attach those guilty of an offence which was a royal plea, and to bring them before the king's justices.[64] Even this may only represent a mild modernisation of established procedures; David I had earlier commanded that his *judex* of Fife should be present in the court of Dunfermline abbey 'so that pleas and justice should be transacted justly'.[65] These provisions seem to have had content. The quitclaim in the court of the prior of Coldingham, by which Liulf and his heirs renounced their rights in Reston Parva in favour of Adam son of Cospatric, was also witnessed by Walter Olifard *justicia regis*, and Robert de Burneville, sheriff of Berwick.[66] Again, when in the 1220s Patrick of Nawton quitclaimed the lands of Moncreiffe to David de Munehtes and his heir in perpetuity in the court of Philip de Moubray, there were present not only Philip's court but also the king's chancellor Master Matthew, Bredi Portanache, who was then *judex*, probably of Strathearn, and a number of other dignitaries with no tenurial right to be there.[67]

William's assize was concerned with criminal matters, ensuring that the pleas of the crown were transferred to the king's court, but the examples just given show that there is no need to see the supervisory role of the king's officer in ensuring that the lord's court did not default in justice as excluded in relation to the secure tenure of land. That royal protection was extended to the holding of land is evident even before the reign of David I. In 1110, Alexander I twice ordered the prior of Durham not to commence actions concerning the lands of Swinton in Berwickshire except when the king came into that part of the country or gave an order either orally or by his letters.[68] Later in the twelfth century, David I commanded the sheriff of Roxburgh to hold lands disputed by the monks of Durham and the earl of Dunbar until he came into the district.[69] The most celebrated case of David's reign is that in which c. 1128 the king responded to complaints made by the *célidé* of St Serf's Island in Loch Leven against 'the furnace and fire of all iniquity', the knight Robert the Burgundian, who had deprived them of the fourth part of Kirkness. The dispute was resolved in the court of Fife and Fothrif, presided over by the earl of Fife, 'great judge in Scotia', and two *judices*, who ordered the restoration of the *célidé*.[70] Although this was clearly the earl's court in action, the office of earl had a predominantly public character at this period, and the proceedings were commanded by the king.

There are other examples of David's intervention in disputes over land – for example, Dunfermline abbey's recovery of the shire of Kirkcaldy which the late Constantine, earl of Fife, had withheld from them by force (*vi*).[71] However, neither this case nor that of Robert the Burgundian has a lordship element, since all the parties had direct relationships with the king.[72] A dispute in which a lordship element does seem detectable is the restoration to the priory of Coldingham by Swain, the priest, of lands in Fishwick, Prenderguest, Coldingham and Lumsden, inasmuch as the estates named were all held of the king by the priory.[73] It looks like a downward claim to restoration where the lord needed the assistance of royal authority. Accordingly, this case rather goes against the model of all-powerful lords exercising authority through self-sufficient courts, especially as Swain the priest is hardly likely to have been able to exert the 'force' which was used by Earl Constantine against Dunfermline abbey. By way of contrast, however, we may point to the acknowledgement of William de Vieuxpoint that he had unjustly occupied lands in contention between him and the monks of Coldingham in the time of King David, seemingly obtained by the monks without royal assistance and leading to the restoration of the priory.[74]

It may be, however, that ecclesiastical lordship was not quite the same thing as its secular counterpart, and that it had more need of outside help to protect its rights. A late example of an ecclesiastical lord having difficulty in exercising jurisdiction over a lay tenant is the dispute between the abbey of Arbroath and the king's baker, Nicholas of Inverpeffer, who held his lands of the abbey, but who had been put in by the king. In 1249, the abbot was trying (unsuccessfully, it would appear) to disinherit (*exheredare*) Nicholas, perhaps for the same reason that gave rise to another dispute between them twenty years later, the tenant's reluctance to pay suit at the abbey's court. The 1249 litigation did not take place before the abbey's court, however, but in front of ecclesiastical judges delegate. Nicholas, with his place in the royal household, was too influential a tenant to be justiced even by such a powerful superior as the abbey of Arbroath; the king was to be his 'defender' (*defensorem*), presumably meaning not that he sought the king's warrandice but that he claimed the king's protection, perhaps by means of royal brieves of prohibition.[74a] In this example, then, both lord and tenant sought outside help; their world was anything but closed. It may be, too, that ecclesiastical lords were more often mindful of tenants' claims to security, even where the tenant's free status was doubtful – so, for example, sometime around 1200, the bishop of St Andrews, having been requested by the lessee of his estate at Arbuthnott in the Mearns to eject a *scoloc* Gillandres, refused to do so when he learned that Gillandres was *nativus de terra*.[75]

Some sense of the force and power which secular lords might bring to bear can be obtained from cases where it was directed against ecclesiastical tenants; but once again the evidence also shows that this exercise of lordship was subject to some external constraint. Sometime between 1162 and 1174, Uhtred, son of Fergus of Galloway, granted Kirkgunzeon to Holm Cultram abbey. He subsequently took a large part of the land back and granted it instead to Walter Berkeley. In response to the abbey's complaint, the king commanded an inquest to be held, following which Walter granted the land back to Holm Cultram, and the king gave his confirmation.[76] The story seems to illustrate lordly discretion as to his tenants; Uhtred, although a member of a Celtic dynasty, was a feudaliser who exercised Anglo-Norman forms of lordship in his dealings with outsiders such as Holm Cultram and Walter Berkeley.[77] He seems to have suffered no adverse consequences as a result of his role in the affair; indeed, he convened the inquest ordered by the king. The abbey was finally restored, and in that sense Uhtred's lordship was ultimately subjected to royal control; but this may only have been after his death in 1174. Another instance of an ecclesiastical tenant being subjected to a secular lord's change of mind is found at the very end of the twelfth century, when William of Hownam took back from Melrose abbey the lands of Raeshaw which he had previously granted to them under a royal confirmation.[78] The circumstances are unclear, but the abbey obtained help, not from the king, but from papal judges delegate. Lordship over ecclesiastical tenants was, to say the least, not purely a matter between the parties to the relationship.

An intriguing instance of the interaction of the lord's court with the king's is found in a recently-published charter of Alan of Galloway as lord of Cunningham, to be dated c. 1225. In this charter, Alan confirmed Hugh of Crawford in the third part of the toun of Stevenston, which had been sold to him by Margaret, daughter of Adam Loccard. Margaret had quitclaimed the lands and rendered them to Hugh in Alan's court *per lingnum* (sic) *et baculum*, but for greater security she also gave Hugh her charter of quitclaim in the king's court.[79] Alan was here acting as the feudal lord in a lordship which had been feudalised since the reign of David I, and which he held by virtue of his de Moreville mother. However, he was also the lord of Galloway, where he exercised great powers not definable simply in feudal terms. Was it the exercise of this power which Margaret and Hugh were anticipating and attempting to forestall by drawing in the king's court? If so, why did Alan allow it to be recorded in his charter in favour of Hugh? The charter also distinguishes between the symbolic transfer in Alan's court and the handing-over of the written record in the king's, the latter being to ensure that the sale was 'held and firmly observed in perpetuity'. This surely hints at the potential inability of Alan's court on its own to sustain Hugh's title. It may not have been Alan who was being forestalled here so much as some possible claimant in the king's court who would be able to undo what had happened in Alan's court. A plausible speculation might point to the uncertainty over who would inherit the aging Alan's lordship on his death. It is not known whether his legitimate son Thomas was still alive at the time of the charter to Hugh; otherwise, and assuming that neither Alan's brother nor his illegitimate son (both confusingly also called Thomas) needed to be taken into account, Alan's patrimony would be divided among his three daughters and fall under the control of their husbands. Hugh may not have been concerned so much about Alan's court, therefore, as the courts of those who would succeed him, who might not be disposed to accept the validity of the sale. If this interpretation is correct, then we may still see this document as evidence of feudal power; but it also shows royal authority as the most effective protection against that power's abuse.

Alan's charter makes no reference to warranty, despite the obvious concern of Margaret and Hugh to guard against future challenges to their transaction. The concept of the lord's obligation of warranty or (in the language of later Scots law) warrandice owed to his tenant was certainly well established in Scotland before the end of the twelfth century, even though it was not necessarily a standard or even a very common clause in charters, whether royal or private. *Glanvill's* account of warranty, in which the obligation arises from homage without any need for an express grant, later found its way into *Regiam Majestatem*, and probably reflects the twelfth-century position in Scotland.[80] The content of the obligation appears clearly enough in a knight-service charter of David I, where the king promises Walter of Ryedale that if he or his heirs are unable to warrant Walter and his heirs in the lands granted against any just claim, then the king or his heirs will give to Walter or his heirs an exchange of a value to their reasonable satisfaction.[81] There is no suggestion here that the king's obligation would always compel him to find against any claimant to the land other than Walter; rather the reverse. Where we find express warrandice clauses in charters, it is submitted, the reference is to the grantor's obligation to make an exchange in the event of a successful challenge to the grantee's title. This is clearly what it means in the thirteenth century and later, even when it seems to be expressed in reverse, as in a charter of 1248 by Patrick, earl of Dunbar, in favour of Melrose abbey: 'And if anyone makes a claim against the said abbot and convent of Melrose, and we and our heirs defend them so that the said lands are lost to them by judgment we or our heirs will give to the said challengers a reasonable extent in our demesne or elsewhere in a competent place to the value of the said lands'.[82]

An important feature of the charters mentioned in the previous paragraph is that they both expressly affect not just the grantor and grantee but their heirs as well. Dr Stringer also found that when Earl David granted express warrandice, he bound himself and his heirs to warrant the grantee and his heirs.[83] The rise of mutual heritability of warranty obligations has been an important element in the debate in England over when inheritance became a clearly automatic legal right as opposed to an expectation based on custom but subject to the lord's discretion.[84] Express warrandice clauses are rare in twelfth-century Scottish charters, so when we find them it may be that they represent efforts to clarify what would otherwise be uncertain; in other words, it might be that early warrandice was not definitely heritable on either side. Then the lord's heir would not be bound to uphold his predecessor's grant, and the position of the tenant, and even more so that of the tenant's heirs, would be so much the less secure. On the other hand, as warrandice clauses became more regular, they continued to refer to the heirs of both parties. This may show that heritable warrandice had always been the norm, and perhaps the legal rule as well, assuming some mechanism to enforce it. More analysis of lay charters in particular is needed before this question can be answered with confidence; but it would at least be one situation where the availability of royal justice favouring security of tenure and heritability could play an important role, as in England. In later law, certainly, there was a royal brieve of warrandice of charter, the origins of which probably lie in the king's protection and ad hoc royal interventions when warrantors failed to fulfil their obligations.[85]

Dr Stringer has argued that the rarity of express warrandice clauses in twelfth-century grants reflects a world in which the tenant who had his lord's grant was less likely to be successfully challenged than in England, either in his lord's court or elsewhere, and so did not need the reassurance of an explicit statement of the lord's support for his tenure: the implied obligation would normally be enough.[86] It seems impossible to verify or challenge this statement conclusively, given the evidence which we have; but the arguments against Milsom's view that warrandice tied a lord irretrievably to the tenant he had chosen[87] seem equally applicable to the Scottish situation, especially if the lord could order a duel to be held in his court to determine which of two claimants had the better right to hold of him, or if the king could intervene to ensure that justice was done to a claimant. The presence of express warrandice clauses in twelfth-century grants is probably to be explained by the parties' awareness of other possible claims which might be made good in some forum, and against which precautions required to be taken. An example may be the grant with express warrandice made by the Countess Ada to Newbattle abbey in 1153 x 1159. The abbey was to hold as Robert son of Geoffrey had held; was warrandice expressed in case Robert or his heirs made a later claim?[88] However, twelfth-century Scotland saw nothing like the English Anarchy of the 1140s, creating the sort of uncertainty and insecurity of tenure in which express warranty obligations began to become more regular. The rise of warrandice clauses so that they became more common in thirteenth-century Scotland suggests that conditions were changing, perhaps as a result of a more active land market and the development of more regular royal justice, both of which may have tended to reduce the certainty flowing from a lord's grant of land.[89]

THE REGULARISATION OF ROYAL JUSTICE TO 1300

Early royal justice was first and foremost the responsibility of the king himself. A royal court presided over by the king can be seen in action from the reign of David I onward, although the description *curia regis* does not appear in surviving sources until the reign of William the Lion.[90] The work of William's *curia* largely conformed to the model of the courts of lesser lords already discussed. Land might be formally granted by the king in his court, or it might be resigned back into his hands by his tenants.[91] In contentious matters, the function of the court seems more often than not to have been to confirm quitclaims and compromises between the parties, rather than actually to determine their respective rights.[92] It is in William's *curia*, however, that we first see the jury in regular use, acting as witnesses to the truth of a disputed matter. The patronage of a church is proved to belong to the bishop of Glasgow by the testimony of *'probos et antiquos et legitimos testes'*.[93] The *Melrose Chronicle* tells of a dispute between the abbey and the men of Stow which was settled by Richard de Moreville and twelve other faithful men, in the presence of the king and his brother, bishops, earls and barons.[94] The jury has clearly developed by the beginning of the thirteenth century, when the abbeys of Kelso and Melrose were disputing the boundaries of certain lands. The king became involved, and with the agreement of the abbots he caused an inquest *per probos et antiquos homines patrie* into the matter, after which, the parties having been convened in the king's full court at Selkirk, it was held that the debateable lands belonged of right to Kelso, the result being explicitly stated to have followed the testimony of the responsible old men of the neighbourhood.[95]

The twelfth-century *curia regis* is the recognisable forerunner of the thirteenth-century *colloquium*, and thus also of the Scottish parliament, although sittings were still sometimes identified as being of the *curia regis* rather than of a *colloquium* in the reigns of the two Alexanders.[96] When we reach the parliaments of John Balliol in the early 1290s, it is still possible to see at work the court in which the king's feudal lordship is exercised.[97] Macduff, who has intruded upon the lands of Rires and Creich which the king is holding in ward until the earl of Fife attains full age, is attached to answer to the king. John de Soules offers his homage to the king and seeks entry into lands to hold as tenant-in-chief. Is Alexander of Abernethy entitled to inherit certain barony lands, or can his father's wife show an alternative right? The bishops, earls and barons of the parliament inform the king of a grant of land made to Ingram de Umfraville and his wife by Alexander III, and the king's rights in the land are carefully defined. The earl of Carrick resigns his earldom, and asks that his son Robert be made earl in his place; the king takes sasine of the earldom and then grants it to Robert, who gives his homage.

The term *curia regis* was not only applied to sessions at which the king himself happened to be present, however. The justice or justiciar (henceforth 'justiciar') did some of the king's judicial work, for both David and Malcolm IV refer to hearings before the king or his justiciar as being alternatives of equivalent authority.[98] A reference to a court held before Roland, son of Uhtred, justiciar perhaps of Galloway in the 1190s, as *'curia domini regis'* underlines this viceregal role of the justiciar. There are at least two thirteenth-century references to the justiciar's court as *curia domini regis*, in 1221 and 1247 respectively.[99] Courts other than those of the justiciar were similarly described in this period. An example is a court held before the chamberlain at Forfar in 1228.[100] We may also note what appears to be a description of Berwick burgh court as *curia domini regis*, probably in the thirteenth century.[101] A document from the reign of Alexander II, probably of 1233 x 1235, refers to another case in the *curia domini regis apud Berwic in plano comitatu*. The case was begun by royal brieve addressed to the sheriff of Berwick, and this, together with the reference to the 'full county', makes it certain that it is his court, rather than that of the burgh, which is being described as the king's court here.[101a]

In none of the examples of the use of the phrase *curia regis* just discussed is there any suggestion of the king being present in the court, and it seems that, in Scotland as in England, that was not necessarily implied by the use of the phrase. The implication to be drawn is rather that the court was held in the king's name by a royal officer exercising royal jurisdiction.[102] The growth in the number of such courts in the twelfth and thirteenth centuries can surely be taken as a sign of a corresponding development in the regularity with which royal justice was used in the kingdom in this period. Sheriff and burgh courts had emerged in the reign of William I, if not before, and their development along with that of the justiciar and the chamberlain may be attributed to the arrival of the Anglo-Norman knights, the burgesses and the religious men of the various monastic houses, most of whom owed their presence in Scotland to royal patronage and who would certainly have expected to receive the protection of royal justice. Perhaps it is significant that two twelfth-century royal charters giving the right to be sued only before the king or his justiciar were grants to a burgess and to an ecclesiastical foundation respectively.[103] By the mid-thirteenth century, most of Scotland had been divided up into sheriffdoms,[104] which were in turn grouped into three justiciary districts – Scotia, Lothian and Galloway – through which the justiciars passed regularly on circuit, or ayre.[105] By the end of the thirteenth century, a court was a standard feature of the burgh polity, and burghs were found throughout Scotland. The chamberlain ayre served a function somewhat equivalent to that of the justiciar in the landward areas, while the Court of the Four Burghs paralleled the *colloquium* or parliament.[106]

Another sign of the regularisation of royal justice is thirteenth-century and later references showing the king issuing brieves *de cursu* commanding his officers to do justice in their courts.[107] The phrase '*de cursu*', translated as 'coursable' in later Scots,[108] means that the brieves in question were issued by the king's chapel, or writing office, in certain standard forms, each designed to meet a particular situation. References to 'letters in the form of the king's chapel' can probably be taken as an alternative way of referring to brieves *de cursu*. They were obtainable from the chapel on payment of a small fee,[109] and were contrasted with brieves *de gratia* (of grace), which were fashioned specially to meet the requirements of an individual case. The existence of brieves *de cursu* before the end of the thirteenth century is powerful evidence of the regularisation of, and steady demand for, royal justice in this period. Sheriff McKechnie and Willock have discussed the emergence of particular forms in the thirteenth century,[110] while Barrow and Harding have pointed to even earlier periods for the origins of others.[111] In many cases, the development appears to be connected with a policy of making the jury the basis of decision-making under the brieve. The jury was rarely described as such: a variety of names was used, including visnet, recognition, inquest and assize. According to developed usage, where the findings of the jury were to be reported back for further action elsewhere, it was known as an inquest; where its findings were put directly into effect, it was known as an assize. Probably before the end of the thirteenth century, the styles of the coursable brieves were being gathered together in collections which almost certainly had as their original the style book of the king's chapel itself.[112] The two earliest of these have been published under the title *The Register of Brieves*, which is an echo of the English *Registrum Omnium Brevium* (1531) rather than the contemporary name for such collections;[113] nevertheless, they, along with another, later example published as *Formulary E* and yet another which is unpublished,[114] will henceforward be referred to as the 'registers' for the sake of convenience.

Taken altogether, therefore, the rise of royal justice in Scotland in the twelfth and thirteenth centuries shows many parallels with the same phenomenon in England: an increasing number of royal courts, the use of royal writs to start litigation there, and the employment of juries as a rational method of determining where truth lay. Furthermore, the king's courts asserted superior rights over the feudal or baronial courts. Already in the twelfth century, lords' courts operated to some extent within the constraints imposed by royal power, although this probably meant different things in different parts of the country. In this early period, royal power itself was limited, but well before the end of the thirteenth century the king's jurisdiction was being exercised much more regularly and systematically, principally through a system of local courts linked to central administration by means of the brieve system and the visitations of the justice and chamberlain ayres.

LATER MEDIEVAL FEUDAL COURTS

The claim of royal justice to superiority did not, however, have the same effect on the feudal or baronial courts as it did in England inasmuch as these courts survived as an integral part of the Scottish legal landscape of the fourteenth and fifteenth centuries, enjoying and exercising wide jurisdictions. The jurisdiction varied from the relatively slight powers of the small landowner who had tenants, through the wider civil and criminal jurisdiction epitomised in a grant *in liberam baroniam,* to the widest jurisdiction of all, obtained by means of the grant *in liberam regalitatem.* As will be discussed more fully later in this chapter, there was a good deal of overlap between these franchisal jurisdictions and the jurisdictions of the sheriff and the justiciar, showing that royal justice was not able to eliminate feudal justice (if indeed it ever wished to). This was underlined by the continuing significance of replegiation, a process which enabled a lord to claim personal jurisdiction over a tenant who had been brought before another court, including those of the king, provided that his own court had sufficient jurisdiction to deal with the matter in issue.[115] Not only does this illustrate the relative power of feudal jurisdiction in later medieval Scotland, it also underlines the continuing practical importance of the lord-tenant relationship within the legal system.

There was a good deal of continuity between these baronies and regalities, and the earlier knights' fees and lordships, not least in the general retention of the feature of territorial compactness, which, as previously noted, is suggestive of a relatively high degree of autonomy.[116] Further, the regality was a jurisdiction from which generally the king's officers could be excluded and where the king's writ did not run, although by no means all regalities had exactly the same privileges.[117] The fact that baronies and regalities were granted freely by the kings of the later Middle Ages shows, however, that they were not regarded as necessarily inimical to royal authority, and it cannot ever have been royal policy to deprive landowners of their jurisdictions, either directly or indirectly. Indeed, it is quite clear that some regalities – for example in Galloway – were granted to facilitate the control of what were difficult areas. Their greatest importance was in the field of criminal justice. In its internal administrative structure, a regality often closely paralleled the kingdom, being entitled, as an inquest of 1320 put it, *'justiciarium suum, camerarium, cancellarium . . . ad modum regis'*.[118] Much as had already happened with the king's court, the lord no longer administered justice through a single court, but delegated its functions to officers who held courts in his name.

Unquestionably, the jurisdiction which a lord exercised over the tenants who held land of him remained important. As late as the mid-fifteenth century, it was possible for Robert lord Fleming and Gilbert lord Kennedy to consider the possibility of action in Robert's baron court of Lenzie to determine a dispute between them over lands in the barony which Gilbert claimed to hold of Robert.[119] This would have been a proprietary case, had it taken place in Robert's court. Examples of the exercise of the disciplinary power to recognosce the lands of tenants can also be found in the fourteenth and fifteenth centuries, although it is not always clear what the justification for the lord's action is. Generally speaking, however, we learn of the recognition because the tenant alleges some abuse of process in another forum.[120] One further use made of recognition by lords was linked with proprietary issues. In 1476, Sir William Knollys, preceptor of Torphichen, recognosced lands lying within the burgh of Edinburgh below the castle wall which were 'debatable betuix Robert of Cochrane for his part and the said Schir William as ourelord of the samyn'. The matter was clearly one of property, for later one Robert Thomson put in his claim to the lands, and the case ended up before the auditors of causes and complaints in parliament.[121] Between 1416 and 1425, Melrose abbey and the Haigs of Bemersyde were embroiled in a dispute over territory at the marches of their respective properties of Redpath and Bemersyde. The lands in question formed part of the estate of Redpath; Melrose claimed to be proprietors, while the Haigs asserted that they had common rights. The land was held of the earl of Douglas as lord of Lauderdale, and he recognosced the lands in dispute before, having inspected charters, he put Melrose in possession once more subject to a pledge or *borgh*. This was clearly a preliminary to a decision on the merits of the case as a whole; still later, the earl held an assize to establish where the boundaries of the two estates lay.[122] The purpose of the recognition was to establish the most recent lawful possession, and to give the possessor the benefit of defending any action which the other party might later care to raise. Something similar to the Redpath case may lie behind the recognition which James Douglas the elder of Dalkeith made concerning the lands of Crossraguel, Lanarkshire, on the death of his brother, Henry, who was also his tenant; it seems that a dispute had broken out between James and Henry's widow over the tutory of Henry's minor heir, and so it may have been uncertain who had the better right to administer the lands.[123] Whether or not either of these cases was ultimately determined in the lord's court or the king's, it is clear that, at the least, the lord's superiority continued to give him an important role to play when disputes broke out over lands held of him.

Lords also retained a pivotal role in the transfer of land, whether by way of alienation or inheritance. Although subinfeudation was a frequent mode of transfer, so were substitutions by which the selling tenant would resign his lands to the lord in favour of the buyer. The lord's position was reinforced by his ability to recognosce lands alienated without his licence.[124] Similarly, his rights on inheritance were not limited to the uplifting of casualties, since until the heir was identified and given sasine the lord held the land. It is clear that the lord was bound to effect the infeftment of the heir and the alienee in whose favour lands had been resigned, but it is also apparent that he was not invariably a mere cypher in a conveyancing mechanism. Most important of all was the development of the casualty of non-entry, under which the lord recovered payments from the heir calculated on the basis of the period during which the latter had failed to seek infeftment by the lord. The origins of this casualty are obscure, but it was regularly enforced in the fifteenth century.

The concepts of feudalism may have been reinforced by the academic study of law which many Scots made at continental universities in the fourteenth and fifteenth centuries.[125] Most of these students were churchmen, but the church was itself a feudal lord and regularly sought enforcement of its feudal rights through its own courts and those of the king. In 1382, there came before the sheriff court of Aberdeen an action falsing a doom given by the baron court of the bishop of Aberdeen against John Crab, one of his tenants. It was argued for the bishop that '*quando controversia vertitur inter dominum et vassallum super feodo vel tenemento quod in curia domini debet huiusmodo questio terminari*' (when a controversy arises between lord and vassal concerning the fee or tenement, such a question ought to be determined in the lord's court).[126] The contention was supported by reference to numerous authorities, including an 1158 constitution of the Emperor Frederick Barbarossa which had been incorporated in the *Libri Feudorum*.[127] As the pleader cited the *Libri Feudorum* elsewhere in his argument,[128] it seems probable that the reference to Frederick's constitution was also from that source. In addition, however, it was argued that the hearing of the case was in accordance with the general customs of the realm.[129] The lawyer who drafted these arguments may have been William de Spynie, a graduate of Paris in canon law, who finished his ecclesiastical career as bishop of Moray and who compiled the *Registrum Moraviense*, which is notably full of feudal material such as styles for homage and fealty, and statements as to when a tenant may be deprived of his fee for delicts against the superior.[130] The *Libri Feudorum* was also cited in an argument about the fealty which the abbey of Lindores owed to the earl of Douglas in respect of certain lands, in which the earl began proceedings against the abbey in his own court.[131] Possibly these citations of the *Libri Feudorum* were unusual, but the work's influence may be detectable in the gradual formalisation of the rules concerning alienation, whereby the tenant who gave away too much would lose the whole to his lord.[132] Finally, a lord who needed legal authority to deprive his tenant of his lands for default of service could find it in the *Libri Feudorum* as well as in indigenous sources.[133]

Both the Crab case and the dispute between Lindores and Douglas ended up in the king's courts. The protection of royal justice was invoked again when Alexander Stewart, lord of Badenoch, 'sitting as lord amongst his vassals and subjects', held his regality court of Badenoch at the standing stones of Easter Kingussie in October 1380. He claimed that the bishop of Moray held certain lands of him. Standing outside the court, the bishop denied Alexander's superiority and asserted that he held of the

king, whose court he invoked. Alexander's court pronounced decree
against the bishop, but the matter was in fact resolved the next day
following deliberations by Alexander with his council (rather than his
court) in his castle of Ruthven. The decree of the court was cut out of its
roll and burned.[134] These dramatic events illustrate many points, of which
the most important are the continuing significance of the lord's court in
lord-vassal questions, the difficulty with which even as powerful and
forceful a lord as Alexander Stewart (better known to history as the Wolf
of Badenoch and the destroyer of the bishop of Moray's cathedral at Elgin
in 1392) might be faced in compelling another influential party to accept
his legal superiority, the interaction between the formality of the lord's
court and the informality possible in his council, and, most crucially here,
the role of royal justice as a means of controlling injustice in the lord's
court.

THE EFFECTIVENESS OF LATER MEDIEVAL ROYAL JUSTICE

The view that the survival of the powerful and active feudal courts just
discussed can be explained by the failure of later medieval royal justice
seems at first sight to gain support from contemporary legislation. There
are a number of fourteenth- and fifteenth-century enactments concerned
with wrongdoing by royal officers of law, in particular the justiciars and
sheriffs, which, taken out of context, convey an unhappy impression of
their persistent ineffectiveness and inefficiency, not to say dishonesty. Set
against a general historical background, however, the enactments take on
a different character, being often contemporary with either a change in
government or the conclusion of some major political crisis. So, in 1357,
David II was requested to hold an ayre to check particularly that royal
officers had not conducted themselves fraudulently or unfaithfully.[135] This
enactment was passed by a council meeting within one month of David's
return from eleven years of captivity in England.[136] Default in the keeping
of the common law was attributed to the king's officers in 1399 by a
council general at which the duke of Rothesay was appointed lieutenant
to the enfeebled Robert III.[137] In 1404, the duke of Albany was appointed
king's lieutenant by another council general, which also enacted that
justiciars and sheriffs should be appointed and should not neglect to
hold their courts at the due times.[138] Twenty years later, on the return of
James I, again from captivity in England, parliament laid down 'that thar
be maide officiaris and ministeris of lawe throu all the Realme that can and
may halde the law to the kingis commonis'.[139] In 1440, following what has
been described as a complete collapse of law and order after the death of
the lieutenant-general exercising royal authority during the minority of
James II, a general council signalled the return of normality by ordering
justice ayres to be held.[140] When James II reached his majority in 1450 and

took up the responsibilities of government, parliament proclaimed general peace and asked the king to appoint officers capable of punishing those who infringed it. 'Juste men . . . that kennys the law' were to be appointed, and justice ayres were to be held.[141] Finally in 1488, following the dethronement and death of James III on the field of Stirling, it was ordained that all those who held offices such as those of justice and sheriff under the late king were to be replaced by the new king's own appointments.[142]

The pattern which emerges from this perspective is regular proclamation by new governments of intention to rule justly by the conventions of the period, exercising justice through the work of officers such as the justiciar and the sheriff. These enactments seem to be part of contemporary political rhetoric, similar to the other statements which were often made at the beginning of a new reign or at the end of some crisis, that justice would be done to rich and poor alike, and that holy mother church should be protected. Of course, the proclamations were more than just rhetoric; the passage of such statutes enabled new governments to appoint their own men to positions of authority if necessary and so consolidate their grip upon the kingdom. It may be, in other words, that, rather than using these statutes to deduce that sheriffs and justiciars did not in fact hold courts and ayres or that they were chronically fraudulent and inept, we should see them as indications of the importance of these royal officers and their customary role in good governance and the administration of justice. This is not to say that all royal officers holding courts in this period can safely be regarded as paragons of judicial virtue. In December 1388, for example, Alexander Stewart, earl of Buchan, was accused of negligence in the administration of his office of justiciar north of Forth, and was dismissed by a council general.[143] The 'negligence' seems to have consisted in a failure to hold courts and ayres 'when and where he should'; perhaps he preferred to operate primarily out of his lordship of Badenoch, for the justice clerk, William Chalmer, was also his secretary there.[144]

Describing the later medieval judicial system, Cooper wrote of 'a rather chaotic welter of ill-defined and overlapping jurisdictions – the Justiciar, the Deputes for the Justiciar, Lords of Regality, the sheriffs and the barons'.[145] This surely overlooked the existence by the second half of the fourteenth century, if not before, of a clear hierarchy of courts in which the feudal jurisdictions of barony and regality had a place below that of the king for purposes of appeal. The dooms of barony courts could be falsed in the sheriff court, as illustrated by the case of John Crab against the bishop of Aberdeen in 1382, while there was also an appeal from the sheriff to the justiciar, and from there to parliament.[146] A case of 1370 shows that the dooms of regality courts could also be subjected to review in parliament.[147] Similarly, in burghs, an appeal structure led to the chamberlain ayre and the burgh parliament, the Court of the Four Burghs.[148] The continuation of these structures through the fifteenth century can be readily demonstrated from references later in this book and other sources. On one view, the structure suggests the subordination of the feudal to the royal courts. On another possible approach, however, it might be better seen not so much as a process of subordination as one of integration, where feudal and royal jurisdiction were not fundamentally in conflict. Baronies and regalities were obtained by royal grant, after all, and what the king had given he could take away if the holder did not or could not exercise it adequately – as probably happened, for example, in Thomas Fleming's regality and earldom of Wigtown in the 1360s,[149] and as was regularly threatened as a sanction by legislation should lords with regalian powers fail to implement them properly.[150]

Something of the old idea of royal power to rectify wrongdoing, in particular in lords' courts, survived not only in remedies such as falsing the doom, but also in a number of brieves recorded in the later 'registers' and still in use in later medieval practice. There were, for example, the brieves *furche* and *meminimus*, by which the king would command barons to give sasine of lands held of them. The problem with which the brieves dealt was that of the heir who could not get the baron of whom he held to infeft him. *Furche* closed with the threat that if the baron did not comply then the sheriff would give sasine instead, and there was a style for such cases addressed to the sheriff.[151] The brieve was in use in 1456, when George, earl of Angus, under threat of a brieve *of furche*, agreed to give sasine to Walter Ogilvy of Campsie and not to pursue him thereafter (presumably for a non-entry fine).[152] A century earlier, in 1354, Robert Symple had claimed to hold lands of the Hospitallers in their court at Balantrodach, saying that if they did not do him full justice (*complementum iuris*) there, he would impetrate letters in the form of the king's chapel to have justice. Fearful of losing their privileges, the Hospitallers granted Symple an assize by which he vindicated his rights.[153] It is possible that *furche* was one of the remedies Symple had in mind. There are other cases of this kind. The brieve of the king's chapel which William Wedderburn presented in the court of the prior of Coldingham in 1425 commanded the prior to give sasine of the lands of Swinton,[154] and in 1451 William Douglas of Drumlanrig presented the earl of Douglas with a royal brieve of sasine, seeking entry to the lands of Hawick which he held of the earl.[155] In both these cases, however, by contrast with that of Symple, the recipient of the brieve refused to obey, in the Coldingham case because the lands were held in chief of the priory of Durham, in the Douglas case because the earl stood under the king's respite.[156] Finally, it is possible that something similar *to furche* may lie behind the intriguing brieve under the white wax by which in 1445 Robert lord Erskine was ordered, following a decreet of the auditors of causes and complaints, to render *complementum iusticiam* to the widow Ada Crab in respect of lands which she claimed to hold of him and of which she was being deprived by Alexander Chalmer, burgess of Aberdeen. The brieve also concludes with an old formula justifying royal intervention: Erskine is to act so that no further complaint of default of justice comes to the king.[157]

It is clear from all this that we have to find some way of describing a system in which royal justice coexisted with strong and active feudal courts. We owe most of what we know at present about the later medieval royal courts in general to Dickinson.[158] Dickinson's own assessment was extremely gloomy: 'now, too, the office of sheriff had become largely heritable in the houses of the nobility; and the ayres of the justiciars (which in earlier times had checked and supervised the inferior courts) were often in abeyance, or held only here and there at wide intervals of time'.[159] However, the gloom may have been taken too far. Thanks to his work on the sheriff and burgh courts, for example, we can say that in both there were three sittings per annum of the head courts at which all those who owed suit in the court, either as the king's tenants-in-chief in the sheriffdom or as burgesses, would normally be present. There were also intermediate courts held at much shorter intervals with a lesser attendance of suitors. Each had a well-defined jurisdiction in the later period. The position regarding brieves will be discussed at length later; but it should be noted here that generally brieves were led at the head courts. Both courts also heard civil actions raised by simple complaint, which were much more numerous than cases begun by brieve, to judge from surviving records. These included cases of debt and other obligations, claims of damage for various wrongs, and actions relating to the possession of goods; in addition, the burgh court dealt with the regulation of the burgh's trading life. In criminal matters, the sheriff court had a much wider jurisdiction than that of the burgh court, which was very limited. In many burghs, however, this changed as grants of shrieval jurisdiction were obtained.[160] The principal features of the sheriff's criminal jurisdiction were theft and slaughter *chaudmelle*, although slaughter on forethought felony came under the sheriff's power if the killer was taken red-handed.[161] This jurisdiction was cognate with that of the baron court, leading to the possibility of replegiation there from the sheriff; but the evidence suggests that the jurisdiction of the baron in cases of homicide was in decline by the end of the fifteenth century.[162] The baron's civil jurisdiction also closely paralleled that of the sheriff, meaning that the prospective litigant had a choice of forum; the selection may have depended on what needed to be achieved.[163]

The few fragmentary records of sheriff and burgh courts which survive from before 1500 support this picture of the way in which these courts generally functioned. We have no real warrant for supposing that the sheriff and burgh courts met less than regularly, or that they did not discharge a great deal of business. Both courts also had full complements of administrative staff – mairs or sergeands to execute summonses and judgments, clerks to keep the written records, dempsters to pronounce the dooms, and so on. In view of Dickinson's emphasis on the inadequacies of the sheriffs themselves, two further points are worth noting: first, that very often the court was presided over by the sheriff depute rather than the sheriff; and second, that the court continued to be constituted, and its judgments given, by the suitors as a body rather than by the individual presiding over its proceedings. The personal failings of the sheriff, if indeed these existed, may not have been particularly important to the smooth running of the court as a result. In fact, like the burgh court, the court can be seen as most probably giving effect to the values of the community from which the suitors and jurors came. Of course, corruption and abuse were not thereby prevented; the point is that the quality of the court's work cannot be measured simply by looking at who held its principal office. The brieve of right was competent in both the sheriff and the burgh courts; how they handled that jurisdiction seems a better test of their effectiveness.

Most of the remainder of this chapter is, however, devoted to discussing the effectiveness of the justiciar and his court. The justiciary is extremely important for present purposes, since it was in the justiciar's court that the brieves of novel dissasine and mortancestry were determined. In a very brief article on the history of the High Court of Justiciary published in 1959, Dickinson unfortunately had no space to discuss such matters as the organisation, structure and personnel of the medieval justiciary.[164] Happily, the gap is now filled for the twelfth and thirteenth centuries by Barrow's detailed study,[165] but the later medieval period remains little known, the fullest discussion still being that in Baron Hume's *Commentaries on the Criminal Law of Scotland.*[166]

In seeking to repair the gaps in our knowledge, the starting point must be Barrow's article, which brings the history of the justiciarship down to c. 1306, and the conclusions of which were summarised earlier in this chapter.[167] When we look at the justiciary between 1306 and 1500, a considerable degree of continuity, not to say conservatism, is readily apparent. First, the justiciarship continued to employ a regional division in its administration, based on the line of Forth. In the autumn of 1305, Edward I had introduced a new scheme with four rather than the traditional two or three zones. These were Lothian, Galloway, the country between the Forth and the Mounth, and the country north of the Mounth.[168] It may be that Robert I adopted this scheme at least in part, to judge from the appearance of a justiciar 'from the waters of Forth to the mountains of Scotia' in 1310.[169] In 1309, however, the northern justiciar was designed '*ex parte boreali aque de Forth*',[170] and in 1312 we find a justiciar 'from Forth to Orkney', subsuming the two northern regions of Edward's 1305 scheme.[171] References to a northern justiciar and to a justiciar of Lothian are frequent thereafter, but no mention is ever made of a justiciar of Galloway.[172] It seems therefore that under Robert I the justiciary returned to its simplest form of a twofold division between north and south; this it retained until the end of our period. Only at the end of the reign of David II did the terminology describing this division become settled as 'the justiciar [either] north [or] south of Forth'. Throughout the reign of Robert I, and most of that of David II, the southern justiciarship was said to be 'of Lothian';[173] only in 1368 do we find the justiciar for that region being described as '*ex parte australi aque de Forth*'.[174] From 1368, the usage is substantially unvarying until the beginning of the sixteenth century. In the first half of the fourteenth century, we also find the justiciar of Scotia, the justiciar north of the Scottish sea, and the justiciar of Scotia north of Forth.[175] By and large (and some of the exceptions are of interest[176]), the usage 'justiciar north of Forth' was standard thereafter.[177] It seems clear, however, that these changes in style do not betoken any substantial adjustment to the original system of dividing the country in two for justiciary purposes.

The second point of continuity is the operation of the ayre system. Between 1300 and 1500, the expectation remained that justice ayres would be held twice in the year in each region, as many parliamentary and other enactments demonstrate. The justiciars were to 'pass throu the cuntre', 'twiss in the yere', 'anys on the girss and anys on the corne', a practice 'eftir the auld lawis', hallowed by 'auld use and custom'.[178] The evidence for the later medieval ayre is broadly consistent with this principle, in that records tend to fall into two groups in relation to time, one being the first half of the year, the other the period from July to October. We know that ayres were held twice in the year in 1358, 1381, 1454, 1470, 1492, 1495, 1498 and 1500.[179] This may not seem an impressive tally, but there is abundant evidence for the activity of the justiciars throughout the fourteenth and fifteenth centuries, and we are surely entitled to assume that this activity was conducted so far as possible in accordance with the norms which the system laid down for itself. However, some historians have doubted whether practice did in fact follow theory. One has commented that 'ayres tended to be few and infrequent',[180] while Dickinson noted that 'a system which works well has no need of frequent legislation, but at least seven acts enjoining the ayres to be held yearly, or generally, or diligently, were passed between 1458 and 1488'.[181] In fact, there are at least eleven enactments between 1404 and 1491 which refer to the holding of ayres in the kind of terms mentioned by Dickinson. In assessing their significance, we should first join with Ranald Nicholson in observing that such acts at least suggest 'that against the general background of curial ineptitude the ayres stood out as being worthy of respect'.[182] Some of the eleven acts are among those already discussed, being among the proclamations of new governments declaring either an intention to rule justly or the restoration of peace and normality. This would account for statutes enjoining the holding of justice ayres in 1404, 1440, 1450 and 1488.[183] In this interpretation, therefore, justice ayres fall to be regarded as part of the ordinary routine of royal government, or as an aspect of normality, rather than as occasional events. Careful scrutiny in context of two more of these statutes, passed respectively in March 1458 and in May 1491, also suggests that they cannot be explained as reactions to a failure to hold ayres. In the first of these, parliament enacted 'that justice ayris be haldin and continewyt yerly out throu the realme for gude of the commounys'.[184] Nicholson states that 'it was presumably because of lapses in the holding of justice ayres'[185] that this statute was passed; but, if so, it is strange that in the same parliament the king was congratulated on his success in the administration of justice which had driven wrongdoers from the land.[186] Moreover, evidence from the exchequer rolls suggests that the ayres were held regularly throughout the 1450s, and that the king himself was an active participant.[187] The statute cannot therefore be taken as meaning that ayres did not then take place; it seems more likely to have been an endorsement of current successful practice.

A similar comment may be applied to the act of 1491, which simply ordained that 'airis be set and haldin'.[188] It has been remarked of James IV, then king, that he drove the ayres 'as they had never been driven before'.[189] While the implied comment on the period before James's accession may be questioned, it is true that in his reign we have for the first time clear evidence of ayres being held regularly.[190] It is found mainly in the treasurer's accounts, where they record the king's spending as he moved round the country with the ayres. Thus the king was with the justice ayre in the autumn of 1488, the spring of 1489 and also of 1490, and again in July 1491.[191] Others may well have been held in the period, but, since the king apparently did not participate in them, they have left no trace in the records of his finances. However, enough has survived to indicate that, whatever may have lain behind the statute of 1491, it was not lapses in the holding of the ayres.

We come in consequence of this discussion to the remaining half-dozen statutes with a rather more optimistic view of the regularity of justice ayres in the fifteenth century than has been taken previously. An immediately striking feature of this group of enactments is that they were all passed in the period 1479–88; that is, during the last ten years of the reign of James III. James was a troubled king throughout this period, and to some extent these statutes reflect his particular problems. Thus, for example, the principal emphasis of the act of 1479 is not so much on failure to hold ayres as the demand that the king should himself participate.[192] James was frequently criticised for his lack of involvement with the processes of justice; but this need not imply that consequently there was no justice to be had at all. Certainly, in the 1460s and the 1470s there were regular justice ayres.[193] In the 1480s, James was also attacked by parliament for his readiness to grant remissions and respites to convicted criminals, and it is in this context that the statutes anent justice ayres are to be found. A brief glimpse of the extent to which James did in fact grant remissions is provided by the treasurer's account for 1473.[194] It is significant that these remissions or compositions were given following an ayre on the south-west circuit in the autumn of 1473. This suggests that ayres were a prerequisite for remissions, in the sense that generally a remission would only be necessary upon a conviction.[195] Such a view would seem to be borne out by the parliamentary enactments under discussion: they seek the 'scharpe executioun of justice' against criminals, that is, they prefer punishment to mercy.[196] As can be seen from the mid-fifteenth-century tract, *Ordo Justiciare*, which lists all the matters then within the competence of the justiciar, his court dealt with the major crimes which lay beyond the powers of sheriff and baron courts, as well as many other matters assigned to it by statute.[197] It can therefore be argued that the problem manifested by these parliamentary complaints of the 1480s is not the lack of justice ayres but a concern over the disposal of those convicted in the ayres.

Nonetheless, the ayres may have been held less regularly for a time in the 1480s, possibly following the major political crisis which engulfed the king in 1482–3. In March 1482, the auditors of causes and complaints ordered that an inquest be held on certain matters at the next justice ayre of Peebles. The inquest was held, but not until February 1485.[198] There had been a coup against the king in the summer of 1482, from which he only recovered the following spring. It cannot be said, however, that the coup leaders failed to hold the ayres. One of them was Archibald, earl of Angus, who was forced to resign as justiciar at the conclusion of the crisis in March 1483.[199] It has often been noted as a puzzling fact that his name is conspicuous by its absence from the witness list of royal charters in the autumn following the coup, despite his prominent role in it.[200] The explanation may be that he was conducting his justice ayre at the time. If so, the point that ayres were part of the normal routine of government is reinforced. Apart from the case of 1485, however, we have no further evidence that ayres were being held until 1487.[201]

Too much has been inferred from the statutes of the fifteenth century regarding the frequency of justice ayres. Any conclusion upon this question based upon these statutes alone, be it positive or negative, would be dangerous, as is clearly shown by the examples of 1458 and 1491. There is scope for differing interpretations as they stand; the validity of such interpretations must be tested against a deeper investigation of the sources for the period. In the absence of regular records before 1500, our sources are bound to give us an uneven picture; for example, references to the justice ayres are found in the financial records, as we have seen, but these depend on factors such as the king's participation and the survival of the relevant parts of the records themselves. The exchequer rolls mention justice ayres when recorded in the sheriffs' accounts, but there are serious gaps in the sheriffs' accounts. The evidence to be gleaned from private muniments is equally random in its nature. Yet what survives from these sources is substantial evidence that justice ayres – and indeed other courts – were held regularly, and that they formed a significant part of the government structure of medieval Scotland.[202] They were clearly taking place under Robert I, and, while the period after his death in 1329 may have seen substantial dislocation of the system south of Forth, there is plenty of evidence for ayres in the north at that time. During the personal reign of David II, there is ample evidence that ayres north and south of Forth were a steady source of revenue, and the same is true for Robert II and Robert III, despite the low esteem in which these kings are often held. The picture is less clear for the Albany governorship, the personal reign of James I and the minority of James II, but references to ayres, and references which assume that they are being held, can be found in sufficient quantity to justify the belief that in fact they were a regular event.

Most important of all is the fact that we can demonstrate an almost continuous succession of justiciars from c. 1306 down to the end of the reign of James IV.[203] The evidence shows that the justiciars of the fourteenth and fifteenth centuries were, like their predecessors, drawn from the ranks of the magnates. Generally speaking, they were also men prominent elsewhere in royal government. Thus they cannot be described as 'professional' judges in the sense that they spent their working lives solely in a judicial capacity. It is quite clear that, especially in the fifteenth century, many held office for short periods – say a year or perhaps only for one ayre – but more than once in their careers. As early as 1344, it was clear that the office was not to become heritable.[204] Justiciarships appear therefore to have been delegated from time to time to members of the king's council. Although some held office for long periods, the justiciars were indeed a 'part-time, lay magistracy'.[205] Proof positive of their legal knowledge is all but impossible, and there are in general no external *indicia* such as, for example, university degrees in law or membership of professional groupings (for there were none) to help us. On the other hand, if we ask how these men came to be part of the king's government, and why specifically they were appointed to carry out justice ayres, the answer must be that they were deemed fit for the task by the standards of the time – whatever these may have been and however different from our own or those of other countries then and now.

The justice ayres continued to involve journeying from sheriffdom to sheriffdom and holding a court composed of the sheriffdom's suitors in the main town of each one, although sometimes, like other courts, it would move to outdoor locations for particular cases. The ayre might be in the sheriffdom for several days, and an ayre as a whole took months rather than weeks to complete. At least in civil matters, the justiciar and the suitors seem to have been responsible for decisions on the law, while the assizers would deal with the facts of cases.[206] Although, once within a sheriffdom, the staff of the local sheriff would be used for matters like the service of summonses and the execution of judgments,[207] setting up and administering an ayre involved a good deal of work by others who had to be specifically employed for the task.[208] On the criminal side, an ayre would be preceded by the presentment procedure, with the clerks of the justiciary touring through the sheriffdoms making up the 'porteous roll', a list of those who would be indicted before the justiciar.[209] Then the ayre had to be proclaimed at least forty days in advance of its arrival in each sheriffdom, to permit the summoning of the suitors and of potential litigants.[210] Once the ayre was under way, it seems to have kept in touch with central government, with messages for continuations being received and the 'estreitis' being sent back.[211] From all this, it can be seen that an efficient communications system was essential to the successful operation of an ayre.

The point is underlined when we consider that the justiciar did not go round his circuit all by himself. As was remarked at the time of the dismissal of the earl of Buchan in 1388, he had to have sufficient power to make his authority apparent and felt (although it was also through having sufficient of his own, in the language of another statute in 1424, that an officer of the law could be appropriately punished for any misdeed).[212] All the later medieval justiciars were major figures in Scottish political society, normally closely associated with, if not actually related to, the king, as well as major landowners able to command a considerable allegiance in consequence. It may be the pomp and display with which the justiciar proceeded through the countryside that lies behind a statute of 1450, which ordained justices and others to 'ryde bot with competent and esy nowmer to eschew grevans and hurting of the pepyll'.[213] However, this display was not simply a matter of show; many of the people with the justiciar had functions to perform in connection with the ayre. The clerk of the justiciary has already been mentioned; he can be found in attendance on ayres, keeping the records and having custody of the seal of the justiciary.[214] A statute of 1488 appointing justiciars also directed 'that our soverane lord send certane wise lordis and persouns of his consale . . . to be assessouris and consalouris to thaim'.[215] This may well reflect what had been normal practice in the past. For example, in 1349 several members of the king's council were with the justiciar of Scotia north of Forth when he held full court at the standing stones of Rayne in the Garioch.[216] Again, in 1466 most of the royal council seem to have been in court at the Dumbarton tolbooth when Gilbert lord Kennedy and Robert lord Fleming litigated before the justiciars south of Forth.[217] The presence of the council probably meant that the king was not far away, and royal participation in the ayres seems to have been important. The alleged failings of James III in this respect have already been mentioned, but, given the length of time involved in an ayre, there must have been some practical difficulties for any king. Nonetheless, a royal presence was commanded by statute in 1440.[218] In 1457, James II ordered the sheriff of Forfar to summon Thomas Cullace 'to compeir befoir us and our counsaile at Dunde the secunde day of the nixt justice aire of Anguss',[219] while during the ayre of Aberdeen in November that year seven men were summoned to compear before the king and his council on a certain day of the ayre to answer for an alleged error made by them in the service of a brieve of inquest.[220] In 1498, the council accompanied a northern justice ayre, holding its own judicial sessions in parallel with those of the justiciar.[221]

In short, a justice ayre could be an impressive display of the king's power and authority in the localities, and it would not be short of the best advice and support of which royal government was capable in this period. The evidence for the justiciar's activities does not support the conclusion that royal justice was weak and irregular in the later medieval period. Perhaps the major flaw of the justice ayre system, however, was its failure to deal adequately with the far north and west. The northern ayre began at Inverness and typically wended its way east and south through Elgin, Banff, Aberdeen, Inverbervie, Forfar, Perth and Cupar. In the south, the ayre started at Edinburgh, moved into the Borders at Lauder, Selkirk and Peebles, and went on to Lanark and from there to Dumfries, Kirkcudbright and Wigtown. Finally, Ayr, Dumbarton and Stirling would be visited, with the last two perhaps being most often dealt with by justiciars specially commissioned for the purpose.[222] In the north and west, by contrast, royal justice was represented by sheriffs and lieutenants with justiciary powers, generally drawn from the local magnates.[223] In 1504, parliament sought to make new arrangements for the visitation of justice ayres in Argyll and the Isles, remarking that 'the pepill ar almaist gane wild'.[224] Like much else in the 1504 parliament relating to the west, this statute should probably be taken as an indication of royal determination, following the suppression of the Lordship of the Isles, to take firmer control of the area through what seemed the most appropriate machinery (incidentally another indicator of the effectiveness, at least in royal eyes, of the ayres).[225] So royal power was still not absolute or uniform over the whole kingdom, and the distinction between the core where royal government was at its most effective, and the periphery, where it was less so, remains a valid one, even if the core was far more substantial than in the twelfth or thirteenth century.

Yet even here, the weakness of royal justice should not be overstated. The king's principal lieutenants in fourteenth- and fifteenth-century Argyll were the Campbells, a kin group increasingly closely associated with royal government, culminating in the career of Colin Campbell, a lord of parliament who became the first earl of Argyll in 1457, acted as a justiciar in the 1460s and became chancellor in 1483. Campbell control of judicial affairs in Argyll was hardly likely to be damaging to royal interests. Similarly, William, the fifth earl of Ross, held the northern justiciarship possibly for as long as twenty years in the reign of David II, while Alexander, lord of the Isles and earl of Ross, was also northern justiciar from 1439 to 1443 and possibly up to his death in 1449. The suggestion that both men combined the advancement of their own power with that of the crown has to be qualified, since each acted during a minority and, in Ross's case, while the king was a prisoner in England (the earl suffered a dramatic fall from grace on the king's return). The late medieval Lordship of the Isles was certainly a classic example of a self-contained and largely autonomous lordship which quite clearly preserved its own legal order wholly distinct from that of the Scots common law in the absence of any regular royal justice. The appointments of Alexander and William may nonetheless show that one aim of central government was to deploy local power towards its own ends, however imperfectly that may have been achieved in these cases.[226]

CONCLUSIONS

This long chapter began with an inquiry into whether Milsom's feudal world could be found in Scotland. Undoubtedly there existed in the twelfth and thirteenth centuries courts in which lords and their tenants put a tenurial relationship into effect; for example, in his court the lord could recover lands from the tenant who failed to render the services due for them, and probably it could also be decided who should hold a disputed tenancy. The evidence does not allow us to say how much autonomy the court had in these processes. Probably it varied considerably, even without taking account of the possibility that outside influences might be brought to bear, in particular royal justice. This outside influence was growing in the twelfth and thirteenth centuries, but the essence of the Scottish court system throughout the medieval period was a partnership, or a multitude of partnerships, between the centre and the localities, rather than a conflict. Private jurisdictions were recognised and used by the king as a principal means to the achievement of law and order. However, the theory of the system was plain; where justice lay in private hands, it was subject to royal correction and control. The general pattern of the practical application of this theory, traced in this chapter, is also clear. Royal justice, and the forms in which it intervened in the courts of private lords, was regularised and systematised. It is in this context that the use of royal brieves to initiate litigation in disputes over land must be set.

NOTES

1. See H. L. MacQueen, Taws of Galloway'.
2. G. W. S. Barrow, *Kingdom*, pp. 279–361; Barrow, *ANE*, passim; The pattern of lordship and the feudal settlement in medieval Cumbria', *Journal of Medieval History*, i (1975), p. 1; 'Badenoch and Strathspey, 1130–1312', *Northern Scotland*, viii (1988), p. 1.
3. See W. C. Dickinson, *Fife Ct Bk*, pp. 347–68.
4. For this see *RRS*, i, pp. 44–9; *RRS*, ii, pp. 39–42; A. A. M. Duncan, *Kingdom*, pp. 160–3, 168–9, 204–5. The development of sheriffs and sheriffdoms is mapped in *Atlas of Scottish History to 1707*, ed. P. McNeill and H. MacQueen (Edinburgh, 1996).
5. G. W. S. Barrow, *Kingdom*, pp. 83–138; *RRS*, i, pp. 49–50; *RRS*, ii, 43–7; A. A. M. Duncan, *Kingdom*, pp. 169–70, 203–4.
6. On the feudal settlement, see G. W. S. Barrow, *Kingdom*, pp. 279–310; Barrow, *ANE*, passim; A. A. M. Duncan, *Kingdom*, pp. 135–42, 175–85.
7. *ESC*, no 54; for the ten knights, see *RRS*, ii, no 80.
8. G. W. S. Barrow, 'Pattern of lordship', pp. 121–4.
9. G. W. S. Barrow, *Kingdom*, p. 295. See further ibid., pp. 296–303; Barrow, *ANE*, pp. 64–141; K. J. Stringer, *Earl David*, pp. 81–91; V. Chandler, 'Ada de Warenne, queen mother of Scotland (c. 1123–1178)', *SHR*, lx (1981), pp. 125–9.
10. Note, however, that in later Scots law only tenants in ward and relief had an automatic obligation of suit: *Fife Ct Bk*, p. lxxiii.
11. *RRS*, ii, pp. 48–9.
12. Fraser, *Annandale*, i, no 4; *CDS*, i, p. 107.
13. *RRS*, ii, 49–50.
14. *St A Lib*, p. 247 (x 1183); and see further above, p. 43.
15. See G. W. S. Barrow, *Kingdom*, pp. 69–82.
16. Ibid., p. 283; idem, *ANE*, pp. 84–90.
17. *AB Coll*, pp. 407–9.
18. *CA Chrs*, i, no 35.
19. See *Inchaff Chrs*, nos 5, 9, 25, 39 and 43.
20. *RRS*, ii, p. 48.

21. See *Moray Reg*, no 179, recording a legal argument in 1398.
22. *CA Chrs*, i, no 10.
23. *Kel Lib*, nos 103, 109, 112 and 474. See *also APS*, i, p. 375 (c. 13).
24. *Arb Lib*, ii, no 2.
25. See below pp. 39–40, on disciplinary jurisdiction.
26. R. M. Maxtone-Graham, 'Showing the holding', passim.
27. *ND*, no 370.
28. *ND*, no 388. Note that the first witness to the quitclaim is Walter Olifard *justicia*, who was justiciar in Lothian from c. 1178 to c. 1188; and the second is Robert de Burneville, sheriff of Berwick from at latest 1174 to c. 1190.
29. *Moncreiffs*, ii, appendix, no II. For the date, see G. W. S. Barrow, *ANE*, p. 136.
30. *Inchaff Chrs*, nos 91–2. On Tristram, see A. A. M. Duncan, *Kingdom*, pp. 448–9.
31. *ND*, no 175.
32. *ND*, no 379. See also nos 380 and 381.
33. *ND*, no 389.
34. *ESC*, nos 49, 153; *RRS*, i, no 243; *RRS*, ii, nos 27, 197 and 513.
35. *APS*, i, p. 375 (c. 12); see also ibid., p. 377 (c. 20).
36. *Melr Lib*, i, no. 325.
37. *ND*, nos 397 and 398.
38. R. Bartlett, *Trial by Fire and Water: the medieval judicial ordeal* (Oxford, 1986), pp. 26–33, 106–9, 114–16.
39. W. Fraser, *Annandale*, i, no 6.
40. *ND*, nos 210, 211, 220.
41. *ND*, no 272.
42. *ND*, no 308.
43. *ND*, no 215.
44. *Coldstream Chrs*, no 1.
45. *Coldstream Chrs*, no 16.
46. *RRS*, v, p. 408 (c. 8); *APS*, i, pp. 468–9 (c. 8).
47. *APS*, i, pp. 321–2 (*Assise Regis David*, cc. 21–3).
48. See A. Harding, 'Brieves', pp. 120–1; *RRS*, i, pp. 64–5; *RRS*, ii, p. 72; *RRS*, v, p. 101.
49. See below, chapter 4, for full discussion.
50. See e.g. the discussion of the brieves *de compulsione* below, chapter 4, and the texts from *Omne Gaderum*, *Leges Portuum* and *Liber de Judicibus* collected *in APS*, i, pp. 734–5.
51. *RM* (*APS*) II, 58, 67; *RM* (*Cooper*), II, 63, 73; *Glanvill*, IX, 1, 8. Note however that the second of the *RM* chapters omits a passage in *Glanvill*, providing for forfeiture of the tenant's fee. See further on these chapters below, pp. 115–20.
52. K. J. Stringer, *Earl David*, especially at pp. 81–91, 102–3; also 'The charters of David, earl of Huntingdon and lord of Garioch: a study in Anglo-Scottish diplomatic', in *Nobility Essays*, especially at pp. 75–7.
53. *Chron Holyrood*, p. 142. Cf. A. A. M. Duncan, *Kingdom*, p. 191.
54. G. W. S. Barrow, *Kingdom*, p. 291.
55. K. J. Stringer, *Earl David*, pp. 107–10.
56. G. W S. Barrow, 'Pattern of lordship', pp. 130–2; K. J. Stringer, *Earl David*, pp. 56–103, especially pp. 60–8.

57. K. J. Stringer, *Earl David*, pp. 102–3.
58. G. W. S. Barrow, *Kingdom*, p. 294.
59. *ESC*, nos. 74, 179, 209.
60. *RSS*, i, no 258.
61. *RSS*, ii, nos. 179, 507.
62. See P. J. Hamilton Grierson, 'Falsing the doom', *SHR*, xxiv (1927), p. 1 for discussion.
63. *APS*, i, p. 375 (c. 12).
64. *RRS*, ii, no 80.
65. *ESC*, no 105.
66. *ND*, no 388.
67. *Moncreiffs*, ii, appendix, no II.
68. *ESC*, nos. 26, 27.
69. *ESC*, no 120.
70. *ESC*, *no SO*.
71. *ESC*, no 94.
72. G. W. S. Barrow, *Kingdom*, p. 280, thinks Robert the Burgundian may have been infeft by either King Edgar or King Alexander I; see also A. A. M. Duncan, *Kingdom*, pp. 137–8, 167–8.
73. *ESC*, no 236.
74. *ND*, nos. 115, 116.
74a. *Arb Lib*, *i, no 250*.
75. *Spalding Misc*, v, pp. 210–13. *Scoloc* seems to be a term for serf or peasant.
76. See *Records and Register of Holm Cultram Abbey*, ed. F. Grainger and W. G. Collingwood (Cumberland and Westmorland AAS Records Series, vol. vii, 1929), nos. 120–3; *RRS*, ii, no 256 and note; also no 540.
77. R. C. Reid, in *Wigt Chrs*, pp. xix–xxi.
78. See *Met Lib*, nos 131–3; *RRS*, ii, no 382; T. M. Cooper, *Cases*, no 7.
79. The charter is published as Document No 6 in Appendix 1 to K. J. Stringer, 'Periphery and core in thirteenth-century Scotland: Alan Lord of Galloway and Constable of Scotland', in *Medieval Scotland: Crown, Lordship and Community*, ed. A. Grant and K. J. Stringer (Edinburgh, 1992).
80. *Glanvill*, IX, 4; *RM* (*APS*), II, 62; (*Cooper*) II, 67. See further S. J. Bailey, 'Warranties of land in the reign of Richard F, *Cambridge Law Journal*, ix (1945–7), pp. 193–6.
81. *RRS*, i, no 42, a better version of *ESC*, no 222.
82. A. A. M. Duncan, *Kingdom*, pp. 407–8. For the quotation, see *APS*, i, p. 409.
83. K. J. Stringer, 'Charters of David', p. 90; *Earl David*, p. 224.
84. See S. E. Thorne, 'English feudalism', pp. 200–7, and P. R. Hyams, 'Warranty', pp. 467–74.
85. For the brieve of warrandice of charter, see below, pp. 124–5.
86. K. J. Stringer, 'Charters of David', pp. 90–1.
87. See above, pp. 14–15.
88. *Newb Reg*, no 69. See also the repeated royal confirmations in *RRS*, i, no 136, and ii, nos. 61 and 91.
89. A. A. M. Duncan, *Kingdom*, pp. 407–9. Dr Stringer casts doubt on just how commonplace express clauses were in the thirteenth

century in 'Charters of David', p. 91.
90. *ESC*, nos 130 and 182; *RRS*, ii, nos 35 and 105.
91. *RRS*, ii, nos 85 and 496.
92. *RRS*, ii, nos 236, 249, 364, 483 and 519. For adjudications by the *curia regis*, see ibid., nos 84, 353 and 440.
93. *RRS*, ii, no 249.
94. *Chron Melr*, p. 44.
95. *RRS*, ii, no 440.
96. See, in addition to the examples in *APS*, i, pp. 405–10, 419–29, K. J. Stringer, 'Periphery', Appendix I, no 6, discussed above, p. 45.
97. *APS*, i, pp. 445–9.
98. *ESC*, no 248; *RRS*, i, nos 121 and 220.
99. W. Fraser, *Douglas*, iii, no 285; *ND*, no 126.
100. *Arb Lib*, i, no 229.
101. *Kel Lib*, i, no 34.
101a. *JLH*, iv (1983), p. 48*.
102. Thus neither baron nor a regality court would have been described as a *curia regis*, and we may properly distinguish other courts such as those of the justiciar and the sheriff as 'royal', albeit that 'all legitimate secular courts derived their authority from the crown': G. W. S. Barrow, 'Popular courts in early medieval Scotland: some suggested place-name evidence', *Scot Studs*, xxv (1981), p. 2.
103. *ESC*, no 248; *RRS*, i, nos 121 and 220.
104. See *Fife Ct Bk*, pp. 347–68; *RRS*, i, pp. 45–9; *RRS*, ii, pp. 39–42; A. A. M. Duncan, *Kingdom*, pp. 160–3, 169, 204–5, 596–7.
105. G. W. S. Barrow, *Kingdom*, pp. 83–136; and further above pp. 58–65.
106. See *Abdn Ct Bk*, pp. cxvii–lv; H. L. MacQueen and W. J. Windram, 'Burghs', pp. 213–14 for further references.
107. See *SHS Misc*, ii, pp. 31–2 ('The Scottish King's Household'); J. Stevenson, *Documents*, p. 169 (the Treaty of Birgham, 1290); E. L. G. Stones and G. G. Simpson, *Edward I*, ii, p. 97.
108. See *Morton Reg*, ii, no 222 (p. 214; 1466); W. Fraser, *Lennox*, no 53; M. Napier, *'The Lanox of Auld': An Epistolary Review of 'The Lennox' by Sir William Fraser* (Edinburgh, 1880), p. 68 (1492); *Family of Rose*, p. 179 (1502). In the last two citations, read 'coursable' for 'conisabill' and 'conrisabill' respectively.
109. *RRS*, vi, no 306. For discussion, see *RRS*, v, pp. 213–14.
110. H. McKechnie, *Brieves*, pp. 7–14; I. D. Willock, *Jury*, pp. 31–7.
111. *RRS*, i, pp. 49, 62–7; *RRS*, ii, pp. 71–5; A. Harding, 'Brieves', pp. 115–31.
112. See *RRS*, v, pp. 258–61 for an important discussion by Professor Duncan.
113. *Reg Brieves* passim; see also *Form E*. For the *Registrum Omnium Brevium*, see J. H. Baker, *IELH*, p. 202.
114. *Form E*; Cambridge University Library MS, Ee.4.21, f. 272ff.
115. On this, see *Fife Ct Bk*, pp. 344–6; and, for examples, *Panm Reg*, p. 169; W. Fraser, *Grandtully*, nos. 84, 85, 87; *Pais Reg*, p. 257
116. See generally the introductions to *Carn Ct Bk* and *Dunf Ct Bk*; also A. Grant, 'Thesis', pp. 109–54, and 'Crown and nobility', pp. 46–7; *RRS*, v, pp. 39–44.
117. See A. Grant, 'Thesis', pp. 112–14; P. G. B. McNeill, *'Discours Particulier'*, pp. 90–3.

118. *RRS*, v, no 172. See further *Dunf Ct Bk*, pp. 8–10, and A. Grant, 'Thesis', pp. 113–14.
119. SRO, *Ailsa muniments*, GD 25/1/97; NLS, *Fleming of Wigtown papers*, Ch. 15561.
120. See e.g. *APS*, i, pp. 552–3 (1385); *Moray Reg*, no 291 (*1395*); *Newb Reg*, no 283 (1425); *Laing Chrs*, no 117. See further below, pp.116–18.
121. *ADA*, p. 54.
122. See *Melr Lib*, ii, nos 540–5.
123. *Mort Reg*, ii, no 194. See further below, pp. 219, 232.
124. Further on this, see A. Grant, 'Thesis', pp. 197–211, and 'Crown and nobility', pp. 43–4; and below, pp. 117–18.
125. On this, see D. E. R. Watt, 'Scottish university men in the thirteenth and fourteenth centuries', *Scotland and Europe 1200–1850*, ed. T. C. Smout (Edinburgh, 1986), pp. 7–9; L. J. Macfarlane, *Elphinstone*, pp. 53–122; R. J. Lyall, 'Scottish students and masters at the universities of Cologne and Louvain in the fifteenth century', *Innes Review*, xxxvi (1985), p. 55.
126. *Abdn Reg*, i, pp. 148–9.
127. See *Libri Feudorum*, II, 55. Frederick's constitition is printed in translation in D. Herlihy, *Feudalism*, pp. 237–9. Other passages in the *Libri Feudorum* to the same effect are I, 10 and 18; II, 16, 20 and 34 (often referring to a 1037 law of the Emperor Conrad II, also printed in translation in D. Herlihy, *Feudalism*, pp. 108–9). See further O. F. Robinson et al., *IELH*, pp. 53–4.
128. *See Abdn Reg*, i, pp. 146–53.
129. *Abdn Reg*, i, pp. 148–9, 153.
130. See P. G. Stein, 'Roman law', pp. 37–9; *Moray Reg*, nos. 299–302 (in the last of which many feudal authorities are cited); see also the homages being given at nos. 285–8.
131. *Lind Chrs*, no 149. For the citations of the *Libri Feudorum*, see p. 203.
132. See *Libri Feudorum*, I, 5 and 13; II, 9 and 24.
133. *Libri Feudorum*, I, 21; II, 24 and 28.
134. See *Moray Reg*, no 159; and further A. Grant, 'The Wolf of Badenoch', in *Moray: Province and People*, ed. W. D. H. Sellar (Scottish Society for Northern Studies, 1993).
135. *APS*, i, p. 492.
136. R. Nicholson, *LMA*, pp. 163–5.
137. *APS*, i, p. 572.
138. *SHR*, xxv (1956), p. 135 (cc. 1 and 2).
139. *APS*, ii, p. 3 (c. 6).
140. *APS*, ii, p. 32 (c. 2); A. I. Dunlop, *The Life and Times of James Kennedy Bishop of St Andrews* (Edinburgh, 1950), p. 318.
141. *APS*, ii, p. 35 (c. 2).
142. *APS*, ii, p. 207 (c. 6).
143. *APS*, i, p. 556.
144. *Moray Reg*, no 159. See further A. Grant, 'The Wolf of Badenoch'.
145. T. M. Cooper, *Papers*, p. 234.
146. P. J. Hamilton Grierson, 'Falsing the doom', p. 6.
147. *APS*, i, p. 535.
148. See H. L. MacQueen and W. J. Windram, 'Burghs', pp. 213–14, and notes thereto, for further references.

149. A. Grant, *Independence and Nationhood*, pp. 152–3.
150. See *APS*, i, pp. 548, 551, 571; ii, pp. 23 (c. 1), 49 (c. 16).
151. *Reg Brieves*, pp. 42–3 (nos 29, 38), 57 (nos 56–9); *Form E*, nos 24–5.
152. W. Fraser, *Douglas*, iii, no 432 (1456). See also *HMC*, xv, p. 8.
153. *SHR*, v (1908), p. 23.
154. SRO, *Swinton charters*, GD 12/22. See also GD 12/25.
155. SRO, *Crown Office writs*, AD 1/53.
156. For further discussion of the earl's reason for refusal to comply with the king's brieve, see H. L. MacQueen and A. R. Borthwick, 'Cases', p. 141 and note.
157. SRO, *Mar and Kellie papers*, GD 124/6/4. See further below, pp. 201, 221.
158. See his introductions to *Fife Ct Bk*, *Carn Ct Bk* and *Abdn Ct Bk*.
159. W. C. Dickinson, 'Administration of justice', p. 345.
160. H. L. MacQueen and W. J. Windram, 'Burghs', pp. 214–15.
161. On these different types of slaughter, see now W. D. H. Sellar, 'Forethocht felony, malice aforethought and the classification of homicide', in *Legal History in the Making*, ed. W. M. Gordon and T. D. Fergus (London, 1991), pp. 43–60.
162. See W. C. Dickinson's comments in *Carn Ct Bk*, pp. cvii–iii.
163. *Carn Ct Bk*, pp. civ–vii. Note that the baron court, unlike the sheriff, had no jurisdiction in spuilzie (*Melr Lib*, ii, no 579).
164. W. C. Dickinson, 'High Court of Justiciary', in *ISLH*, pp. 408–12.
165. G. W. S. Barrow, *Kingdom*, pp. 83–138.
166. I have used the second edition, 2 vols (Edinburgh, 1819), ii, pp. 1–14.
167. See above, p. 49.
168. E. L. G. Stones, *Relations*, no 33 (*APS*, i, pp. 119–22).
169. *Abbotsford Misc*, i, pp. 53–6; *Lindores (Abbotsford)*, pp. 11–13.
170. *RRS*, v, no 12.
171. *HMC*, v, p. 626.
172. Note that the designations of Gilbert lord Kennedy as justiciar of Galloway in 1459 (*ER*, vi, p. 574) and of Mark Haliburton as clerk of the justiciary of Galloway in 1457 (*ER*, vi, p. 353) are not revivals of the thirteenth-century justiciary but an aspect of the administration of crown lands, the Douglas forfeiture in 1455 having brought their lordship of Galloway into the crown patrimony (R. Nicholson, *LMA*, p. 378).
173. See the references to Robert Lauder the elder as justiciar of Lothian in H. L. MacQueen 'Thesis', pp. 326–7; also *Melr Lib*, ii, no 421; *RRS*, v, no 163, and vi, nos 101, 219 and 237. *ND*, no 326, gives the seal of the office of justiciary of Lothian in 1366.
174. *RRS*, vi, no 503. Note that we have the clerk of the justiciary south of the Forth in 1362: *RMS*, i, no 100 and note; cf. A. L. Murray, 'The lord clerk register', *SHR*, liii (1974), p. 127.
175. W. Fraser, *Menteith*, ii, no 29; *RRS*, v, nos 156, 311; *APS*, i, p. 511; *RRS*, vi, nos 3, 70 and 234; *SHR*, ix (1912), p. 239; *Dunf Reg*, nos 352, 376; *Abdn Reg*, i, pp. 79–81, 86; *RMS*, i, appendix 1, no 144; W. Fraser, *Southesk*, ii, no 36.
176. For fifteenth-century justiciars 'of Scotia', see H. L. MacQueen, 'Thesis', pp. 60–1; H. L. MacQueen and A. R. Borthwick, 'Cases', p. 150.

177. Early references to the 'justiciar north of the Forth' include *Moray Reg, Cartae originates*, no 18; *Dunf Reg*, no 376; *Panm Reg*, p. 169; *RMS*, i, no 161, and appendix 1, no 28; *RMS*, ii, no 3717; *RRS*, v, nos 12, 140, 202, 285; vi, nos 33, 50, 230 and 462. In one northern document, Alexander, lord of the Isles, is designed as justiciar 'this side (*citra*) Forth' (*Abdn Reg*, i, p. 241). See also, for a thirteenth-century justiciar north of the Forth, M. O. Anderson, *Kings and Kingship in Early Scotland* (Edinburgh, 1973), p. xvii, note 3.

178. For these quotations from fifteenth-century legislation, see *APS*, ii, pp. 32 (c. 2), 35 (c. 2), 170 (c. 4) and 225 (c. 10).

179. H. L. MacQueen, 'Thesis', pp. 69–87, provides the evidence on which this sentence is based.

180. Dickinson/Duncan, *Scotland*, p. 98.

181. W. C. Dickinson, 'High Court of Justiciary', p. 408.

182. R. Nicholson, *LMA*, pp. 427–8.

183. See above, pp. 54–5.

184. *APS*, ii, p. 49 (c. 14).

185. R. Nicholson, *LMA*, p. 383.

186. *APS*, ii, p. 52.

187. H. L. MacQueen, 'Thesis', pp. 77–8, surveys some of the evidence.

188. *APS*, ii, p. 225 (c. 10).

189. Dickinson/Duncan, *Scotland*, p. 252.

190. H. L. MacQueen, 'Thesis', pp. 83–7.

191. *TA*, i, pp. 102–5, 130–1, 140, 150; *ER*, x, pp. 243, 366.

192. *APS*, ii, p. 111 (c. 2).

193. H. L. MacQueen, 'Thesis', pp. 78–81.

194. *TA*, i, pp. 6–10.

195. See C. H. W. Gane, 'The effect of a royal pardon in Scots law', *JR*, xxv (1980), p. 21.

196. *APS*, ii, pp. 104, 118, 165, 170 and 176. See also ibid., p. 201, and N. A. T. Macdougall, *James III*, pp. 99, 120 and 201–3.

197. For the *Ordo Justiciare*, see *APS*, i, p. 706. See also W. C. Dickinson, 'High Court of Justiciary', p. 409.

198. *ADA*, p. 98; *Peebles Recs*, no 16.

199. *APS*, xii, p. 33.

200. R. Nicholson, *LMA*, p. 511; N. A. T. Macdougall, *James III*, p. 167.

201. *ER*, ix, pp. 380, 460; *ADC*, i, p. 233; SRO, *Acta dominorum concilii*, CS5/16, f. 6.

202. For what follows, see H. L. MacQueen, 'Thesis', pp. 69–77.

203. See H. L. MacQueen, 'Thesis', pp. 326–34, for a list from c. 1306–1513.

204. See J. M. Thomson, 'A roll of the Scottish parliament 1344', *SHR*, ix (1912), p. 239.

205. T. M. Cooper, *Papers*, p. 227.

206. See H. L. MacQueen and A. R. Borthwick, 'Cases', pp. 148–9.

207. See for example *Mort Reg*, ii, no 223.

208. The *Ordo Justiciarie* of the 1450s (so dateable because of its references to William Sinclair, earl of Orkney) gives a useful picture of the administration of a justice ayre (*APS*, i, pp. 705–8).

209. *ER*, vi, p. 98 is one example. The porteous roll is referred to in 1473 (*AB Ill*, iv, p. 407). See also R. K. Hannay, *College of Justice*, p. 328,

and J. Irvine Smith, in *ISLH*, p. 429.

210. See for example *Pitfirrane Writs*, no 24, and *TA*, i, pp. 173, 182, 184, 200.

211. *TA*, i, pp. 53, 184, 237, 239, 241.

212. *APS*, i, p. 556 and ii, p. 3 (c. 6).

213. *APS*, ii, p. 36 (c. 8).

214. For the clerks of the fourteenth and fifteenth centuries, see H. L. MacQueen, 'Thesis', pp. 119–20.

215. *APS*, ii, p. 182.

216. *Abdn Reg*, i, pp. 79–81.

217. SRO, *Ailsa muniments*, GD 25/1/102.

218. *APS*, ii, p. 32 (c. 2).

219. *Brechin Reg*, i, no 88.

220. *AB III*, iw, pp. 205–13.

221. *TA*, i, p. 318; *ER*, xi, pp. 316★, 333★; *ADC*, ii, pp. 93–211, especially pp. 210–11.

222. On these circuits, see H. L. MacQueen, 'Thesis', pp. 88–91.

223. For these lieutenancies, see e.g. *RMS*, i, no 556 (1373); *HMC*, iv, p. 485 (no 235); W. Fraser, *Eglinton*, ii, no 35 (1430).

224. *APS*, ii, p. 249 (cc. 3–5).

225. See above, p. 3.

226. See on this paragraph W. D. H. Sellar, 'Celtic law', pp. 3–4, and references there given; A. Grant, 'Scotland's "Celtic fringe" in the late Middle Ages: the Macdonald Lords of the Isles and the kingdom of Scotland', in *The British Isles 1100–1500*, ed. R. R. Davies (Edinburgh, 1988), pp. 121–2, 127–8, 132–3; B. Webster, 'David II and the government of fourteenth-century Scotland', *TRHS*, xvi (1966), p. 125.

3

Men of Law and Books of Law

In 1473, parliament was much concerned to deal with the obscurity of the law, one of the causes of which was declared to be 'the gret diversite now fundin in divers bukis put in þe divers persounis that ar callit men of law'.[1] This chapter examines who the men of law were, and the contents and nature of their books. The purpose is twofold. The first is to deal with Cooper's contention that the conditions for the intellectual development (as distinct from the actual enforcement) of the law did not exist: 'it has never yet proved possible to construct a first-class system of Common Law without a first-class system of judicial organisation and a skilled body of lawyers to work it'.[2] In Cooper's view, medieval Scots law lacked not only the judicial organisation but also the skilled body of lawyers, particularly in the courts.[3] We have dealt with the point about judicial organisation; now we turn to the men of law. Fifteenth-century sources refer often to 'men of law', earlier records to '*jurisperiti*', men skilled or learned in the law. This section examines the use of men of law as pleaders and representatives on behalf of litigants in the Scottish courts. Although it was normal for parties in a litigation to act for themselves, it was also not unusual to be represented. As we shall see, these representatives came from the ranks of both clergy and laymen. The idea that a cleric might be learned in the law is not surprising; but it has been generally assumed that this could not normally be true of a layman. In this section, some of the evidence about the *jurisperiti* and men of law is examined, and it is argued that, at any rate in the fourteenth and fifteenth centuries, they always included laymen as well as clergy. Accordingly, although the secular courts discussed in the previous section were staffed by laymen, it does not follow that in this world there could be no significant legal development or discussion; on the contrary, the framework existed for sophisticated legal argument and debate.

In looking also at the books made and used by these men of law, we are not only identifying the materials on which these arguments were based, but we are also studying the nature of the evidence for the law itself, on which much of the discussion in the succeeding chapters will be based.

Two other points may also be made at the outset. First, it is clear that kings legislated from at latest the reign of David I on a wide range of matters, and this was an important source of law. Second, the medieval men of law included no great jurists; Scots law did not produce a *Glanvill* or a *Bracton*. The writing on law was chiefly derivative and confined to statements of the rules found in legislation and other sources. The really striking feature for the purposes of this book is that *Glanvill* was a major source for *Regiam Majestatem*, the principal book of the later medieval law. In other words, the leading account of the law of late twelfth-century England, written just as Henry II's reforms transformed the Milsomian world, seemed to a later medieval Scot to provide an appropriate framework on which to base a statement of his own law. So this aspect points us once again at the central theme of this book: to what extent did Scottish conditions in the later Middle Ages in fact reproduce those described in *Glanvill*?

THE MEN OF LAW

When someone went to law in the fifteenth-century courts, it was in company, if we may judge from legislation seeking to restrict the practice of coming to court 'with multitude of folkis and armys'. Supporters, often carrying weapons (this is what seems to be meant by 'armys') which they were supposed to lay aside as they entered the court, came from obligations of kinship or as lords supporting their men; or, if the litigant was a great man, as his familiars or as members of his household and council.[4] A not uncommon clause in bonds of manrent provided that the grantor would support his lord in all his actions, often referring explicitly to litigation.[5] The legislation did not seek to abolish these practices, only to limit the numbers coming and to make them do so in 'sobyr and quiet maner', but its repetition at intervals throughout the fifteenth century may suggest a continuing difficulty. So in 1466, for example, Robert lord Fleming refused to compear in person at the justiciar's court in Dumbarton because he had heard that his opponent, Gilbert lord Kennedy, had come to court with an army.[6] However, in among the crowd of supporters accompanying a litigant, there might also be found his lawyers or, as contemporaries would have put it, his men of law. *Prelocutors* and advocates are mentioned among the allowable companions in an act of 1428, while when the thane of Cawdor and Hugh Rose of Kilravock agreed to settle their differences in 1492, they were to use the advice of certain persons and 'quhat men of law it plese them to tak with them'.[7] The courtroom atmosphere suggested by fifteenth-century legislation may not seem particularly conducive to the effective deployment of the skills of a man of law, yet it is clear that his role, already well established, was a by no means insignificant element in medieval litigation.

Clearly also to be included among the men of law are the notaries who drew up legal documents and whose attestation gave such documents especial force as evidence and record of formal transactions or other acts such as the giving of sasine or the taking of procedural steps in court. The notaries have been the subject of much recent work, showing them to have been a feature of the Scottish scene from at latest the thirteenth century, and increasing significantly in number and importance after 1400.[8] Notaries might be clerics or laymen, and they might have studied arts or law at a university. Their participation and interest in the common law of Scotland is evident in a number of ways, not least in the extent to which members of this branch of the legal profession seem to have been principally responsible for the penning of the legal manuscript collections or books to be discussed later in this chapter.[9] Thus the treatise *Omne Gaderum* claims in its preface to have been composed in 1425 by William Kinnaird, clerk of St Andrews diocese and notary public by imperial authority, while Alexander Foulis, one of the most prominent notaries of the mid-fifteenth century, was responsible for the compilation of one of the legal manuscripts now held in the National Library of Scotland.[10]

Men of law representing and pleading for others in court are variously described as 'advocate', 'forespeaker' (*prelocutor* in Latin sources), 'attorney' (*actornatus*) and 'procurator' (*procurator*). These appear to be technical terms with a specific content, the most general being 'advocate'. A forespeaker or *prelocutor* is one who speaks despite the presence in court of his client, while an attorney or procurator represents a client who is absent.[11] The distinction is very clear in the record of the litigation between Gilbert lord Kennedy and Robert lord Fleming in 1466, where the absent Fleming is represented by procurators, while Kennedy is present but has his *prelocutor* advance his case.[12] The term forespeaker seems to originate in the Anglo-Saxon *forespeca*,[13] whose function was to make the formal statement of claim with which a case would be opened; if he made a mistake, the client could nonetheless continue, 'since it is generally possible to amend in another person's mouth what may not be amended in his own'.[14] In England, the *forespeca* evolved into the *narrator* or *conteur*, 'who could harmlessly blunder',[15] since his words would not bind his client; there also emerged the attorney, who did stand entirely in his client's shoes and bound him by what he said and did.[16] If this was the early pattern in Scotland, it had been lost sight of in the later Middle Ages, since the function of the forespeaker or *prelocutor*, like that of the attorney or procurator, clearly extended to the conduct of an entire litigation and not just to uttering the statement of claim. The attorney is found from the thirteenth century on,[17] the term being seemingly borrowed from England, but it was often replaced by the canon law 'procurator' in the fifteenth century.

Pleading involved more than the ability to be articulate in pursuit of a claim. As has been shown elsewhere, it was intimately connected with procedure.[18] It involved the statement of a claim, often (but not always) in set forms of words, by or for the party raising the action; and the entry on the other side of defences, or 'exceptions', which might be met in turn by 'recounters'. Exceptions might be in law (that is, an argument that the pursuer's claim as stated gave rise to no legal remedy), dilatory (objections to the form in which the action was brought, rather than to its substance) or peremptory (the allegation of a fact not referred to in the original statement of claim which gave a different legal colouring to the situation there set out). Dilatory exceptions had to be pleaded first; they included exceptions against the judge, against the court, against the brieve or summons with which the action was begun, and against the day and place of the action. Further, the dilatory exceptions had to be pleaded in a particular order; once one was invoked, the right to refer to earlier kinds was lost. The purpose of pleading peremptory exceptions was to define the issue to be determined by the court. An example from 1368 illustrates the technique. John, son of Walter, sued Thomas Scott, alleging that Scott had wrongfully turned out his cattle on John's pastures and deforced John's sergeant. Scott's answer was not to deny the facts stated by John but to aver that the lands belonged to his lord, which fact, if proved, would tend to put John rather than Scott in the wrong.[19] There might also be pleas in law, that is, as to the precise content or meaning of particular legal rules. A system of forms of action, based on various different styles of initial writ or brieve, offered much scope for this kind of pleading, turning on the precise meaning of the words used in the brieve. What was dissasine? What was a free holding, and how did it differ from a fee? Courts dealing with brieves of novel dissasine, mortancestry and right must have had to answer these questions, and others like them; and, from the answers that they gave, the substantive law evolved.

While no doubt in practice the forms of pleading were much less rigid than this bare summary suggests, there can be no doubt that it demanded considerable skills and knowledge of procedure and the general law. That procedure was obviously influenced by Romano-canonical procedure as found in the church courts. Church lawyers were employed in the secular courts and formed a significant element among the 'men of law'. Attention has been drawn to the clerics who were pleading in the sheriff courts of Fife and Aberdeen in the early sixteenth century.[20] There can be no doubt that this had been quite normal throughout the medieval period. From the thirteenth century on, many clerics were primarily what could safely be termed practising lawyers. The classic example is Adam Urry of Glasgow diocese, who died in 1288 repenting of his devotion, contrary to God's command, to laws and statutes when he should have been more concerned with the cure of souls.[21] No doubt there were many others like him, *jurisperiti* learned in the canon and the civil laws who put their skills at the disposal of lay as well as ecclesiastical clients in litigation.[22] Thus Harvey and John of Strathanery, both clerks, were appointed joint and several attorneys to pursue the brieve of dissasine which the heirs portioner of the barony of Fithkil in Fife raised against the abbot and convent of Dunfermline around 1319.[23] In 1348, a justiciary court at Forfar took '*consilio jurisperitorum*' concerning the interpretation of a royal grant of teinds to the priory of Restenneth, and their advice is surely reflected in the court's reference to the rule drawn from Roman law, '*quia nullus plus iuris transferre potest in alium quam possidet in seipso*'.[24] Perhaps it was from such lawyers that David II obtained the many authorities of the civil law which he put to the earl of Ross in the 1360s and which the earl was unable to answer.[25] We have already seen very learned arguments drawing on the civil, canon and feudal laws being put to secular courts, probably by ecclesiastical lawyers, round about 1380. Admittedly these were on behalf of ecclesiastical clients – the abbey and convent of Lindores in one case, the bishop of Aberdeen in another – but presumably it was thought that the secular courts to whom the arguments were addressed would be prepared to listen to them.[26]

Should we be sceptical about the capacity of the secular courts to comprehend such arguments, or, bearing in mind the difficulties of the earl of Ross in dealing with David II's civilian citations, of the ability of lay parties to reply in kind? Perhaps not. For example, James Douglas of Dalkeith, a litigious landowner prominent in the second half of the fourteenth century, owned '*libros civiles*' (books of the civil law?) in the 1390s.[27] Books may be owned without being read or even referred to, of course, but in the fifteenth century there is evidence showing a layman familiar with the texts of Roman law. One David Reid, who acted as advocate in a number of cases in the middle of the century, once referred a justiciar's court to Justinian's *Codex* in support of a proposition that a dead man might be convicted of treason. The text is a statute of Marcus Aurelius, which is quoted verbatim in a document recording this and other pleas put forward by Reid in the case.[28] Little is known of David Reid, and his educational background is obscure, but he does not seem to be designated 'Master' in any source, suggesting that he had never graduated from any university which he may have attended. One swallow does not make a summer, but it cannot be assumed that laymen at any time during the period with which we are concerned were unable to deal with the learned laws, or that a secular court would have been blinded by the science of ecclesiastical lawyers pleading before them.

The presence of the ecclesiastical lawyers within the secular system ensured that the learned law did filter through into the secular law, as is evident, for example, in a number of aspects of procedure which will be referred to later. William de Spynie's learned arguments for the bishop of Aberdeen against John Crab were based on the civil and canon as well as the feudal laws, although directed towards questions arising between a lord and his vassals. Fifteenth-century legislation often reflects canonical and civilian influences, a classic instance being the series of acts anent prescription beginning in 1469, although another act of 1450 makes it clear that this branch of the law had already been received before that date.[29] The famous act of 1424 providing that 'gif there be onie pure creature for fault of cunning or expenses that cannot nor may not follow his cause the king for the love of God sail ordain the judge before quhom the cause suld be determined to purwey and get a leill and wyse advocat to folow sic pure creatures causes'[30] probably reflects a well-established practice in the canon law.[31] The accepted exclusive jurisdiction of the church in matrimonial and testamentary matters, and in questions of status, had an important effect on secular law, with regard for example to the definition of an heir for the purposes of succession to land. The identity of the heir could turn on questions of legitimacy, which in turn might depend on questions of marriage; both topics were matters for the canon law. It is easy to see, therefore, how the ecclesiastical lawyer could bring his learning to bear inside the secular system.

However, as the example of David Reid reminds us, laymen as well as ecclesiastics were pleaders in the secular courts. Laymen had much opportunity to become acquainted with law and court practice if they wished. Many must have developed knowledge of the law by virtue of their regular attendance as suitors and members of assizes and inquests at courts royal and baronial, which would have enabled them to echo the well-known boast of Hervey de Glanville in the shire court of Norfolk and Suffolk in the mid-twelfth century:[32]

> Worthy and wisest men, it is long ago that I first heard the charters of Saint Edmund, which have been read here now, and they were always authoritative until this very day. For I want you to know that I am, as you see, a man of very advanced age. I remember many things which happened in the time of King Henry, and before that, when justice and right, peace and good faith, flourished in England . . . Indeed, I truly declare, attest and demonstrate that fifty years have passed since I first took to frequenting hundreds and shires with my father, before I was a householder and afterwards up until now.

The point of the boast was the knowledge and wisdom in legal affairs which Hervey had acquired as a result of his long experience in the courts, and to which the court now should defer.[33] Men like Hervey must also have been found as suitors and assizers in the Scottish courts throughout

the Middle Ages, and their existence may explain the frequent references
to 'weakness' or 'debility' with which a court would defer taking a
decision; an experienced and knowledgeable suitor, or group of suitors,
was absent, and the court was reluctant to determine matters without
them.[34] There is the tantalising possibility of some form of institutional
training in the native law, at least by the beginning of the sixteenth
century, when an entry in the register of the privy seal in 1508 records a
crown letter of gift of lands in Trotternish that was made to one
Coinneach, son of William, 'to hald the said Kanoch at the skolis and for
to lerne and study the kingis lawis of Scotland, and eftirward to excers
and use the sammyn within the bondis of the Ilis'.[35] The reference to
schools brings to mind the celebrated act of 1496 commanding all
barons and freeholders to send their eldest sons to 'the sculis of art and
jure sua that thai may have knawlege and understanding of the lawis'.[36]
This was to enable them more effectively to discharge their functions as
judges in the sheriff and baron courts, and so cannot simply be a
reference to the learned laws studied at the universities then developing
at St Andrews, Glasgow and Aberdeen.[37] In general, however, it seems
likely that most of the lay pleaders and notaries to be found at work in
this book would have learned most of their law from experience of the
practice of the courts rather than in any more formal setting.[38]

The aptitude which could be shown around the courts might explain
the rise of some to prominence in the general administration of the law,
as justiciars, sheriffs and royal councillors, and the use of others as
forespeakers and attorneys. No doubt the legal and forensic ability which
a man might demonstrate in the pursuit and defence of his own legal
interests – a commonplace practice throughout our period – could also
lead to requests being made for him to represent others in court. An
example may have been Hugh Rose, baron of Kilravock 1494–1517, who,
according to his family's historian, 'appears to have been skilled in the
laws, acting for himself and his friends'.[39] In earlier periods, however, it
may be that a man was asked to speak on another's behalf as a friend, a
kinsman or an influential patron, or simply as an articulate and persuasive
negotiator, as much as a person who knew the law.

Recent writing[40] has given prominence to a number of laymen who in
the later fifteenth century were pleading on behalf of others with sufficient
regularity to be considered professional advocates in that they formed 'a
group of men who were recognised as having specific, professional skills
in the representation of litigants and who spent much of their time and
derived much of their income from putting those skills at the disposal of
litigants'.[41] However, the activity of laymen as pleaders can be taken much
further back than the later fifteenth century. The 'registers' of brieves give
styles for royal letters of attorney (*de attornato*) in which named individuals

are given the authority to act for a named principal in his *loquelis placitis et querelis*.[42] There are a number of examples of the use of such letters of attorney in court actions, and many were in favour of laymen.[43] The practice of representation in court seems well established in the fourteenth century even though it is not always possible to say that the representatives had been appointed under a brieve *de attornato*. For example, there are *prelocutores* in several of the cases recorded in the Aberdeen burgh court roll for 1317; in another, a party constitutes 'his attorney and procurator'.[44] In the case of John, son of Walter, against Thomas Scott in 1368, discussed earlier in this chapter, Scott's *prelocutor* was his lord John Lindsay.[45] In 1356, David II inspected a charter by which William Troup granted lands to John Gray of Broxmouth 'for his faithful *subsidio et consilio'* which had enabled Troup to recover certain lands from Thomas Murray.[46] Had Gray pleaded Troup's case in court, and was this grant his fee? A few years later, Colin Campbell agreed to act for Gilbert of Glassary '*in suis justis agendis*', perhaps including his legal affairs.[47] The earl of Ross was represented by attorneys in his litigation with Sir David de Anand in 1368.[48] Alan Lauder, who in 1374 received a pension for his labours 'in the office of clerk of the rolls of the justiciary south of Forth',[49] was *prelocutor* for William Borthwick in another case before parliament in 1368.[50] Another possible example of a layman of this period with legal skills is William Chalmer, justice clerk from 1369 until at least 1398 and secretary to Alexander Stewart, earl of Buchan and justiciar north of Forth in the late 1380s.[51] Chalmer was also John Crab's *prelocutor* in his dispute with the bishop of Aberdeen in which William de Spynie displayed his learning on the other side.[52] Walter Bower tells us of Sir John Ramornie, *prelocutor regis* under Robert III (1390–1406) and a *causidicus disertissimus* (a very eloquent pleader).[53]

Fifteenth-century legislation touches on pleaders a number of times. In 1426, parliament laid down that only 'honest and sufficient persons of discretion' should be admitted as 'attournays' in the justice ayre, while in 1430, again following a Romano-canonical model, it set out the oath of calumny to be sworn by 'advocatis and forspekaris in temporalle courtis pledande'.[54] In 1455, rules on the costume of those men of law who were 'forspekaris for the cost' were prescribed by parliament, but were apparently only to apply in time of parliament or general council.[55] While it would be wrong to read this legislation as evidence for a legal profession, it is clear that the practice of representation by others was common enough to require a modest degree of regulation.

Many of the cases raised by the brieves of right, novel dissasine and mortancestry which will be studied in detail in the succeeding chapters of this book involved lay pleaders, being either the parties themselves or others presumably retained for the purpose. For example, Thomas

Graham of Thornuke was 'forespekare' for Margaret Mundell in a mortancestry case in 1455, and it may have been the same Thomas Graham who made several arguments and points of law on behalf of John Blair of Adamton in his action of mortancestry just a few months earlier.[55a] Alexander Skene was his father's procurator in a brieve of right case in 1458 and again in 1460.[56] Sir Thomas Cranston and David Guthrie of Kincaldrum, both termed 'forespekares', conducted a debate on the law of warrandice in an action of mortancestry in 1465,[57] and the latter opposed the learning of David Reid with some of his own in another mortancestry dispute in 1466.[58] Guthrie is an excellent early example of the emerging class of lay legal professionals: he was justiciar south of Forth by 1471 and justiciar of 'Scotia' in 1473, as well as Lord Clerk Register from 1468 to 1473 and ex officio a member of the royal council when it acted judicially. Admittedly, Guthrie was exceptional in that he was a graduate in arts of both Cologne and Paris, but it was not for that learning that he came to hold the offices he did.[59] William Richardson and Alexander Spens represented Andrew Bisset and John Dishington in their prolonged litigation during the 1470s, which turned on a number of points about pleading and procedure in the brieve of mortancestry. Richardson acted for the king and the sheriff of Fife before the parliamentary auditors in 1479, while Spens was a parliamentary auditor in 1478.[60]

MEN OF LAW AS ROYAL OFFICERS

The important point about the examples just mentioned is that in them we can see laymen arguing legal and factual points of some complexity, as the later discussion of the brieves of right, mortancestry and novel dissasine will make clear. The same laymen, or laymen like them, constituted the secular courts of medieval Scotland, whether as members of the king's council in its judicial sessions, or as justiciars, sheriffs, baillies and barons, or as suitors. If we take the justiciars, for example, it is clear that many of these men were seen as having talents which fitted them for the work. The inference that these included knowledge of, and skill in, the law may now seem reasonable. In the fourteenth century, Robert Erskine, Archibald Douglas and William Dishington not only presided in justice ayres but were also appointed to the parliamentary committee to deal with matters touching common justice in 1370.[61] Alexander Stewart, earl of Mar, sat judicially in various cases before parliament (1430), council general (1422) and council (1424), while Robert Lauder of the Bass and Edrington, and Thomas Somerville of Carnwath, may be found sitting with him in some of these cases.[62] All were justiciars in the reign of James I. John lord Lindsay of the Byres, William lord Somerville and Laurence lord Abernethy in Rothiemay are others who were both justiciars and members of conciliar and parliamentary sederunts dealing with legal actions in the middle of the fifteenth century,[63] and Lindsay was appointed a lord of session in 1458.[64] The rather fragmented judicial records of council and parliament under James III show his justiciars (who included David Guthrie, as already mentioned) active there also.[65] The justiciars of James IV included John lord Glamis, Robert lord Lyle, John lord Drummond, Laurence lord Oliphant, Andrew lord Gray and George Gordon earl of Huntly. All held other judicial positions apart from that of justiciar, not just under James IV but also under James III. In particular, Glamis, Oliphant, Drummond and Lyle acted as auditors of causes and complaints in the parliaments of James III, while Gray was sheriff of Forfar and, under James IV, a fairly regular member of the king's council in its judicial sessions.[66] A number of justiciars became chancellor: William Sinclair earl of Orkney, Andrew lord Avandale, Colin Campbell earl of Argyll and George earl of Huntly would in consequence have been much involved in the judicial work of the king's council as well as in the legal work of the king's chapel.

Laymen can also be seen acting in the various commissions to examine the laws which were set up by parliament in the fifteenth century. Thus in 1426 'sex wise and discrete men of *ilkane of the thre estatis* [emphasis supplied] the quhilkis knawis the lawis best' were to look at various aspects of the law with a view to reform.[67] Something similar was proposed in 1473, with the commission to consist 'of ilk state . . . twa persounis of wisdome conscience and knawlege'.[68] It is unlikely that the representatives of the estates of the barons and freeholders, and of the burgesses, were of merely nominal assistance to the clergy on these committees. In 1481–2 a commission was set up to investigate the law of purpresture;[69] as well as a number of clergy, it included the earl of Argyll (a former justiciar soon to be chancellor),[70] John Drummond laird of Stobhall (later Lord Drummond and a justiciar), Robert lord Lyle (justiciar and council judge), Sir John Ross of Montgrennan (king's advocate and a regular council judge),[71] Master Richard Lawson (a regular judge and pleader before the council, and justice clerk)[72] and Alexander Foulis, the leading notary.[73] In this commission, we can see the lay professionals being set to work in their specialist field.

It is impossible, therefore, to accept Cooper's sweeping view that the laymen who presided over the later medieval Scottish courts were 'masquerading as judges and engaging casually in the discharge of judicial duties in intervals snatched from their major preoccupations as territorial magnates, or statesmen, or ecclesiastical dignitaries'.[74] We have to consider the possibility that these laymen knew a good deal of the law of Scotland and perhaps even knew something of the law of Rome and of the church, deriving that knowledge from experience as landowners, courtholders, suitors, litigants and advocates. In addition, the law might be derived from books, and it is to these books and their contents that we now turn.

What were the sources of the law practised in the courts by the men of law? In a customary system, we might expect to find it embodied primarily in an oral tradition passed on from generation to generation, perhaps with particular individuals established as the repositories of the law to whom others deferred. That this formed an element of medieval Scots law there need be no doubt. The recollection of the president of the court, the suitors and the forespeakers or procurators must have served in the place of any formal doctrine of precedent. There are virtually no private collections of decisions by any court surviving from the period before 1500 comparable to the later practicks. The only one of which I am aware is in the Bute manuscript, one of the earliest collections of legal materials now surviving. Under the heading *Ordo Justiciarie* (which was later used as the title of a another short manual narrating the jurisdiction and the procedure of the justiciar's court) are reported half a dozen cases, all apparently before the justiciar and to be dated to the fourteenth century.[75] The men of law also failed to produce anything comparable to the English Year Books, probably reflecting the generally local nature of their training and practice in matters of native law, quite distinct from the Inns of Court legal education out of which the Year Books came. While arguments from silence or near-silence are dangerous when in general we have so little evidence about the medieval legal system, it may well be that oral tradition generally sufficed in place of written records of decisions. In the fifteenth century, and probably earlier, litigants would often obtain notarial instruments recording steps in procedure or the verdicts in cases which they had brought, but this seems to have been either for the purposes of record as litigation went along so that a party's position could not be prejudiced later on, or to have the verdict put into effect. Although such instruments are often the only evidence for these cases now available to us, there is nothing to suggest that they were used by lawyers as records of precedents for later use in court; they were preserved in the litigant's muniments, usually as part of a set of titles to land or other important rights.

Where such instruments are extracts from court books, they are also evidence that court records were kept.[76] However, very little survives from before 1500, even though we know that from the thirteenth century on there were justiciary records, and our earliest remaining burgh court records date from 1317.[77] It is almost inconceivable that the sheriff courts did not keep records of some sort from the same period, for otherwise the detailed accounting which the sheriffs can be seen making in the exchequer rolls from the mid-thirteenth century on would have been impossible. The non-survival of such records is probably to be explained by their passage through various hands over time, as personnel changed.[78] It is difficult to imagine that the records would have been usable as a source of information, after a certain interval of time had passed, without indexing and cataloguing systems, which were almost certainly beyond the capacity of the bureaucracy of the courts in this period. In any event, it may have been difficult to create and maintain an archive in which records could be kept and maintained. The clerks and their assistants may therefore have been relatively indifferent to material recording acts of their courts occurring before their time, and the survival of these records was thus at best a matter of chance.

EARLY LEGAL TEXTS

The law of the Middle Ages in Scotland was not simply an oral affair, primarily dependent on unwritten customary tradition for its content and survival. Written law certainly existed, probably from the beginning of our period, and became important by at latest the thirteenth century. Our evidence for this is found in some forty manuscripts, all but one dating from the fourteenth century or later, and containing a wide range of legal texts and what purports to be legislation of kings from Malcolm MacKenneth (c. 1005–34) on.[79] The earliest such manuscript, the Berne, can be dated c. 1270; others which will be regularly referred to in the rest of this book include the Ayr and Bute manuscripts.[80] An understanding of the contents and significance of these manuscripts is beset with thorny problems, not all of which can be confronted here; but some discussion is required, both for the light which the manuscripts can throw on the development of medieval Scots law in general, and on the written law as a source for contemporaries in particular.

First, it is surprising that the manuscripts reveal no substantial body of written law in the Celtic tradition comparable to that found in Wales and Ireland, although medieval chroniclers referred to the laws made by Kenneth mac Alpin, first king of Scots 840–58,[81] and there is a late reference to the laws of 'Renald McSomharkle'[82] – presumably Ranald son of Somerled, *'dominus Innse Gall'* in the second half of the twelfth century.[83] Whatever these may have been, nothing survives in the legal collections. The so-called *Leges inter Brettos et Scotos* seem to stem from the Celtic tradition and may have been written initially in a Celtic language. Their first appearance, however, is in a French version in the late thirteenth-century Berne manuscript, while a little later a Latin version found its way into *Regiam Majestatem*.[84] It is often argued that the Celtic legal tradition was an oral, pre-literate one, even in the later Middle Ages, but the *Leges inter Brettos et Scotos* suggest an alternative hypothesis: a written tradition of Celtic law which did not survive because it was never sharply distinguished from the Anglo-Norman customs introduced in the twelfth century, and both traditions were absorbed in the developing common law. Other material which survives among the *leges Scocie* of the Berne manuscript certainly suggests that legislative activity in the twelfth and thirteenth centuries took Celtic law and institutions for granted, so to speak, and deployed it within the developing legal system rather than sweeping it aside.[85] Another example of this blending of traditions may be found in the forest laws of the twelfth and thirteenth centuries, where Gilbert has drawn 'a picture . . . of native landholders learning of and then copying the Normans' idea of a forest as a hunting reserve and of Normans adopting some native customs . . . Earlier customs not only survived in, but also influenced the hunting arrangements of, twelfth- and thirteenth-century Scotland'.[86] The contrast with Ireland and Wales, where the Celtic legal traditions were those of a conquered people denied access to the laws of their Anglo-Norman conquerors by the exceptions of Irishry and Welshry, is an important one.

Some manuscripts contain a text entitled *Leges Malcolmi Mackenneth*, which purports to be enacted by Malcolm II, who reigned from 1005 to 1034.[87] It opens with an obviously anachronistic account of how the king granted away the whole of his kingdom to his barons subject to the feudal casualties of ward and relief, reserving for himself only the moot-hill of Scone; this story is also found in Fordun's *Chronica Gentis Scottorum*, completed in 1364.[88] The body of the text deals with the fees of royal officers, who were certainly unheard of in eleventh-century Scotland. As it stands in the manuscripts, the text must have been compiled in the fourteenth century.[89] There is no evidence to show that the link with Malcolm II had any basis in fact, but it shows how later medieval lawyers liked to see their law stretching back into the remote past, fortified by its association with good and successful kings. Equally, the reputation of kings was enhanced by lawmaking; the thirteenth-century Melrose chronicler commented of Kenneth mac Alpin, unifier of Dalriada and Pictavia, that he was called the first king, not because he was [the first], but because he first established the Scottish laws which they call the laws of mac Alpin'.[90]

THE LEGISLATIVE TRADITION

Legislative activity, presumably although not certainly reflected in written texts of some sort, is evidenced in sources other than the legal manuscripts from the reign of David I, the epitome of the good and successful Scottish king. David engaged in lawmaking in relation to burghs, for a charter of his grandson William I refers to three 'assizes' of David establishing certain burghal trading monopolies.[91] John Gilbert has inferred the issue of further assizes containing new forest laws,[92] and there seems to have been another assize concerned with the process of perambulation.[93] There also survive references to David's statute (*statutum*) anent the forfeiture of teind-defaulters in Scotia.[94] The word assize seems here to imply not a simple royal edict but a pronouncement on the law made with the assent of or at an assembly of the king's barons, if the parallel English usage is anything to go by.[95] Statute is also a word of obscure meaning in the twelfth century, as we have already seen with the English *statutum decretum* on division of lands among heiresses, and the *statutum regni* on distraint, but it does seem to carry the idea of an addition to the existing law made with the king's authority, and with the support of his court.[96]

In these assizes and statutes, and in innovations in the administration of justice such as the establishment of justices (later justiciars) and sheriffs, lie the roots of the later medieval tradition associating David with lawmaking and the foundation of the law as it was subsequently known. Although lawmaking is not highlighted in contemporary accounts of David's kingship other than that of his friend Ailred of Rievaulx, the tradition was established before the end of the thirteenth century. By c. 1270, the *Leges Quatuor Burgorum* was similarly attributed expressly to David, although almost certainly the work was compiled after his reign, perhaps as late as the thirteenth century.[97] In 1305, Edward I appeared to embrace the whole of Scots law under 'the laws of David', although recognising that there had been amendments and additions by later kings;[98] probably not long afterwards, the compiler of *Regiam Majestatem* stated in the prologue that it had been composed at David's command.[99] It is unlikely that by doing so he intended to pass off the work as actually written under David; rather, it was a statement that this was a book of the good old law as it had been since the foundation of that law by the king. The failure of later, more literal-minded ages to grasp this point was to lead to centuries of debate on the 'authenticity' of *Regiam* as a source of law, both historical and formal, a matter to which we will return later in this chapter. In the fourteenth century, the tradition developed further with the grouping in the legal manuscripts of miscellaneous old laws under the heading *Assise Regis David*, although the choice of which laws should be included varied greatly from one compilation to another.[100] Fifteenth-century parliaments stated more than once that laws relating to measures and to fishing were originally statutes 'maid be king David', one being the *Assisa de Mensuris et Ponderibus* attributed to the king, the other apparently an assize included in the *APS* version of the *Assise Regis Willelmi*.[101] Later still, in a story given in some of the legal manuscripts, David became a Justinianic figure who had

> chesit out xxiiii clerkis of the wysest and mast able of all his kynrike
> and gert thaim swere apon haly relykis that thay suld passe twa and
> twa in cumpany togidder oure all the kynrikis of the crystyndome

and wryt up all the lawys of ilke land bath in burch and on land and geff tham day of twa yheris to cum again. And quhen thai come agayn thai fande the kyng at the new castell apon tyn . . . And thare he mad and stabblist all his lawys of Scotland bath in burch and on land be hale assent of al his prelatis lordis barounis burges and commouns.[102]

The tale is as improbable as that of Malcolm MacKenneth, but the tradition reflects the genuine importance of David's reign as a period of legal innovation in Scotland, recorded in writing shortly after if not during his reign, and making its way into the hands of posterity as a result.

A similar although less elaborated tradition attached itself to the name of King William, again taking its starting point from undoubted legislative activity in his reign. Much of that was in confirmation of his grandfather's assizes relating to burghs, although he may have added laws for the protection of those travelling to burgh fairs.[103] In a brieve relating to teinds, the king wills that whatever was enacted (*statuit*) in King David's days, especially with regard to the church, is to be justly maintained,[104] while another refers to William's assize of Galloway, which apparently provided for the pursuit of thieves.[105] The tradition associating William with written laws led not only to the *Assise Regis Willelmi*, another miscellaneous collection of varying content which nonetheless undoubtedly contains some genuine assizes of the king's reign, but also the *Constitutiones Regis Willelmi sive Constitutiones Portuum*, a compilation of mainly burghal material headed by William's 1209 charter to Perth.[106] This was in turn incorporated into a much larger work, the *Leges Portuum*, which has a further, as yet little explored, relationship with the later work known as the *Liber de Judicibus*.[107]

Discussing the legislation of William's son Alexander II (invariably described as statutes, as is also the case with later kings), Duncan has commented that[108]

> legal hacks of a later date persistently attributed to David I that innovatory and codifying role which belonged to Alexander II and his time . . . The idea that such *written* material was relevant to the practice of law seems to have arisen in the reign of Alexander II and to have been complementary to the king's role in reforming judicial practice by 'statute'.

Although it is true, as we shall see, that important innovation occurred by way of legislation in the reign of Alexander II, it would seem, however, to be the reign of William in which the written tradition of the later Middle Ages really begins. Nothing survives of the texts of David's undoubted assizes, although it seems more likely than not that they were promulgated in some written form; perhaps the reason is because they were re-enacted and re-embodied in William's assizes, which formed the authentic texts for the compilers of legal material at work in his reign and after. Certainly, some of William's legislative texts survived, as indeed did some of Alexander II's; they can be verified as genuine mainly through internal references but sometimes also as a result of comment in other contemporary sources.[109] This is not to lessen the importance of Alexander's reign in Scottish legal history, but simply to observe that the change to which Duncan rightly draws attention can be pushed back to William's time and has antecedents in David's. The significance of written law advances alongside the expansion in the role and forms of royal justice discussed earlier in this book.

There is a rather puzzling gap in the written tradition when we come to the reign of Alexander III, explicable perhaps in the light of the consolidatory and relatively conservative character of his reign viewed from the perspective of legal development, but nonetheless surprising given the later tendency to look back to his time as a golden age of peace and justice.[110] It is less surprising that John Balliol also made little impact on the legal tradition. With the accession of Robert I, however, we have a legislating king whose statutes, notably those enacted at Scone in 1318, found their way into lawyers' collections and were still referred to in the fifteenth century.[111] Indeed, from this time on, kings legislated regularly through parliaments and general councils, and it is possible to see the legislative tradition being built upon and reworked, particularly in the fifteenth century.[112]

Inevitably, this process left much confusion in the lawyers' collections, our main evidence for legislation before 1466, the year from which official parliamentary record survives, and the texts must be treated with caution. Even where we can be confident of the text, we must also bear in mind that statutes were open to interpretation by the men of law. In 1428, parliament uttered the classic legislator's complaint, providing that ma man interprete the statutis uthir wayis than the statut beris and to the entent and effec that thai war maid of befor ande as the makaris of thaim undirstude'.[113] Although this is the doctrine of literal interpretation in accordance with the legislative intent, more or less as it is understood today, the fact that it was necessary to make this statement may say much about the attitude of fifteenth-century practitioners to statutes.[114] Unquestionably, however, these acts were law and were an important source for the lawyers of the period. Indeed, some of those enacted in the fifteenth century have survived as law to the present day.

REGIAM MAJESTATEM

Fifteenth-century lawyers also looked on the non-legislative texts found in their collections as forming part of the law. Of these, the most important to contemporaries was the one known from its opening words as *Regiam Majestatem*. Indeed, it was so important that often the title would be given, not merely to the treatise itself, but to the entire volume of the lawyer's collection, a tradition perpetuated by the title of Sir John Skene's 1609 edition of the medieval texts. *Quoniam Attachiamenta*, also known as the *Leges Baronum*, probably had the greatest significance after *Regiam*. Yet, from the point of view of later legal historians, the value of *Regiam* as evidence of the law of medieval Scotland is uncertain. The principal reason for this is the fact that the greater part of the treatise is drawn from *Glanvill*. The significance of this has already been noted,[115] and it is reinforced by the fact that *Glanvill* was also deployed in the compilation of the *Liber de Judicibus*.[116] *Glanvill* was therefore an important text in Scotland; the problem is to elucidate why this was so.

Since about 1600, when the relationship between *Regiam* and *Glanvill* became clear once more,[117] the issue of how far the law of late twelfth-century England was also the law of medieval Scotland has been the subject of debate which has often been coloured by issues of national prejudice. Given the general lack of evidence for medieval Scots law, there has been a tendency to suspect statements in *Regiam* unless they can be independently verified from another source. Modern scholarship has dwelt on the problem of origins and date, setting aside the question of its use in practice, or even denying that it was intended for practical use at all. In the two volumes which Walker has lately devoted to medieval Scots law, extensive use is made of *Regiam* as a source for the period before 1286, consistently with his view that the treatise is a product of the reign of Alexander III, but virtually none for the period from 1286 to 1488, presumably because he believes that it was no longer relevant in practice as a source of law. The remainder of this chapter will endeavour to show that *Regiam* continued to be used as a source of current law by later medieval lawyers, who seem to have been, and probably were, either unaware of or unconcerned by the problems of the work's origins, save inasmuch as they believed it to have been promulgated by David I and so be the good old law of the land. It is therefore legitimate for the historian to use the evidence of *Regiam* in discussing the law of the period, as will be done in later chapters of this book. However, there are a number of pitfalls which must be identified and, where possible in the current state of knowledge, avoided. Fixing the date and original text of *Regiam* does not exhaust our difficulties. It is vital to realise that *Regiam* itself has a history, and that the text was not absolutely static or settled. We have to understand as much as possible about *Regiam's* development in order to be able to use it properly; and the same is true of the other treatises found in the legal manuscripts.

The important facts which seem to be established by modern research on *Regiam* are, first, a date of composition somewhere in the fourteenth century after 1318, most likely in the reign of Robert I (the *terminus ante quem* is the early fifteenth century, the date of the earliest surviving text, which is in the Bute manuscript); second, that the Romano-canonical section in Book I was derived from the *Summa in titulos decretalium* of the mid-thirteenth century canonist Goffredus da Trano, and suggests that the compiler was a canonist; and third, that the attribution of the Scottish laws which conclude Book IV is often late, unsupported by any internal evidence, and so cannot be used to date the text as a whole.[118] Alan Harding has sought to open up a new understanding of *Regiam*, taking us away from a centuries-old preoccupation with its status as a source of Scots law to a realisation that the object of the compiler may have been not to give an account of the law but to use the structure of a law book to sustain an image of the Scottish people under the jurisdiction of their king at a time when their national identity was under external threat, another pointer to the reign of Robert I.[119] Peter Stein has hinted at an official rather than a private origin;[120] in this connection, it is interesting to note the canonical origins of the phrase '*regia majestas*', and the fact that it first appears in Scotland in documents of Robert I, possibly in imitation of French usage.[121]

Our starting point is the fifteenth-century statutes which refer to *Regiam*. It can surely be taken that these show the text as authoritative at this period. In 1426, we have the well-known provision 'that sex wise and discrete men . . . the quhilkis knawis the lawis best . . . sal se and examyn the bukis of law of this realme that is to say Regiam Maiestatem and Quoniam Attachiamenta and mend the lawis that nedis mendment'.[122] It is sometimes suggested that the final words just quoted imply that neither *Regiam* nor *Quoniam* was regarded as authoritative but required amendment to make them so. It is more probable, however, that the 1426 project was similar in nature to those discussed in the reign of James III. In 1469, a commission was appointed by parliament to consider 'the reductioune of the kingis lawis, Regiam Majestatem, actis, statutis and uther bukis to be put in a volum and tobe autorizit and the laif to be distroyit'.[123] Four years later, parliament was again considering 'the mending of the lawis, for the declaracioun of divers obscure materis that ar now in our lawis and that daily occurs'. The king was requested to appoint a commission of two people on the matter, 'for the cleirnes of the said materis to be had'. Two points were of concern: first, 'the daily materis . . . that as yit thare is na law for the decisioune of thame'; second, and more interesting for present purposes, 'the gret diversite now fundin in divers bukis put in be divers persounis that ar callit men of law'. The solution to this second problem was that 'thar be a buke maid contenand al the lawis of this realme that sail remain at a place quhare the lafe may have copy and nane uther bukis be usit.[124]

This is the most explicit statement of the essential problem with any legal text in a manuscript tradition – the sheer variety and inconsistency of the texts, and the consequent lack of certainty which might result. Such inconsistency might arise for any number of reasons, some of which were nicely summarised by T. F. T. Plucknett:[125]

> Sometimes an obscurely written word in the original has been variously misunderstood by long successions of copyists. More often (and this is essentially so in a long and laborious task) the copyist works mechanically, heedless of the sense of his text – which indeed he may not comprehend . . . Sometimes a scribe is too ambitious and may introduce 'corrections' into a text which is actually quite accurate – if only he had understood it. More often he is tricked by his eyesight. Thus it is extremely common for the same word (especially in a technical work) to occur twice in close proximity. The scribe will copy a phrase ending with the first occurrence of the word, and at the next glance at his exemplar he will continue copying from the second occurrence of the word, thus omitting the intervening passage. In the sesquipedalian jargon of the textual critics this is familiarly known as homoeotelenton, which is deemed to be a special case of haplography.

Deliberate change by the copyist in an effort to bring material up to date can also be detected. Gilbert has found instances of such updating in the manuscripts of the *Leges Forestarum*, while David Fergus has observed evidence of deliberate change in the development of *Quoniam Attachiamenta*, although this cannot be decisively linked to the act of 1426 requiring its examination and amendment.[126] It is in this sense that the act's 'mendment' should be understood, nevertheless, as a process to reinforce the existing authority of *Regiam* and other works by a process of updating and harmonisation, rather than to give them the status of a source for the first time.

An illustration of official updating may be by the commission which in 1481 investigated the 'under and mysty' law of purpresture.[127] *Regiam* is indeed uncertain on the point at issue. An early chapter states that the brieve or plea of purpresture pertains to the justiciar's court.[128] A later chapter confirms the justiciar's jurisdiction where the purpresture is against the king, but adds that there may be purpresture against other lords, which they may deal with in their own courts.[129] The question for parliament in 1481 was whether any lord with less than baronial jurisdiction had the right to deal with purpresture. The conclusion of the commission, reported to parliament in 1482, was that only barons had this power.[130] But clearly *Regiam*, drawing as it was on the simple terminology of twelfth-century English lordship found in *Glanvill*, was inadequate for the relative complexities of late medieval Scottish tenures and jurisdictions.[131]

Regiam was also a starting point for reform. The clearest examples of this are to be found in the reign of James III. In 1471, parliament passed a statute permitting reduction of the retours of inquests on the grounds of 'partial malice or ignorance'. This was already provided for in *Regiam*, but the precise procedure to be followed was not clear. The act spelt out a remedy before the king's council, but stated that the false assize was 'to be punyst eftir the forme of the kingis lawis in the first buk of his maieste contra temere jurantes super assisam'.[132] Four years later, parliament was extending these provisions to criminal assizes, with the punishment again to be 'efter the forme of the auld law contenit in the buk of Regiam Maiestatem'.[133] Finally, in 1487, a lengthy statute against 'trespassouris' concluded with the provision that those convicted should be 'punist efter the forme of the kingis lawis and of Regiam Maiestatem and the statutis maid be king James the first and king James the secund'.[134]

There are a number of other aspects to the history of *Regiam* which have scarcely been touched upon in modern discussions. There is for example the issue of its structure. All the printed versions since Skene's edition divide the work into four books, and it has been suggested that this may be the result of the influence, 'direct or indirect', of Justinian's *Institutes.*[135] However, the story cannot be a simple one. The evidence of the manuscripts shows that, like the versions of *Glanvill* from which it was probably copied, early versions of *Regiam* were not divided into books at all, while in the fifteenth century it was commonly divided into three books rather than four.[136] The four-book tradition ran alongside this one, however, first appearing in the early Bute and Cromertie manuscripts, albeit with a capitulation which was continuous from beginning to end. This structure is found in some later fifteenth-century manuscripts before apparently becoming the dominant pattern in the sixteenth century.[137] The picture is therefore complex and, while Justinianic influence cannot be ruled out – it is apparent for example in the way in which the words with which the treatise begins meld *Glanvill's 'regiam potestatem'* with the *Institutes' 'imperatoriam majestatem'* – the question of when first and from what source does not yield to easy answers.

Another important event in the history of the treatise was its translation from Latin into Scots, seemingly carried out in the fifteenth century. The earliest manuscript with a Scots text of *Regiam*, the Auchinleck manuscript, has been dated to around 1455.[138] The development of Scots as a language of the law has not yet received the attention which it deserves, although David Sellar has pointed out the earliest recorded use of the vernacular in legal proceedings before parliament in 1390, and the gradual shift of legislative language from Latin to Scots, completed at the beginning of the active reign of James I, has been noted by various others.[139] Lyall has lately drawn attention to early fifteenth-century

translations into Scots of the *Leges Burgorum* and the *Laws of Oleron* in
the Bute manuscript, as well as the increasing use of the vernacular for
charters and other legal documents from the last quarter of the fourteenth
century.[140] Gilbert and Fergus have also discussed the Scots translations
of, respectively, the *Leges Forestarum* and *Quoniam Attachiamenta*,[141] while
the recently-published gild court book of Dunfermline contains a
vernacular version, seemingly written down in the first half of the fifteenth
century, of some chapters of the thirteenth-century *Statuta Glide*.[142] The
translation *of Regiam* is obviously part of this story of developing legal
writing in the vernacular, reflecting the language of the courts and daily
business. As we have it in the Auchinleck manuscript, the translation
seems to stem from the tradition of some 190 chapters numbered
consecutively, although it is also divided into four books.[143]

The translation of *Regiam* into the language of daily life suggests some
practical purpose for the work. This is supported by the evidence we have
showing the manuscripts passing from hand to hand in the fifteenth
century.[144] The books were bought – not to say written – for use. A little
earlier, towards the end of the fourteenth century, there is evidence that
a copy of at least some of the written law of Scotland was in private hands.
The testaments of James Douglas of Dalkeith, drawn up in 1390 and
1392, both bequeath 'all my books, both of the statutes of the Scots realm
and of romances' to his eldest son, also James.[145] Douglas was, as we shall
see later on, a regular litigant throughout his career, and it is tempting to
suppose that this copy of the Scots statutes had been put to frequent
practical use. Its importance to him is certainly suggested by the fact that
he chose to leave the book to his heir. The statutes may well have included
Regiam Majestatem, so often portrayed in the later Middle Ages as an act
of King David, as well as, perhaps, versions of the *Assise Regis David*, the
Assise Regis Willelmi and other acts attributed to later Scottish kings.

Although Cooper was unable to identify any use of *Regiam* in court
earlier than 1501,[146] there are in fact several references to it of fifteenth-
century date, showing the work and others being cited to and indeed
apparently followed by the Scottish courts. The sources in which these
references are found are of two types. First there is the notarial instrument, drawn up at the request of one or other party to a litigation,
recording some procedural step or decision taken by the court in question. Some of these instruments give us a relatively full picture, going
beyond the formalities to describe what was said for the parties before the
court determined its course of action; it is in these kinds of document that
we find mention *of Regiam*. A less well-known type of document is what
appears to be a pleader's *aide-mémoire*, seemingly informal notes of pleas
to be presented to the court by or on behalf of one of the parties to the
litigation. These documents lack any formalities of execution or address,

and for that reason probably do not represent early samples of written pleading but were instead drawn up to assist the pleader in his oral presentation to the court. Certainly they cite authority for the propositions stated, and among these authorities *Regiam* finds a place.

An example of this type of document, dating from March 1473, relates to the great dispute at this time over the succession to the earldom of Lennox, in which two of the claimants were John Stewart lord Darnley and John Haldane of Gleneagles. They were in dispute before the king's council, and the document states the pleas for Darnley. Several points are made, for one of which *Regiam* is cited as follows:[147]

> Item, quhair it is allegit be the said Johne of Haldane that he was enterit in the said erldome be gift of the Kingis Hienes, and, be that titill, was in possessioun of the sammyne, it may be weile understandin that, sen it is perfitly knawin that thir landis war into the kingis handis be resoun of warde, sen the deide of Erle Duncan that deid last possessour of the said erldome, thair mycht na persoune haiff possessioune of thir landys be gyft of the kingis heenes, be thir causys, so quhen the said Erle Duncan dissesyt, the rycht se deit with hym, and the keping of the landys, with the ayr of the sammyne, came into the kingis handis, as superior and cheyff lord; and thair may na superior clath, seys, na possess na persoune of the landys cummyne in thair handys be deid of thair tenandis, for thai ar callit custos terrarum; and heyrto concordis the kingis lawis in libro 2° Regie Maiestatis, capitulo xxxi°, de heredibus maioribus quid facere debent post mortem antecessorum suorum licet enim domini possunt faciant.[148] Alsua it is writtin into the sammyne buk, capitulo xxxiiii°, quam potestatem habent domini in heredibus hominum suorum et in eodem habetur nichill tamen de hereditate alienare possunt ad remanentiam.[149] And the sammyn effec is said, capitulo xxxvii°, ad quod tenentur custodes heredum: restituere tenentur et custodes heredum ipsis heredibus hereditates instau-ratas.[150] And sua thair may na thing cum betwene the deid of the antecessour and the entre of the ayr that may stop the ayr of his entre: heyrfor the pretendit gift maide to Johne of Haldane had na strenth, na yit thair mycht na sesyng na possessioune folow thairupone; ergo, the respet is nocht hurt.

There is incidentally a tantalisingly close relationship between the citations of chapter numbers given in this document and the chapter references in a manuscript of c. 1439 now preserved in the National Library of Scotland, with only one minor variation. It seems probable that a text of *Regiam* closely related to the 1439 version was being used by the pleader in this case.[151]

Another example of this kind of document, which has been lying unpublished in the Montrose burgh archive, has been noted by Alan Borthwick in his recent doctoral thesis. This appears to be a set of instructions drawn up by the burgh for its forespeaker David Reid in a case before the chamberlain ayre in 1448. Reid, whom we noted earlier in this chapter, was, among other things, to rely on certain propositions 'as the king's statutes bear witness in the book of the king's majesty'. As Borthwick points out, the text in question is found not in what we now call *Regiam Majestatem*, but among the acts of David II.[152] The reference bears out the point already made that in the medieval period the title *Regiam Majestatem* could refer not just to the particular text but to all the matter commonly found within a single manuscript.

An example of the notarial instrument recording an argument in court may be found among the documents relating to a dispute between the Cawdor family and the Campbell earl of Argyll at the very end of the fifteenth century.[153] The dispute arose as the unintended result of manoeuvrings by William, thane of Cawdor, to divert his estate away from his heir, also William, to his second son John. The thane granted the fee of his properties to John, who predeceased his father, leaving only two baby girls to succeed him. The Crown took the girls into feudal wardship; when the elder, Janet, died, wardship of the survivor, Muriel, was granted to Archibald, earl of Argyll. As Muriel's tutor-dative, Argyll raised a brieve of inquest in Inverness sheriff court, seeking service to the lands of Cawdor. The brieve was addressed to one John Stirling as sheriff *in hac parte* and opposed by the thane and his son Andrew. Their *prelocutor* was John Calder, precentor of Ross, who challenged Stirling as a suspect judge and supported his case with a citation of '*libro tercio Regie Maiestatis*'. The instrument then purports to quote a passage to the effect that the *judex delegatus* cannot act unless *the judex ordinarius* (here the sheriff principal of Inverness) has refused to act or there is just cause. I have not been able to trace this passage in any of the printed versions of *Regiam* or other old laws, although that is not to say that there is no such passage in any tradition of *Regiam*. In any event, the court held against the argument; in due course, Muriel was married to a Campbell and the Cawdor lands became part of that family's heritage.

The most interesting examples of the use of *Regiam* and *Quoniam* in a fifteenth-century litigation are in a great case between Gilbert lord Kennedy and Robert lord Fleming in the 1460s. The details of this case are discussed elsewhere in this work;[154] for present purposes, it suffices to say that Kennedy was suing Fleming by brieve of mortancestry for certain lands in the barony of Kirkintilloch. The case ran through various procedural stages between 1462 and 1466, culminating in pleas before the justiciary court at Dumbarton in autumn 1465 and spring 1466. An undated memorandum survives recording, in its own words, 'the resonys that Robert Flemyng allegis quhi the landis of Kirkintilloch quhilkis quhilum pertenyt to Johne Kenedy knycht ar eschete to him as fee and heretage and at Gilbert Kenedy may nocht succede to the landis be any law of Scotland or be law canon or civile'.[155] The first of these reasons is given as follows:

> A reson is be law of Scotland quhat man that is convicit of felony or grantis in jugement felony and speciale that is hurtyng to the kingis maieste he forfatis al his gudis movabil and immovabil as the law in the buk of Regiam Maiestatem Rubrica de convicto de felonia Notandum quod si quis de felonia intelligatur convictus vel confessus in curia, Si de domino Rege in capite tenuerit, omnes res suis mobiles domini Regis sunt terra vero per annum in manus domini regis remanebit elapso quoque anno terra ad dominum de cuius feodo est revertetur.[156]

There are other notarial instruments in the Fleming of Wigtown papers which record arguments advanced in court in 1465 by Fleming's forespeaker, David Reid, identifiable with the David Reid already mentioned who acted for Montrose in 1448.[157] Although the record of his arguments on Fleming's behalf does not mention citation *of Regiam*, there is a virtual quotation from a well-known passage in the text comparing the brieves of novel dissasine and mortancestry as respectively brieves of possession and property, and saying that the former touches only freehold (*liberum tenementum*) while the latter touches fee and freehold.[158] These principles are then used to mount a technical attack on the lawfulness of the summons by which Fleming was called to defend the action of Kennedy.

Regiam was not used only in Fleming's interest. Kennedy too had a forespeaker in David Guthrie, another already identified as an early lay lawyer.[159] In the pleading at Dumbarton in April 1466, he referred the court to two passages in *Regiam*. No specific references are given in the notarial instrument recording his argument; there are simply quotations *'prout declaratur in libro Regie Maiestatis'* and a reference to *'alio capitulo iuxta finem'*.[160] The two points made are, first, that Fleming had agreed to the case proceeding in an indenture displayed to the court and so, following what is Book I chapter 11 of the *APS Regiam*, the brieve should proceed to an assize without delay; second, following Book IV chapter 51, which is indeed near the end of the work, that Fleming's absence from court should not stop the assize. All this is recorded in a notarial instrument drawn up by Alexander Foulis, who in 1454 had compiled a manuscript collection of laws containing both a *Quoniam* and a *Regiam* in the three-part tradition of the text, with the first two parts being capitulated continuously, and the third part containing a new series of chapter numbers.[161] Was this text in court at Dumbarton in April 1466? Another interesting feature of the pleading in this case is that both parties also referred to material other than *Regiam*. Guthrie cited what the instrument calls *Attachiamentis*, that is, *Quoniam Attachiamenta*, as further authority for the propositions just mentioned. As already noted, Reid's pleadings for Fleming drew the attention of the court to a constitution of Marcus Aurelius to be found in Justinian's *Codex*, as well as to a statute of James I. Elsewhere we can find fifteenth-century and earlier evidence of the citation of the *Leges Burgorum*.[162]

It seems clear, therefore, that pleaders of the period did have recourse to the material in the manuscripts, and that it was of unquestioned authority in the courts. So when in 1456 a body of eight judges made reference to 'the books of the law' in reducing proceedings in Aberdeen sheriff court on a brieve of right, we can take it that these books included *Regiam* and *Quoniam*, with perhaps others besides.[163] With the exception of the Cawdor case, it is possible to identify the passages in *Regiam* and other works which are cited in the references just discussed. It is striking that where, as in the Lennox case, there is mention of specific chapter numbers, not only can these not be squared with any of the printed editions, but there also appears to be no exact manuscript equivalent either. This brings us up against the problem of citation within a tradition of discordant manuscripts, and the importance of rubrics as identifiers. In the manuscripts, the chapter headings are given special prominence by being written in larger characters and sometimes in different-coloured or bolder ink. In the cases, it seems, these rubrics were used for citation purposes. Once again, the practical use of these texts is evident; ready reference was facilitated by these techniques.

Some brief conclusions may now be offered. The simple point is that *Regiam Majestatem* and many of the other works found in the legal manuscripts were used as works of authority in fifteenth-century Scottish legal practice. The evidence does not suggest critical use, for example, distinguishing between Glanvillian and non-Glanvillian sections. All of *Regiam* possessed authority, at least potentially. The difficulties lay rather in achieving consensus on the text and in interpreting its meaning; difficulties which it is also necessary to face today by working with the manuscripts themselves, in the absence of satisfactorily critical editions of many of the texts. We are not therefore absolutely free to use the evidence of *Regiam* and the other works as a source for the laws of Scotland up to 1500 and beyond; the manuscripts require analysis, and then other evidence must be used to buttress conclusions suggested by the texts thus considered. Nevertheless, it is certain that the texts, and in particular *Regiamy* are of the first importance in the study of the later medieval law.

NOTES

1. *APS*, ii, p. 105 (c. 14).
2. T. M. Cooper, *Papers*, p. 226.
3. Note, however the comments in T. M. Cooper, *Papers*, pp. 231–2.
4. See *APS*, ii, p. 3 (c. 5) in the light of *APS*, ii, p. 16 (c. 10); also *APS*, ii, pp. 51 (c. 29), 176 (c. 3) and 177 (c. 9).
5. J. M. Wormald, *Lords and Men*, pp. 68–9.
6. NLS, *Fleming of Wigtown papers*, Ch. 15,566.
7. *Family of Rose*, p. 155.
8. J. Durkan, 'The early Scottish notary', in *The Renaissance and Reformation in Scotland*, ed. I. B. Cowan and D. Shaw (Edinburgh, 1983), pp. 22–40.
9. R. J. Lyall, 'Books and-book owners in fifteenth-century Scotland', in *Book Production and Publishing in Britain 1375–1475*, ed. J. Griffiths and D. Pearsall (Cambridge, 1989), p. 239.
10. See *APS*, i, pp. 186–7, 192. The Foulis MS is NLS, Adv MS 25.4.10. See further, on Foulis, H. L. MacQueen and A. R. Borthwick, 'Cases', pp. 150–1, and above, pp. 83, 97.
11. G Donaldson, 'The legal profession in Scottish society in the sixteenth and seventeenth centuries', *JR*, xxi (1976), pp. 2–3.
12. SRO, *Ailsa muniments*, GD 25/1/102.
13. M. T. Clanchy, *From Memory to Written Record: England 1066–1301* (London, 1979), p. 221.
14. *Leges Henrici Primi*, p. 156 (46, 6).
15. S. F. C. Milsom, *HFCL*, p. 40; see also P & M, i, pp. 211–12.
16. P & M, i, pp. 212–14; P. A. Brand, *The Origins of the English Legal Profession* (Oxford, 1992), pp. 43–9.
17. See e.g. *Arb Lib*, i, no 294 (1253) (T. M. Cooper, *Cases*, p. 1).
18. See H. L. MacQueen, 'Pleadable brieves, pleading and the development of Scots law', *LHR*, iv (1986), p. 403.
19. *APS*, i, p. 505.
20. T. M. Cooper, *Papers*, p. 232; G. Donaldson, 'Legal profession', pp. 7–8.
21. *Chron Lanercost*, p. 124.
22. P. G. Stein, 'Roman law', pp. 22–8, 31–45; G. W. S. Barrow, *Kingdom*, pp. 135–6, note; D. E. R. Watt, 'Scottish university men in the thirteenth and fourteenth centuries', *Scotland and Europe 1200–1850*, ed. T. C. Smout (Edinburgh, 1986), pp. 7–9; S. D. Ollivant, *Official*, pp. 51, 60–2. See also the later medieval example of Bishop Elphinstone, discussed in L. J. Macfarlane, *Elphinstone*, pp. 53–122.
23. *Dunf Reg*, no 352.
24. W. Fraser, *Southesk*, ii, no 36.
25. A. Fraser (ed.), *Frasers of Philorth*, ii, appendix, no 12.
26. *Lind Ch*, no 149; *Abdn Reg*, i, pp. 143–55; and see above, p. 53.
27. *Mort Reg*, ii, nos 193 and 196.
28. NLS, *Fleming of Wigtown papers*, Ch. 16,632. See also Justinian's Code (C.9.8.6.2).
29. *APS*, ii, pp. 37 (c. 18) and 95 (c. 4).
30. *APS*, ii, p. 8 (c. 24).
31. See J. A. Brundage, 'Legal aid for the poor and the professionalization

of law in the Middle Ages', *JLH*, ix (1988), p. 169; also C. N. Stoddart, 'A short history of legal aid in Scotland', *JR*, xxiv (1979), p. 170; and Brand, *English Legal Profession*, pp. 104, 154.

32. H. M. Cam, 'An East Anglian shire-moot of Stephen's reign', *EHR*, xxxix (1924), p. 570.

33. For suit in medieval English county courts, see R. C. Palmer, *County Courts*, pp. 56–88.

34. For 'professional' suitors and assizers, see *Fife Ct Bk*, App. E; I. D. Willock, *Jury*, pp. 90–6. Cf. the 'judges' among the suitors in English county courts discussed in R. C. Palmer, *County Courts*, pp. 59–76.

35. *RSS*, i, no 1564, commented upon in J. Bannerman, 'The Scots language and the kin-based society', in *Gaelic and Scots in Harmony: Proceedings of the Second International Conference on the Languages of Scotland*, ed. D. S. Thomson (Glasgow, 1990), p. 13.

36. *APS*, ii, p. 238 (c. 3).

37. Note however the tentative suggestion in J. J. Robertson, *'De Composicione Cartarum'*, *Stair Misc I*, p. 82, that there was university teaching in secular law in Scotland.

38. It may be worth noting that lawyers generally still place greater value on practical as against academic training in the law.

39. *Family of Rose*, p. 66. The comment is by Mr Hew Rose, minister of Nairn, who in 1683–4 wrote a MS history of the family of Rose of Kilravock, based on documents not all of which still survive.

40. T. M. Cooper, *Papers*, pp. 231–2; G. Donaldson, 'Legal profession', p. 7; A. L. Brown, 'The Scottish "establishment" in the later fifteenth century', *JR*, xxiii (1978), pp. 103–4; H. L. MacQueen and A. R. Borthwick, 'Cases', pp. 149–51.

41. P. A. Brand, 'The origins of the English legal profession', *LHR*, v (1987), p. 35; also idem, *English Legal Profession*, pp. vii–viii.

42. *Reg Brieves*, pp. 35–6, 53; *Form E*, pp. 47–8. Cf. P & M, i, p. 213. It is worthy of note that in the Ayr and Bute registers (but not in *Form E*) the brieves *de attornato* appear at the beginning, which may be indicative of the interests of the original compilers.

43. *Dunf Reg*, no 352; *Arb Lib*, i, no 347. See also *Arb Lib*, i, no 294 for a layman appearing for his wife as *'attornatus coram justitiario constitutus'* in 1253.

44. *Abdn Recs*, pp. 1, 8, 10, 11–12, 14.

45. *APS*, i, p. 505.

46. *RRS*, vi, no 139.

47. *Panm Reg*, ii, p. 175.

48. *APS*, i, p. 504.

49. *RMS*, i, no 456; *HMC*, v, p. 611.

50. *APS*, i, pp. 505–6.

51. For Chalmer's career, see *RMS*, i, no 295; *Moray Reg*, no 159 and p. 210.

52. *Abdn Reg*, i, p. 145. Further on Chalmer, see E. L. Ewan, *Townlife in Fourteenth-Century Scotland* (Edinburgh, 1990), index refs *sub nom* Chalmer, William, and A. A. M. Duncan 'The Laws of Malcolm MacKenneth', p. 269.

53. *Chron Bower*, viii, p. 40.

54. *APS*, ii, pp. 9 (c. 9), 19 (c. 16). On the oath of calumny, see D. Baird Smith, 'A note on *juramentum calumniae*', *JR*, li (1939), p. 7, and M. P. Clancy, 'A further note on *juramentum calumniae*', *JR*, xxxi (1986), p. 170.

55. *APS*, ii, p. 43 (c. 12).

55a. H. L. MacQueen and A. R. Borthwick, 'Cases', pp. 127–36; R. C. Reid, 'Coschogill writ', p. 132.

56. *APS*, xii, p. 25, no 46; *AB Coll*, p. 284

57. H. L. MacQueen and A. R. Borthwick, 'Cases', pp. 136–7.

58. *SRO, Ailsa muniments*, GD 25/1/102.

59. H. L. MacQueen and A. R. Borthwick, 'Cases', p. 149. See also A. R. Borthwick, 'Thesis', pp. 293–5, for Guthrie's father Alexander as 'a man of legal skills'.

60. *ADA*, pp. 71, 72 (Richardson); ibid., p. 23 (Spens).

61. *APS*, i,p. 508.

62. See *Pais Reg*, p. 70; W. Fraser, *Carlaverock*, ii, no 31; and *RMS*, ii, no 146 (*APS*, ii p. 28, no 6) for the relevant sederunts. On Somerville, see further H. L. MacQueen and A. R Borthwick, 'Cases', p. 150, and A. R. Borthwick, 'Thesis', p. 44.

63. *AB Ill*, iv, pp. 205–13; W. Fraser, *Grant*, iii, pp. 259–60; W. Fraser, *Pollok*, i, no 35; *Scone Lib*, no 213 (*APS*, xii, p. 22, no 4). On William lord Somerville, see A. R. Borthwick, 'Thesis', p. 296.

64. *APS*, ii, p. 47.

65. For the auditors and council judges under James III, see T. M. Chalmers, 'Thesis', pp. 170–83, 235–50; L. J. Macfarlane, *Elphinstone*, pp. 98–9.

66. See, for all those named, A. L. Brown, 'Scottish "establishment"', pp. 100–1; T. M. Chalmers, 'Thesis', pp. 172, 180–5, 265–6, 459, 462; L. J. Macfarlane, *Elphinstone*, pp. 112, 116, 174–6, 421–2. For Gray as sheriff of Forfar, see *RMS*, ii, nos 1806, 2257; *ER*, xi, p. 330*.

67. *APS*, ii, p. 10 (c. 10).

68. *APS*, ii, p. 105 (c. 14).

69. *APS*, ii, pp. 133, 141.

70. T. M. Chalmers, 'Thesis', pp. 247–8.

71. A. L. Brown, 'Scottish "establishment"', p. 99; N. A. T. MacDougall, *James III*, p. 300; T. M. Chalmers, 'Thesis', pp. 172–3, 187, 237, 245; L. J. Macfarlane, *Elphinstone*, pp. 99, 174, 422.

72. A. L. Brown, 'Scottish "establishment"', pp. 103–4, and T. M. Chalmers, 'Thesis', pp. 173–4, 237, 239, 245–6. See also R. K. Hannay, *College of Justice*, p. 313.

73. H. L. MacQueen and A. R. Borthwick, 'Cases', pp. 150–1.

74. T. M. Cooper, *Papers*, p. 227.

75. NLS, MS 21,246, f. 123. The reports are scattered through the *Fragmenta Collecta* of *APS*, i. This *Ordo* is discussed in A. A. M. Duncan, 'The Laws of Malcolm MacKenneth', pp. 260–1, 271–3. For the later *Ordo*, see *APS*, i, pp. 705–8.

76. See e.g. W. Fraser, *Melville*, iii, no 41 (sheriff court book of Forfar, 1452); *Laing Chrs*, no 179 (sheriff court book of Berwick, 1480).

77. For references to the rolls of the justiciary from the mid-thirteenth century on, see G. W. S. Barrow, *Kingdom*, p. 99, and *ND*, no 326; for burgh court records, see I. Flett and J. Cripps, 'Documentary

sources', *The Scottish Medieval Town*, ed. M. Lynch et al. (Edinburgh, 1988), pp. 24–8.

78. Cf. the rolls (admittedly not full records) kept by the English county courts from not long after 1200: R. C. Palmer, *County Courts*, pp. 38–40, 153.

79. See generally *APS*, i, pp. 177–210. Many other MSS have since been discovered; see for an up-to-date picture *QA (Fergus)*, pp. 11–15.

80. The Berne and Ayr MSS are preserved in the SRO, call nos PA 5/1 and PA 5/2 respectively. For the Bute MS, see note 75 above.

81. A. O. Anderson, *Early Sources*, i, p. 270; *Chron Melrose*, p. 224; *Chron Fordun*, i, p. 151; *Chron Wyntoun (Laing)*, ii, p. 84; *Chron Bower*, ii, p. 294.

82. *Monro's Western Isles of Scotland*, ed. R. W. Munro (Edinburgh, 1961), p. 57.

83. See *Acts of the Lords of the Isles*, p. 280.

84. For the *Leges* texts, see *APS*, i, pp. 663–5. See further A. A. M. Duncan, 'Regiam', p. 204; H. L. MacQueen, 'Alexander III', pp. 90–4; 'Laws of Galloway', pp. 135–6.

85. H. L. MacQueen, 'Alexander III', pp. 88–95.

86. J. M. Gilbert, *Hunting*, pp. 24–6.

87. *APS*, i, p. 709.

88. *Chron Fordun*, iv, c. 43. See further *Chron Bower*, ii, pp. 414–17, and editorial note on p. 501.

89. See A. A. M. Duncan, 'The Laws of Malcolm MacKenneth', pp. 241–4.

90. A. O. Anderson, *Early Sources*, i, p. 270.

91. *RRS*, ii, no 475.

92. J. M. Gilbert, *Hunting*, pp. 243–4.

93. See *Arb Lib*, i, no 229; *APS*, i, p. 91; T. M. Cooper, *Cases*, pp. 21–2; a reference of 1227 commented on by *APS*, i, p. 53; I. D. Willock, *Jury*, p. 12; and G. W. S. Barrow, *Kingdom*, p. 73 and note.

94. *RRS*, ii, nos 71, 281. The *statutum* is apparently extended south of the Forth, to Loquhariot, Midlothian, in the time of William I: see *RRS*, ii, no 124.

95. H. G. Richardson and G. O. Sayles, *Law and Legislation from Ethelbert to Magna Carta* (Edinburgh, 1966), pp. 101–4; W. L. Warren, *Governance*, p. 108.

96. See above, p. 12; further H. G. Richardson and G. O. Sayles, *Law and Legislation*, pp. 34–5, and the same authors' *The English Parliament in the Middle Ages* (London, 1981), xxv, pp. 1–3.

97. H. L. MacQueen and W. J. Windram, 'Burghs', pp. 209–11.

98. E. L. G. Stones, *Relations*, p. 125; *APS*, i, p. 122.

99. *RM (APS)*, Prologus; *RM (Cooper)*, Prologue.

100. See *APS*, i, pp. 315–25, but note also the description of the manuscripts and the Table of Authorities, ibid., pp. 177–265.

101. *APS*, ii, pp. 12 (c. 22), 119 (c. 6), 221 (c. 16). For the assizes, see *APS*, i, pp. 374 (c. 10), 673. Note also the attribution to David of the *Assisa de Tolloneis*, and the *Assise Panis Vini et Cervisie* (*APS*, i, pp. 667, 675). The fifteenth-century legislation seems also to take account of an act of 1318 apparently amending the Davidian material (*RRS*, v, p. 409 (c. 11); *APS*, i, p. 469 (c. 11)).

102. *APS*, i, p. 194, note.
103. For William's assizes in relation to burghs, see *RRS*, ii, nos 442 and 475.
104. *RRS*, ii, no 124.
105. *RRS*, ii, no 406. For comment, see H. L. MacQueen, 'Laws of Galloway', p. 135.
106. See A. A. M. Duncan, *Kingdom*, pp. 185–6, 200–3; P. G. Stein, 'Roman law', pp. 10–11; H. L. MacQueen and W. J. Windram, 'Burghs', p. 211.
107. P. G. Stein, 'Roman law', pp. 13–14; W. J. Windram, 'What is the *Liber de Judicibus?*', *JLH*, v (1984), p. 176.
108. A. A. M. Duncan, *Kingdom*, p. 541.
109. Ibid., pp. 185, 200–3, 539–41; H. L. MacQueen, 'Alexander III', p. 87.
110. H. L. MacQueen, 'Alexander III', pp. 74–6.
111. See p. 111 for references to King Robert's statutes in the fourteenth century; also *SHR*, xxix (1950), pp. 3 and 5 for reference to 'Robert the Browsys statutis', and 'the statut of king Davy' (i.e. David II).
112. See, for discussion, I. E. O'Brien, 'Thesis', ch. 1; also A. A. M. Duncan, *James I King of Scots 1424–1437*, 2nd ed. (University of Glasgow Scottish History Occasional Paper, 1984) pp. 1–3. See for examples the weights and measures statutes cited above, note 101, and the statutes on 'coming to court in quiet and sober manner', discussed above, p. 75.
113. *APS*, ii, p. 16 (c. 11).
114. The statute may even be countering a view that statutes should be interpreted consistently with the *ius commune:* see O. F. Robinson et al., *IELH*, pp. 116–18. For further discussion of the later medieval and early modern theories of the relevance of legislative intent in statutory interpretation, ultimately derived from Roman law, see I. Maclean, *Interpretation and Meaning in the Renaissance: the context of law* (Cambridge, 1992), pp. 142–58.
115. See above, pp. 5, 75.
116. W. J. Windram, '*Liber*', p. 177.
117. See H. L. MacQueen, '*Glanvill* resarcinate: Sir John Skene and *Regiam Majestatem*', in A. A. Macdonald *et al.* (eds), *The Renaissance in Scotland* (Leiden, 1994).
118. For these propositions, see A. A. M. Duncan, '*Regiam Majestatem*', passim; P. G. Stein, 'The source of the Romano-canonical part of *Regiam Majestatem*', *SHR*, xlviii (1969), p. 107.
119. A. Harding, '*Regiam Majestatem* amongst medieval law books', *JR*, xxix (1984), p. 97.
120. P. G. Stein, 'Roman law', p. 21; 'Romano-canonical part', p. 112.
121. See *RM (Cooper)*, p. 58; *Reg Brieves*, p. 39 (no 17); *RRS*, v, pp. 76–7 and 282; ibid., nos 13, 66, 140, 416, 559, 566. See also for *regia majestas* in the reign of David II, *Moray Reg*, no 153.
122. *APS*, ii, p. 10 (c. 10).
123. *APS*, ii, p. 97 (c. 19).
124. *APS*, ii, p. 105 (c. 14).
125. *Early English Legal Literature* (Cambridge, 1958), p. 54.
126. J. M. Gilbert, *Hunting*, p. 245; *QA (Fergus)*, pp. 97–9, 111 note.
127. *APS*, ii, p. 133.
128. *RM (APS)*, I, 4; *RM (Cooper)*, I, 5.

129. *RM* (*APS*), II, 68; *RM* (*Cooper*), II, 74.
130. *APS*, ii,p. 141.
131. See further on purpresture below, pp. 118–20.
132. *APS*, ii, p. 100 (c. 9). See *RM* (*APS*), I, 13; *RM* (*Cooper*), I, 14.
133. *APS*, ii, p. 111 (c. 4).
134. *APS*, ii, p. 176 (c. 3).
135. P. G. Stein 'Roman law', p. 15; A. Watson, *Legal Transplants*, p. 31. Cf. A. Harding, '*Regiam*', p. 105.
136. For this, see *APS*, i, pp. 185, 186, 187, 191, 194 and 198–9.
137. See *APS*, i, pp. 185, 193, 195, 196, 200, 203, 204, 205.
138. NLS, Adv MS 25.4.15, described in *APS*, i, 188.
139. W. D. H. Sellar, 'Courtesy', p. 9; A. A. M. Duncan, *James I*, p. 2.
140. R. J. Lyall, 'Vernacular prose before the Reformation', in *The History of Scottish Literature: Origins to 1660*, ed. R. D. S. Jack (Aberdeen, 1988), pp. 164–5. The translations are in the Bute MS: see *APS*, i, p. 183. Professor Stein thinks it possible that the Scots version of the *Leges Burgorum* preceded the Latin one ('Roman law', p. 9), but with respect this seems an untenable point of view.
141. J. M. Gilbert, *Hunting*, pp. 279–90; *QA* (*Fergus*), pp. 38–9.
142. *The Gild Court Book of Dunfermline 1433–1597*, ed. E. P. D. Torrie (Scottish Record Society, vol. 12), pp. xii, 150–4.
143. See description in *APS*, i, p. 188.
144. See *APS*, i, p. 181 note; R. J. Lyall, 'Books and book owners', pp. 242–5.
145. *Mort Reg*, ii, nos 193 (p. 171) and 196 (p. 181).
146. *RM* (*Cooper*), p. 3.
147. W. Fraser, *Lennox*, ii, no 62.
148. *RM* (*APS*), II, 32; *RM* (*Cooper*), II, 42.
149. *RM* (*APS*), II, 36; *RM* (*Cooper*), II, 42.
150. *RM* (*APS*), II, 38; *RM* (*Cooper*), II, 42.
151. The MS is Adv MS 25.4.13, where the chapters cited in the plea are respectively chapters 31, 35 and 37 of Book II. The rubrics are also not quite as cited in the plea (see ff. 44r–45r). For a description of the MS, see *APS*, i, pp. 185–6.
152. A. R. Borthwick, 'Thesis', p. 341. For the act of David II, see *APS*, i, pp. 498, 509, 535, and further below, p. 221.
153. *Cawdor Bk*, p. 104.
154. See below, pp. 179–83; also my 'Kin of Kennedy', passim.
155. NLS, *Fleming of Wigtown papers*, Ch. 16,632.
156. *RM* (*APS*), II, 49; *RM* (*Cooper*), II, 55.
157. NLS, *Fleming of Wigtown papers*, Chs 15,563 and 15,564. See above, pp. 78, 96–8, and below, p. 112.
158. *RM* (*APS*), IV, 40; *RM* (*Cooper*), Supplement no 22 (pp. 295–6).
159. See above, p. 112.
160. SRO, *Ailsa muniments*, GD 25/1/102.
161. NLS, Adv MS 25.4.10; see description in *APS*, i, pp. 186–7.
162. For references, see H. L. MacQueen and W. J. Windram, 'Burghs', p. 227 note 94.
163. *AB Ill*, iii, p. 8 (also SRO, Calendar of Charters, ii, no 345A, RH6/345A). Dr Borthwick suggests that the eight judges constituted a session rather than being simply arbiters: see 'Thesis', pp. 282–3.

4

Pleadable Brieves and Free Holdings

ORIGINS AND EARLY DEVELOPMENT

Before the end of the thirteenth century, it was thought to be a rule of the Scottish common law that no freeholder could be made to answer for his lands except by an action begun by the king's brieve. The rule is found in the earliest manuscript of the *Leges Burgorum*, the Berne manuscript, which is dateable to c.1270:[1]

> If anyone is challenged for his lands or tenement in a burgh, he need not answer his adversary without the lord king's letters unless he freely wishes it. And he who is so challenged can resort to delays and to reasonable essonzies, once, twice and three times. And at the fourth day he shall come to warrant his essonzies and to answer before the bailies whoever they may be from time to time.

In 1296, Alexander Macdonald of Islay wrote to Edward I of England about the situation in Kintyre, and remarked that 'many people say that according to the laws of England and Scotland no-one ought to lose his heritage unless he has been impleaded by brieve and named in the brieve by his own name'.[2] The law of England had been clear since the time of *Glanvill*[3] – no man could be made to answer for his freeholding without a royal writ – so, if the phrase 'many people say' implies a measure of doubt as to the proposition which follows, as seems possible, it can only have related to the Scottish situation. There can, however, have been little doubt that the brieve rule was already established in burgh law, as the Berne manuscript indicates, for in 1317 it was successfully invoked in an action before Aberdeen burgh court raised by simple complaint rather than by brieve.[4] William Duncan sued Philip Gaydon, alleging *wrang et unlaw* in Philip's retention of a house against parties to whom William had leased it. In the pleading, it emerged that the house had been held by Philip's parents *in maritagium* – that is, jointly and heritably, but inalienably until the third generation after the original couple to whom the property had been so granted – yet nevertheless Philip's father had sold the house to William. Philip argued that his possession was based on a heritable title derived from the tenure of his parents, and that accordingly he did not have to answer William's complaint unless it was made by a letter of the king's chapel. The court upheld Philip's argument and dismissed the case.

The first establishment of the rule in Scotland was not therefore as a result of an enactment by parliament in 1318 which stated that 'no one is to be ejected from his free holding [*liberum tenementum suum*] of which he claims to be vest and saised as of fee without the king's pleadable brieve or some similar brieve nor without being first reasonably summoned to a certain day and place for his free holding'.[5] The statute may have been necessary, however, to eliminate some uncertainty as to the rule's application outside the burghs. We will return shortly to the question of how such uncertainty might have arisen; but first it should be asked why it was thought necessary to resolve the uncertainty in 1318. Indeed, it is surprising to find such a provision in the legislation of that 'conservatively feudal'[6] king Robert I, for the rule it embodies is usually seen by English legal historians as 'anti-feudal' in effect if not in intention, in that it seems to have destroyed the jurisdiction of lords' courts in England over land disputes, which in 'feudal theory' was an exclusive one.[7] Robert I, by contrast, is usually seen as 'revitalising' the feudal institutions of the barony and the regality, with their extensive franchisal powers.[8] What then lies behind the act of 1318?

One explanation may be the political background to the act. Following his victory at Bannockburn in 1314, Robert I had his parliament declare that all who would not come into his peace would be forfeited.[9] Thus those who held lands in both Scotland and England had to choose to which crown they would in future give their allegiance; those who chose to be subject to the English king would lose their lands. This had happened to many even before 1314, and the lands had been granted out instead to supporters of King Robert. Coupled however with the return of former owners to Scottish allegiance after 1314, a complex situation arose. Barrow's full review of the handling of this situation leads him to the conclusion that 'King Robert held fast to the principle that there should be no disinheritance of men and women claiming property by hereditary right, provided that they were prepared to swear allegiance to him', and that 'the king's dealings with regard to property and the services rendered by its holders were informed by a spirit of conservatism and restoration'.[10] Such a policy must, however, have led to clashes between the returning disinherited and those who had benefited from forfeiture of their lands. Duncan has drawn attention to an interesting case in 1315 involving an unusual grant of express warrandice by the king, which anticipates the possibility of a challenge to the title of a grantee receiving lands formerly owned by opponents of Robert I. The grant was of the sheriffdom and burgh of Cromarty, the beneficiary Sir Hugh Ross, and, as Duncan remarks, 'the anticipated source of challenge was the Mowat family, heritable sheriffs of Cromarty in Alexander III's reign'. Mowat may have sought recovery in 1315 and 1316, with some limited success in respect of his sheriffship, although by 1321, 'offended at his treatment by the king', he had deserted once again to England.[11] This dispute between Mowat and Ross may even have been the immediate cause of the act of 1318. Duncan has also noted a burgage charter in which 'the new tenant was promised that the old, if restored, would give satisfaction by redeeming the land at the king's ordinance and will, together with compensation for buildings erected, assessed by an assize'.[12] No doubt there were also compromises. An instructive example is that involving the loyal Adam Marshall, who was given the barony of Manor in Tweeddale on the forfeiture of its owner, Alexander Baddeby, in 1309.[13] Baddeby reentered Scottish allegiance after Bannockburn, and Manor was divided between him and Adam, presumably by agreement.[14] In 1323, however, Baddeby unsuccessfully sought restoration of the whole from the king.[15] It is surely against a background where the king's loyal adherents were uncertain about being able to retain their new properties against the returning disinherited that parliament enacted in 1318 that no man could be put out of his free holding without the king's pleadable brieve. There was nothing 'anti-feudal' about this; it was a move in the interests of security of tenure and the status quo. Those in possession could only be put out by due process of law, a due process best ensured by compelling the use of procedure under certain well-defined royal brieves.

We can now return to the question of how doubt and uncertainty might have arisen by 1296 about whether or not the brieve rule was part of the law of Scotland, which in turn requires consideration of how it had found its way into the law of the burghs. *Regiam Majestatem* follows *Glanvill* in stating that the requirement of a brieve in cases concerning free holdings was '*secundum consuetudinem regni*'.[16] It seems improbable, however, that the origins of the rule are to be found in the background of Milsom's immoveably biased lord's court, tied to sitting tenants by the obligations of warranty. Although our evidence and knowledge for the operation of warrandice in twelfth- and thirteenth-century Scotland are alike sketchy, it does not seem that only the king's command could open up questions about a holding as a result of its existence. Rather, the fact that warrandice had sometimes to be expressed suggests that doubts over the validity of a tenancy could exist and be made live, even when the lord was the king.[17]

Another obvious point is that the rule could hardly have developed before judicial procedures on royal brieves became reasonably regular. As early as 1110, the king could order that actions should only be commenced before him personally, or when he gave either a written or oral command.[18] Judicial processes were certainly held on the orders (which may or may not have been written) of David I, Malcolm IV and William I, and the examples which we have all relate to disputes over land.[19] Many of these processes involved perambulations of disputed boundaries, and by early in the thirteenth century, if not before, the brieve of perambulation was becoming established.[20] The brieve *de nativis* was another royal command in writing which had assumed regular form in the course of the twelfth century,[21] and there may have been other brieves which gave effect to the royal power to intervene in matters concerning justice.

Harding has argued persuasively that the roots of the Scottish rule requiring brieves to make a man answer for his lands lie in twelfth-century grants of the king's protection which included commands that the beneficiary should enjoy quiet possession of his lands, that his causes should be treated as the king's own, and that he should not be impleaded except before the king or his justices, and at the king's command.[22] If we couple this with the general willingness of the king to remedy defects of justice and to order that judicial processes be held, it can be seen that twelfth-century conditions provided fertile ground in which there could germinate the seed of the idea that a royal brieve was needed to eject a sitting tenant. It was in such a context that the English rule took shape as a custom, according to *Glanvill*,[23] and there might have been a similar customary development in Scotland.

This suggestion will not suffice as an explanation of the origins of the brieves rule, not least because there is no evidence that the rule was observed in Scotland in the twelfth century or even early in the thirteenth. It might even be suggested that there is evidence that the rule was unknown as part of Scots law at that time. Between 1206 and 1208, Melrose abbey and Patrick, fifth earl of Dunbar, were locked in litigation over rights of pasture in Sorrowlessfield between the Gala and Leader Waters, which the earl was alleged to have violently occupied. The case was begun before ecclesiastical judges delegate, but the earl argued that, as the case concerned a lay holding, it ought to be heard before a secular court: *actor sequi debeat forum rei.* The abbey countered successfully that according to the custom of these parts a layman could be convened before an ecclesiastical tribunal in respect of lands granted in alms. Nonetheless, the case was eventually settled in the king's full court at Selkirk.[24] Had the 'custom of these parts' been that the abbey required a royal brieve to make the earl answer in court, however, reference to it might have been expected on the earl's side. It may be that such a plea lurks behind the record's Romano-canonical formulation that the pursuer should use the defender's forum, but on balance this seems less likely than that the brieves rule was not yet even arguably part of Scots law.

Whatever its origins, the English rule rapidly became inextricably bound up with the law and procedure of the writs of right, novel disseisin and *mort d'ancestor*. If we postulate a thirteenth-century origin for the brieve rule in Scotland, as it is argued must be done, then it is inherently probable that the development was influenced by an awareness of English law. It will be shown in later chapters that the pleadable brieves to which the rule compelled recourse in disputes over land – the brieves of novel dissasine, mortancestry and right – were themselves introduced to or developed in Scotland in imitation of English models.[25] It is most likely that the rule came into Scots law in the same manner, and that its arrival was connected with the brieves themselves. Certainly, Alexander Macdonald of Islay was well aware of the English rule in 1296. With one exception, we do not know whether this transplantation of forms of action was accomplished by a series of legislative or executive acts, or in some other way, but so evident is the use of the English models that it seems unlikely that the Scottish brieves evolved independently from pre-existing native ones into the final versions which certainly existed by 1300. However, this does not mean that the transplant of the brieve rule occurred in a similar manner. It might otherwise be difficult to explain the uncertainty about its place in the law which may be discernible in Alexander Macdonald's letter. If uncertainty existed, it can best be explained, it is submitted, by the fact that the brieves of right, mortancestry and, in particular, novel dissasine were in use in Scotland, that their English origins were well known, and that in some sense the brieve rule could be seen as probably (but not as clearly as might have been the case after some legislative act) following from the existence of the brieves themselves.

As will be shown in the following chapter, the brieve of novel dissasine was most probably introduced in Scotland as the result of legislation in 1230.[26] The brieve was an order that a person who had been ejected from lands 'unjustly and without a judgment' should be restored to them. What obviously followed from this was that in order to eject a person lawfully from lands it was necessary to obtain a judgment. Nothing in the brieve said that the judgment had to follow a process begun by brieve, but an action begun by royal command and taking place in the king's court was perhaps less likely to be challenged later as lacking the qualities of a just judgment. Similarly, mortancestry gave a remedy against an intruder sitting on lands to which the bearer of the brieve had a hereditary claim. The implication was that the claimant could not simply go in and eject the intruder; he had to use the king's brieve if he wished to avoid an action of dissasine. Finally, the brieve of right provided a general action for other types of claim to land. The king's brieves therefore provided a comprehensive structure of remedies by which land might be recovered; they were used as such; and novel dissasine was a powerful incentive to use them. In this context, and given the origins of the actions, an argument that the custom of the land now made it necessary to use the brieves in claims for land was certainly an intelligible one.[27]

Such arguments must have been reinforced by the place of the brieve rule in the burgh laws.[28] If the model suggested for the development of the rule in the landward areas is accepted, however, the burghs present something of a problem, for neither novel dissasine or mortancestry was available in the burgh courts. The brieve of right was the principal remedy for the burgess out of his lands.[29] It is possible that the rather stronger statement of the brieve rule in the burgh laws is to be explained as a result of the fact that, on its own, the brieve of right did not so clearly imply the need to use brieves in all cases. Moreover, there was in the burghs an action equivalent to novel dissasine called 'fresh force'.[30] No royal brieve was involved in raising the action; the scope of the brieves rule therefore did not extend to it. One explanation might be that fresh force developed before the brieves rule; certainly, it was known in England very early in the thirteenth century, and might have been borrowed from there at that time.[31] A second possibility is that fresh force was conceived more as a remedy against wrong than as a means of recovering land to which otherwise the rule would have applied, or as a genuinely possessory remedy which was normally followed by an action about the right. It certainly seems to be linked to the idea found in the *Leges Burgorum* that a dispossessed person should be immediately restored before any question of right was discussed.[32] However, the existence of this remedy without brieve, along with the absence of novel dissasine and mortancestry, may have compelled an earlier articulation and settlement of the brieves rule in burgh than in the landward areas. How, when and by what authority this articulation and settlement occurred lies out of our sight, but it is suggested that it cannot have been much before the middle of the thirteenth century.

The existence of the brieve rule may also underlie the development of the brieve *inhibicionis domini regis pro homine vexato ad curiam Christianitatis* found in the 'registers' of brieves. This was a command to a church court not to act in a dispute over a lay tenement, 'because the cognition of the cause ought by law to pertain to our royal court'.[33] There are several thirteenth-century examples of both royal prohibitions and renunciations of the right to resort to such prohibitions, suggesting that this was an important weapon in jurisdictional struggles between the church and laymen.[34] It was most likely to emerge when the jurisdiction of the king's courts had been regularised, and is a sign of the development of forms of action which the king wished to see used. It may even be that one of the impulses behind the visible regularisation of procedures and forms of action taking place in the reign of Alexander II was to provide a secular alternative to ecclesiastical jurisdiction. It is clear that this was a major issue early in the reign of his successor.[35] There were many laymen who, like the earl of Dunbar in the early 1200s, found themselves summoned to answer for land before judges delegate when they would have preferred to be in a lay forum perhaps more responsive to their position. Similarly, if like Melrose abbey in the Dunbar case an ecclesiastical pursuer had difficulty in making church jurisdiction stick, the development of regular forms of royal justice as another means of protecting and asserting property rights may not have been unwelcome.

THE BRIEVE RULE IN THE FOURTEENTH AND FIFTEENTH CENTURIES

Whatever its earlier origins, from 1318 the source of the rule that no man need answer for his lands without the king's brieve was taken to be the statute of Robert I. Thus, in 1382, it was said to be 'according to the statute of King Robert' that he who had held 'for years' ought not to be expelled from possession without a pleadable brieve.[36] Similarly, in 1398, the bishop of Moray argued that 'according to the statute of King Robert' only by pleadable brieve could his church of Moray be put out of its immunity from suit at the sheriff court of Inverness, a freedom held for years and more.[37] On another occasion, sometime in the reign of Robert II, it was argued that 'according to the statute of the last King Robert no-one ought to be ejected from any land of which he claims himself to be vest and saised without a pleadable brieve'.[38]

As these references make clear, the brieve rule survived until the end of the fourteenth century. As already noted, it is found in *Regiam;* it is also cited with little comment in *Quoniam.*[39] It was referred to in the interesting legal battle which developed over the succession to the Douglas lands after the death without male heirs of the second earl, James, in the battle of Otterburn in 1388. His sister Isabella was his heir at law, and her husband Sir Malcolm Drummond seems to have obtained sasine of the lands on her behalf. In terms of a tailzie of 1342, however, the earl's illegitimate cousin, Archibald Douglas, was the heir entitled to take the lands and the earldom. Archibald showed the tailzie and established his rights in parliament in 1389, when it was also declared that those wishing to pursue alternative claims to the lands should proceed by pleadable brieves.[40] A little earlier, in 1369, the prior and monks of Pluscarden in Moray were engaged in a litigation over a claim to multures; they alleged that they had had peaceful possession for forty days and more and that, accordingly, it was 'against the customs of the realm' for them to be put out 'without a pleadable brieve'.[41]

The requirement of brieves in cases concerning freehold survived into the fifteenth century. The first piece of evidence for this is an undated document in Scots which, to judge from the script, is of at least the mid-fifteenth century.[42] The relevant part of it runs as follows:

This is the answer that we, Wylzame the Grame, Richard the Grame and Henry the Grame, makis tyll our soverayne lorde the kyngis letter, the quhylke chargyt us to compeyr the xii day of July tyll answar apon the landis of Hutton and to bryng wyth us charteris and documentis to schaw. And in the fyrst, we clame the sayde landis wyth thair pertynence our fee and herytage, and haf beyne this hundreth yeris and mare, and we in pesabyll possessioun this xx yeris, and we understande that he that is yere and day in peseabyll possessioun in any land clamande it of fee and herytage he aucht nocht to ga owte of his possessioun forowte the kyngis brefe pledabyll.

In his recent doctoral thesis, Alan Borthwick has also drawn attention to a prolonged litigation between the burghs of Dundee and Montrose in the mid-fifteenth century. The issue concerned the trading bounds of each burgh. In the course of this dispute, reference was made to the rule requiring a pleadable brieve to eject a man from his fee and heritage, probably by David Reid, who was procurator for Montrose.[43] Finally, Borthwick has also noted a case before a chamberlain ayre in Montrose in 1456, where the claim of one Janet Inchmedan to a tenement in the burgh was successfully repelled by reference to the need for a pleadable brieve in such causes.[44] All three references make the survival of the brieve rule until the mid-fifteenth century quite certain.

The rule almost certainly also applied within regalities, even though the king's writ did not run within these franchises. Robert I made two grants of land in regality to Thomas Randolph, 'with the four complaints belonging to our royal crown and with all pleas and complaints both in common indictments and in pleadable brieves'.[45] It seems highly probable that this meant that the lord of regality was empowered to issue pleadable brieves within his regality wherever the king would have done so elsewhere. We know that in the sixteenth century the regality chancery of the archbishop of St Andrews had styles for the brieves of right, mortancestry and others, running in the name of the archbishop but otherwise exactly similar to those issued by the king.[46] There are examples of the use of the archbishop's brieve of right within the city and regality of St Andrews.[47] In 1413, a brieve of mortancestry was issued in the regality of Arbroath abbey.[48] In 1455, a brieve of mortancestry was led in the regality of Drumlanrig, while in 1433 a brieve of dissasine was presented to the justice ayre of the regality of the earldom of Atholl.[49] A brieve of distress was issued by the chancery or chapel of the regality of Garioch in 1407.[50] In other words, the regality was a microcosm of the kingdom, with its own chapel issuing pleadable brieves, and the rule requiring such brieves in cases of freehold was almost certainly operative there as well. A 1358 grant of David II to the warden of the mint gave him jurisdiction over all pleas concerning his men, excepting only those of the crown and of freeholding.[51] Although this is not expressly said, the latter exception is presumably because such pleas had to be begun by brieve in the royal courts, and the king had determined not to grant a franchise of that sort to this beneficiary.

FREE HOLDING IN SCOTS LAW

It was only where a man had a free holding (*liberum tenementum*) that he received the protection of the brieves rule as formulated in 1318. What was the nature of a free holding or 'frank tenement', as *liberum tenementum* came to be translated in legal Scots? The matter was discussed in some detail by Cooper and Dickinson in two articles published in 1945, and has received little attention since.[52] Cooper brought together material from *Regiam* and other sources, and concluded that by the reign of Robert I *liberum tenementum* was used in correlation with the term *feodum*, or fee, to describe an interest in land which would endure only for the holder's lifetime. *Feodum* or fee, by contrast, described heritable interests which would pass to the current holder's heirs on his death. Cooper finished his article by asking whether this interpretation of *liberum tenementum* in the context of the private law of landownership applied also in public law, specifically to the right of freeholders, or *libere tenens*, to attend parliament. It was this question which Dickinson sought to answer. He pointed out that initially the prime distinction between the freeholder and other occupiers of land was that his holding was free, with an obligation of suit at his lord's court, that is, parliament in the case of the king's tenants-in-chief. In the fourteenth century, some of the king's freeholders became barons, so giving rise to a distinction between them and other freeholders; but the latter were those who held in chief of the king in fee and heritage alone, without the jurisdictional privileges conferred by a grant *in liberam baroniam*. However, the phrase *liberum tenementum* was not used to describe the holding of such a *libere tenens*. *Liberum tenementum* was used in the fourteenth and later centuries to describe the holding of a person where *the feodum* or fee was held by another. This could best be illustrated by a practice that developed in the second half of the fourteenth century and subsequently became customary among landowners, whereby the holder of a fee resigned his lands to the superior in favour of another, typically a son. The superior would then grant the fee to the son subject to the reservation of a *liberum tenementum* in favour of the father.[53] Thus the fiar of the lands became 'not the person who holds a fief, but the person who has a reversionary right to a fief which is subject to a liferent'.[54] This conclusion is reinforced by the apparent fact that the holder of the *liberum tenementum* continued to act as owner of the land by, for example, paying suit at the superior's court. In this way, the holder of a *liberum tenementum* could appear to be a *libere tenens*, causing conceptual confusion which is apparent in the later writings of Skene and Craig on the subject.

A *Regiam* passage discussed by Cooper shows how the compiler conceived the *liberum tenementum* as part of the fee.[55] The man who had *liberum tenementum* might also have the fee; but the man who had the fee might have given the *liberum tenementum* away. *Regiam* suggests that the nature of the remedy against dispossession might vary according to the nature of the right claimed, an aspect of the passage which will be given detailed consideration in subsequent chapters. The crucial point for present purposes is that when the act of 1318 said that no-one was to be put out of his *liberum tenementum* without the king's brieve, it was not intended to confer rights only upon one who had a mere freeholding or frank tenement and nothing else; a fiar in possession had a *liberum tenementum*, and he could not be ejected therefrom unless by action begun by pleadable brieve.

This conclusion is also borne out by a passage found in some of the legal manuscripts which proclaims itself to be a statute of Robert I, and which Cooper termed 'a mature formulation of theory'.[56] It states that there may be three interests in land: possession, as when one holds land in security; *liberum tenementum*, when one has lands for the term of one's life; and fee, when a man may not have recourse or entry to his land until after the death of him who has the *liberum tenementum*. The passage concludes that all three interests may be claimed by one person and gives as an example of someone who ought to have possession, *liberum tenementum* and fee, the person ejected unjustly from his heritable lands.

When we turn to the cases in which the statute or rule was pleaded or referred to after 1318, it can be found in use to defend those claiming to hold by a heritable title; for example, in the Hutton case, the rule was stated as being that anyone 'in peseabyll possessioun in any lande clamande it *of fee and herytage* [emphasis supplied] . . . aucht nocht to ga owte of his possessioun forowte the kyngis brefe pledabyll'.[57] In the fourteenth-century dispute over the Douglas inheritance, the rule was again invoked in favour of one sitting on a heritable title, although the order of inheritance was subject to the limitation of a charter of tailzie.[58] All the other fourteenth-century references to the rule were made on behalf of ecclesiastical foundations where church lands or rights were under dispute. In such situations, it was wholly inappropriate to talk either of heritage or of holding for a lifetime, yet the 1318 statute clearly applied.[59] The ecclesiastical cases throw other interesting light on what might be covered by the concept *liberum tenementum*, since in them the brieves rule was being invoked to protect claims to multures and to immunity from suit of court.

DISCIPLINARY JURISDICTION

The rule that no man could be made to answer for his freeholding without a pleadable brieve was not, however, universally applicable. A lord exercising what Milsom termed his 'disciplinary jurisdiction' over his tenants could bring them to court without a brieve for proceedings which could deprive them of their lands.[60] Milsom drew his analysis of this jurisdiction in England from *Glanvill*, in which very clear statements are made as follows:[61]

If anyone does anything to the disinheritance of his lord and is convicted of it, he and his heirs shall by law lose the fee which he holds of him. The same rule will apply if anyone lays violent hands on his lord to hurt him or do him an atrocious wrong (*atrox iniuria*), and this is lawfully proved against him in the proper court. But I put this question: is anyone bound to defend himself on such charges against his lord in his lord's court; and *may his lord distrain him to do so by award of his court without a command from the lord king or his justices, or without a writ from the lord king or his chief justice?* [emphasis supplied] The answer is that anyone may lawfully bring his man to trial and distrain him to come to his court by judgment of his court; and . . . the whole of the fee which he holds of that lord shall be at the lord's mercy. I also put this question: may a lord distrain his man to come to his court to answer a complaint by the lord that he is withholding service, or that some of the service is in arrears? The answer is that he may lawfully do so, *even without a command from the lord king or his justices* [emphasis supplied] . . . If the tenant is convicted of the charge, he shall by law be disinherited of the whole fee which he holds of that lord. (IX, 1) . . .

When it is a question of rendering reasonable aids, lords may by judgment of their own court, as of right and *without any precept from the lord king or the chief justice* [emphasis supplied], distrain their tenants by the chattels found on their fees or, if necessary, by the fees themselves, provided that the tenants are dealt with justly in accordance with the judgment and reasonable custom of the lord's court. (IX, 8)

Both these passages were later incorporated in *Regiam*, retaining the emphasis on the lord's power to bring a tenant into court to answer for his defaults and perhaps to lose his lands, without first obtaining the king's brieve. Perhaps significantly, however, the compiler of *Regiam* restricted the lord's power to distrain for aids to the tenant's chattels, omitting *Glanvill*'s alternative of distraint by the fee 'if necessary'.[62] Was this because this particular aspect of distraint by the fee had fallen out of use by the time the compiler was at work?

Reference has already been made in an earlier chapter to a number of thirteenth-century examples of tenants resigning lands in their lords' court *pro defectu servicii.*[63] It seems likely, if not certain, that these resignations had been preceded by the exercise of a disciplinary jurisdiction by the lord in his court, and in none of the cases is there any reference to such process having been initiated by brieve. *Quoniam* discusses the failure to perform services in some detail, explaining that the lord may summon the tenant to his court and ultimately recognosce – that is, take back into his own possession – his lands, but it is not suggested that he requires any brieve to do so.[64] A text for which there is only late manuscript authority, but which is attributed to the reign of Robert II and is said to give the opinions of the *jurisperitorum regni* on when the lands of tenants may justly be recognosced, allows recognition for services to the lord superior to whom the service is owed, again without mentioning the brieve rule.[65] Examples of this process specifically related to default of service are hard to find in the later medieval period, presumably in consequence of the declining importance and significance of military service.[66] Recognitions certainly occurred, however, although it is not clear whether or not this was for default of service or some other obligation owed to the lord. An example is the doom of the baron court of Dirleton by which William Fenton was put out of his lands of Fenton in the constabulary of Haddington around 1385.[67] A statute of 1401 laid down rules on the procedure to be followed by the lord's court in such cases, which probably amounted to no more than a restatement of the existing law.[68] That the exercise of this power of control had given rise to problems is suggested by the act's reference to 'wilful and secret' recognitions by lords which vex the lieges in their heritage; it is interesting that in the example just mentioned William Fenton complained that the court of Dirleton had acted while he was absent. The emphasis throughout the act is on the need for due, open and public process; but no mention is made of any need for a brieve, although the result of the procedure was to deprive the tenant of his lands. Nor are brieves referred to in any of the other examples of recognitions known to me.[69]

In England, however, the writ rule eliminated the lord's power to distrain by the fee for services. As Milsom tells the story, the problem case was not where the tenant was simply in arrears with an admitted service, but where he disputed the service claimed by the lord. By *Bracton's* day, the lord needed a writ in such cases.[70] The logic seems to have been that possession of the land was in issue, so that, although the lord's right only gave him the land in security of his claim, and did not destroy the tenant's rights, the tenant was entitled to the protection of the writ rule. Moreover, the possibility of the lord disinheriting the tenant so that he regained full right in the land, recognised by *Glanvill* in the passages quoted above, seems to have disappeared in the course of the thirteenth century, presumably for the same reason.[71]

The reason for the contrasting non-application of the brieve rule to such cases in Scotland is not clear, but two tentative suggestions may be made. First, recognition did not involve the tenant being permanently deprived of the lands; as the act of 1401 made clear, if it was not already so, the lord took possession only until the tenant repaired his default, or showed himself ready to do so if default were established, whereupon the tenant might regain possession of the lands pending resolution of his dispute with the lord.[72] Once again, William Fenton's case in 1385 may be an illustration: after the doom of the baron court against him had been given, he was restored to possession of Fenton subject to a pledge (*borgh* in Scots), pending an appeal against the judgment.[73] The act did not stop lordly abuse. In 1426 James Douglas younger of Dalkeith recognosced Carlops from his tenant David Menzies of Vogrie, and infeft Alan Erskine instead, an action which led Menzies to complain, successfully, in parliament.[74] An example of what the 1401 act intended to happen may be found, however, in proceedings in 1438, where the earl of Douglas, having as lord of Lauderdale recognosced lands in Lauder from Gilbert Lauder, returned him to possession subject to the finding of a *borgh* by Gilbert.[75]

A second reason why the brieve rule may not have come into play to restrict the lord's disciplinary powers was that the issue in disciplinary cases was not the ownership of the tenant's land, but the commission of wrongs against the lord. The loss of the land if the wrong was established was the penalty and not the issue at the centre of the dispute. Another striking point, however, is that *Regiam* is the only source to speak of full-scale disinheritance of the tenant so that he could never be restored to the land; and it is possible that this power, if it ever existed in Scotland, was indeed eliminated by the brieve rule.

The opinion of the *jurisperitorum regni* on the lord's powers of recognition attributed to the reign of Robert II also mentions unlicensed alienation as a possible cause of action.[76] Recognition of a tenant's lands for unlicensed alienation was another lordly power with an obvious disciplinary nature, since the tenant who sold his lands or part of them without his lord's consent would lose his holding completely. As in England, where the versions of Magna Carta issued in 1217 and 1225 included a provision that no man might alienate so much of his land as to disable him from performing the services due to his lord, this power might be linked to recognition for default of service, inasmuch as the tenant alienating his lands was reducing his capacity to render his services.[77] There are undoubted examples of the exercise of this right by lords in medieval Scotland, perhaps following the lead of the king, and there is no evidence to show that it was curtailed by the brieve rule.[78] If the earlier suggestion about the possible influence of the *Libri Feudorum* on later

Scots feudalism is correct, then that work's emphasis on the lord's right
to control alienation by the tenant may have played some part in its
development in Scotland.[79] In England, the right to control alienation
evolved after Magna Carta, as lords strove to protect first the services,
later the incidents, against the prejudice which might be caused by
alienation, enabling the lord, if he was quick enough, either to forestall or
to eject the purchasers. These rights remained important until the statute
Quia Emptores in 1290, which took away the power of lords to control
tenants' alienations. Novel disseisin, rather than the writ rule, seems to
have been the mechanism for controlling the exercise of the power in the
period between 1217 and 1290.[80] In Scotland, there was no *Quia
Emptores*, and the lord's consent to alienation remained important, with
one practical effect being that transfer of land was normally by resignation
to and regrant by the lord, or by confirmation. Another was the possibility
that an original grant might contain a clause or phrase recognising that
the tenant might be succeeded by 'assignees' – that is to say, licensing
alienation in advance.[81] The lord's court seems to have retained this
element of its disciplinary jurisdiction throughout the fifteenth century;
in 1497, Sir Simon Preston of that ilk falsed the doom of the baron court
of Coulter concerning his alienation of lands in the barony which he held
of Robert Menzies of Enoch. The baron court had decreed that for this
the lands should be recognosced in the baron's hands.[82]

Feudal discipline seems also to link two other areas in which the
Scottish lord could take action without brieve in his court against the
tenant and his lands, purpresture (or 'purprision', as it was rendered in
Scots) and 'showing the holding'.[83] The discussion of purpresture in
Regiam is lifted almost straight from *Glanvill*.[84] It is defined as encroachment by a tenant upon the demesne of his lord. The lord can summon the
offending tenant to his court, and conviction leads to forfeiture of the
lands held of the lord by the tenant. For this reason, Milsom includes
purpresture in his discussion of the lord's disciplinary jurisdiction.[85] In
Glanvill, however, there is a form of royal writ by which such actions were
begun, and Biancalana has suggested that it was originally a royal action
which the king made available to lords.[86] There is accordingly a difficulty
in seeing the action as part of a lord's pristine disciplinary jurisdiction.

Glanvill's writ was edited out by the compiler of *Regiam* in taking over
the substance of his comments about purpresture, although in an earlier
chapter he did refer to the existence of a *'breve seu placitum de
purpresturis'*.[87] Both the Bute and *Formulary E registers* do contain a brieve
commanding that an inquest be held on whether a purpresture had been
committed.[88] The style is, however, concerned only with purpresters on
the king's lands, and it is retourable. Brieves of purpresture are found in
no other formulary. Purpresture was undoubtedly part of Scots law from

the thirteenth century, and the 1292 inventory of the royal archives mentions a great roll which recorded, amongst other things, inquests of purpresture, perhaps ordered by brieves like the one in the registers, with the wrong presumably being committed on the king's lands.[89] A classic example of purpresture by encroachment on royal superiority rights can be found in 1416, when William Douglas of Old Roxburgh was summoned before the council for disturbing the king's tenants of the barony of Cessford. Douglas justified his actions by claiming that the barony was held in chief of him, not the king, but was commanded to answer for his purpresture.[90]

Later medieval evidence shows that landowners other than the king could use the action, but there is no evidence of any brieve. The classical model of purpresture survived into the later fifteenth century. The 1481 commission on purpresture, mentioned in an earlier chapter, confirms that the account in *Regiam* was still the basic source for the law, albeit one in need of clarification, and that the action was heard in lords' courts; no mention is made of any brieve.[91] On 20 October 1478, Sir John Sandilands of Calder led a process of purpresture in his baron court of Calder against his tenant Andrew Dury, who held the lands of Wester Corsewood in the barony. Dury had uplifted rents in Wester Corsewood although 'unorderly enterit clamand and vouchand blanschferme quhare he suld hafe haldin warde and releif'; he had also withheld a suitor from Sandilands' court, and been art and part in the misdeeds of other tenants, 'in disherising and dishonoring' of their lord. For all this, Dury forfeited his lands: an excellent example of disciplinary jurisdiction still at work. However, Sandilands' efforts were in vain, for two years later council declared the process void, since 'na process of forfature of purprisioune suld be led for sic causis'.[92] The case has various points of interest, not least that the tenant Dury, by claiming to hold blenche rather than in ward and relief, was in fact claiming to hold for less service than the lord asserted to be due. In Milsom's interpretation of the Glanvillian world discussed earlier, this in itself would have been a cause of disciplinary forfeiture. In late fifteenth-century Scotland, however, the lord Sandilands was not concerned to have military service; he wanted his casualties and rents, and he tried to bring the case against his tenant by means of purpresture. Even more interestingly, in the end he was unsuccessful. Disciplinary jurisdiction was still a reality, then, but external controls had already limited its scope and were continuing to do so.

Purpresture had, however, become a concept which had expanded outside the lord-tenant relationship well before this time, if indeed it had ever been so restricted. In 1357, Arbroath abbey successfully sued Laurence of Garvock, burgess of Aberdeen, for purpresture by the removal of stone from the abbey's lands of Nigg. The abbey brought its case before the king's council, and it is not clear what, if any, tenurial link it had with Laurence.[93] From this, we might argue that purpresture had become a broader concept than that described in *Glanvill* and *Regiam*, as an action available against strangers failing to recognise the claims of lordship. Following *Glanvill*, *Regiam* stated that in such cases the lord should use either the brieve of right or the brieve of novel dissasine.[94] Another case in 1383 illustrates purpresture in a context where feudal discipline cannot have been involved, when the bishop of Moray found certain burgesses of Elgin committing purpresture in his lands of Kinneddar by unloading a small boat of its cargo (presumably without paying toll) and placed them under arrest.[95] The case out of which the debate about the law arose in 1481, leading to the appointment of the parliamentary commission on the subject, was also not one between a lord and tenants, but rather a dispute about the right to uplift rents from the lands of 'Rausburn'.[96]

Milsom sees the English writ *de purpresturis* as something of an oddity requiring explanation in that purpresture was clearly part of the lord's disciplinary jurisdiction and therefore no writ ought to have been necessary. The writ emerged, he suggests, because the action challenged the tenant's right, not to his own tenement (although the disciplinary jurisdiction would forfeit that), but to the land upon which he was alleged to have encroached. Confusion of thought therefore suggested that there should be a writ, in accordance with the general rule.[97] Scottish lawyers seem to have avoided this confusion, even when the wrongdoer was not a tenant and so not liable to disciplinary forfeiture. In the fifteenth century, there were doubts about jurisdiction in purpresture, but it is apparent that the action remained competent in baron courts and does not appear ever to have required a brieve, even when brought against a non-tenant. It may be that this can be reconciled with the brieve rule by the suggestion that such a defender would not be in possession of the land in question, but be simply one passing through and seeking to evade the lord's rights, as in the Kinneddar case of 1383; or who came on to it to uplift material, as in the Nigg case of 1357, or rents, as in the Rausburn case of 1480.

'Showing the holding' was an action by which, in its developed form, a lord compelled his tenant to display the charters on which he held his lands. In 1957, R. M. Maxtone-Graham showed that the main purpose of the action was to enable lords to ascertain the terms on which tenants held their lands and to ensure the preservation of their written titles. The tenant who failed to produce his charters or who was shown to be holding in a way inconsistent with their terms lost his lands, which looks very much like an exercise of disciplinary powers over tenants. Elsewhere, Maxtone-Graham demonstrated that, no matter what *Quoniam* might suggest to the contrary by its close juxtaposition of the brieve rule with its comments on showing the holding, no brieve was required to compel the tenant to show his holding in his lord's court. He concluded that 'unless a very narrow construction be put on [the rule] – that no one with an ex facie valid title can be evicted without royal brieve – it cannot be said to express the law of Scotland'.[98] Manifestly, as this chapter demonstrates, the rule *was* part of the law of Scotland into the fifteenth century; indeed, it was invoked by the Grahams of Hutton, in the pleading quoted earlier, in response to a summons to show their charters in the king's council.[99] So, some explanation must be sought of when the brieves rule did apply, and of when it did not, to cases of showing the holding.

The English equivalent to showing the holding was, as Milsom has shown, a *quo waranto* inquiry in the lord's court.[100] Paul Hyams has offered a persuasive reconstruction of the nature of such inquiries in the twelfth century before the rise of the common law. They occurred most frequently after 'the lord's recent succession or recovery of control from some rival'. Charters were not essential, although, as they became more common, so they became conclusive proof of tenure and the service attached thereto.[101] However, with the rise of the common law in the later twelfth century, lords increasingly brought these inquiries in the king's courts rather than their own, beginning their actions by royal writ. In some cases, this seemed to be made necessary by the rule requiring writs in freehold cases; a tenant had been put in by the previous lord and had sufficient seisin as a result to resist the new or restored lord's *quo waranto* action without writ.[102]

This model requires us to face Maxtone-Graham's question again, but also may lead towards an answer. The first point is that 'showing the holding' was probably, perhaps even certainly, older than the brieve rule, so that the latter took shape in a world where the former was an already established process. Further, the aim of the process was not so much to challenge tenants' titles as to enable a lord to take stock of his tenants and the services which they owed him. It was administrative, but also disciplinary; the lord would be enabled to enforce the services which were shown by the inquiry to be owed. If the services had not been provided, the lord could recognosce, and the brieves rule was inapplicable to cases of this type. Charters were probably not of the essence to begin with; it would be sufficient if the lord's court could remember the grant and sasine given to the tenant. However, if the tenant had not even this to justify his presence on the land, then why should he be allowed to stay? As an interloper, he should go, and the brieves rule would not protect him when it became part of the law.

The action of showing the holding, at least in its developed form of the later medieval period, seems to go further than this, in allowing the lord to challenge the title shown. The case of 1382 in which the bishop of

Aberdeen required John Crab to show his charters for the lands of Murthly is the supreme example. Here, Crab showed his charters, the validity of which was then challenged by the bishop, apparently successfully, on a variety of grounds. No question was raised about the bishop needing to begin his action by brieve. Twice, indeed, reference is made to the brieve rule in the documents about the case, but one is on behalf of the bishop rather than the tenant Crab. Having recovered the lands, if anyone now sought a brieve of inquest in the king's chapel against the bishop, it should be rejected on the grounds that he could only be ejected from his possession by pleadable brieve.[103] The other reference to the brieve rule, however, allows the tenant to invoke it against the lord who has refused to accept the charter which in fact justifies the tenant's holding, and now seeks to eject him.[104] Perhaps this was the nature of the claim of the Grahams of Hutton to the protection of the brieves rule. It may be possible to understand Crab's and other cases of the same nature as succeeding against the tenant on the basis that the charters shown did not justify the manner of his possession. Thus Crab's charter was from a previous bishop who could not bind a successor; it had insufficient consent from the canons of the cathedral; it lacked *causa*; and anyway Crab was not complying with the obligations it imposed upon him.[105] The charter on its face showed that the holding was illicit; Crab's possession was that of an interloper, and he could not be protected by the brieves rule.

This discussion of recognition, purpresture and showing the holding has demonstrated the continuing vitality of the lord's disciplinary jurisdiction in medieval Scotland, and has also shown that it was not constricted by the brieves rule. It may give support to Milsom's argument that this jurisdiction was exercised without writ in twelfth-century England before novel disseisin and the rule requiring writs to put out a landholder. We cannot jump too quickly to this conclusion, though. How far was Scottish law and practice affected by literal readings of *Regiam*'s Glanvillian passages allowing the lord to exercise his jurisdiction without the king's brieve? Was it also affected by the insistence of academic feudal law, to which reference was certainly made in John Crab's case, that disputes between a superior and his vassal should be tried in the superior's court? It seems that the brieves rule was, as Maxtone-Graham suggested, of comparatively narrow scope; it protected those on land with title to be there which justified the manner in which the land was actually held.

THE PLEADABLE BRIEVES

What were the pleadable brieves? *Regiam* contains a chapter '*De his quae placitantur per brevia*', which lists the brieves of right, *de nativis*, mortancestry, novel dissasine and distress.[106] *Quoniam* has another, slightly longer list of brieves '*communiter currentibus que sunt placitabilia*'.[107] This includes all those mentioned in *Regiam* while adding the brieves of convention, *de liberando hominem de plegiagio, de proteccione regis infricta* and warrandice of charter. Neither list mentions any of the brieves termed 'retourable' in medieval sources, the main examples of which are the brieves of inquest (for the service of heirs to land), tutory (to determine entitlement to be tutor-at-law of a fatherless child) and idiotry or furiosity (to determine the sanity of a particular individual and the identity of a tutor or curator for that person). With these brieves, the sheriff was commanded to hold an inquest to determine the answers to questions asked in the brieve itself, and then return, or 'retour', the result to the king's chapel, where the next step of process would be taken.[108] This clearly distinguished such brieves from the pleadable ones, where the determination of the assize was implemented by the court in which the case had been heard. The distinction had probably emerged before the end of the thirteenth century, for the 'register of brieves' in the Ayr manuscript is headed with the description 'chapters of the chapel of the king of Scots both of letters to be pleaded in courts and of brieves to be sent by the king from chancery'.[109] Although this is not entirely clear – it cannot mean that 'letters' were distinct from 'brieves', for example – some difference is being made between judicial and administrative royal documents which turns on pleading in court.[110] Pleading was itself a technical concept, as pointed out in an earlier chapter, and so it is not surprising to find that the brieves which gave rise to such pleading early became a distinct category.[111]

As I have argued in more detail elsewhere,[112] the pleadable brieves must also be distinguished from another group of brieves which at first sight appear similar in that no retour was made or required after the verdict of the assize. These brieves concern the declaration of boundaries between lands (perambulation, lining in burghs), or the division of a piece of land between two or more persons each entitled to a share of it (terce for widows entitled to a life right in one third of a deceased spouse's lands, with the heir taking the remainder, and division to partition land, for example, between heirs-portioner). The key distinction here seems to be that, under these brieves, the assize always had to carry out the task assigned, whereas in the pleadable brieves the parties determined the actual issue to be put to the assize by the exchange of pleas or exceptions. The pleadable brieve simply set out an issue in very broad terms – that the defender was occupying lands belonging to the pursuer, or had failed to pay a debt, for example; once the case was in court, the parties would be able to narrow the question down to a more specific issue to be answered by the assize through the pursuer making his statement of claim setting out the grounds of his right, and the defender explaining his position.

To which of the pleadable brieves did the brieve rule compel potential pursuers seeking the recovery of lands to have recourse? Of those listed in *Regiam* and *Quoniam*, it is possible to eliminate the brieves *de compulsione*, *de nativis* and *de proteccione regis infricta*. It is convenient to start with the brieves *de compulsione*: distress, convention, warrandice of charter, and relief of caution. They may be taken together in this way, since many features of form show a common ancestry. All use the verb '*compellatis*' as the instruction to the judge (typically the sheriff or the bailies of the burgh). A debtor is to be compelled to pay, perform his reasonable agreements, fulfil his obligation of warrandice or relieve his cautioner from liability, while the officer to whom the brieve is addressed is to act so that the king hears no further complaint of default of justice.[113] The theory of a common origin is reinforced by the discussion in *Quoniam* where it is stated that the procedure in the various brieves *de compulsione* (apart from warrandice of charter) is identical.[114] Warrandice is treated separately because it necessarily affects other actions, the raising of which prompted the bringing of the brieve.[115] Harding argues persuasively that the origin of the brieves of debt lies in the king's protection against non-payment of debt and, perhaps, indiscriminate poinding, an argument strongly supported by the appearance of the *compulsio* form as a clause in the royal letters of protection found in the 'registers' of brieves, as well as by the 'default of justice' formula with which the brieves conclude.[116] Probably the first pleadable compulsion brieve was the action for debt, and the other forms merely elaborated on that original. Thus the brieve of distress is the first of the compulsion writs in the Ayr manuscript 'register' (where there are seven different forms altogether), the Edinburgh manuscript (where there are ten) and the Bute manuscript (where there are eleven).

The legal issues with which each of these brieves dealt are quite clearly to do only with personal rather than real rights, and so they may be excluded from the ambit of the brieves rule. Nevertheless, these brieves could touch upon disputes relating to land, and a proper understanding of their scope is of some importance for the present work. This is most obviously true of the brieve of warrandice, whereby a person challenged for possession of his lands sued the author of his title to enforce the obligation of warrandice contained in the charter granting him the lands. A court action challenging the pursuer's title would have been the normal prerequisite for this brieve. This is borne out by *Quoniam* which also states that bringing the brieve will sist that action. If the claim of warrandice succeeds, then the author of the title will be brought into the principal action as defender.[117] A brieve in the Bute manuscript entitled *supersessio* instructs the justiciar to sist a process of mortancestry before him while the defender brings an action before the sheriff on a brieve of warrandice.[118] An example of this is found in a document of 1372 in which the earl of March acknowledges before the sheriff of Edinburgh that James Douglas of Dalkeith has presented him with a royal brieve of warrandice after being impleaded for the lands of Morton in the justiciar's court. The earl accepts his liability to warrant Douglas in that court.[119]

When the brieves of distress, convention and relief of cautioners can be found in the sources, it is clear that they are being used to enforce debts and contracts in both the sheriff and burgh courts.[120] What is of most interest, however, is the process of execution which followed continued default by the debtor after the decree of the court against him. According to *Quoniam*, payment of the debt or performance of the contract had to follow within fifteen days, otherwise the pursuer would be entitled to seek satisfaction from the debtor's moveables.[121] Moreover, it seems, the creditor could move ultimately against the debtor's heritage also, at least from the late thirteenth century onward. Thus, in 1290, lands in the *villa* of Berwick were sold by the owner to his creditors, Kelso abbey, under judicial compulsion of the lord king's bailies.[122] It is not stated whether this was the culmination of proceedings under a brieve of distress; indeed, the first explicit evidence of such a brieve is twelve years later.[123] Kames, Erskine and Ross all believed that the brieve of distress was introduced in the reign of Alexander II, and that a statute attributed to that king by Skene permitted execution against the debtor's heritage if his moveables proved insufficient to satisfy the creditor's claim.[124] In preparing the *Acts of the Parliaments of Scotland*, however, Thomas Thomson did not print the statute among those of Alexander II, presumably because he found its text only in two late manuscripts, and there are no internal reasons for supposing it to be authentic legislation of any thirteenth-century king.[125] On the other hand, however, several pieces of later medieval evidence show that the principle of the 'statute' operated in practice under the brieve of distress. For example, in May 1442, Gilbert Menzies brought such a brieve against John Tulloch and his son Wat in the sheriff court of Kincardine at Inverbervie. Having obtained judgment, Gilbert and the sheriff-deputes were unable to find goods of the defenders to satisfy it, and obtained the king's precept to have a '*strop*' put on their heritage. The lands were then offered for sale at the next four head courts of the sheriffdom. Finally, in January 1444, Gilbert again presented royal letters to the court and sought fulfilment of the judgment. The sheriff-depute appointed an assize to 'prise' as much of the lands to Gilbert as would satisfy him, after which heritable state and sasine was given. Finally, all this was confirmed by the king in July 1450.[126]

It is worth noting, especially in the light of earlier discussion of the lord's disciplinary jurisdiction over his tenant's lands for default of service, that execution against heritage, as opposed to moveables, seems to have required further royal authorisation. *Quoniam* implies that the brieve itself was sufficient warrant for execution against the debtor's goods,[127] while in a case of 1452 on a brieve of convention, once the pursuer had obtained judgment, the sheriff ordered his mair to compel the fulfilment of the contract according to law.[128] This throws interesting light on the act of 1469, which states that 'quhare the dettoure has na moveable gudis bot his lande, the schireff before quham the saide soume is recoverit be the brefe of distres sail ger sell the lande to the availe of the det and pay the creditour'.[129] Was a purpose of this provision the removal of a formality of execution against heritage? Certainly, in general, the act made such diligence easier, because it enabled the creditor to claim entry automatically from the superior of whom the debtor held the lands where previously entry could have been refused. This presumably is why Gilbert Menzies had to obtain a royal confirmation under the great seal when he carried out his apprising in the 1440s; without it, he would not have been properly entered or infeft. Proceedings against heritage in satisfaction of debt are relatively common from 1469 onward, no doubt because they had become more readily available and enforceable.[130] Even so, the debtor might not be put out of his lands forever; the act gave him seven years to pay his debt and redeem them before they were lost to the creditor in perpetuity.

The 1469 act also shows the context of lordship within which the brieve of distress functioned. The act opens with an account of 'the gret herschip and distructiounis of the kingis commonis, malaris and inhabitaris lordis landis throw the force of the brefe of distres, that quhare ony soumes ar optenit be virtu of the said brefe upoun the lord awnare of the ground, that the gudis and catal of the pur mennis inhabitaris of the ground ar takin and distrenzeit for the lordis dettis quhare the malis extendis nocht to the avail of the det'.[131] The tenants offered assistance by the act of 1469 were not freeholders holding of the lord in question, however, but those possessing on tacks and customary tenures who would have enjoyed little protection either from the lord or the lord's creditors under the general law before 1469. This also seems to confirm the authenticity of a passage in *Quoniam* to the effect that the creditor could seize the cattle of a debtor's husbandmen (*husbandorum*).[132] The act provided specifically that 'fra hyne furth the pure tenandis sal nocht be distrenzeit for the lordis dettis forthir than his termes mail extendis'.[133] This liability of tenants for the debts of their lord may be another explanation of the familiar clause in royal letters of protection, prohibiting poinding of the beneficiary for another's debts, although it is difficult to see how twelfth-century and later peasant tenants could have afforded such royal letters.[134]

We know that actions of debt might be brought without brieve, and the question arises of why a creditor should indulge in the expense and trouble of obtaining one. *Quoniam* offers three reasons: first, the defender could not claim his lord's court; second, the creditor did not need to make his claim in formal words; and third, neither party could be amerced.[135] Again this points us back to the origins of the brieves in the king's protection, inasmuch as recovery of debts is facilitated, and the possibility of injustice in the court having jurisdiction over the debtor can be avoided.

Harding also finds the origins of the brieve *de nativis* in the king's protection,[136] but at no stage did the brieve *de nativis* lead to the ejection of the defender from his freeholding. It was essentially a personal action, brought by the pursuer to recover '*nativos et fugitivos homines suos*', his serfs who had fled from the lands to which their status bound them.[137] The model of the English writ of naifty was clearly important in the evolution of the brieve, from 'general confirmations of seigneurial rights, warnings to other lords', into a tool for the commencement of litigation.[138] *Regiam* and *Quoniam* explain that when one claims another to be his native bondman by brieve *de nativis*, the defender's status is established either by the evidence of his relations or by an assize.[139] This latter procedure was used before the sheriff of Banff in 1364, when the bishop of Moray sued by a '*breve de capella domini nostri regis super nativis*', and recovered '*nativos homines suos . . . per meliores et fideliores patrie assysam*',[140] There are one or two other earlier cases which may have involved a brieve *de nativis*,[141] but it seems likely that in the latter part of the fourteenth century it fell into desuetude with the disappearance of the status of serfdom and the idea that a man and his children could be thirled in perpetuity to labour in the place of their birth.

As found in the Bute and Edinburgh formularies and in *Quoniam* the brieve *de proteccione regis infricta* takes a deceptively simple form.[142] It is addressed to the sheriff and commands him to summon a named person to appear 'before the king', to answer there concerning his breach of the king's protection '*cum equis vi et armis*', and to have done to him what justice demands. *Quoniam* makes it clear that here the sheriff was acting as an officer of the justiciar's court, in which the brieve was actually pursued. The form is thus rather like that of English writs returnable by the sheriff before the king's justices – the only one of the Scottish brieves to take this style. *Quoniam* goes on to explain that with this brieve only the fourth day is peremptory; that is, the defender had three essonzies before he needed to make any appearance in court. The pursuer then made a statement of claim in which, according to *Quoniam*, he had to specify precisely the time, place and manner of the wrong done to him, and assess or quantify his damage.[143] Again according to *Quoniam*, the pursuer had also to state that this was done in defiance of the king's protection, unjustly and contrary to the law of the land. The case proceeded on the finding of an assize, and if the defender was found guilty he was in the king's mercy as well as liable to the pursuer in damages.[144]

What then did this vaguely-expressed brieve seek to remedy? It has been persuasively argued by Harding that the brieve *de proteccione regis infricta* 'plays the same role in Scotland as the writ of trespass in England'.[145] The link between the two is found in their phraseology: the breaking of the king's peace *cum vi et armis*, with force and arms. This raises the question of how far the similarity can be taken. Could the brieve be used to try questions of title to land, as began to happen with English trespass writs about 1400?[146] There is unfortunately, but unsurprisingly, no direct evidence. In 1368, an action by a brieve *de proteccione regis infricta* was raised in the justiciar's court at Lanark. It was alleged that the defender had wrongfully pastured his cattle on the pursuer's land. The defender claimed that the pastures belonged to his lord, John Lindsay, and that he ought not to answer for his lord's fee and heritage on a brieve *de proteccione regis infricta*.[147] A possible interpretation of this is that in 1368 the brieve was regarded as inappropriate for claims to land. There also survives a statement of claim alleging a breach of protection which clearly involves only a personal wrong. It follows closely the form suggested by *Quoniam*, stating the date and place of the wrong as well as the manner of it: the defender 'wrangwisely and aganis the law' took away twenty-one beasts of various kinds not belonging to him, worth ten pounds sterling. This, it is alleged, broke the king's firm peace and protection, causing 'il, molest, wrang and greif to the pursuer, who assesses his 'schame and skath' at four hundred pounds.[148]

The brieve itself may well have been superseded after 1430, when parliament passed a statute concerning 'the brief of the breking of the kingis proteccioun'. If a person was under the king's protection and it was broken, 'fra he haf complenzeit to the schiref', then that officer was to summon the infringer to appear before him at his next head court, 'til answer to this party anentis the breking of the kingis proteccioun'. Whether or not the defender compeared, the sheriff was 'to ger it to be knawin be ane assise gif the kingis proteccioun be brokyn or nocht'. If the defender was found guilty, penalties were to be the same as under the brieve: liability to pay the king's unlaw, and to 'assith' the pursuer.[149]

On the face of it, this statute transfers jurisdiction to the sheriff which had previously pertained to the justiciar. It appears to dispense with any need for a brieve to commence the litigation. Instead, the procedure is commenced by simple, perhaps oral, complaint and judicial summons. No essonzies are allowed. Given that justice ayres took place at most twice in any year, it can be seen that the essonzies available against the brieve could delay the hearing of the case for a considerable period of time. Since the head courts of the sheriffdom were held thrice a year, the statute seems to provide greatly increased opportunity to use the concept of breach of the king's protection to found an action. However, some caution must be exercised before drawing this conclusion too readily. There is a clear relationship between the brieve *de proteccione regis infricta* and claims of *wrang and unlauch*, which were certainly being brought without brieve in the burgh court of Aberdeen in 1317.[150] It can also be inferred from an act of 1318 that actions of *wrang and unlauch* (also described as actions of *torte et non raysoun*) were known in other courts at this period.[151] Two of the cases in Aberdeen concerned defamation, while the third was an unsuccessful claim in respect of possession of land, which was repelled by reference to the brieves rule, as noted earlier in this chapter.[152] There is a significant comparison to be made with the situations to which the brieve *de proteccione regis infricta* was applied in the 1368 case and the statement of claim which constitute virtually our sole evidence on the matter. These dealt with what slightly later law would have called wrongful occupation and spuilzie respectively.[153] The first appearance of such nomenclature in Scotland is in the mid-fifteenth century, significantly after the passage of the act of 1430.[154] We will return to these and similar actions in a later chapter, but it may be that their development owes something to an attempt to clarify and define categories within the broad idea of breach of protection.[155] We remain uncertain about much in the development of trespassory notions in medieval Scots law, and in particular about when and why a pursuer might have used the brieve *de proteccione regis infricta* rather than making a complaint of *wrang and unlauch*. So far as our extremely limited evidence goes, however, it seems that in the fourteenth century both actions were regarded as inappropriate for the recovery of land, and that the brieves rule did not bring the brieve *de proteccione regis infricta* into play.

This leaves us with the brieves of right, mortancestry and novel dissasine. The next three chapters are devoted to a detailed discussion of these brieves, which were clearly remedies for the recovery of land, the use of which was made necessary by the brieves rule, and which survived into and beyond the fifteenth century. The treatment will not be strictly chronological, in order to assist clarity of analysis and argument. Much about the brieves, particularly the question of origins, is uncertain, and requires inference back from the relatively knowable of the later medieval period to the unknown of the earlier period. Equally, each brieve throws light upon the others at various stages of their development. The third following chapter therefore attempts to draw together the strands of the arguments set out in the preceding two, and to make some further conclusions, in particular on origins, purpose and functions of the brieves considered as a group in the context of medieval Scottish society.

NOTES

1. *APS*, i, p. 341 (c. 43). The Berne MS is SRO, PA 5/1.
2. PRO, *Ancient correspondence*, SC 1/18/147, printed *SHR*, 1 (1972), pp. 15–16, calendared *CDS*, v, no 152.
3. *Glanvill*, XII, 2, 25.
4. *Abdn Ct Bk*, pp. 10–14.
5. The best text is now *RRS*, v, p. 413 (c. 25). See also *APS*, i, p. 473 (c. 25).
6. The phrase is G. W. S. Barrow's: *Bruce*, p. 262.
7. See e.g. R. C. van Caenegem, *Birth*, pp. 26–7; M. T. Clanchy, *England and its Rulers*, pp. 143–4.
8. See G. W. S. Barrow, *Bruce*, pp. 282–3, 292; R. Nicholson, *LMA*, p. 111; *RRS*, v, pp. 39–44.
9. *RRS*, v, no 41 (*APS*, i, p. 464).
10. G. W. S. Barrow, *Bruce*, p. 270.
11. *RRS*, v, p. 74.
12. *RRS*, v, pp. 73–4.
13. *RRS*, v, no 5.
14. See *RRS*, v, no 60 for the grant to Adam.
15. *RMS*, i, appendix 1, nos 95–6. See further G. W. S. Barrow, *Bruce*, pp. 278–9.
16. *RM* (*APS*), III, 23; *RM* (*Cooper*), III, 25. Note that this follows *Glanvill*, XII, 25. The statement of the rule in *Glanvill*, XII, 2, is found in *RM* (*Cooper*), III, 20, but not in the parallel chapter of *RM* (*APS*) (III, 17), which follows the earliest MS in this respect. See however Cooper's note on this text.
17. See above, pp. 45–7.
18. *ESC*, nos 26, 27; see also no 121.
19. *ESC*, no 80; *Newb Reg*, no 3; *RRS*, ii, nos 232, 540; G. W. S. Barrow, *Kingdom*, p. 81.
20. See, in addition to references in the previous note, e.g. *Arb Lib*, i, nos 228, 229; *Dunf Reg*, no 193; *Newb Reg*, nos 119 and 170; *Soutra*, no 32.
21. See below, p. 127.
22. A. Harding, 'Brieves', pp. 128–9.
23. *Glanvill*, XII, 2, 25.
24. *Melr Lib*, i, nos 101–5; T. M. Cooper, *Cases*, no 6; Cooper, *Papers*, pp. 81–7.
25. See below, pp. 136–210, passim.
26. See below, pp. 137–8.
27. Recent writers on English law have linked the origin of the writs rule with novel disseisin: see J. Biancalana, 'Want of Justice', pp. 448–9 note 56.
28. Note that none of the borough custumals printed in *Borough Customs*, ed. M. Bateson, 2 vols (Selden Society, 1904–6), other than that of Waterford in Ireland (i, p. 235), refers directly to the writ rule.
29. See below, pp. 155–6, 176–7, 199–201.
30. See below, pp. 155–6.
31. D. W. Sutherland, *Novel Disseisin*, p. 26 note.
32. *APS*, i, p. 352 (c. 99).
33. *Reg Brieves*, pp. 46 (no 64), 55 (nos 23–7); *Form E*, nos 4–7.

34. *Moray Reg*, pp. 459–61; J. Robertson, *Concilia*, ii, pp. 242–6; *Inchcolm Chrs*, nos 21, 25: *Beauly Chrs*, no 5; possibly also *Inchaff Chrs*, no 110, where Walter *pistorem* and Hawys his wife renounce all remedies in favour of Inchaffray, including 'royal letters [?of prohibition]'.

35. See G. W. S. Barrow, *Kingdom*, pp. 90–2; M. Ash, 'The Church in the reign of Alexander III', in *Scotland in the Reign of Alexander III*, ed. N. H. Reid (Edinburgh, 1990), p. 37.

36. *Abdn Reg*, i, p. 155.

37. *Moray Reg*, p. 209.

38. *Moray Reg*, p. 379.

39. See above, p. 107; *QA (Fergus)*, ch. 20; *QA (APS)*, ch. 18; *QA (Cooper)*, ch. 25.

40. *APS*, i, pp. 557–8. For background, see R. Nicholson, *LMA*, pp. 201–2.

41. *Moray Reg*, no 153.

42. *HMC, Various Collections*, v, p. 77; corrected from SRO, RH4/124/1.

43. A. R. Borthwick, 'Thesis', pp. 340–2. On Reid, see above, pp. 78, 96–8.

44. A. R. Borthwick, 'Thesis', pp. 344–5.

45. *RMS*, i, appendix 1, nos 31 and 34; *RRS*, v, no 389 (p. 634).

46. *St A Form*, i, pp. 251–4.

47. SRO, ADC, CS 5/12, f. 129v, and ff. 152r–153r. See further below, p. 210.

48. SRO, *Forglen muniments*, GD 185/2/2/1.

49. See R. C. Reid, 'Coschogill writ', p. 132; *CA Chrs*, ii, no 128. The regality of Drumlanrig was held by the earls of Douglas in regality; the Douglases of Drumlanrig held of the earl in barony.

50. *Abdn Reg*, i, p. 212.

51. *RRS*, vi, no 170. The grant only survives in the form of a late translation of the original.

52. T. M. Cooper, 'Freehold in Scots law', *JR*, lvii (1945), p. 1; W. C. Dickinson, 'Freehold in Scots law', JR, lvii (1945), p. 135. See also A. Grant, 'Thesis', pp. 204–7.

53. For two examples antedating Dickinson's earliest instance of this practice, see *RRS*, vi, nos 266 and 269. The device is not explicable as a means of avoiding the casualties of ward and relief, since supcriors would hardly have agreed to it otherwise, and indeed often carefully reserved these casualties in the transaction. It may have avoided the casualty of non-entry, however. Probably it was also used to minimise other inheritance formalities (e.g. service of the heir), or to divert lands away from the heir: see A. Grant, 'Thesis', pp. 206–7.

54. W. C. Dickinson, 'Freehold', p. 146.

55. *RM (APS)*, IV, 37 (and see also IV, 40); *RM (Cooper)*, Supplement no 19 (see also no 22); T. M. Cooper, 'Freehold', pp. 2–3. As Cooper notes (*RM (Cooper)*, pp. 41 and 297), the source of these passages appears to be an English treatise of the thirteenth century, *Articuli qui in narrando indigent observari* (as to which see P & M, ii, p. 45 note).

56. *APS*, i, p. 722; T. M. Cooper, 'Freehold', p. 3.

57. *HMC, Various Collections*, v, p. 77.
58. See above, p. 111.
59. See above, p. 111.
60. S. F. C. Milsom, *LFEF*, pp. 25–7.
61. *Glanvill*, IX, 1 and 8. Note that there is no reference, negative or otherwise, to the writ rule in the other *Glanvill* passages (VII, 12 and 17) cited by S. F. C. Milsom, loc. cit., previous note, which deal specifically with the tenant's felony and the unchaste heiress. On these passages, see also P. A. Brand, 'Lordship and distraint', pp. 5–6.
62. The omission is there from the Bute MS on, so does not seem to be a piece of late editing: see e.g. NLS, MS 21,246, f. 45r; Adv MS 25.4.13, f. 57r–v; Adv MS 25.5.10 (Cromertie), f. 57r; BL, Addit MS 18,111, f.45r–v.
63. See above, pp. 39–400.
64. *QA (Fergus)*, ch. 33; *QA (APS)*, ch. 30; *(Cooper)*, ch. 47. See also ch. 16 *(Fergus)* [ch. 14 *(APS)*, ch. 18 *(Cooper)*] (lands maybe escheat to their lord if tenant commits murder) for another example of feudal discipline.
65. *APS*, i, p. 733 (c. 22). This text is quoted in Sir James Balfour, *Practicks*, ii, pp. 482–3; and in J. Skene, *DVS*, sv 'Recognition'. It is probably to be linked to the increasing use of recognition by royal government in the later fifteenth century, discussed in R. Nicholson, 'Feudal developments', pp. 16–20. On recognition for failure of service, see also Thomas Craig, *JF*, III, 5, xxiii.
66. See above, ch. 1.
67. *APS*, i, pp. 552–3.
68. *APS*, i, p. 575.
69. See, in addition to material already cited, *Moray Reg*, no 291; *Newb Reg*, no. 283; *Mort Reg*, ii, no 194; *Laing Chrs*, no 117.
70. S. F. C. Milsom, *LFEF*, pp. 30–1; see also P. A. Brand, 'Lordship and distraint', pp. 14–15.
71. D. W. Sutherland, *Novel Disseisin*, p. 82. S. F. C. Milsom, *LFEF*, p. 11 note, characterises this position as 'the factual result of external control'.
72. *APS*, i, p. 575.
73. *APS*, i, pp. 552–3. See, on further proceedings in this case, below, pp. 135 (note 154), 233.
74. *Newb Reg*, no 283. For the 'Karlenlippis' of this document as Carlops, Midlothian, see W. J. Watson, *The Celtic Place-Names of Scotland* (Edinburgh, 1926), p. 140.
75. *Laing Chrs*, no 117.
76. *APS*, i, p. 733 (c. 22).
77. Chapter 39 of Magna Carta 1217 (chapter 32 in the 1225 reissue) is reproduced in *Omne Gaderum (APS*, i, p. 731 (c. 4)). See also Thomas Craig, *JF*, III, 3, for reasoning of this kind justifying recognition for alienation.
78. See e.g. *Familie of Innes*, p. 64 (1377); A. Grant, 'Thesis', pp. 202–4; *RRS*, vi, nos 251, 253, 469; W. Fraser, *Southesk*, ii, no 56; *ADC*, i, p. 22; R. Nicholson, 'Feudal developments', pp. 16–19; C. Madden, 'Royal treatment of feudal casualties in late medieval Scotland', *SHR*, lv (1976), pp. 184–7. The treatment in R. Burgess, *Perpetuities*

in *Scots Law* (Stair Society, 1979), pp. 58–60, is useful, but the medieval 'statutes' mentioned should be treated with caution.

79. See *Libri Feudorum*, I, 5, 13; II, 9, 24, 34, 38–44, 52, 55; and see above, p. 53.
80. D. W. Sutherland, *Novel Disseisin*, pp. 86–96; see also S. F. C. Milsom, *LFEF*, pp. 113–21.
81. A. Grant, 'Thesis', pp. 197–211.
82. *Prot Bk Young*, nos 875 and 896; see also, for another recognition for alienation in a baron court, no 895.
83. They are so linked by Thomas Craig, *JF*, III, 5.
84. *Glanvill*, IX, 11; *RM (APS)*, II, 68; *RM (Cooper)*, II, 74.
85. S. F. C. Milsom, *LFEF*, p. 11 note 1, pp. 26–7.
86. J. Biancalana, 'Want of justice', pp. 480–1.
87. *RM (APS)*, I, 4; *RM (Cooper)*, I, 5.
88. *Reg Brieves*, p. 59 (no 71); *Form E*, no 20. The full text is as follows in Bute (NLS, MS 21,246, f. 12v):

    Inquisicio de purprestura

    Rex etc. Sciatis quod constituimus tales loco nostri ad faciendum diligentes et fidelem inquisicionem per probos et fideles et antiquiores homines patris si aliqua purprestura sit facta super terras nostras de K per A de B vel per quoscumque alios quantum qualiter et a quo tempore et quid per dictam inquisicionem diligenter et fideliter factam esse inveneritis sub sigillis eorum et quorundam aliorum qui dicte inquisicioni intererunt faciende ad capellam nostram mittatis et hoc breve quare etc omnibus et singulis mandamus quatinus dictis talibus loco nostri constitutis in premissis sitis intendentes et respondentes presentibus etc. See also, on this brieve, *RRS*, v, pp. 106–7.

89. *APS*, i, pp. 114–15.
90. *HMC*, xiv (3), pp. 15–16.
91. *APS*, ii, pp. 133, 141; see above, p. 83.
92. *ADC*, i, p. 74.
93. *RRS*, vi, no 152.
94. See passages in both works cited above, p. 120.
95. *Moray Reg*, no 290.
96. *ADA*, p. 91; *ADC*, i, pp. 45, 59.
97. S. F. C. Milsom, *LFEF*, p. 27.
98. R. M. Maxtone-Graham, 'Showing the holding', pp. 254–5. For *Quoniam*, see *QA (Fergus)*, ch. 20; *QA (APS)*, ch. 18; *QA (Cooper)*, ch. 25.
99. See above, p. 112. The plea is not noted in R. M. Maxtone-Graham's article.
100. S. F. C. Milsom, *LFEF*, pp. 45–54.
101. P. R. Hyams, 'Warranty', pp. 460–2 (quotation on p. 461).
102. This is the situation in S. F. C. Milsom's Countess Amice case: see *LFEF*, pp. 45–7, and P. R. Hyams, 'Warranty', pp. 494–6.
103. *Abdn Reg*, i, p. 155.
104. *Abdn Reg*, i, p. 154.
105. *Abdn Reg*, i, pp. 144–5, 150–2. See also, on alienation of church lands to laymen in the canon law, M. Cheney, 'Inalienability in mid-twelfth century England', *Proceedings of the Sixth International Congress of Medieval Canon Law 1980: Monumenta Iuris Canonici Series C* (Vatican, 1985), vii, p. 467.

106. *RM (APS)*, I, 4; *RM (Cooper)*, I, 5.
107. *QA (Fergus)*, ch. 36; *QA (APS)*, ch. 33; *QA (Cooper)*, ch. 49
108. For retourable brieves, see I. D. Willock, *Jury*, pp. 109–21.
109. Reg Brieves, p. 33.
110. See, for inconclusive discussion of this heading, *RRS*, v, pp. 104–5.
111. See above, p. 77, any my article cited in the next note.
112. H. L. MacQueen, 'Pleadable brieves', pp. 416–17.
113. For styles, see *Reg Brieves*, pp. 37–9 (nos 11–17), 53–4 (nos 5–17); Form E, nos 103–13; *QA (Fergus)*, pp. 199–202, 209–10; *QA (APS)*, chs 49–51, 56; *QA (Cooper)*, chs 49–51, 55.
114. *QA (Fergus)*, ch. 36; *QA (APS)*, ch. 34; *QA (Cooper)*, chs 50, 51.
115. *QA (Fergus)*, ch. 40; *QA (APS)*, ch. 38; *QA (Cooper)*, ch. 55.
116. A. Harding, 'Brieves', p. 128; *Reg Brieves*, pp. 35 (no 1), 55 (nos 28–32); *Form E*, no 43.
117. *QA (Fergus)*, ch. 40; *QA (APS)*, ch. 38; *QA (Cooper)*, ch. 55.
118. *Reg Brieves*, p. 61 (no 96).
119. *Mort Reg*, ii, no 130.
120. See e.g. *Abdn Ct Bk*, pp. cxxv note 5, 133, 232, 237; SRO, *Crown Office writs*, AD 1/52; *Ayr Burgh Court Book 1428–1478*, f. 77v; *Kel Lib*, ii, no 397; W. Fraser, *Wemyss*, ii, no 49; W. Fraser, *Melville*, iii, no 41; *RMS*, ii, no 375; *APS*, i, p. 735 (c. 8).
121. *QA (Fergus)*, ch. 36; *QA (APS)*, ch. 34; *QA (Cooper)*, ch. 49.
122. *Kel Lib*, i, no 44. See further W. Stevenson, 'The monastic presence in Scottish burghs in the twelfth and thirteenth centuries', *SHR*, lx (1981), p. 103.
123. *Kel Lib*, ii, no 397.
124. Lord Kames, *HLT*, ii, pp. 57–63; J. Erskine, *Institute*, II, 12, ii; W. Ross, *Lectures*, i, p. 397.
125. See *APS*, i, p. 734 (c. 1), and 'Table of Authorities'.
126. *RMS*, ii, no 375. For further detail of this case, see A. R. Borthwick, 'Thesis', pp. 364–6.
127. *QA (Fergus)*, ch. 36; *QA (APS)*, ch. 34; *QA (Cooper)*, ch. 49.
128. W. Fraser, *Melville*, iii, no 41.
129. *APS*, ii, p. 96 (c. 12).
130. R. Nicholson, 'Feudal developments', pp. 11–16; cf. R. Burgess, *Perpetuities in Scots Law* (Stair Society, 1979), p. 56.
131. *APS*, ii, p. 96 (c. 12).
132. *QA (Fergus)*, ch. 36; *QA (APS)*, ch. 34; *QA (Cooper)*, ch. 49.
133. *APS*, ii, p. 96 (c. 12).
134. See e.g. *Reg Brieves*, pp. 35 (no 1), 55 (no 28); A. Harding, 'Brieves', p. 121; *RRS*, v, p. 101.
135. *QA (Fergus)*, ch. 36; *QA (APS)*, ch. 34; *QA (Cooper)*, ch. 49.
136. A. Harding, 'Brieves', p. 128.
137. For styles, see *Reg Brieves*, pp. 36 (no 5), 53 (no 12), and *QA (Fergus)*, pp. 208–9; *QA (APS)*, ch. 55; *QA (Cooper)*, ch. 56; see also *RRS*, i, pp. 63–4, and ii, p. 71.
138. See P. R. Hyams, *Kings, Lords and Peasants in Medieval England* (Oxford, 1980) pp. 230–2, for a discussion of the relationship of the English writ of naifty with the brieve *de nativis*. The quotation is from these pages also.
139. RM (APS), II, 8; RM (Cooper), II, 11; QA (Fergus), ch. 41; QA (APS), ch. 39; QA (Cooper), ch. 56.

140. *Moray Reg*, no 143.
141. See e.g. *RMS*, i, appendix 1, no 67; *Dunf Reg*, no 379.
142. See *Reg Brieves*, p. 56 (no 41); *Form E*, no 48; *QA (Fergus)*, pp. 207–8; *QA (APS)*, ch. 54; *QA (Cooper)*, ch. 54.
143. *QA (Fergus)*, ch. 39; *QA (APS)*, ch. 37; *QA (Cooper)*, ch. 54. See also, on this, an act of 1318: *RRS*, v, p. 411 (c. 17); *APS*, i, p. 471 (c. 17).
144. For all this, see *QA (Fergus)*, ch. 39; *QA (APS)*, ch. 37; *QA (Cooper)*, ch. 54.
145. A. Harding, 'Brieves', p. 134. For trespass in England, the *locus classicus* is S. F. C. Milsom, *Studies*, pp. 1–90; see also A. Harding's introduction to *Shropshire Roll*, pp. xxxii–lviii; and *Select Cases of Trespass from the King's Courts 1307–1399*, ed. M. S. Arnold (Selden Society, 2 vols, 1985, 1987).
146. D. W. Sutherland, *Novel Disseisin*, pp. 169–203.
147. *APS*, i, p. 505.
148. *Mort Reg*, i, appendix 1, no 10.
149. *SHR*, xxix (1950), p. 9, correcting dating in *APS*, ii, 22 (c. 1). On assythment, see R. Black, 'A historical survey of delictual liability in Scotland for personal injuries and death', *Comparative and International Law Journal of Southern Africa*, viii (1975), p. 53, and J. M. Wormald, 'Bloodfeud', pp. 62, 80–6, 89–90.
150. *Abdn Ct Bk*, pp. 8, 10, 11. See further H. L. MacQueen and W. J. Windram, 'Burghs', pp. 216, and notes.
151. *RRS*, v, p. 411 (c. 17); *APS*, i, p. 471 (c. 17). See further, on this act, H. L. MacQueen and W. J. Windram, 'Burghs', p. 216. The idea of *wrang and unlauch* went back at least to the time of Alexander II: see *APS*, i, p. 402 (c. 11).
152. See above, pp. 105–6.
153. *APS*, i, p. 505; *Mort Reg*, ii, appendix 1, no 10. On spuilzie and wrongful occupation, see below, pp. 222–8.
154. See *APS*, ii, pp. 32 (c. 2), 36 (c. 7), and 47 (c. 2), and *AB Ill*, iv, p. 43 (spuilzie); *Arb Lib*, ii, no 123 and *APS*, ii, p. 51 (c. 25) (wrongful occupation). Note several references to spoliation in a case abut the withholding of mutures in 1369 (*Moray Reg*, no 153), and that William de Fenton was *exspoliatus* of his tenement of Fenton in 1385 (*APS*, i, p. 552).
155. Note however that the general concept of *wrang and unlauch* still survived, at least in burghs, in 1455 (*APS*, ii, p. 43 (c. 9)).

5

The Brieve of Novel Dissasine

ORIGINS AND EARLY HISTORY

In translation of the Latin text of the original, the brieve of novel
dissasine (Latin *nova dissasina*, 'new dissasine' in Scots) runs thus in the
fourteenth-century formularies:[1]

> The king to the justiciar [north or south] of Forth. By his grave
> complaint A has shown us that B unjustly and without a judgment
> dissaised him of the lands of C with the pertinents in the tenement
> of D within the sheriffdom of E, of which he was vested and saised
> for days and years as of fee. Wherefore we command and ordain
> that you take from the foresaid A safe and secure pledges for the
> pusuit of his claim, and that you cause to be recognosced by good
> and faithful men of the neighbourhood justly and according to the
> assize of the land if it is as the said A has shown us. If through the
> said recognition held justly and according to the assize of the land
> you find it to be so, cause the foresaid A justly to have sasine of the
> said lands of C with the pertinents and without delay take for our
> use the amercement pertaining to us from the foresaid B for the
> unjust dissasine made by him. But if by the same recognition held
> justly and according to the assize of the land it appears otherwise
> to you, take to our use the amercement pertaining to us from the
> foresaid A for his unjust complaint.

The dependence of this style on the English writ of novel disseisin is
readily apparent from comparison:[2]

> The king to the sheriff, greeting. N has complained to me that R,
> unjustly and without a judgment has disseised him of his free
> tenement in such-and-such a vill since my last voyage to Normandy.
> Therefore I command you that if N gives you security for prosecut-
> ing his claim, you are to see that the chattels which were taken from
> the tenement are restored to it, and that the tenement and the
> chattels remain in peace until the Sunday after Easter. And mean-
> while you are to see that the tenement is viewed by twelve free and
> lawful men of the neighbourhood, and their names endorsed on this

writ. And summon them by good summoners to be before me or my justices on the Sunday after Easter, ready to make the recognition. And summon R, or his bailiff if he himself cannot be found, on the security of gage and reliable sureties to be there then to hear the recognition. And have there the summoners, and this writ and the names of the sureties.

The earliest reference to a remedy for dissasine in the Scottish royal courts seems to be in a statute of 1230, the wording of which closely parallels the style of the brieve set out above, and which has generally been accepted as authentic.[3] It is however clear that an enactment included in the *Assise Regis David*, laying down that brieves of novel dissasine and mortancestry are always to be determined by an assize, cannot possibly be legislation of David I, accurate though its statement of the law is.[4] There is no evidence of any brieves dealing with such questions earlier than the reign of Alexander II, or indeed of any forerunners in style of the brieve as it appears in the formularies of the Ayr and Bute manuscripts. It is also inherently unlikely that novel dissasine was known as such in Scotland before the introduction of novel disseisin in England in the 1160s. The assize may reflect genuine legislation of a later period, or may perhaps even be a version of the 1230 act itself, since the brieve refers to 'recognition justly and according to the assize of the land', and the use of a recognition or jury is also at the heart of the 1230 statute.

The 1230 statute on dissasine reads as follows in translation:

> The lord king Alexander also enacted at the said day and place that if anyone should complain to the lord king or his justiciar that his lord or any other person has dissaised him unjustly and without a judgment of any tenement of which he was previously vest and saised, and shall find pledges for the pursuit of his claim [*de clamore suo prosequendo*], the justiciar or the sheriff by precept of the king or the justiciar shall cause it to be recognosced by good men of the country if the complainer [*conquerens*] makes a just complaint. And if it shall be recognosced and proved, the justiciar or the sheriff shall cause him to be resaised of the land of which he was dissaised, and the dissaisor shall be in the king's mercy. If however it shall be recognosced that the complainer has made an unjust complaint, the complainer shall be in the king's mercy of ten pounds.

The statute is found in the *Acts of the Parliaments of Scotland* as part of a group of enactments stated to have been made at Stirling in 1230 in the presence of the magnates of the realm, including Thomas de Melsanby, prior of Coldingham, William Comyn, earl of Buchan and justiciar of Scotia, and Walter Olifard, justiciar of Lothian. Although the printed text does not correspond in this respect with the earliest manuscripts of the legislation, the names mentioned held the offices in question in and around 1230. William and Walter were indeed justiciars of Scotia and Lothian respectively, and Thomas was prior of Coldingham.[5] It seems unlikely that their names were added gratuitously in the later manuscripts, and it is probable that all three played an important role at the *colloquium*. The presence of the two justiciars at the making of the statute on dissasine, which was to confer an important new jurisdiction on their courts, is certainly significant. The policy behind the statutes considered as a group seems to be to consolidate the use of the jury in judicial proceedings, reflecting the general trend away from the use of combat and the ordeal as a mode of proof following the prohibition of the latter by the fourth Lateran Council in 1215.[6] It is tempting to suppose that the draftsman of this text had in front of him not only the style of the English writ but also the now lost assize which introduced novel disseisin in England, the fruit of what *Bracton* described as the work of 'many wakeful nights'.[7]

The statute enacts that when complaint is made to the king or his justiciar of dissasine from any tenement in which the complainer claimed to have been infeft, a royal writ is to be sent to the justiciar or the sheriff commanding them to determine the justice of the complaint. This is to be done by means of a recognition – that is, an assize or jury. Barrow has drawn attention to a case before the justiciar of Lothian, brought by Mariota of Chirnside and her son Patrick, son of Richard, against the priory of Coldingham for one ploughgate at Renton, and begun 'by the lord king's brieve of recognition' before 1242. He has suggested that, since it came before the justiciar and involved a *recognition* it may have been a case begun by a brieve of dissasine.[8] On the grounds that it too involved a *recognitio*, a case before the sheriff of Berwick sometime between 1233 and 1235 is another possible early example of the brieve.[9] This case is especially interesting in that the pursuers claimed rights of estovers in a wood at Reston in Berwickshire, which belonged to the defenders, the priory of Coldingham. In English law, estovers was the common right of tenants to take wood from the lord's estate so far as necessary for the repair of houses, hedges and agricultural implements.[10] The writ of novel disseisin was used from its earliest beginnings in the twelfth century to protect common rights of pasture, and the author of *Bracton* argued that it could be used for common rights of all sorts, including estovers.[11] If the view in *Bracton* was ever adopted in practice, it was obscured in the course of the thirteenth century and the second Statute of Westminster had to declare in 1285 that the assize could be used to recover estovers before the king's justices.[12] Prior to 1285, interference with estovers was dealt with by *quod permittat* writs before the sheriff, which were sometimes known as 'the little writs of novel disseisin' because they were pleaded without an assize in the county court.[13]

Can a parallel with England be drawn here, given that the Reston case was heard before the sheriff? The answer is probably not. Apart from the fact that there is no evidence for any *quod permittat* form in the admittedly much later Scottish formularies, the act of 1230 does suggest that the justiciar might issue a brieve of dissasine himself, saving the complainer the need to approach the king's chapel, and in it direct that the case be heard by the sheriff. That such a procedure was followed may be borne out by a letter of Hugh Barclay, justiciar of Lothian, written in 1262, in which he states that he has issued 'two pairs of the king's letters of dissasine' to John Scott of Reston.[14] Unfortunately, it is not stated in which courts the actions will be heard. Another document dated 2 August 1247 narrates how Adam Spott impleaded Ranulf of Buncle 'by precepts of the lord king of Scots and of lord David de Lindsay then justiciar of Lothian' for certain lands in Buncle. The case was commenced in the 'county (*comitatu*) of Berwick', which suggests the sheriff's court, although a final settlement was reached in the 'court of the king of Scots' before Lindsay the justiciar.[15] Possibly, then, this was a case heard initially before the sheriff on a brieve issued by the justiciar. Such a power did have an English parallel, although it should not be pressed too far: 'if the disseisin had been committed during a general eyre in the county, the justices in eyre could issue the original writ themselves, saving the offended party a trip to Chancery'.[16] Perhaps, then, the pursuers in the Reston case of the 1230s had obtained a brieve of dissasine from the justiciar addressed to the sheriff and were using procedures first made available by the act of 1230.

Another early case of dissasine, this time before the justiciar's court, may be the action in which Gilbert, son of Samuel, impleaded Maeldomhnaich, earl of Lennox, 'by letters of the lord king' for the lands of Monachkenneran in 1235.[17] The lands in question were attached to the church of Kilpatrick which the earl had subinfeudated to Paisley abbey. The rector of the church was the earl's younger brother Dougal, who alienated the lands to Gilbert. Gilbert's title was completed by a confirmation from Earl Maeldomhnaich. In 1233, the abbey recovered the lands by action before papal judges delegate, but Gilbert remained contumaciously absent from the proceedings, and the secular arm had to be brought against him to enforce the judgment. Perhaps the earl had been compelled as a result of this to eject Gilbert, and the latter's reaction had been to bring a brieve of dissasine. The case was settled with the earl agreeing to pay Gilbert sixty silver marks for the renunciation of his claim. Later, perhaps in the 1270s, the dean and archdeacon of Dunblane instructed Laurence, dean of Lennox, to go 'to the pleas of the lord king at Dumbarton', probably meaning a justice ayre being held there, and inhibit actions begun 'by letters of the lord king of perambulation or of

recognition' against the abbot and convent of Paisley and their lands.[18]
Assuming that the 'or' (*vet*) is disjunctive, the 'letters of recognition' may
have included brieves of novel dissasine.

It is certainly arguable from much of this early evidence that at least
one of the reasons for the introduction of the brieve of novel dissasine in
Scotland was to provide a remedy for tenants dissaised by their lords. We
saw in an earlier chapter that the ejection of tenants by lords was certainly
not unknown before 1230.[19] The act of 1230 which apparently introduced the brieve begins: 'If any man complains to the lord king or his
justiciar that his *lord* [emphasis supplied] or any other has dissaised him
unjustly and without a judgment . . .'. The brieve was a remedy for
dissasine, enabling a person who had had sasine of a tenement to recover
it where his ejection was unjust and without a judgment. The act of 1230
provided that if dissasine 'be recognosced and proved, the justiciar or the
sheriff shall cause him to be resaised of the land of which he was dissaised',
while the brieve instructed that the successful pursuer should 'justly have
sasine of the lands'. To have sasine was to have been put into possession
of land by the grantor, typically although not invariably the lord of whom
the lands were to be held. From the twelfth century on, the giving of
possession occurred symbolically; that is, the grantee received symbols of
the land – earth and stone, rod and staff- from the grantor in a ceremony
on the lands themselves.[20] Equally, the tenant resigned his holding by
returning possession symbolically to the lord, and it is interesting to note
that in 1248 the tenant could be said to be dissaising himself by this
process.[21] Sasine and dissasine were therefore general concepts closely
related to the relationship between lord and tenant. Before a dispossessed
person could bring novel dissasine, therefore, he had to have established
the relationship of sasine between himself and the land's lord prior to the
ejection; and what he sought through the remedy was a restoration of that
relationship. The person whose actings were most likely to affect the
relationship of sasine was clearly the lord.

A case of a lord being sued by his tenant, perhaps for dissasine, is the
action of Gilbert against the earl of Lennox for the lands of
Monachkenneran in 1235. The feudal dimension is also quite apparent
in the case where Mariota of Chirnside and her son Patrick sued the
priory of Coldingham for a ploughgate at Renton. Patrick's father Richard
(who was presumably Mariota's husband) is designed 'of Renton' in the
record of the case. Lands in Renton would have been held of the priory.[22]
If this was a case of dissasine, what we may be seeing is a dispossessed
tenant and tercer suing their lord to get back into their lands. Finally, the
claim of Adam of Spott in 1247 may well have been one to hold the lands
in issue of the defender Ranulf, who was the lord of the estate of Buncle
in which the lands lay.

There is also a strong feudal background to the case in which Eda, Mary and William of Paxton sought to enforce a right of estovers in the wood of Restonside against the priory of Coldingham. Estovers, as already mentioned, was a right which tenants had to take wood for certain purposes from the lord's lands. This is clearly what was meant in the Restonside case, where the pursuers were allowed reasonable estovers for the construction of houses, hedges and ploughs; another document allows us to see that other tenants of the priory also enjoyed such estovers in Restonside.[23] Milsom has argued that the use of novel disseisin to protect such rights of common is important evidence of the action's 'feudal orientation', because typically the common, whether it was a pasture, wood or some other, would be controlled by the lord.[24] Clearly, there is just such an orientation in this estovers case. However, the picture is not simply one of the lord excluding his tenants from their rights. Part of the background to this case seems to be a dispute between Coldingham and its mother house of Durham over the superiority of Paxton and Auchencrow, probably because the properties had fallen into the possession of female heirs. The dispute was settled in 1235, when it was agreed that the heirs of Paxton and Auchencrow owed homage, relief and marriage to Durham rather than to Coldingham.[25] At the time of the case before the sheriff of Berwick, therefore, the question of who was the lord from whose lands estovers could be claimed was unclear, and it is conceivable that the dispute arose initially as a result of the refusal of the family of Paxton to acknowledge Coldingham's superiority. It is also possible that the family had sought to exercise estovers in Coldingham's woods of Restonside, which lay around Auchencrow. The matter was settled on the basis that the Paxtons should enjoy estovers not in Coldingham's wood of Restonside but only in the estate of Auchencrow, and that the priory's foresters would protect that right. Lordship and its claims thus explain much in this case, but the denial of Coldingham's superiority may well be why the matter could not be dealt with in the prior's court but only in the king's.

None of this evidence seems clearly to involve the exercise of disciplinary jurisdiction by a lord. It is striking that both the act of 1230 and the form of the brieve of novel dissasine omit certain phrases found in the writ of novel disseisin and emphasised by Milsom in his argument that the purpose of the assize was to control lordly action against the tenant's fee. The writ orders the sheriff to reseise the tenement in question of its chattels, and to attach the defendant's bailiff. The reference to chattels points to distraint – the lord has taken first the chattels and then the fee – while at the time the writ was invented, only lords would have bailiffs.[26] The fact that neither the 1230 act nor the brieve mentioned chattels or bailiff does not mean that disciplinary jurisdiction was not a target for the early novel dissasine; but it tends to suggest that wider aims lay behind its introduction.

Similarly, it does not follow from the fact that these brieves were used against lords that they were the only possible defenders. The act of 1230 (a date long after the assizes had lost their feudal orientation as a primary feature in England), while it refers to lords as perhaps the prime examples of likely dissaisors, does not restrict the operation of the remedy to such cases, but states that it will operate whenever one is dissaised by another unjustly and without a judgment. There is a hint that unjust dissasine is a breach of the king's peace in the reference which the act makes to the losing defender's liability to be 'in the king's mercy', that is, subject to a fine. Following *Glanvill*, *Regiam* enables a lord to use novel dissasine against a tenant committing purpresture, provided that the time bar for the action has not elapsed.[27] Legislation in 1318 dealing with the brieve states that current practice at that time enables the person dissaised to bring the action directly against a good-faith third party infeft in the land after the original dissasine.[28] There was hardly likely to be any existing tenurial link in the land between such parties, although the infeftee might have been put in by a dissaising lord. An example of a case involving the grantee of a dissaisor who was not the lord of the dissaisee may however be found as early as 1231 in a series of documents recording the settlement in the justiciar's court at Roxburgh of a dispute over the lands of Swinewood, Berwickshire, between Coldingham priory on the one hand, and Patrick, son of the earl of Dunbar, and his father on the other.[29] There was no tenurial link between the parties, so far as we can tell, although they were near neighbours, the Dunbar lands extending all around the priory's Berwickshire estates from East Lothian into the Merse. In a quitclaim which his father confirmed, Patrick the son acknowledged that his ancestors had unjustly occupied and detained Swinewood. The implication seems to be that Patrick was in occupation in consequence of his father's grant, and that the priory had pursued its action against the former. There is nothing which says directly that this action was raised by any brieve, let alone the brieve of novel dissasine; but there are a number of interesting points about it which suggest that it was such a case. First, there is the apparent nature of the priory's claim: unjust occupation by Patrick. Then there is the involvement of the justiciar's court, although it is not clear why a case involving lands in the sheriffdom of Berwick should have been heard at Roxburgh. Next, there is the position of the priory. A brieve of right might seem the more appropriate action for the recovery of lands which had passed from an original dissaisor to subsequent grantees, and indeed Patrick expressly acknowledged the priory's '*plenum ius*', language partially (but, importantly, not exactly) echoing the '*plenum rectum*' of the brieve of right. However, that brieve, at least in its mature form, required the pursuer to show a heritable title,[30] which of course the priory, as a body incapable of having heirs, did not possess, even though it had held Swinewood since c. 1100 by virtue of a grant from King Edgar to which reference was made in court.[31] Finally, there is the evidence of the 1318 legislation already referred to. As will be discussed in more detail below, that legislation also suggests that in actions against the dissaisor's grantee, the brieve of novel dissasine was only competent so long as the dissaisor was still alive (a precisely similar rule operated in England).[32] This may then explain the role in the case of Patrick's father, the earl of Dunbar, as the original dissaisor of the priory.

If this explanation of the nature of the Swinewood litigation is accepted, then a number of other interesting points may be made about the possible intentions behind the introduction of the brieve of novel dissasine in 1230, just a year before Patrick and the priory reached their settlement. As already noted, Thomas de Melsanby, then prior of Coldingham, is one of those specifically named as participating in the *colloquium* of 1230, alongside Walter Olifard, who was the justiciar before whom the 1231 settlement was made. Evidently, the priory had had difficulties with the Dunbar family over Swinewood for some considerable time before 1231, but may have had significant legal problems to overcome before the lands could be recovered. It is not clear upon what grounds the Dunbars rested their occupation of Swinewood, but there seems to have been no question of their holding it of the priory. The priory court would therefore have been ineffective against occupiers who refused to acknowledge its jurisdiction. Even if the Dunbar possession rested on an unrecorded lease from the priory, it might have been extremely difficult to compel such a powerful tenant to submit to the prior's court. The first alternative resort in such circumstances might have been the ecclesiastical courts, but the earl of Dunbar had already in his long career shown other religious pursuers what a formidable opponent he could be in resisting the jurisdiction of the church and claiming the protection of the king's courts.[33] Within the king's courts there was the limitation of the brieve of right that a heritable title was required. It is not inconceivable, therefore, that at least one of the motives of some members of the *colloquium* of 1230 was the provision of an efficacious royal remedy in this very case.

As shown by the other thirteenth-century cases already mentioned, however, if protection of the interests of Coldingham priory was a factor in the legislation of 1230, it backfired inasmuch as the priory's tenants and others were probably able to exploit the new brieve against them. A tentative conclusion on the reasons for the act of 1230 is that, important and illuminating though this feudal context is in understanding the brieve of novel dissasine and its introduction, it does not provide a complete explanation. The brieve increased the capacity of the king's courts to protect the church against dispossession, an important matter as ecclesiastical pursuers found it increasingly difficult to force secular defenders to accept ecclesiastical jurisdiction. From the point of view of such pursuers, the brieve may well have looked like a possessory remedy, the resolution of which would still leave open to the defeated defender the raising elsewhere of proprietary issues. It may even have been to avoid this possibility that Coldingham was so careful to obtain Patrick of Dunbar's acknowledgement of its '*plenum ius*'.

If all this argument is valid, then early dissasine was not merely the breaking of a relationship between a lord and his tenant. Otherwise, it would be hard to understand how the intervention of a third party without reference to the lord could affect the tenant's sasine. Sasine was not merely an abstract legal concept but a state of fact connected with the land itself. It was like seisin in England, constituted not just by symbolical delivery but by possession following thereupon, and dissasine was exclusion from visible possession and enjoyment of land.[34] It did not follow that the dissaisor gained sasine; all that had happened was that the dissaisee had lost his sasine. However, the brieve of novel dissasine compelled a rather more sharply defined answer to the question of what sasine was, because only those who had had it could use the remedy. It is from the brieve's introduction in the thirteenth century that we should trace the story of sasine as a legal concept.

NOVEL DISSASINE OR DISSASINE?

It is striking how closely the form of the brieve of novel dissasine, as it appears in the 'registers' and *Quoniam*, follows the wording of the act of 1230 which speaks, as do the styles, of the pursuer's complaint that he has been dissaised by another unjustly and without a judgment, and requires that a recognition of the good and faithful men of the neighbourhood should be held to make inquiry into the matter. If the complaint is found to be true, the pursuer is to be restored to his former sasine; if not, he is to be put in the king's mercy. It seems a reasonable conclusion that the brieve took on its form immediately or very soon after its introduction. If so, many of the thirteenth-century brieves and cases which have been thought to be examples of the brieve of novel dissasine must be set on one side, particularly where the brieve in question is retourable and so not pleadable. An example is the case in 1262 where an inquest before the sheriff found Robert Cruik to have deforced the burgesses of Peebles of their common of Waddenshope by various acts, including the construction of a house and ploughing.[35] The royal brieve which initiated this process was retourable, and not in the style of novel dissasine. It is not known what action followed upon it; it is certain that the brieve was not one of dissasine. The same can be said of three other retourable brieves from the reign of Alexander III: one by which the sheriff of Traquair was to investigate and report on whether the abbot and convent of Melrose were being deforced by a diversion of the Gala Water into a new course; another by which Alexander Comyn, justiciar of Scotia, was to inquire how Hector (a Latinisation of Gaelic Eachann) of Carrick came to be ejected from the lands of Auchensoul; and the last one by which the sheriff of Roxburgh was to find out who had plundered the land of Horndean in the hands of James Gifford.[36]

We may note here, however, a curious brieve of King John in 1294, in which he commanded Geoffrey Mowbray, justiciar of Lothian, to ensure that the abbot and convent of Melrose were not dissaised (*disseysitos*) by William Douglas of the common way through Douglasdale, possession of which they had recovered before the Guardians at Edinburgh. If the justiciar found that the monks were being disturbed, he was to bring the matter before the king and his council.[37] The brieve has echoes of novel dissasine: apart from the use of the word 'dissaised' already referred to, it opens with a narrative of the monks' grave complaint, it refers to restoration justly and without delay, and the justiciar is involved. However, the brieve is clearly not pleadable; it is an order to maintain a judgment already made, contempt of which will lead to further proceedings, not before the justiciar, but before the council, of which the justiciar is merely the executive officer. The case looks very much like one in which novel dissasine might have been used, however; its apparent non-use may be explicable by reference to the special circumstances of the interregnum following the deaths of Alexander III and the Maid of Norway. Just possibly, on the other hand, the case before the Guardians may have been an appeal from a lower level at which the brieve of novel dissasine had been used but reference to which was unnecessary at this late stage in the proceedings. However it is interpreted, the brieve should not be seen as an example of either the style of, or first-instance jurisdiction in, brieves of novel dissasine at the end of the thirteenth century.

The form appears to have been identical whether the brieve was called one of novel dissasine, as in the 'registers' and *Regiam*, or simply dissasine, as in *Quoniam*. The earliest direct reference, in 1262, is to the 'king's letters of dissasine'.[38] In the fourteenth century, there are references both to brieves of dissasine (as when the portioners of the barony of Fithkil sued Dunfermline abbey in 1319,[39] and when Thomas Hay of Loquhariot claimed the lands of Middleton from his neighbour William Borthwick in 1368[40]) and to brieves of novel dissasine. Thus the 1318 legislation speaks in two chapters of the brieve of novel dissasine,[41] while in 1312 the abbey of Arbroath and its men were given temporary exemption from all suits or complaints to be brought against them, excepting only actions begun by brieves of novel dissasine or terce.[42] This last may suggest that the 'novel' element had substantive consequences in that the action might become time-barred, as in England. However, the only Scottish source to refer explicitly to a time-limit beyond which novel dissasine was not available is *Regiam*, which, in a passage borrowed from *Glanvill*, states that the time-limit was fixed periodically by the king's council.[43] It is perhaps important that by 1230, when the Scottish remedy was introduced, English law had begun to relax the strictness of the requirement that the disseisin be 'novel' or recent. In that year, an English plaintiff could sue on a disseisin ten years old, while from 1276 to 1546 the time-limit beyond which novel disseisin could not go was May 1242. Thus, as Sutherland remarks, 'in the fourteenth and fifteenth centuries the assize was for practical purposes free of any time limitation'.[44] In the absence of any specific evidence on time-limits in Scotland, it may well be that in fact there never were any, but that does not mean that the word 'novel' was wholly without significance. A document of 1434 which refers to two separate actions in the previous year, one begun by brieve of dissasine, the other by brieve of novel dissasine, suggests that there was some kind of formal distinction based on 'novelty'. This thought is supported by the fact that the ejection complained of under the brieve of dissasine had occurred seventy years previously.[45] Unfortunately, the source tells us nothing about the other brieve, but it seems reasonable to suppose that there the ejection of the pursuer had been a rather more recent event. One further point which may have a bearing on the interpretation of the references here is that the brieve of dissasine had been obtained from a regality chancery, while the brieve of novel dissasine was royal; in other words, the distinction was merely that between the styles which happened to be used in two different writing offices at that time.

THE 1318 LEGISLATION

Whatever interpretation we place upon the significance of the word 'novel' when used in this context, the 1433 cases show that an action of dissasine could reach a long way back in time by the fifteenth century. A careful study of the 1318 legislation on dissasine suggests that this was also the case in the thirteenth and early fourteenth centuries. There are two acts dealing with the brieve of novel dissasine, of which the first, chapter 13, is relevant to the point under discussion. The Latin of the act is far from straightforward, so it is given here as well as my translation which follows below:[46]

> Item ordinatum est et assensum quod quia ante ista tempora breve de nova dissasyna non solebat impetrari nee portari nisi super tenentem ita bene ubi tenens intravit per feffamentum alterius sicut per dissasynam et iniuriam suam propriam vult dominus rex et

statuit quod de cetero ita bene nominetur in brevi de nova dissasyna dissasytor sicut tenens eius et infeodator si sit vivus. Et si plures dissaisytores faciant unam dissasynam et principalis dissasytor moriatur antequam dissasytus habuerit statum suum recuperatum propter hoc non perdat dissasytus recuperacionem suam per breve de nova dissasyna quamdiu invenire poterit tenentem in vita aut dissaisitorem qui fuit ad dissasynam factam. Et si tenens ita infeodatus impetraverit breve de warencia de carta pendente assisa penes suum infeodatorem vel heredes suos si voluerit propter hoc tamen non minus capiatur assisa ad primum diem placiti. Et si assisa transient pro queralante quilibet dissaysiencium teneatur dissaysito ad dampna sua secundum tempus quo tenuit tenementum post dissaysinam factam. Et quicunque inventus fuerint dissay-sitores cum vi et armis post istud statutum publicatum sit adiudicatus ad prisonam et grave amerciamentum ad voluntatem regis. Et istud statutum de dissaysina facta teneat locum tantummodo post statutum editum et non ante.

Item, it is ordained and agreed that, whereas before this time the brieve of novel dissasine was not wont to be impetrated or taken out except against a tenant both where the tenant entered by the infeftment of another and where he entered by his own dissasine and wrong: the lord king wills and enacts that from now the dissaisor and infeftor if he is living shall also be named in the brieve of novel dissasine as well as his tenant. And if several dissaisors carried out a dissasine and the principal dissaisor has died before the person dissaised has recovered his estate, the dissaisee shall not on account of this lose his recovery by brieve of novel dissasine so long as he can find a living tenant or a dissaisor who was at the making of the dissasine. And if the tenant so infeft impetrates a brieve of warrandice of charter pending the assize against his infeftor or his heirs if he so wishes, on account of this, nevertheless the assize shall be taken at the first day of pleading. And if the assize holds for the complainer, the dissaised shall have his damages for each dissasine in accordance with the time of the holding after the dissasine. And whenever after the publication of this statute dissaisors are found to have acted with force and arms, it shall be adjudged to imprisonment and to a grave amercement at the will of the king. And this statute of dissasine shall have force from the time of the proclamation of the statute and not before.

This differs not only from Cooper's rather free translation of this statute but also, in one important aspect, from my own previously-published interpretation.[47] This is made necessary by one small but important change to one word in Duncan's new edition of the text. The singular '*nominetur*' has replaced the previous edition's '*nominentur*' in the statute's first substantive section. Cooper took the passage available to him – '*vult dominus rex et statuit quod de cetero ita bene nominentur in brevi de nova dissasyna dissasytor sicut tenens eius et infeodator si sit vivus*' – to mean 'It is hereby enacted that it shall be competent for the future to call as defenders to a brieve of novel dissasine (a) the original intruder, (b) the person in actual possession of the lands, and (c) if he is still alive, the person from whom the lands were derived by the person in actual possession'. As the verb *nominentur* was in the subjunctive form and in a *quod* clause following words of command, it was suggested in 1983 that the sentence ought to be translated 'they *shall be* named'. In other words, the act was not merely permitting the pursuer to call the dissaisor and infeftor as defenders, it was compelling him to do so. The conversion of the verb into a singular form suggests a further modification. Like Cooper, in 1983 I thought that the plural implied that '*dissasytor*' and '*infeodator*' might be separate persons, a reading which the complex structure of the Latin seemed to support. The singular must mean, however, that '*dissasytor*' and '*infeodator*' are alternative ways of referring to one person whose activities explain how the current tenant came to be possessed of the land. As will emerge, this reading simplifies the sense of the act considerably. The section thus begins by explaining current practice, that the brieve is only used against one who entered either by his own wrongful dissaisine or through infeftment by another. As already noted, this seems to mean that before 1318 the current possessor of the lands was named as the dissaisor in the brieve, regardless of whether or not it was he who had originally ejected the pursuer. However, the act states that this practice is to be changed: the original dissaisor and infeftor (if alive) is to be named as a defender alongside the current possessor.

We can best understand the significance of this provision by looking at thirteenth-century English developments. To begin with, one disseised in England could only name his disseisor as defendant, but success in this action enabled him to recover from any third party put in after the disseisin. About 1212, though, a new rule emerged, that the plaintiff should name both disseisor and any such third party in his writ, since the old law in effect meant that the latter could be put out of his holding without writ and by judgment in a suit to which he was not a party. Donald Sutherland has argued that this new rule was also a consequence of the lengthening time-limits within which the assize could be brought. The old rule had come to operate unfairly, 'for the third party who was holding the land might have come in years after the disseisin and held in good peace for a long time before the assize was brought'.[48] Towards the end of the thirteenth century, in another reflection of the expansion of the time limits, English law was further developed to meet the contingency of feoffees intermediate between the disseisor and the current tenant, requiring the plaintiff to name them if they were alive.[49] Novel disseisin was thus available even though so much time had passed that feoffees of the disseisor had died and their heirs had come into possession. It was however always essential to name the disseisor: 'the form of the original writ was never adapted . . . to make any room for a defendant who was named simply because he was tenant and not because he was supposed to be guilty of disseisin'.[50]

The 1318 act can therefore be seen as a second attempt to solve a problem created by the lengthy period which might elapse between a dissasine and the raising of an action in respect of it, and within which the impetration of the brieve was competent in Scotland. The first solution had been sharply distinct from that developed in England, inasmuch as the tenant infeft after but not otherwise a participant in the dissasine could apparently be the sole defender in the subsequent action. If it is correct to say, as has been suggested above, that the brieve introduced in 1230 was substantially in the form found in the later formularies, then it is clear that in the thirteenth century the Scottish courts adopted a wide approach to the concept of dissasine, covering not only actual ejection but also keeping-out. The solution of the 1318 act, however, was adoption of the English rules as they had stood since the late thirteenth century; as we shall see, this characterises the whole of the act. The solution did not, however, remove the idea that the mere tenant could be liable for dissasine; he remained a person who had to be named in the brieve, a point of some importance elsewhere in the act.

The next provision deals with dissasines carried out by several persons. If the principal dissaisor were to die before the dissaisee had recovered his estate, then the action could be brought against any living person who had taken part in the dissasine, or who was a tenant of the lands in the life of the principal dissaisor. Again, passage of time between the dissasine and the raising of the action is implied. The act was following English precedent established in the reign of Edward I, and, as Sutherland notes, the development allowed the assize to be used long after the original disseisin.[51] The point is reinforced when it is noticed that here the act makes an exception to its earlier provision about who should be named in the brieve and called as defenders. Actions may be directed against one who has become a tenant after dissasine by a group without bringing in any of the other parties involved. However, we can derive one time-limit, albeit not an especially severe one, from this provision. The act expressly states that it is to prevent the dissaisee losing his right of action on account of the death of the principal dissaisor that he is enabled also to sue the other participants or the tenant. The implication is that the brieve of novel dissasine was only competent during the lifetime of the dissaisor, a rule

similar to that of English law. It looks as though this rule was part of Scots
law both before and after 1318.

There is perhaps also a feudal dimension still evident in this part of the
legislation of 1318. The dissaisor who put one person out of, and another
into, sasine of a tenement would most typically be a lord exercising
control over who should be his tenants, while the group of dissaisors
could conceivably be the lord's court, or following, or officers, with the
principal dissaisor referred to in the act being the lord himself or his
steward.[52] On the other hand, the thirteenth-century evidence on novel
disseisin in England shows that disseisors were often accompanied by
large groups made up of 'their lords, friends, relatives, retainers, and
hirelings, all making up a gang or an army, whichever one cares to call it,
of whatever size seemed to be needed for the job'.[53] Such cases were
certainly not courts at work. A possible Scottish example is the ejection
from her lands of Christiana, lady of Esperston, by the Templars, probably
during the reign of either Alexander III or John Balliol. Here, the Templars
claimed title by virtue of a grant from Christiana's deceased husband,
although she maintained that he had had no authority to make it and that
it could only endure for his lifetime. The Master of the House of the
Temple came with his followers (*clientibus suis*) and expelled Christiana.
She was later resaised (*resaysita*) after an inquiry begun by letters in the
form of the king's chapel, which may well have been a brieve of novel
dissasine.[54] Again, it is clear that the group involved in this case was not
a court giving judgment and putting it into effect, but was rather
supporting the claim of one who believed himself to have a valid title and
was acting against another who in his view was an interloper.

The act goes on in its third provision to discuss the position of the
tenant. It seems clear that a tenant is generally still to be regarded as a
potential defender; in other words, that the concept of dissasine still
includes, as it did before the act, keeping out someone who had been
ejected from his land. He may be liable as a co-defender with the dissaisor,
or on his own as a result of the death of those involved in the original
dissasine, in particular the principal dissaisor. The act states that the
tenant may if he wishes take out a brieve of warrandice of charter against
the person who infeft him, or his heirs. The reference to the heirs of the
infeftor is explained by the fact that the most likely infeftor would be the
now deceased principal dissaisor; assuming that the tenant had held the
lands in issue of him, his heirs would now be the superiors and so liable
to warrant the tenant's title. However, the act continues by providing that
although the tenant may call a warrantor in this way, nevertheless the
assize is to proceed against him at the first day of pleading. It was of the
essence of novel dissasine in Scotland, as in England, that no essonzies,
or excuses from appearance, were allowed to the defender and that the

case should be determined on its first day in court.[55] We can see this rule in operation in 1433, when it was only with the consent of the pursuer that his case of dissasine was continued to a second day.[56] Nothing was to delay the action, and the Glanvillian rule that the tenant who calls a warrantor in disseisin loses the action immediately is found in *Regiam* also.[57] Thus the warrantor could not take over the defence of the action in place of the tenant. In thirteenth-century England, however, it became possible for the tenant to start a separate action against his warrantor by the writ *warantia carte*: if he lost in the assize, he would then be able to recover from his warrantor lands elsewhere of equal value to those from which he had just been put out.[58] This is the position which the Scottish act seems to achieve. The rationale of the original rule that the defender could not call a warrantor must have been that a mere dissaisor had no title to be warranted, or alternatively that as the pursuer's lord he had no need of a warrantor; but when the remedy became available against tenants who had ex facie valid infeftments to show, such reasoning lost much of its force. The calling of the warrantor ensured that the real wrongdoer was brought to court to have liabilities to both dissaisee and tenant enforced against him. It is not known when the brieve of warrandice of charter was introduced; it appears in the Ayr manuscript as a form of writ *de compulsione* in the name of King Alexander, implying a thirteenth-century date.[59] Other evidence shows that generally the effect of raising a brieve of warrandice was to sist or suspend the principal action:[60] the effect of the 1318 act was therefore to preserve the special position of dissasine with regard to warrandice, but also to permit the deflection of the burden of the action from the tenant.

It has been said that the 1318 act altered procedure in dissasine 'in favour of the dispossessed pursuer'.[61] Our interpretation of its provisions so far suggests a different conclusion, that the act favoured the sitting tenant who had come in after the dissasine. In general, the pursuer had to search out the other parties involved and bring them into his action. A crucial consequence was the spreading of the pains of losing the action, either by use of the brieve of warrandice in the case of the tenant infeft after dissasine, or by the allocation of damages among the parties involved.[62] This is provided for by the act, the effect of which is that the dissaisee is to recover damages from each of the dissaisors in proportion to the time which each of them spent in the lands. This would have had the effect of reducing the tenant's liability, and again underlines the point that actions of dissasine knew no formal time-limit. We do not know how the quantum would have been assessed – *Regiam* states a maximum of ten marks, but *Quoniam*, which is supported on this point by a case of 1430 in which the pursuer was awarded 100 marks by way of damages, allows recovery of the whole of the pursuer's loss through his exclusion.[63]

If it is asked why the legislators of 1318 should have wished to give this kind of protection to tenants who had entered their lands after a dissasine, the political situation of the time, in which Robert I was ready to restore those disinherited during the recent wars to their lands if they were ready to enter his allegiance, should be borne in mind. As already noted in the previous chapter,[64] such a policy must have led to clashes of interest between those put out in the wars through their English allegiance and those who had gained possession as a result, in which perhaps the former might have raised actions of dissasine to recover their lands. It is surely against a background where the king's loyal adherents (and their tenants) were uncertain to what extent they would be able to retain their new lands against the returning disinherited that chapter 13 of the 1318 legislation was enacted. This would explain its preoccupation with old dissasines. A similar rationale may well underlie chapter 19, the other act of 1318 dealing with dissasine: the defender here, as also in brieves of right and mortancestry, was to have full opportunity to consider the case against him and to state his own position.[65] The traditionally rapid procedure of the brieve of novel dissasine was to be slowed so that it could deal justly with the complex questions of title and possession which were thought likely to arise in the context of 1318.

The final provision of the act lays down that those who are found to be dissaisors *cum vi et armis* after the publication of the statute are to be imprisoned and are also liable to a major amercement or fine at the king's will. That dissasines could be violent is evident from the graphic details of which we learn in the document recording the expulsion from her lands of Christiana, lady of Esperston, mentioned earlier. She resisted her ejection by the Master of the Temple and his followers, first by barring her door against them and then, when they broke in, by clinging to the lintel; she was finally removed when one of the followers struck off one of her fingers.[66] The reference in the act to *vi et armis* is a reminder that dissasine is conceived of as a wrong rather than as a proprietary remedy, a point to which we shall return shortly, while the references to imprisonment and fines also suggest its criminal aspect. This appears to add to the Glanvillian rule stated in the act of 1230 and *Regiam*, and echoed in the brieve itself, that the guilty defender must pay a fine to the king's use, by imposing a stricter penalty on those who dissaise with violence.[67] Was this intended to deter those of the disinherited who might be tempted to self-help? If so, it may well stand alongside chapter 25 of the 1318 legislation which affirmed the rule that no man was to be put out of his freehold without the king's brieve, and directed the claims of the disinherited along the path of the common law.[68] Chapter 13's provisions on violent dissasine ought also to be interpreted in the light of the act of which it is part and which was intended to create joint liability between the original dissaisor and those deriving title to the lands from him. Such subsequent tenants were also dissaisors liable under the brieve, but they did not dissaise *cum vi et armis*; that would be most likely to happen in the act of ejecting the person now impetrating the brieve. Thus it would be the original dissaisor rather than the current possessor who would be liable to this penalty. Again, therefore, the policy of protecting the tenant is apparent; it is also noteworthy that in the framing of this reform, an English provision, the first Statute of Westminster of 1275, was being followed.[69]

In all this reform, it is clear that the legislators were dealing with technical law in a technical way; but the real motivating force is not an abstract concern with the technicalities of the law, but a need to deal with the complex political situation of the time. The technicalities of novel dissasine were adjusted to assist in the settlement of King Robert's Scotland. Despite the continuing hostilities with England, English law remained a source for borrowing, and the act suggests the draftsman's familiarity with both Edwardian legislation and the thirteenth-century case law on the assize of novel disseisin.

THE LATER MEDIEVAL POSITION

If, to begin with, the sheriff's jurisdiction in dissasine was coextensive with that of the justiciar, as the evidence discussed at the beginning of this chapter suggests, this had ceased to be the position by the early fourteenth century and perhaps before. In the fourteenth century 'registers', the brieve is always addressed to the justiciar.[70] *Regiam* and *Quoniam* both state that the action pertains to his court.[71] On this point, the treatises are supported by the few later medieval cases for which evidence survives. In 1319, the abbey of Dunfermline and the portioners of the barony of Fithkil were involved in a boundary dispute. The portioners, dissatisfied with the result of an earlier brieve of perambulation, brought another action by a brieve of dissasine, which was begun in the justiciar's court.[72] In 1342, an assize held in the full court of the justiciar at Inverbervie found that Sir William Mowbray had dissaised the abbot and convent of the abbey of Arbroath unjustly and without a judgment of various lands in the Mearns.[73] Thomas Hay of Loquhariot brought his brieve of dissasine against William Borthwick in 1368 in the justiciar's court at Edinburgh.[74] In 1430, Mariota Cunningham recovered the lands of Balwill and Ballaird from Susanna and Donald Christison by brieve of novel dissasine in the court of the justiciar south of Forth at Stirling.[75] Finally, the two cases of dissasine in 1433 were both heard before the justiciar north of Forth at Perth.[76] A final confirmation of the position can be found in a minor treatise probably written in the 1450s, the *Ordo Justiciarie* which explains details of procedure in the justiciar's court. This gives a form of summons '*super Breve de Nova Dissaisina*', whereby the sheriff is ordered to bring the defender before the justiciar's court.[77]

When we look at these fourteenth- and fifteenth-century cases, it is harder to find any feudal dimension. Most of the cases of dissasine seem in fact to be contests between tenants-in-chief, rather than between tenants and lords, and to be about rights in lands rather than the recovery of possession. The dispute between the portioners of Fithkil (now Leslie in Fife) and Dunfermline abbey in 1319 involved rights of common in the lands of Goatmilk and Caskieberran (now in Glenrothes, Fife, just across the river Leven from Leslie). However, there would appear to have been no tenurial link between the parties. Rather, both had rights and the question concerned their mutual extent. The boundaries within which each could exercise their rights were initially determined by a brieve of perambulation, but clearly the result left the portioners with a smaller area than they had expected. The brieve of dissasine seems therefore to have been brought to claim ejection from ground in which they claimed common rights and to be essentially a dispute between neighbours. Interestingly, it was held that the matter could not be reopened in this way.[78] The case *of Hay of Loquhariot v William Borthwick* in 1368 was also a dispute between neighbours about rights in adjoining lands. The lands under dispute were those of Middleton, which lie all around what are today the farm ofLoquhariot and the village of Borthwick in Midlothian. The evidence shows that the two families were constantly at odds about each other's rights in Middleton, and that the brieve of dissasine raised by Hay in 1368 was only an incident in a long story about the definition and extent of these rights.[79]

Nevertheless, it is important not to lose sight of the potential relevance of feudal power as a source of dissasine in the later medieval period. The act of 1401 defining the right of the lord to recognosce his tenant's lands for various breaches of feudal discipline – default of service, unlicensed alienation, felony and others – talks of 'wilful and secret' recognitions, which must often have been dissasines made unjustly and without judgment.[80] Recognition did not necessarily involve the permanent deprivation of the tenant, inasmuch as the lord was bound to hold the land pending the tenant's remedying his default, but clearly, just as with distraint (as distinct from forfeiture) of the fee in thirteenth-century England, novel dissasine would control the steps taken by the lord.[81] However, no examples have been found where such actions formed the basis for a claim using the brieve. It may be that the relative decline of the importance of services, so that it was not often necessary to take disciplinary action, explains this; alternatively, distress of the tenant's goods may usually have sufficed, or lord and tenant were generally able to resolve disputes without resort to formal process. It was, after all, in the best interests of both to do so. On the other hand, there are cases on record where complaint was made of the lord's abuse of the power to recognosce lands.[82] It may be significant that the tenant in these cases does not seem to have made use of novel dissasine, but looked instead for remedies from the king's council and parliament. In some of them, the tenant might have been in difficulty with the brieve; for example, William of Fenton had been initially ejected by a judgment, and his subsequent repossession of the land had been subject to a *borgh*, so perhaps novel dissasine would not have helped him.[83]

It should also be kept in mind that a tenant could dissaise a lord, but the survival of purpresture into the later medieval period as a remedy in the lord's court may have made the brieve of novel dissasine an unnecessary procedure in many such cases.

BURGH COURTS AND FRESH FORCE

The brieve of novel dissasine seems never to have been used in the burgh courts. There is a broad parallel with the English novel disseisin, which was also not used in borough courts. Instead, the English burgess used an action called fresh force.[84] In Scotland, similarly, there does seem to have been an action of fresh force available in the burgh court. A chapter in the *Leges Burgorum* declares that he who has been ejected from possession of lands without proper authority or judgment should be restored before any other claim to the lands is heard,[85] while a fragment found in many of the later legal manuscripts said *in gremio* to be a statute of Robert I lays down a procedure '*super deforciatione recenli in burgo*'.[86] This seems to modify what is said in the *Leges Burgorum* in that the person complaining of recent ejection is to have his case heard immediately upon the debateable ground by an assize, to determine not just the possessory question of expulsion and restoration but also that of ownership, 'so that he against whom it is decided shall never be heard thereupon afterwards'. This is an interesting change, to which we will return later;[87] whether or not it was truly legislation of Robert I or any other king, two cases of *recens deforciamentum* were heard before assizes in Aberdeen burgh court in 1399, both proceeding upon the pursuer's complaint and giving of a pledge rather than upon a royal brieve, and in 1448 'fresch force' by a wrongful distress was alleged in Ayr burgh court.[88] It seems clear that this was the action which served the burgess in place of novel dissasine.

The brieve of right, which as shown in a later chapter was the principal remedy for the recovery of lands in burgh,[89] may have been used to deal with complaints of ejection such as would otherwise have been the subject of a novel dissasine. The complaint which the brieve of right remedied was deforcement, which might well have included dissasine. In one respect, however, as the law developed, the brieve of right in burgh may have proved inadequate, and that would be in the provision of a remedy for ejection for those whose title was not heritable and who were accordingly not within the terms of the brieve. The fragment attributed to Robert I mentions two interests in land which were not heritable – holding in security of a debt or holding for one's lifetime only – presumably indicating that these might be recovered by the action of fresh force. It may not be too far-fetched, therefore, to see this action as a later introduction, almost certainly borrowed from England and intended to cure a defect in the operation of the brieve of right in burgh. The chapter in the *Leges Burgorum* about the immediate restoration of a dispossessed person before any inquiry as to his right refers to the rule in some versions as an assize of Newcastle-upon-Tyne,[90] and may represent a first attempt at a solution by borrowing, with the Robert I fragment on fresh force being a further development of the law. This reconstruction is speculative and not susceptible of proof, and it would be rash indeed to try to provide it with a chronology; but it would explain what seem to be our only certain facts, that the dispossessed burgess had two remedies for his restoration, the brieve of right and the action of fresh force, and did not use the other brieves available in the landward areas, novel dissasine and, as we shall see, mortancestry.

FEE AND FREEHOLD

The style in the Ayr manuscript for the brieve of novel dissasine says that the pursuer must have been vest and saised of the lands as of fee or as of terce (*dote*) or by a rent (*firma*) whose term has not yet expired.[91] This last suggests an interesting contrast with England where only the life-tenant and tenant *pur auter vie*, and not the mere termor, were protected in their seisin by the assize.[92] There is no further Scottish evidence on this point, although the converse case of the lessee who stayed on after the expiry of his lease might have been an example of a dissasine. A possible instance of this is a case in 1341 when, having recovered lands of which Sir William Mowbray was dissaising them unjustly and without a judgment, the abbot and convent of Arbroath began leasing them out, apparently resuming what had been normal practice with these lands since the middle of the thirteenth century.[93] Mowbray may well have been a tenant who stayed on too long.

  Returning to the issue of the sasine which the pursuer had to show that he had enjoyed, in *Quoniam* the brieve states that the pursuer must have been vest and saised as of fee,[94] while in the Bute style the formula is, simply, that the pursuer was vest and saised of the lands.[95] It is difficult from this limited evidence to draw any clear picture of what interest in the lands a pursuer had to show he held before the dissasine. Something can perhaps be made, however, of a *Regiam* passage which states that the brieve of novel dissasine 'touches only *liberum tenementum*'.[96] We have already seen that in later medieval Scotland '*liberum tenementum*' meant in effect any life interest in land, whether or not that interest was heritable, a common example from the fourteenth century onwards being the liferent which fathers often reserved to themselves when granting the fee of their lands to their sons in order to minimise inheritance formalities.[97] In England, the assize protected freeholdings – that is, any tenancy for life, whether that life was the tenant's or that of another person[98] – and it would be surprising if the Scottish brieve was not of at least comparable scope. Terce, the widow's liferent of part of her estate, is specifically referred to in the Ayr manuscript as recoverable by brieve of novel dissasine. If so, there would seem no reason for not offering similar protection to the widower in his right of courtesy. When in 1368 Robert Stewart, lord of Menteith, complained before king and parliament that Archibald Douglas was excluding Stewart's wife from her terce of a former marriage, it was successfully argued that he should have recourse not to parliament but to the common law in the justiciar's court.[99] Was it the case that the appropriate remedy, given that the lady had already been served to her terce, would have been a brieve of novel dissasine? It may also be possible to draw some parallel with the burghal action of fresh force, which could be used to recover land which the pursuer was holding for his lifetime only, or as security for a debt.[100]

What seems to emerge from this is a fuller understanding of what contemporary writers meant when they spoke of dissasine as a possessory remedy. It was not that the pursuer need only be someone who had had possession, with or without right thereto. Rather, it was that the pursuer did not have to show a heritable title, or fee, the nearest thing in medieval land law to outright ownership. Medieval jurists battled to fit the realities of landholding into the sharp Romanist contrast of ownership and possession; if heritable title was ownership, all else must be possession only.[101] However, even in Scotland with its relatively simple structure of interests in land, that dichotomy did not fit the facts of legal life. To say that a man was not a proprietor did not preclude his having some other interest in or claim to the land; many of these he could recover in the event of dispossession, even from the heritable proprietor, by the brieve of novel dissasine. Indeed, it may not have been uncommon for, say, a tercer to recover against the person who held the fee. It is a long way from that, however, to say that someone who had gained possession without any shadow of right could bring the brieve successfully when he was turned out by the true owner. Sutherland has shown us that, no matter what *Bracton* might have said, in England the mere wrongful possessor was not normally protected by the assize against disseisin by the true owner.[102] It is probable that the position was the same in Scotland. In any case, it is clear that novel dissasine in Scotland was far from functioning as a merely 'possessory' remedy. As Maitland remarked, 'a possessory action is likely to lose some of its possessory characteristics if the plaintiff is suffered to rely on ancient facts'.[103] It is clear from the 1318 legislation that, even before that time, the action enabled a challenge to another's title to land if its ultimate source lay in a dissasine of the pursuer by someone who was still alive and, from 1318, named in the brieve. That event need not be and often was not a recent one; again we can refer to the 1433 case where the action was brought seventy years after the dissasine. Similarly, the burghal action of fresh force, perhaps initially conceived of as possessory in character, certainly became a proprietary remedy, perhaps as early as the reign of Robert I. The supposed statute of his reign laying down the procedure '*super deforciatione recenti in burgo*' modifies what is said in the *Leges Burgorum* in that the person complaining of recent ejection is to have his case heard immediately upon the debateable ground by an assize, to determine not just the possessory question of expulsion and restoration but also that of ownership, 'so that he against whom it is decided shall never be heard thereupon afterwards'.[104] Whether or not this is legislation of Robert I, the language of the text was echoed in Ayr burgh court in 1448, when in a 'fresh force' case the court determined which party had right and declared that the losing party should 'nocht be herd . . . in tyme to cum'.[105]

THE BRIEVE DE AQUEDUCTU

In 1434, parliament enacted a statute which introduced the brieve *de aqueductu* into Scottish practice. The form of the brieve as laid down by parliament was clearly modelled on, and in effect a variant of, novel dissasine. It began by narrating the pursuer's grave complaint that he had been disturbed and molested unjustly and without a judgment in his possession of the waterway at his mill. The court was instructed to restore him to his possession if the complaint was true. The brieve was clearly seen as 'possessory'; although the pursuer might be restored to his former possession, the brieve explicitly provided that the defender could still seek his rights 'in form of the common law, or by brieve of our chapel or in other ways according to the law of the realm'.[106] However, the statute did not provide for the brieve to be addressed to any particular court, and in practice it seems to have been heard in the sheriff court rather than the justiciar's.[107]

To understand the meaning of the brieve *de aqueductu*, some account of the technology of medieval mills is necessary. Mills were commonplace in Scotland, having a crucial role in a range of important activities such as the grinding of grain, the fulling of cloth, and brewing and distilling. They were driven by water power, drawing on Scotland's abundant rivers and streams. There were usually several mills along any given waterway; but, in order for any one mill-owner to create greater control over and power in the flow of water to his mill, it was often necessary to build dams and artificial lades, which would gather the water and then redirect it at greater speed, thereby increasing the mill's capacity. John Shaw's description of the methods used in early modern times to ensure a mill's water supply could doubtless be applied to the medieval period as well:[108]

> Normally an artificial water-course or *lade* was drawn off from a stream and, having been applied to the water-wheel, returned thereto. Under the simplest arrangement, part of a stream was diverted to a mill without the use of a dam . . . Where several springs and small streams lay within the catchment area, simple *gather-dams* might be constructed, while on larger streams a *dam-dyke* of peats, divots, or loosely piled boulders was usually built.

Jean Gimpel has explained why the deployment of this technology caused disputes between neighbouring mills throughout medieval Europe. 'The height of the dam was of paramount importance, as it determined the fall of the water, which drove the waterwheels. The higher the dam, the higher the waterfall, and the faster the grain would be ground.'[109] If however a downstream owner built a dam for his mill, or raised the height of an existing dam under the guise of repairs, it could have an adverse effect on the mills further upstream. 'The height of the waterfall was also determined by the height of the dams downstream. If the level of the water retained by the lower dam was too high, the upstream dam would not have a waterfall sufficiently high to drive the waterwheels.'[110] Equally, an upstream owner might cut off or reduce the water supply downstream by the creation or expansion of his lade. This certainly seems to be what lies behind the language used to describe situations in which *aqueductu* was deemed the appropriate remedy later in the fifteenth century: 'abstractioune of the water of Northesk fra the alde gang and fra the mylne of Kynnabir' in 1467;[111] wrongful perturbation 'of the mylne layd and draucht of water to the mylne of Drumkow' in 1482;[112] competing claims to 'the mylne dam of Pople' in 1483;[113] and 'wrangwis doune castin of the mylland of Tolgart and stoppin of the watter of the sammyn' in 1491.[114]

Such problems did not arise in Scotland for the first time in the fifteenth century. Thus, in the thirteenth century, Alan de Sinton built a mill on the River Esk downstream from another mill belonging to Dunfermline abbey. His elaborate agreement with the monks shows that all parties were well aware of the downstream proprietor's capacity to damage the upstream mill's power supply, and of the danger that the upstream proprietor might divert the watercourse which powered both mills.[115] As noted earlier in this chapter, Melrose abbey was complaining about a diversion of the Gala Water by some unknown wrongdoer in

1268, probably because one of its mills was adversely affected.[116] Why then did parliament only act in 1434? In England, from the beginning, the assize of novel disseisin seems to have been available for diversions of watercourses.[117] It would be surprising if the Scottish brieve was of lesser scope, especially when, as seems to have been the case, it followed its original in extending to rights of common. A Glanvillian passage in *Regiam* refers to novel dissasine as a possible remedy in the context of diversion of watercourses.[118] Perhaps in 1434 parliament was making the procedures of novel dissasine more readily available, by removing the restriction of the brieve to the justiciar's court in this category of case and enabling it to be dealt with in the more regular meetings of the sheriff court. The economic significance of the mill was such that any debate as to its possession should not be left over until the arrival of the justice ayre. However, parliament did not specify that the brieve must be heard only in the sheriff court; if an ayre occurred before the next head court of the sheriffdom, then it would obviously be more convenient to deal with the matter then. A parallel may be drawn with the development of the viscontiel writs of nuisance or 'little writs of novel disseisin' in thirteenth-century England, allowing the benefits of the assize to be taken in the county court rather than before the king's justices.[119]

The brieve *de aqueductu* must also be set in a feudal context, inasmuch as the mill was one of the characteristic monopolies of lordship, operating as a source of revenue through thirlage and multures, compelling tenants to have their grain ground there and to pay for the privilege. However, it is therefore unlikely that it was a remedy for tenants against wrongdoing lords. If anything, it was more probable that the tenants would be the defenders in any action, having interfered with the lade which powered the lord's mill, perhaps to drive their own in order to avoid the lord's claim to multures. An example may be the action which John, lord Carlisle, brought in the sheriff court of Dumfries by brieve *de aqueductu* against Jasper of Newlands in respect of the mill of Duncow in 1482. Carlisle had been granted the barony of Duncow by James III in 1477, after an eight-year gap following the forfeiture of the former baron, Alexander Boyd.[120] Newlands was almost certainly a tenant of the barony (the estate of Newlands is only a mile or two from modern Duncow), and his claim to the mill may well have sprung from occupation and use during the vacancy. This is the only possible case of this type, however. Part of the reason why they may have been rare can be found in the Glanvillian passage in *Regiam* already mentioned, which holds diversion of water-courses to be purpresture when committed by a tenant against his lord.[121] The lord could therefore deal with the tenant in his own court if he had one, and so, given the survival of purpresture in the fifteenth century discussed in an earlier chapter,[122] had no need of the brieve *de aqueductu*.

The documented cases where *aqueductu* was used suggest that the typical scenario was a struggle between neighbouring lords where an upstream proprietor had made adjustments to the watercourse in order to increase the power of his mill, and had thereby adversely affected the power downstream at his neighbour's mill; or it was a battle over the profits of the mill. *Carlisle v Newlands* was certainly a dispute between near neighbours, whether or not it was also a struggle between a lord and his tenant. In 1467, William lord Graham's mill of Kinnaber, at the mouth of the North Esk, was clearly being deprived of water by William Graham of Morphie's neighbouring mill of Morphie, which was on an offshoot of the river a few miles upstream.[123] The litigation in 1491 over the mill of Tullygarth (also known as Linn Mill[124]) on the Black Devon in Clackmannan was also a contest between the owners of two independent estates, although of a more complex character than the Kinnaber case. James Mushet of Tullygarth had the right to compel the tenants of John lord Drummond's barony of Kincardine in Menteith to use his mill.[125] The right is puzzling, because the two baronies were not linked by any waterway, and this may well explain the resentment with which it was obviously regarded by Drummond, who was thereby deprived of an important source of income. Perhaps the explanation is that Mushet had been granted some sort of security right, as there is other evidence showing his activity as a money-lender.[126] The struggle over the mill of Popple on the Whittingham Water in East Lothian in 1483 is even more obscure; the pursuer, David Lauder of Popple, had a claim to one third of the mill and its profits by virtue of an assignation, while the defender, James Ogill of Popple, was an occupant of the estate who probably claimed the whole.[127] Within a year of the case being remitted to be tried by a brieve *de aqueductu*, however, Ogill and others had cast the mill down and destroyed it, an action for which they had later to 'content and pay' Lauder.[128]

DECLINE OF NOVEL DISSASINE

Brieves of dissasine, novel or otherwise, were still known in mid-fifteenth-century Scottish legal practice and, to judge from the cases in the 1430s and the slightly later *Ordo Justiciarie*, terminology and procedure had changed little since its introduction in 1230. To the best of my knowledge, however, there are no subsequent references to this form of action, and it must be concluded that sometime in the second half of the fifteenth century the brieve began to fall out of use. Obviously, *aqueductu* was still in use at this period, but we cannot draw conclusions from that about novel dissasine, since the former was distinct in some significant ways, most notably in apparently being a matter for the sheriff rather than the justiciar. A statute of 1504 envisages the pursuit of pleadable brieves (note the plural) in the justiciar's court.[129] We know of three pleadable brieves which were taken before the justiciar: *de proteccione regis infricta* (which, it will be recalled, may have been abolished in 1430 and is not mentioned in the *Ordo Justiciarie*), mortancestry (of which, as we shall see, there are examples in the later fifteenth century) and novel dissasine. However, if the last-named was not completely forgotten and in disuse by the beginning of the sixteenth century, its time was running very short indeed. The *St Andrews Formulare* of c. 1520, which contains styles for the brieves of right, mortancestry and *aqueductu*, does not mention novel dissasine at all; nor do the *Formulary E* or the Cambridge MS 'registers' of the early sixteenth century, although the latter gives an *aqueductu* style.[130] Clearly, novel dissasine was no longer employed in the city and regality of St Andrews in the early sixteenth century; in this, the regality probably reflected the situation in the kingdom at large.

NOTES

1. *Reg Brieves*, pp. 40 (no 21), 62 (no 107); *QA (Fergus)*, pp. 205–7.
2. This style is that in *Glanvill*, XIII, 33.
3. *APS*, i, p. 400 (c. 7). Cf. A. A. M. Duncan, *Kingdom*, pp. 539–41; G. W. S. Barrow, *Kingdom*, p. 114.
4. *APS*, i, p. 325 (c. 35).
5. G. W. S. Barrow, *Kingdom*, p. 137; A. A. M. Duncan, 'An interim list of the heads of some Scottish monastic houses before c. 1300', *The Bibliotheck*, ii (1959), p. 8.
6. A. A. M. Duncan, *Kingdom*, pp. 539–41; I. D. Willock, *Jury*, pp. 23–8, 31–2.
7. *Bracton*, f. 164b (iii, p. 25).
8. *ND*, no 378; G. W. S. Barrow, *Kingdom*, p. 115.
9. Durham Dean and Chapter muniments, printed *JLH*, iv (1983), pp. 48*–*9.
10. W. S. Holdsworth, *HEL*, iii, p. 143; vii, pp. 306, 315.
11. *Glanvill*, XIII, 37; *Bracton*, ff. 231 (iii, pp. 187–8), 235b (iii, p. 199); D. W. Sutherland, *Novel Disseisin*, pp. 111, 135 note 1; *Novae Narrationes*, p. lxxxiii. The Norman novel disseisin was also regularly used to protect common rights: J. R. Strayer, 'The writ of novel disseisin in Normandy at the end of the thirteenth century', in *Medieval Statecraft and the Perspectives of History* (Princeton, 1971), p. 6.
12. *Statutes of the Realm*, i, p. 84 (c. 25).
13. D. W. Sutherland, *Novel Disseisin*, p. 63; *ERW*, pp. 32, 72, 85, 215–16, 261; *Novae Narrationes*, pp. lxxxiv–vi, 22, 77–8, 194–6.
14. *Cold Corr*, no 1. The 'pair' probably refers to the brieve of dissasine and to the following summons of the defender to answer in court.
15. W, Fraser, *Douglas*, iii, no 285; cf. W. Ross, *Lectures*, ii, p. 219 note.
16. D. W. Sutherland, *Novel Disseisin*, pp. 64–5.
17. *Pais Reg*, p. 170. For the other details of the case, see ibid., pp. 157–70 and T. M. Cooper, *Cases*, pp. 33–40.
18. *Pais Reg*, p. 176. Laurence was dean of Lennox in 1274 (D. E. R.

Wart, *Fasti*, p. 179)
19. See above, pp. 43–5.
20. G. Donaldson, 'Early Scottish conveyancing', in *Formulary of Old Scots Legal Documents*, ed. P. Gouldesbrough, Stair Society, vol. 36 (Edinburgh, 1985), pp. 165–75. See also W. M. Gordon, *Studies in the Transfer of Property by Traditio* (Aberdeen, 1970), pp. 222–4.
21. *APS*, i, pp. 408–9; *Melr Lib*, i, no 235.
22. *ND*, nos 375–87.
23. *ND*, no 418. 'Estovers' seems also to have been used in medieval Scotland with the wider meaning of 'necessaries, maintenance, support'. See references in C. du Cange, *Glossarium Medieae et Infimae Latinitatis*, and J. Skene, *DVS*, both sv '*Estoverium*'. For an example of a use of the word in this sense in 1238, see *Arb Lib*, i, no 261.
24. See S. F. C. Milsom's introduction to P & M, i, pp. xlii–iii; also *LFEF*, p. 13. See also D. W. Sutherland, *Novel Disseisin*, p. 30.
25. *Cold Corr*, no 239. For Coldingham as superior of Paxton, see *ND*, no 357.
26. S. F. C. Milsom, *LFEF*, pp. 11–13.
27. *RM* (*APS*), II, 68; *RM* (*Cooper*), II, 74; *Glanvill*, IX, 11,13. See J. Biancalana, 'Want of justice', pp. 480–1. On the lack of evidence for time bars in the Scottish novel dissasine, see above, pp. 145–6.
28. *RRS*, v, p. 410 (c. 13); *APS*, i, 470 (c. 13). See further above, pp. 146–53.
29. *ND*, no 126. See also nos 60, 64, 67, 118, 119, 124, 125 and 127–34. For the possible location of the now lost Swinewood, see *RRS*, ii, p. 154. Note *ND*, no 389: '*in campo qui vocatur Swinewde ex australi parte de Aye*' (i. e. on the south bank of the River Eye).
30. On the brieve of right generally, see below, pp. 188–210.
31. *ESC*, no 19, See also no 65.
32. See above, pp. 149–150.
33. See *Melr Lib*, i, pp. 101–5, for a case between Earl Patrick and Melrose abbey which began before the ecclesiastical courts, but ended in the king's; discussed in T. M. Cooper, *Cases*, no 6, and Cooper, *Papers*, pp. 81–7. See above, p. 108.
34. For seisin in England, see P & M, ii, p. 34; S. E. Thorne, 'Livery of seisin', *LQR*, lii (1936), p. 345; A. W. B. Simpson, *Land Law*, pp. 38–44; R. C. Palmer, *The Whilton Dispute 1264–1380* (Princeton, 1984), pp. 31–3.
35. *APS*, i, pp. 100–1; T. M. Cooper, *Cases*, no 59. See also H. McKechnie, *Brieves*, p. 10; I. D. Willock, *Jury*, p. 33; G. W. S. Barrow, *Kingdom*, p. 116; D. M. Walker, *Legal History*, i, pp. 220, 264, 275.
36. *Melr Lib*, ii, appendix, no 13; *CDS*, i, nos 2193, 2680. See also, on these, G. W. S. Barrow, *Kingdom*, p. 116; D. M. Walker, *Legal History*, i, p. 264.
37. W. Fraser, *Douglas*, iii, no 10.
38. *Cold Corr*, no 1.
39. *Dunf Reg*, no 352.
40. *APS*, i, p. 505.
41. *RRS*, v, pp. 410 (c. 13), 412 (c. 19); *APS*, i, pp. 470 (c. 13), 471 (c. 19).

42. *RRS*, v, no 402.
43. *RM (APS)*, III, 32; *RM (Cooper)*, III, 36; *Glanvill*, XIII, 32.
44. D.W. Sutherland, *Novel Disseisin*, pp. 55–7, 139.
45. *CA Chrs*, ii, no 128.
46. The best text is now *RRS*, v, no 139 (p. 410). See also *APS*, i, p. 470 (c. 13).
47. See T. M. Cooper, *Papers*, p. 90; H. L. MacQueen, 'Dissasine and mortancestor', p. 27 and note 38.
48. D.W. Sutherland, *Novel Disseisin*, p. 57.
49. Ibid., pp. 139–41.
50. P & M, ii, p. 56; D.W. Sutherland, *Novel Disseisin*, p. 58.
51. D.W. Sutherland, *Novel Disseisin*, pp. 141–2.
52. Compare S. F. C. Milsom, *LFEF*, pp. 18–20.
53. See D.W. Sutherland, *Novel Disseisin*, pp. 118–25.
54. For the document recording these events, see J. Edwards, 'The Templars in Scotland', *SHR*, v (1908), pp. 23–5 (translation on pp. 17–21). See further G.W. S. Barrow, 'The aftermath of war', *TRHS*, xxviii (1978), pp. 112–14.
55. *RM (APS)*, III, 32; *RM (Cooper)*, III, 36; *QA (Fergus)*, ch. 38; *QA (APS)*, ch. 36; *QA (Cooper)*, ch. 53.
56. *CA Chrs*, ii, no 128.
57. *RM (APS)*, III, 32; *RM (Cooper)*, III, 36; *Glanvill*, XIII, 38.
58. D. W. Sutherland, *Novel Disseisin*, pp. 131, 218; S. F. C. Milsom, *LFEF*, p. 63.
59. See above, p. 124.
60. *RM (APS and Cooper)*, I, 15; *QA (Fergus)*, ch. 40; *QA (APS)*, ch. 38; *QA (Cooper)*, ch. 55; *Reg Brieves*, p. 61 (no 96); and see above, pp. 124–5, and below, pp. 178, 183.
61. Barrow, *Bruce*, p. 297.
62. There seems to be no evidence to show that in Scotland the tenant could vouch a co-defender in novel dissasine as his warrantor and then drop out of the action. Clearly, this would not be possible before 1318 if only the tenant was named as defender; it would have been possible from 1318, but there is no express provision in the act about this. The question arises because such a rule developed in England once it became possible to sue both disseisor and tenant in the one action (D.W. Sutherland, *Novel Disseisin*, pp. 218–19). This was in addition to the action by *warantia carte*.
63. *RM (APS)*, III, 32; *RM (Cooper)*, III, 36; *QA (Fergus)*, ch. 38; *QA (APS)*, ch. 36; *QA (Cooper)*, ch. 53; *JR*, xxxi (1986), p. 125.
64. See above, pp. 106–7.
65. *RRS*, v, p. 412 (c. 19); *APS*, i, 471 (c. 19).
66. *SHR*, v (1908), p. 23.
67. *RM (APS)*, III, 32; *RM (Cooper)*, III, 36; *Glanvill*, XIII, 38; above, p. 137.
68. *RRS*, v, p. 413 (c. 25); *APS*, i, p. 473 (c. 25).
69. *Statutes of the Realm*, i, p. 35 (c. 37); D.W. Sutherland, *Novel Disseisin*, pp. 134, 219–20.
70. *Reg Brieves*, pp. 40 (no 21), 62 (no 107); *QA (Fergus)*, pp. 205–7; *QA (APS)*, ch. 53; *QA (Cooper)*, ch. 53.
71. *RM (APS)*, I, 4; *RM (Cooper)*, I, 5; *QA (Fergus)*, ch. 38; *QA (APS)*, ch. 36; *QA (Cooper)*, ch. 53.

72. *Dunf Reg*, no 352.
73. BL, MS Add 33,245, ff. 156v–157r.
74. *APS*, i, 505.
75. Aberdeen University Library, MS 1160/18/9, f. lr-v, printed *JR*, xxxi (1986), pp. 124–5.
76. *CA Chrs*, ii, no 128.
77. *APS*, i, p. 705. The *Ordo* runs in the name of William Sinclair, earl of Orkney and justiciar south of the Forth. Orkney was chancellor 1454–6 (*British Chronology*, p. 175) and acted as justiciar at that time (*ER*, vi, pp. 386, 433, 485).
78. See *Assise Regis Willelmi*, c. 24 (*APS*, i, p. 379) for a statement that when boundaries have been perambulated, the decision can only be varied by brieve of right.
79. See *RMS*, i, appendix 2, nos 31, 385 and 389; *Yester Writs*, nos 21, 23, 37, 39, 41A, 42–51, 68A, 70A and 106.
80. *APS*, i, p. 575. See above, pp. 116–17.
81. See D. W. Sutherland, *Novel Disseisin*, pp. 82–96.
82. See above, pp. 116–17.
83. *APS*, i, pp. 552–3.
84. A. Harding, *Law Courts*, p. 42; D. W. Sutherland, *Novel Disseisin*, p. 26 note, p. 63; H. L. MacQueen and W. J. Windram, 'Burghs', p. 219.
85. See c. 99 (*APS*, i, p. 352).
86. *APS*, i, pp. 721–2 (cc. 12 and 13).
87. See above, p. 158.
88. *Abdn Ct Bk*, pp. 65, 117; *Ayr Burgh Court Book 1428–78*, f. 52r.
89. See below, p. 200–1.
90. See H. L. MacQueen and W. J. Windram, 'Burghs', p. 223 note 19.
91. *Reg Brieves*, p. 40 (no 21), reading with Cooper (ibid., 15) *nondum* for the original's *dum*, which makes no sense in the context.
92. D. W. Sutherland, *Novel Disseisin*, pp. 12–13, 32, 135–8.
93. BL, MS Add 33,245, ff. 156v–157r; *Arb Lib*, i, nos 247 and 311 for thirteenth-century leases of the lands; *RRS*, vi, no 29 (*Arb Lib*, ii, no 17) for royal confirmation of 1341; *Arb Lib*, ii, no 19 for lease subsequent to 1342 case. The lands were again in dispute in the 1350s: *RRS*, vi, nos 124 and 133, *Arb Lib*, ii, no 27. See also *RRS*, vi, nos 13 and 182.
94. *QA* (*Fergus*), p. 205; *QA* (*APS* and *Cooper*), ch. 53.
95. *Reg Brieves*, p. 62 (no 107) gives only a brief summary of the original.
96. *RM* (*APS*), IV, 40; *RM* (*Cooper*), p. 296 (Supplement, no 22). A similar idea was expressed in the *Leges Portuum*, title 278, and *Liber de Judicibus*, title 106. It is also found in the pleadings *of Kennedy v Fleming* in 1466: see above, p. 97, and below, p. 168.
97. See above, pp. 113–14.
98. D. W. Sutherland, *Novel Disseisin*, p. 30.
99. *APS*, i, p. 505.
100. *APS*, i, pp. 721–2.
101. See, on the proprietary/possessory distinction in thirteenth- and fourteenth-century England, D. J. Seipp, *'Bracton*, the Year Books, and the "transformation of elementary legal ideas" in the early common law', *LHR*, vii (1989), p. 175.

102. D. W. Sutherland, *Novel Disseisin*, pp. 97–104.
103. P&M, ii, p. 52.
104. *APS*, i, pp. 721–2.
105. *Ayr Burgh Court Book 1428–78*, f. 52r.
106. *APS*, ii, p. 22 (c. 2).
107. See *HMC*, vol. 44, xv, 8 (Buccleuch MSS), p. 48 (no 96) (case before the sheriff in 1482); *ADA*, p. 147 (brieve to 'be direct to the schireff in 1491). The style in the 'register' found in Cambridge University Library MS Ee.4.21 is addressed to the sheriff (f. 274v).
108. J. Shaw, *Water Power in Scotland 1550–1870* (Edinburgh, 1984), p. 12.
109. J. Gimpel, *The Medieval Machine* (London, 1979), p. 31.
110. Ibid., p. 31.
111. *ADA*, p. 8.
112. *HMC*, vol. 44, xv, 8 (Buccleuch MSS), p. 48 (no 96).
113. *ADA*, p. 119*.
114. *ADA*, p. 147.
115. See *Dunf Reg*, nos 197, 231; A. A. M. Duncan, *Kingdom*, p. 352.
116. *Melr Lib*, ii, appendix, no 13; see above, p. 145.
117. D. W. Sutherland, *Novel Disseisin*, pp. 63, 216–17; see also J. S. Loengard, 'The assize of nuisance: origins of an action at common law', *Cambridge Law Journal*, xxxvii (1978), p. 144.
118. RM (*APS*), II, 68; *RM* (*Cooper*), II, 74; *Glanvill*, IX, 11,13. On the *Glanvill passage*, see J. Biancalana, 'Want of justice', pp. 480–1.
119. D. W. Sutherland, *Novel Disseisin*, pp. 62–3; R. C. Palmer, *County Courts*, pp. 180–1.
120. See *RMS*, ii, nos 1327 and 1385.
121. See above, p. 160.
122. See above, pp. 118–20.
123. For Kinnaber and Morphie on the border between Forfarshire and Kincardineshire formed by the North Esk, see Ordnance Survey NO 725618 and NO 714643 respectively. The Mill of Morphie is at NO 714629.
124. See *RMS*, i, nos 193 and 194. Linn Mill is at Ordnance Survey NS 928922.
125. See *ADC*, i, p. 343.
126. *ADC*, i, pp. 214, 217, 238, 239, 241.
127. *ADC*, i, p. 72; *ADA*, p. 171.
128. *ADA*, pp. *147, 171.
129. *APS*, ii, p. 254 (c. 41).
130. Cambridge University Library MS Ee.4.21, f. 274v.

6

The Brieve of Mortancestry

In many ways, the story of the brieve of mortancestry (*morte antecessoris*) seems to parallel that of dissasine closely. There is a reference which establishes its existence in Scotland in the mid-thirteenth century. In 1253, Emma of Smeaton sued the abbey of Dunfermline by royal letters of mortancestry, claiming lands in the fee of Musselburgh which had been held by her father.[1] The case was settled, but it is clear that the basis of Emma's action was, as one would expect with mortancestry, a claim to succeed to an immediate ancestor who had died vest and saised in lands which were now being unjustly withheld by some unentitled person. This is the substance of the brieve as it is described in *Regiam* and *Quoniam*[2] and as it appears in the registers, where its form is as follows:[3]

> The king to the justiciar. We command that you cause to be recognosced by the good and faithful and older men of the neighbourhood whether the late A, father of W the bearer of the presents, died vest and saised as of fee of the lands of S with the pertinents in the tenement of K in the sheriffdom of A; and whether the said W, son of the said late A, is the lawful and nearest heir of the said late A in the same lands with the pertinents; and whether there is anything on account of which he ought not justly to recover sasine of the said lands with the pertinents. And if by the said recognition held justly and according to the assize of the land you find it to be so and that G, who, as W alleges, unjustly detains the said lands with the pertinents, says nothing reasonable on account of which the said recognition ought not to proceed of right although he has been reasonably cited to be present at the holding of the said recognition, cause the said W to have such sasine of the said lands with the pertinents justly and without delay as his late father A had of the same lands on the day when he was alive and dead.

The brieve is obviously modelled on the English writ of *mort d'ancestor*, which ran as follows:[4]

> The king to the sheriff, greeting. If G son of O gives you security

for prosecuting his claim, then summon by good summoners twelve free and lawful men of the neighbourhood of such-and-such a vill to be before me or our justices on a certain day, ready to declare on oath whether O, the father of the aforesaid G, was seised in his demesne as of his fee of one virgate of land in that vill on the day he died, whether he died after my first coronation, and whether the said G is his next heir. And meanwhile let them view the land; and you are to see that their names are endorsed on this writ. And summon by good summoners R, who holds that land, to be there then to hear the recognition. And have there the summoners, and this writ.

Regiam states that mortancestry 'touches' fee and freehold, and that in this it 'exceeds' novel dissasine, which touches only freehold.[5] What this means is that in mortancestry the pursuer's claim was necessarily to a fee or heritable title, based as it was on the claim to inherit from a deceased ancestor, whereas, as we have seen, in novel dissasine the title claimed by the pursuer did not need to be a heritable one but merely one of a life interest.[6] Mortancestry thus tended to look further back into the history of a holding than novel dissasine, being concerned not with the sasine of the pursuer but with that of a deceased ancestor. This explains why the assize was to consist of the good and faithful and older men of the neighbourhood, rather than merely of the good and faithful, as in novel dissasine; only the older men could properly bear witness to the state of an ancestor's holding. Something of the idea behind this comes through the testimony in the Monachkenneran dispute settled before ecclesiastical judges delegate in 1233, in which it is clear that the credibility of a witness's statements as to how land should be held was fortified if he spoke from personal observation over several decades. Thus Alexander son of Hugh could tell of the situation sixty years ago and more, when he was a child; Nemias spoke to matters fifty years before, and was reliable because he had been born in the parish where the lands were located; and Thomas Gaskel could testify to the situation over forty years previously, from when he had been brought up in the area.[7] It was men able to give information of this kind who were expected to constitute the assize of mortancestry in its early days.

A potent source of misunderstanding in approaching the brieve of mortancestry has been its confusion since the sixteenth century with the brieve of inquest, as following medieval usage we shall call it.[8] By the brieve of inquest, an individual established his title to inherit a deceased person's lands. This seems always to have taken place in the sheriff court. It was a formal procedure without any defender, the result of which would be retoured to the king's chapel. A precept of sasine would then be issued ordering that infeftment of the heir take place.[9] A brieve of mortancestry, by contrast, was pleadable and not retourable; the brieve was addressed to the justiciar and heard in his court; its aim was not merely to establish a title to inherit but also to rid the lands of an intruder who was summoned to defend the action; and the brieve itself warranted the giving of sasine to the successful pursuer rather than requiring a further precept following the conclusion of the process.

No surviving source gives us a firm indication as to when mortancestry was introduced in Scotland, although Emma de Smeaton's case in 1253 gives a terminus ante quem. A reasonable guess would be that mortancestry came in not long after, or at the same time as, novel dissasine. The two go naturally together. Like novel dissasine, the aim of mortancestry was to provide a relatively speedy process for the recovery of lands; the sources conflict on whether essonzies were either limited or altogether excluded, but it is clear that only the minimum of delay was to be tolerated in putting the matter to an assize. The only procedural factor in which there was a clear contrast with novel dissasine was that a warrantor might be called by the defender.[10] The reference in mortancestry to 'the recognition in accordance with the assize of the land', identical to that in the brieve of novel dissasine, suggests that there was some enactment, now lost, which introduced mortancestry round about the same time as the remedy for dissasine. The gist of it may be preserved by the act in the *Assise Regis David*, which provides that novel dissasine and mortancestry are always to be decided by an assize (here in its sense of jury, or recognition). There may accordingly be some link with the general policy of emphasising the use of the jury which has already been detected in the reign of Alexander II. If the introduction of mortancestry is thus to be linked with that of novel dissasine, a further possibility arises. In the previous chapter, it was speculatively suggested that the 1230 act introducing novel dissasine drew on the lost English ordinance on novel disseisin. If the speculation is justified, it is equally probable that the mortancestry legislation used the Assize of Northampton of 1176, which brought *mort d'ancestor* into English law.

Another clue as to the date of mortancestry's introduction can be found in Robert I's legislation in 1318, when the scope of the action was widened so that it could be brought by a pursuer tracing his right to succeed from grandparents as well as from parents, uncles, aunts and siblings.[11] Until this point, then, Scots law was similar to the position under the writ *of mort d 'ancestor* before 1237, when the person drawing his right from the seisin of grandparents and other more remote relatives was first offered protection by the writs of aiel, besaiel, tresaiel and cosinage (which last went further than even post-1318 Scottish mortancestry actions).[12] This suggests that the initial Scottish borrowing of *mort d'ancestor* took place before that date; it seems probable that, had the transplant occurred after 1237, the Scots would have given the new brieve a wider scope. Again, this points to much the same period as the adaptation of novel disseisin to become novel dissasine.

It is also worthy of note that the brieve of inquest appears to be well developed by the mid-thirteenth century, when the first examples are found.[13] The earliest style for this brieve, which is in the Ayr manuscript, restricts its scope to the inheritance claims of the same categories of relatives as mortancestry,[14] although this limitation later disappeared. So there may be some original link between the retourable inquest and the pleadable mortancestry, both protecting particular inheritance rights.

Maitland noted the 'curious' restriction of the assize of *mort d 'ancestor* to plaintiffs within only a very narrow range of relationships to the deceased tenant. 'There can be no principle of jurisprudence involved . . . the law begins by providing for common cases, and will often leave uncommon cases unprovided for, even though they fall within an established principle'.[15] Biancalana has developed an argument that the choice of particular relationships for protection covered those where 'the criteria of inheritance were sufficiently clear that, if the ancestor had died seised, there was no good reason for a lord to have denied the heir his ancestor's seisin'. Other cases should be left to be worked out in the lord's court.[16] Yet, perhaps a better view may be found in another sentence of Maitland's: 'if the plaintiff must rely on remote kinship, we can not urge that, since the relevant facts must be known to the neighbours, there is no place for trial by battle'.[17] The restriction of relationships was not imposed by the Assize of Northampton, but in the working-out of its principles by the courts and the king's chancery. The key to the assize was the deployment of the jury; the group of relations from which the plaintiff had to trace his claim included only those whose seisin the members of the jury could generally be expected to know about and remember. The list therefore depended on the practical limitations of the jury as a group of witnesses to the facts alleged, and no more than that was involved. Mortancestry was probably introduced in Scotland as part of a move towards the general use of the jury,[18] and the same practical limitations were recognised.

There are perhaps a couple of examples of a brieve of mortancestry pre-dating the case of Emma of Smeaton in 1253. One is the case about estovers already mentioned in the discussion of novel dissasine, and dating from 1233 x 1235. A brieve of mortancestry, like one of dissasine, was one of recognition.[19] What suggests that the brieve of recognition in the estovers case might be one of mortancestry is the word used to describe the parties raising the action. The word is *petentes*, translated in England as 'demandants', and said to be appropriate for *mort d'ancestor* but not for novel disseisin, where instead one speaks of the *querens* or plaintiff. This follows *Bracton's* learning that novel disseisin is a possessory action whereby one complains of an essentially personal wrong while *mort d'ancestor* is petitory and does not necessarily reflect on the conduct of the other party. As Maitland put it, 'the *querela*, as distinct from the *petitio*, often comes from one who is with difficulty persuaded to accept money instead of vengeance, while the *petens* may have no worse to say of his opponent than that he has unfortunately purchased from one who could not give a good title'.[20] In Scotland, it is not clear whether the language used to describe the parties has any significance of this kind. Although the statute of 1230 which introduced novel dissasine spoke of the party who raised the action as the *conquerens*, and the 1318 legislation on the brieve of the *querelante*, and although in 1434 we find the pursuer under a brieve of novel dissasine described as '*prosequens*',[21] all words with overtones of wrongfulness and complaint, in the later medieval period the normal Latin usage to describe each litigant was that of *actor* and *reus*, without any apparent variation among the forms of action.[22] It is not impossible, however, that the word *petentes* shows that the estovers case was one of mortancestry. There are some early thirteenth-century cases where estovers were recovered by *mort d'ancestor* in England,[23] although later this function was taken over by *quod permittat* writs in the nature of *mort d'ancestor* and was not regained under the second Statute of Westminster in 1285.[24] The dispute between Coldingham and Durham over the superiority of Paxton and Auchencrow which, as shown in the previous chapter, underlay the estovers case, may have broken out on the death of the ancestor of the pursuers, raising the question of with whom they should seek entry to the lands. It is significant that the dispute focused on the issues of homage, relief and marriage, all matters suggesting that the issue was the infeftment of a deceased tenant's heirs.[25]

Another possible case from the middle of the thirteenth century is the action which Mariota, daughter of Samuel, raised by royal letters against the bishop of Glasgow concerning the lands of Stobo in Peeblesshire. Mariota and her sister's son both eventually quitclaimed the bishop of the lands; it is thus possible that the basis of her claim was a right of inheritance derived from Samuel. Accordingly, as Barrow has suggested, this may have been a case of mortancestry.[26] If so – and we cannot be sure – then it seems that in its early days mortancestry, like novel dissasine, might be taken in the sheriff court, where Mariota's action was raised. This would again support the contention that the estovers case, which was also determined in the sheriff court, was one of mortancestry.

In England, it seems clear that the assize was directed primarily against lords. This is evident from the text of the relevant chapter of the Assize of Northampton: 'should the lord of the fee deny the heirs of the deceased seisin of the said deceased which they claim, let the justices of the lord king thereupon cause an inquisition to be made by twelve lawful men as to what seisin the deceased held there on the day of his death; and according to the result of the inquest let restitution be made to the heirs'.[27] The Assize also suggests what were the principal cases where difficulty arose with its explicit references to female succession and to under-age heirs in the lord's ward; also mentioned is that the lord should recognise the widow's claim to dower.[28] *Glanvill* is also evidence that a principal problem was the minority of either party; that is to say, not only the underage heir in ward, but also the underage lord. When the defendant is a minor, the assize can be postponed until he comes of age, unless his father held merely in ward. From this latter possibility there may arise an inquiry whether the father of the defendant held in fee or ward.[29]

For Scotland, the position of the lord on his tenant's death provides one convincing context in which the situation remedied by the brieve might arise. When a tenant died, his land reverted to the lord, who had to find a new tenant. We can see this clearly in the twelfth century, at least among tenants-in-chief, in those grants where the king speaks of 'restoring' a deceased tenant's heir to his lands, even though we do not know of any break in the continuity of the tenancy.[30] If the tenant's heir was excluded, or at any rate not put in by the lord, then under the scheme of the brieve the lord became one who was unjustly detaining the lands, and a fortiori where the lord had put a third party in sasine of the lands. *Regiam* takes over *Glanvill*'s account of *mort d'ancestor*, with its emphasis on the problems of minor parties,[31] while the *Leges Forestarum* envisages mortancestry as the remedy of the heir who comes of age having been in ward, and cannot recover his lands from his lord.[32] When in 1253 Emma of Smeaton brought her brieve of mortancestry against Dunfermline abbey, she was in fact suing the superior of whom her father had held the lands.[33] A claim by a tenant against a lord to a right of common may also lie behind Mariota's action against the bishop of Glasgow. Stobo had been part of the bishop's demesne from very early times,[34] and it is described as his manor (*manerium*) in this dispute with Mariota.[35] Between 1208 and 1214, a neighbouring landowner claimed common of pasture in Stobo, and there may have been another such claim in the 1220s;[36] there is at least a chance that this was also what Mariota sought. The tenurial explanation for the introduction of mortancestry is plainly more than a possibility, particularly in the light of the clear instance of Emma's claim in 1253.

Mortancestry involves the idea that there is such a thing as a right to take land following the death of a tenant, at least in certain categories of case. Milsom argues that in England *mort d'ancestor*, while intended only to prevent abuse of power by the lord, had the effect of taking the lord out of the picture of inheritance altogether. The relatively fluid customs which governed inheritance in twelfth-century England were replaced by relatively rigid rules in which the lord played no part of significance, and was deprived of his ability to choose who should be his tenants. The question of how far inheritance customs bound lords in twelfth-century England before the appearance of *mort d'ancestor* is a controversial one, into which it is unnecessary to go in depth here.[37] From early on in the twelfth century in Scotland, grants were commonly 'to the grantee and his heirs', or 'in fee and heritage'. Duncan comments that 'by the late twelfth century most land in Lowland Scotland and in the great straths of the Grampians, held "in feu and heritage" (*in feodo et hereditate*) was understood to pass from father to eldest son provided that the son met certain prior obligations – the widow's portion and the lord's relief.[38] Female succession, with partition among all daughters if there was no male heir, was also an established custom before 1200.[39] Mortancestry clearly did not create such rights; rather, it took them for granted and provided a mechanism for their enforcement. Yet it would be mistaken to see inheritance customs as absolutely settled or uniform even in the reign of Alexander II, and this provides a background against which we can see why lords might go wrong. A customary law of succession might simply not have an answer to a particular problem, or have several alternative answers, one of which would be chosen when a concrete case presented itself. So, in the Great Cause at the end of the thirteenth century, there was much debate as to whether, in the event of the failure of a direct line of heirs, the inheritance customs of Scotland were governed by the principle of primogeniture or proximity, or indeed whether designations of heirs could take effect many generations later.[40] The custom of automatic inheritance was not immutably established until the thirteenth century; we know of land held by Anglo-Frenchmen being bequeathed by testament in the twelfth century, as well as at least once in the burgh of Berwick as late as 1246.[41] The distinction between heritage and conquest (respectively, inherited lands and lands otherwise acquired by the current holder) seems also to have been observed in the twelfth century, inasmuch as the Scottish lands acquired by Anglo-French settlers seem often to have descended to the first holder's younger son while the eldest took the original lands in England, the classic example being the Bruce lordship of Annandale.[42] The other characteristic of conquest, free alienability, was to survive in later burgh law, and the general concept remained part of Scots law until 1874.[43] Finally, there are some twelfth-century examples of claims by inheritance being apparently overridden in favour of outsiders, involving the settlement of Anglo-Normans at the expense of native heirs.[44]

The fluidity and uncertainty of inheritance customs in at least some circumstances is reflected in a number of succession disputes dealt with by William I and Alexander II, in which governing principles as well as facts of descent may have had to be ascertained. The main examples arose from the feudalisation of the Celtic earldoms and provinces. Earldoms such as Atholl, Caithness and Menteith were all the subject of confused and obscure disputes during their reigns,[45] while Alexander had to force the principle of partible female inheritance upon the recalcitrant province of Galloway after the death without a male heir of its lord, Alan of Galloway, in 1234. The men of Galloway favoured the claim of an illegitimate son of Alan, and this feeling was still strong enough at the end of the thirteenth century to trouble Alexander III and to be used by Edward I as a weapon in Scottish affairs.[46] Similarly, in Fife and Carrick, earldoms passed into female hands by virtue of inheritance laws, but the kindred also recognised a male successor as their head or captain, a position which seems to have coexisted with that of the holder of the earldom and even to have received royal recognition.[47]

However, we cannot infer too much about the uncertainty or variability of custom at the lower rungs of the landholding ladder from the king's enforcement of inheritance customs at the elevated levels of earldoms and provincial lordships, especially as the story there is complicated by the integration of Celtic institutions with, or their resistance to, Anglo-French ones. Inheritance laws could here be a political tool, allowing Galloway to be divided and more effectively ruled from the royal point of view, for example, or enabling the conferral of earldoms such as Buchan and Angus upon favoured royal supporters by marriage to the heiress in question, or giving the king wardship and marriage rights, as over the minor daughter of Neil, earl of Carrick, after his death in 1256. Certainly, it cannot be said that the introduction of the brieve of mortancestry was a response to these particular problems; but it is consistent with a royal policy which favoured a particular model of inheritance, a royal policy also evident in the contemporaneous development of the brieve of in-quest. Two of the cases which we have discussed as early examples of mortancestry involve women pursuers, for example, and it may be that one aim of the brieve was to uphold female inheritance in the face of much contrary social pressure.[48] In at least one instance, the brieve highlighted female succession specifically; that is, where the inheritance was claimed on the basis of a deceased sister's sasine. A brother of the full blood – that is, of the same parents – would always have taken before any sister. Therefore, where a claim was based on a sister's sasine, it must have often been by a woman. However, this was not the only conceivable case based on a sister's sasine, since a brother consanguinean – that is, of the same father but another mother – could be postponed until after the death of his half-sister.[49]

Another possible context where mortancestry might have operated was in holdings which hovered uncertainly between the free and the unfree.

Milsom has noted how in England nearly all the early cases on the assize of *mort d'ancestor* were concerned with small peasant tenements. 'One mistake may have been common: sometimes it appears that the tenement concerned . . . had been assumed to be unfree and therefore at the lord's disposal. Nor was this necessarily in the ordinary sense a mistake by the lord and his court: in some of these cases it is clear that the question of the freedom of the tenement is being asked for the first time, precisely because it is only *mort d'ancestor* and novel disseisin that have made it a meaningful question.'[50] Although in Scotland there is no evidence for early use of mortancestry in this context (unless we count Mariota's case against the bishop of Glasgow), a trend towards heritable tenure has been discerned in the thirteenth century where previously holdings had been founded on leases renewed over generations, or on the consent of the lord alone without any written title.[51] In this process, mortancestry may have had a role to play akin to that observed by Milsom, protecting the holdings of rent-paying tenants, the heritability of whose titles would otherwise have been vulnerable to lordly error.

JURISDICTION

As with novel dissasine, a number of the early cases suggest that the sheriff may have had jurisdiction in cases of mortancestry. However, *Regiam*, *Quoniam*, the 'registers' and surviving examples of the use of the brieve from the fourteenth century show that later it pertained only to the court of the justiciar.[52] A brieve in the Bute manuscript directs the sisting of an action before the justiciar in a brieve of mortancestry.[53] In 1321, two justiciars were assigned to hear the cause of John de Mora against Sybil de Quarentely and John Cissor on a brieve of mortancestry. The doom given stripped the defenders of their lands.[54] There survives from 1368 a document following the style of the brieve of mortancestry in the Ayr manuscript almost exactly. It is addressed to three justiciars and commands them to hold a recognition of the good and faithful and older men of the country to see whether the late William Douglas of Liddesdale, uncle of the pursuer, died vest and saised as of fee of lands in Peeblesshire. If so, and if the pursuer, James Douglas of Dalkeith, is his lawful and nearest heir, and if Roger Carruthers with his wife Isabella is unjustly detaining the lands, then the justiciars are to put Douglas into the lands so that he holds as his uncle did on the day when he was alive and dead.[55] Another brieve of mortancestry from the same period, only part of which survives, commands the justiciar south of Forth to recognosce by good and faithful and elder men of the country whether the late John Helbek, brother of the bearer of the brieve, Matthew Helbek, died vest and saised as of fee in Calderside in Lanarkshire.[56] The missing part of the brieve would certainly have gone on to identify the party alleged to be wrongfully occupying the lands. In an interesting document of 1390, Murdoch Stewart, justiciar north of Forth, narrates how Thomas Hay of Errol, the constable, presented a brieve of mortancestry against William Keith the marischal in the full court of the justice ayre at Dundee. An assize of the best and worthiest of the country found that Thomas was the lawful and nearest heir of his grandfather John Keith in the lands of Inverpeffer in the sheriffdom of Forfar, and that William was unjustly detaining them. Thomas was to have the sasine which his grandfather had had on the day when he was alive and dead.[57] This appears to be a classic case of mortancestry and an application of the statutory provisions of 1318. Murdoch Stewart heard another such case in 1397 in his capacity as justiciar north of Forth, when Alexander Murray of Colbyn and William son of John of Badfothal sought to recover the third part of the barony of Badfothal by a brieve of mortancestry. They alleged that Michael Mercer was unjustly detaining these lands. An assize found that the pursuers' grandmother, Marjorie, died saised as of fee of the third part of the barony, and that as Alexander and William were the lawful and nearest heirs they should have sasine and heritable possession.[58] It seems clear that when in 1369 James Douglas of Dalkeith and William Cresswell agreed to have the controversy between them over the lands of Roberton in Lanarkshire settled by a brieve of mortancestry, the case would have been heard in the justiciar's court.[59]

As with novel dissasine, there is no evidence to suggest that mortancestry was ever used in the burgh court, and once again there is a close parallel with the position in England. The exclusion of *mort d'ancestor* from boroughs attracted some comment by English writers. *Glanvill* states that 'for reasons of convenience' it had been enacted that burgage tenures could not be recovered by *mort d'ancestor*, and the king had provided another remedy.[60] The nature of this other remedy is not stated. *Bracton* explains that *mort d'ancestor* was excluded where local custom permitted the purchase of borough lands, because sometimes land which had been bought could be bequeathed by the purchaser in his will so that his heir under the normal rules of primogeniture might lawfully be excluded from them. However, the writer went on to comment that 'as to lands that descend hereditarily the assize could well lie, because they cannot be bequeathed any more than lands lying outside as to which the assize lies, and the reason why it does not is not clear'.[61]

In Scotland, we find in *Regiam* the passage from *Glanvill* that it had been enacted for reasons of utility that burgage could not be recovered by this action.[62] There is however no evidence of such a piece of legislation in Scotland. As to *Bracton's* remarks, there is some evidence that the Scottish burgage could be bequeathed by testament in the first half of the thirteenth century,[63] but this ceased to be the law. Alienability was also restricted to protect the interest of the heir. The burgess could alienate only his conquest – that is, the lands which he himself had acquired or purchased rather than inherited. However, alienation of conquest was prohibited when the burgess was on his death-bed, unless it was necessary through poverty.[64] Heritage could never be sold except in cases of necessity.[65] Necessity had to be determined by the procedures of the *retrait lignager*, which conferred a right of pre-emption upon the heir.[66] Only the heir who had knowingly failed to make use of this right could be prevented from subsequently challenging the validity of a sale to some other person. Where the lands were seized by a creditor in satisfaction of a debt (perhaps the most typical example of a transfer by reason of necessity), then they had to be offered to the debtor's heirs within a year and a day – that is, at the next three head courts. All this shows that there would have been relatively few occasions when the heir of a deceased burgess could not claim to be entitled to the lands of his ancestor by right of inheritance.

From all this, it would seem that the Bractonian puzzlement at the general exclusion of burgage from the ambit of mortancestry might have been echoed in later medieval Scotland. If, however, when mortancestry was introduced, burgage lands could still be bequeathed by testament in Scotland, then the explanation that the remedy had no place in a regime where the heir-at-law did not have an automatic claim may make some sense and be another piece of indirect evidence for the relatively early introduction of the brieve.

MORTANCESTRY AFTER 1300

The fourteenth-century evidence shows that mortancestry was regularly used in this period, in substantially the form in which it appears in treatises and registers. The only hint of change other than by the legislation of 1318 is the disappearance from the records of the idea of the assize consisting of the good and faithful older men, who seem to be replaced by the best and worthiest in the sources dating from the reign of Robert II (1371–88) on. The act of 1318, allowing claims to be based on grandparents' titles, plainly took effect, as the cases of *Hay v Keith* and *Murray v Mercer* show.[67] However, the act's origins, as generally with the legislation on recovery of lands by pleadable brieve in 1318, must surely be found in the context of the attempted settlement in respect of the returning disinherited initiated by Robert I following Bannockburn. The act seems to be in favour of the disinherited, however, by contrast with the other legislation. Before the act, returning disinherited who sought to recover ancestral lands of which they themselves had never been possessed could only have used mortancestry if a member of their own or an immediately preceding generation had died vest and saised. If the relative had not been

infeft on death – if, for example, he had been put out during the wars –
then only the lengthy procedures of the brieve of right would have been
available to his heirs. By permitting mortancestry claimants to go back
one more generation, there was more chance of reaching the time of
peace and settled conditions under Alexander III and an ancestor who
had died in sasine of the lands. The change is probably also a sign of the
change overtaking the jury, which was ceasing to be a group of witnesses
and becoming one of assessors of the evidence led before them. Whatever
the original purpose of the reform, however, it plainly opened up the
remedy for many other claimants later in the century.

Like novel dissasine, mortancestry proceeded without essonzies being
allowed to the defender, although, as we have seen, in 1318 it was laid
down that he should be given an opportunity to hear the brieve and to
consider the case against him.[68] According to *Regiam*, the defender's
failure to compear on the first day did not entail loss of the case but
merely adjournment to a second day.[69] However, *Quoniam* states that if
the defender did not answer the summons, the case was to be decided at
once.[70] *Quoniam* is borne out by two litigations in 1455, in both of which
the defenders apparently failed to compear to answer brieves of
mortancestry, which were at once put to the recognition of an assize.[71]
The rule in *Quoniam* was cited, apparently successfully, in *Kennedy v
Fleming* in 1466.[72] Unlike dissasine, the defender in mortancestry might
have the action sisted by calling a warrantor, and there is at least one
example of this procedure in a case of 1465.[73]

Fifteenth-century evidence, which is much more plentiful than for
novel dissasine in the same period and is found at a much later date,
shows the brieve of mortancestry continuing to be quite distinct from the
brieve of inquest. Thus the brieve of mortancestry raised in 1413 by
Alexander de Irwyn, lord of Drum, was to recover the lands of Forglen
from an interloper, John Fraser, and was determined by an assize before
the justiciar of the regality of Arbroath abbey. Irwyn's successful claim
was based on the heritable sasine of his grandfather.[74] In 1437, William
Douglas, lord of Drumlanrig, recovered from Janet Murray, widow of the
late James Gledstanes, certain lands near Hawick in Roxburghshire in
which his father had died vest and saised as of fee and which Janet now
unjustly detained. The action was begun by brieve of mortancestry and
decided in the justiciar's court.[75] In January 1455, John Blair of Adamton
recovered the lands of Coschogill in the regality of Drumlanrig from
James Lorane, using a brieve of mortancestry.[76] The following March,
Margaret Mundell pursued two brieves of mortancestry against different
defenders before Laurence, lord Abernethy in Rothiemay, justiciar south
of Forth. Brieves to summon the defenders had been sent to the sheriff
of Dumfries by the justiciar and executed by the king's sergeant. Finally,

the assize pronounced a verdict in Margaret's favour.[77] The *Ordo Justiciarie* provides a form for the summons of a defender on a brieve of mortancestry,[78] and something like it must have been used in the virtually contemporary Mundell case. There is an actual example of such a writ from 1467. In it, William Edmonstone of Duntreath, justiciar south of Forth, commands the sheriff and bailies of Lanark to cause the parties to a brieve of mortancestry of the lord king's chapel to compear before him at the next ayre of Lanark for the determination of their case.[79] In January 1465, William Douglas of Drumlanrig, son of the pursuer in the case of *Douglas of Drumlanrig v Murray* (1437) mentioned above, sought other lands in the barony of Hawick by brieve of mortancestry before the justiciars south of Forth, this time from Alexander Gledstanes, probably the son of the previous defender. Douglas relied on the right of his grandfather and succeeded before the assize to which the brieve was put.[80] A year later, Gilbert lord Kennedy recovered lands in the barony of Kirkintilloch from Robert lord Fleming by brieve of mortancestry pursued in the court of the justiciar at Dumbarton. The assize found that Gilbert's grandfather had died vest and saised as of fee in the lands and that Robert was now unjustly detaining them.[81]

In 1471, Andrew Bisset came before the auditors of parliament to false a doom which had been given in the justice ayre of Cupar, Fife, upon a 'brief of mortancestry'. The auditors referred the question to the next parliament, because they could 'nocht now be avisit be the lawys that thai find written to declare quhat order and proces salbe had in the proceding of the said brief.[82] On the face of it, this might suggest that the brieve was becoming less well understood, but other evidence suggests that this was not the problem for the auditors. The next parliament dealt with the matter by passing a statute, the order and form of which were 'to be observit and kepit in al pointis in the proceding of the brief of mortancestrie purchest be Andro Bissate agane the lord of Ardros and now dependand in the justice are of Couper', as well as in the pursuit of pleadable brieves generally. The doubt of the auditors seems therefore to have concerned a general point, rather than being the result of a revival of an outmoded form of action. This is confirmed by the tenor of the statute itself, which deals with the formalities of pleading and falsing the doom rather than anything specific to mortancestry.[83] Bisset's action was still going in 1478, when he again falsed the doom before the auditors in parliament. The auditors declared that the decision of the justice court 'upoun the breve of morthancestre . . . was evil gevin and wele agane sayd . . . for diverse and mony resonis'.[84] There is no sign in the records of this long-drawn-out case that the brieve of mortancestry was even beginning to lose its identity, although we can perhaps see reasons why potential litigants might wish to use other, speedier remedies.

MORTANCESTRY AND TAILZIES

In 1430, parliament enacted that 'fra hyne furth thar sal na bref of mortansister pass fra the kyngis chapel bot in maner and furm as his ordanit in Robert the Browsys statutis, that is to say, of lineale successioune and nocht of taylze'.[85] The policy behind the statute was clearly to restrict the scope of the brieve to claims based on common-law rights of inheritance, rather than allowing it to be used for claims founded on destinations in tailzies. The latter situation had certainly arisen before 1430. The action which James Douglas of Dalkeith brought against Roger and Isabel Carruthers in 1368 is an example. Douglas, it will be recalled, sued in right of his uncle, William Douglas of Liddesdale. Now when William died in 1353, he left a daughter Mary who inherited his lands. In 1351, however, William had granted the lands which were to be contested in 1368 to James, with the proviso that James would take only if William died without male issue. There were several other provisions to ensure the succession of male heirs.[86] Mary Douglas died in childbirth in 1367, which actually left James as the heir of line, entitled to all the heritage that had belonged to William.[87] However, he did not make his 1368 claim as Mary's heir, but directly as William's. James's action was thus based on the tailzie of 1351. Indeed, it seems likely to have been the outcome of a conflict over the lands between James and Mary. If Mary had claimed the lands as heir-general and put in the Carrutherses as her vassals, then if James were her heir he would be bound to warrant their title. If, however, Mary had no right over the lands through the 1351 tailzie, then James could get rid of her infeftees as intruders. Regrettably, we can only speculate as to whether facts like those suggested lie behind our records of this case; but it can be said that James's action appears to be based on his right as heir of tailzie to William rather than on the other right available to him as heir of line to Mary. An action of mortancestry implies, moreover, that James had never had sasine of the lands he claimed.

In England, by this time, the heir of entail was confined to his remedies by the writs of formedon under the statute of 1285, *De Donis Conditionalibus*[88] although it is worth noting that, prior to its enactment, *mort d'ancestor* was competent where the issue in tail were heirs-general and their ancestors had died seised.[89] In Scotland, tailzies were generally in favour of the male line of heirs, and failure of that line seems to have been comparatively rare.[90] This, coupled with the much greater control of alienation exercised by Scottish superiors by contrast with their English counterparts, probably accounts for the lack of difficulties experienced with tailzies in Scotland, and certainly explains why mortancestry continued to be a most appropriate form of action for the heir of tailzie seeking recovery from an intruder. Even after 1430, where the person of the heir-general and the heir of tailzie merged in one man, then mortancestry could still be used without infringing the statute. Thus in 1466, Gilbert lord Kennedy brought the brieve against Robert lord Fleming not only as heir-general but also as heir under a tailzie of 1385.[91]

It was *De Donis* which was primarily responsible for the development of the concept of the fee tail in England and the consequent elaboration of the doctrine of estates in land. It is most unlikely that the Scottish act of 1430 had or was intended to have a similar effect. No new remedy was offered to the heir of tailzie unable to gain entry against an intruder or to use mortancestry as heir-general. This seems to leave the brieve of right as the only available remedy; but, if so, that would not have led a medieval Scots lawyer to suppose that the tailzied fee was different in kind from a fee the succession to which was open to heirs-general. As we shall see, the brieve of right also protected heirs with such a claim. Our lawyer would merely have seen the interposition of a longer procedure between the heir of tailzie and the realisation of his right.

MORTANCESTRY AND LATER MEDIEVAL FEUDALISM

The later medieval cases of mortancestry often look as though they are about abstract questions of title and rights to land rather than being merely a remedy for disappointed heirs against wrongdoing lords. We can see this sometimes in the language of our records: it is the *droit* of a barony which will be settled by a brieve of mortancestry in 1369, and it is *complementum iuris* which the pursuers seek under another such brieve in 1397.[92] Where the background to a case can be worked out in any detail, it is generally a title competition which is laid before us. Take for instance Hay the constable against Keith the marischal for the lands of Inverpeffer in 1390. Hay's claim was based on the sasine of his grandfather John Keith. John's daughter, who must have been his heir, married Hay's father. However, sometime after 1324, we find Robert Keith, the then marischal and head of the Keith family, putting Inverpeffer under a tailzie in favour of his heirs-male after the death of his son John (the same John Keith?). Thus the lands passed to his brother Edward, who in turn was succeeded, sometime before 1351, by his eldest son William, the defender of 1390. No doubt the Keith claim is explained by the strength of feeling in favour of agnatic succession in Scotland. Its illegality is easy for us to see; it would perhaps have been less obvious in 1390 when William was holding by a title over sixty years old which had been the subject of a royal confirmation.[93]

However, none of this means that the brieve had ceased to operate in a feudal context. In the fourteenth century, the pivotal role of the lord or superior in the transfer of tenants' land by inheritance was, if anything, strengthened. Heirs had still to seek entry and receive sasine from him, as the lands were recognosced by the lord on the tenant's death. This explains the development in the later Middle Ages of the casualty of non-entry, payable by an heir who delayed seeking infeftment from the lord.[94] Avoidance of non-entry as well as of the formalities of service of heirs probably explains another development in later medieval legal practice which has already been discussed, the practice of landowners making *inter vivos* grants in fee to their heirs, but reserving a *liberum tenementum* while they lived.[95] If this suggestion is correct, it underlines the continuing reality of the lord's powers on his tenant's death. The abuse of these powers lies behind an act of 1401 which deals with the difficulty experienced by heirs who often find that the lord has infeft someone else.[96] Mortancestry would have provided remedies against such seigneurial wrongs, although it is not mentioned in the statute. Situations of this kind lie behind the litigations over lands in the barony of Hawick which involved the Douglases of Drumlanrig and various members of the Gledstanes family in 1437 and again in 1465. Here, the complicating factor was that the Douglases held the barony of the Earls of Douglas, but twice – between 1421 and 1427, and again between 1444 and 1450 – an heir of the family failed to take immediate entry with the superiors on the death of his father. The earls accordingly held the land until entry was made, and seem to have granted demesne or 'mains' lands in the barony to the Gledstanes on each occasion – grants which could only be reversed on each occasion by a brieve of mortancestry brought by the heir once infeft.[97] Another situation may be illustrated by a final concord made in 1325 by Henry Maule, lord of Panmure, and John of Glassary concerning the lands of Benvie and Balruddery in Gowrie which John held of Henry. Henry had seized Balruddery on the death of his late mother, Ethana de Vaux, who had been holding the lands *in dotem*, but now he recognised that his tenant John was entitled to the *jus* and property.[98] Had it been necessary, John's remedy in this situation was mortancestry.

Later again, in 1466, when Gilbert lord Kennedy brought a brieve of mortancestry against Robert lord Fleming, he was seeking to recover lands which his ancestors had held of the Flemings; it is significant that to begin with the parties seem to have contemplated action in Robert's court. Here, then, the question seems to have been: was Robert entitled to the lands in demesne, or only to a superiority over them? Behind this debate lay rules whose ultimate source was *Glanvill*, the rights of lords to the lands of vassals who had committed treason against the king. Robert alleged that Gilbert's elder brother John, who had been first entitled to the lands, had committed treason against King James I, and that in consequence, following *Regiam*, his heritage went to the king for a year and a day before reverting to the lord. With this argument, we are back in the world of the lord's disciplinary jurisdiction, with the tenant's fee being escheat for wrongdoing. However, it was not enough to win the case for

Robert, whose problem lay in establishing any conviction of John following his mysterious imprisonment at Stirling in 1430 and subsequent disappearance. He, or rather his advisers, sought to circumvent the problem by reference to a statute of Marcus Aurelius allowing the conviction of traitors after their deaths, but this display of learning was insufficient for Robert's purpose. Recovery of the lands came later, and not, it seems, by legal process.[99]

Even when there was no tenurial link claimed between the original parties in a mortancestry case, a feudal dimension could come in if the defender called a warrantor. It would seem from a writ in the Bute manuscript that this would sist the principal action until the warrantor appeared to take over its defence;[100] there is here a significant contrast with the position in novel dissasine. Often the warrantor must have been the superior, and the pursuer's case would then become a claim to hold the lands of him. At least, this is what we can see happening in a case of 1372, where James Douglas of Dalkeith, who had been impleaded in the justiciar's court for his lands of Morton in Dumfriesshire, brought a brieve of warrandice against the earl of March in the sheriff court. The earl, who had granted the lands to be held of him by Douglas only a few years before, accepted his liability to appear before the justiciar.[101] It seems almost certain that the case in that court was one of mortancestry, and that it would now become a question of the pursuer's right to hold of the earl.

DECLINE OF MORTANCESTRY

In conclusion, there can be little doubt that the brieve of mortancestry remained in use as a distinct form of action until the end of the fifteenth century. The sources give us no direct information on its operation after 1478; but, as already mentioned, the act of 1504 on falsing dooms does suggest that some pleadable brieves were still being addressed to the justiciar's court at the beginning of the sixteenth century.[102] The appearance of a style for the brieve of mortancestry in the Cambridge and St Andrews formularies, substantially identical with those in the Ayr and Bute manuscripts and in *Quoniam*, underlines the point that the argument from silence can cut both ways.[103] In the latter part of the sixteenth century, however, neither Balfour nor Skene was aware of any difference between the brieve of mortancestry and the brieve of inquest, and plainly by their time the true nature and effect of the former had been forgotten.[104]

NOTES

1. *Dunf Reg* nos 82–3.
2. *RM* (*APS*), III, 24–5; *RM* (*Cooper*), III, 28–9; *QA* (*Fergus*), ch. 37; *QA* (*APS*), ch 35; QA (*Cooper*), ch. 52.
3. *Reg Brieves*, pp. 40 (no 20), 62 (no 106).
4. This style is that of *Glanvill*, XIII, 3.
5. *RM* (*APS*), IV, 40; *RM* (*Cooper*), p. 296 (Supplement, no 22).
6. See above, pp. 156–8.
7. *Pais Reg*, pp. 165–7; T. M. Cooper, *Cases*, pp. 37–9.
8. The confusion was apparent early in the sixteenth century: although the 'register' in Cambridge University Library MS Ee.4.21 contains a true brieve of mortancestry (f. 273v), its style for the brieve of inquest is headed '*breve inquisicionis morte antecessoris*' (f. 269r). For a brief view of the confusion's consolidation by John Skene which should have been ended by John Erskine's clarification in the eighteenth century, see I. D. Willock, *Jury*, pp. 107–8. The confusion which still flows from T. M. Cooper's comments on the subject in *Reg Brieves*, pp. 13–15, despite correction by H. McKechnie, *Brieves*, p. 11, is evident in D. M. Walker, *Legal History*, i, pp. 108, 265; ii, p. 735. For medieval usage, see e.g. *Reg Brieves*, p. 41 (no 22) ('*generalis inquisicio*); *APS*, ii, p. 253 (c. 40); *ADA*, p. *135; *ADC*, i, p. 34. It is not true to say, as T. M. Cooper does (*Reg Brieves*, p. 14), that the term mortancestry 'is of very frequent occurrence in Scottish charter records of the thirteenth century' as a description of the brieve of inquest or, indeed, at any time before the sixteenth century.
9. The fullest modern account of the brieve of inquest is I. D. Willock, *Jury*, pp. 109–21.
10. On these procedural points, see *RM* (*APS*), III, 24–5; IV, 19; *RM* (*Cooper*), III, 28–9; p. 287 (Supplement no 9); *QA* (*Fergus*), ch. 37; *QA* (*APS*), ch. 37; *QA* (*APS*), ch. 35; *QA* (*Cooper*), ch. 52. See further below, pp. 178, 183.
11. *RRS*, v, p. 413 (c. 23); *APS*, i, p. 472 (c. 23). Note that this act refers only to the '*breve de recognicione*', and not to mortancestry as such; but nonetheless mortancestry must be meant. Mortancestry was a '*breve de recognicione*', according to *RM* (*APS*), I, 4; III, 24; *RM* (*Cooper*), I, 5; III, 27.
12. P&M, ii, p.57.
13. H. McKechnie, *Brieves*, p. 9; I. D. Willock, *Jury*, p. 33.
14. *Reg Brieves*, p. 41 (no 22).
15. P&M, ii, p. 57.
16. J. Biancalana, 'Want of justice', pp. 441, 506–14.
17. P&M, ii, p. 57.
18. I. D. Willock, *Jury*, pp. 23–32; A. A. M. Duncan, *Kingdom*, pp. 539–41; above, p. 138.
19. *RM* (*APS*), I, 4; III, 24; *RM* (*Cooper*), I, 5; III, 27; above, note 11.
20. P&M, ii, pp. 571–2.
21. See *APS*, i, p. 400 (c. 7); *RRS*, v, p. 410 (c. 13) (also *APS*, i, p. 470 (c. 13)); H. L. MacQueen and A. R. Borthwick, 'Cases', p. 124.
22. It may be worth noting here, however, that according to the *Leges Forestarum* (*APS*, i, p. 730) damages were recoverable in a

mortancestry as in a dissasine action, i.e. the action is in essence a complaint about a wrong.

23. *Novae Narrationes*, p. lxxxiii.
24. *Novae Narrationes*, p. lxxxvi; *Shropshire Roll*, p. xxx.
25. *Cold Corr*, no 239; above, p. 141.
26. *Glas Reg*, nos 130, 131 and 172; G. W. S. Barrow, *Kingdom*, pp. 115–16. For another possibility, see below, pp. 201–2.
27. For the text of the Assize, see *Stubbs' Select Charters*, pp. 179–80.
28. I here accept the interpretation of the Assize offered by R. C. Palmer, 'Origins of property', pp. 13–17; cf. J. Biancalana, 'Want of justice', p. 505 note.
29. *Glanvill*, XIII, 2–17.
30. See for examples G. W. S. Barrow, 'The Scots charter', *Studies in Medieval History presented to R. H. C. Davis*, ed. H. Mayr-Harting and R. I. Moore (London, 1985), p. 154.
31. *RM (APS)*, III, 24–5; IV, 40; *RM (Cooper)*, III, 28–32; also p. 295 (Supplement no 22).
32. *APS*, i, pp. 730–1 (c. 3).
33. See *Dunf Reg*, nos 180, 185, 194, 195 and 303.
34. *Glas Reg*, pp. 5, 7, 23, 30, 43, 50, 55.
35. Ibid., no 131.
36. Ibid., nos 104–5, 126–8.
37. See S. E. Thorne, 'English feudalism and estates in land', *Cambridge Law Journal*, xvii (1959), p. 193; J. C. Holt, 'Politics and property in early medieval England', *Past and Present*, no 57 (1972), p. 3; the same author's four presidential addresses to the Royal Historical society on the theme, 'Feudal society and the family in early medieval England', published in *TRHS*, xxii–v; and his 'Magna Carta 1215–1217: the legal and social context', p. 15; S. F. C. Milsom, *Studies*, pp. 231–60; S. D. White, 'Inheritances'; J. Hudson, 'Life grants'.
38. A. A. M. Duncan, *Kingdom*, p. 370.
39. See e.g. G. W. S. Barrow, *Kingdom*, pp. 353–4, *and ANE*, p. 65, for Eschina of Mow before 1177; A. A. M. Duncan, *Kingdom*, p. 372, for Berkeleys c. 1193, and p. 188, for earldom of Buchan c. 1212; K. J. Stringer, *Nobility Essays*, p. 49, for De Moreville lords of Lauderdale 1196; *Panm Reg*, i, p. xvi, for Maules of Panmure 1186.
40. E. L. G. Stones and G. G. Simpson, *Edward I*, i, pp. 13–21; G. W. S. Barrow, *Bruce*, pp. 39–49.
41. *Melr Lib*, i, no 82; A. C. Lawrie, *Annals*, p. 21; T. M. Cooper, *Cases*, no 37. See also the *post obit* gifts made to the monks of Coupar Angus c. 1200 (*CA Chrs*, i, nos 10, 11; *CA Rent*, i, p. 335 (no 42)).
42. G. W. S. Barrow, *ANE*, p. 12. Many of the first Anglo-French settlers were themselves younger sons seeking to establish a patrimony: ibid., pp. 13–29.
43. W. D. H. Sellar, 'Common law', p. 89; and see further above, p. 176–7.
44. G. W. S. Barrow, *ANE*, pp. 22–4.
45. A. A. M. Duncan, *Kingdom*, pp. 178–9, 192–7, 543–6; see also G. W. S. Barrow, 'The reign of William the Lion king of Scots', *Historical Studies*, vii (Dublin, 1969), pp. 34–5 (Menteith), and B. E. Crawford, 'The earldom of Caithness and the kingdom of Scotland

1150–1266', in *Nobility Essays*, pp. 33–7 (Caithness).
46. H. L. MacQueen, 'Laws of Galloway', p. 138.
47. See MacQueen, 'Kin of Kennedy'; pp. 278–81; J. M. W. Bannerman, 'Macduff of Fife', pp. 32–8.
48. For the social pressures, see A. A. M. Duncan, *Kingdom*, pp. 371–4.
49. The law of the half-blood's inheritance stated in P & M, ii, pp. 302–3 survived in Scots law until the Succession (Scotland) Act 1964: see T. B. Smith, *A Short Commentary on the Law of Scotland* (Edinburgh, 1962), pp. 402–3, and W. D. H. Sellar, 'Common law', p. 89. I am grateful to the latter author for help on this point.
50. S. F. C. Milsom, *HFCL*, pp. 136–7, citing *LFEF*, pp. 22–3, 167.
51. A. A. M. Duncan, *Kingdom*, pp. 392–7; see also ibid., pp. 378, 410–12.
52. *Reg Brieves*, pp. 40 (no 20), 62 (no 106); *QA (Fergus)*, pp. 203–5; *QA (APS and Cooper)*, ch. 52.
53. *Reg Brieves*, p. 61 (no 96).
54. *APS*, i, p. 479; *RMS*, i, appendix 1, no 74.
55. *RRS*, vi, no 417.
56. *RRS*, vi, no 503.
57. *Spalding Misc*, ii, p. 319. In my article 'Dissasine and mortancestor', I confused the 'Inverpeffer' of the document with Innerpeffray in Perthshire. Since the case was heard at Dundee in the ayre of Forfar, this was an obvious error. Inverpeffer is just south of Arbroath (NGR NO 5937).
58. *AB Ill*, iii, p. 263.
59. *Mort Reg*, ii, no 107.
60. *Glanvill*, XIII, 11. See also the editor's note on this passage.
61. *Bracton*, f. 271 (iii, p. 295). Cf. *Borough Customs*, i, pp. 243–5.
62. *RM (APS)*, III, 25; *RM (Cooper)*, III, 29.
63. T. M. Cooper, *Cases*, no 37. The contrary view in H. L. MacQueen and W. J. Windram, 'Burghs', p. 220, is therefore wrong for the thirteenth century.
64. *Leges Burgorum*, cc. 21, 42, 101 (*APS*, i, pp. 336, 340, 353). With regard to death-bed, see also *APS*, i, p. 723.
65. *Leges Burgorum*, c. 42 (*APS*, i, p. 340).
66. See H. L. MacQueen and W. J. Windram, 'Burghs', p. 227 note 94 for references; also E. L. Ewan, *Townlife*, p. 94.
67. See above, p. 176.
68. *RRS*, v, p. 412 (c. 19); *APS*, i, p. 471 (c. 19).
69. *RM (APS)* III, 24–5; *RM (Cooper)* III, 28–9.
70. *QA (Fergus)*, ch. 37; *QA (APS)*, ch. 35; *QA (Cooper)*, ch. 52.
71. See H. L. MacQueen and A. R. Borthwick, 'Cases', pp. 127–36; R. C. Reid, 'Coschogill writ', p. 132.
72. SRO, *Ailsa muniments*, GD 25/1/102.
73. *RM (APS)*, IV, 19; *RM (Cooper)*, p. 287 (Supplement, no 9); H. L. MacQueen and A. R. Borthwick, 'Cases', pp. 136–48.
74. SRO, *Forglen muniments*, GD 185/2/2/1.
75. W. Fraser, *Douglas*, iii, no 301.
76. R. C. Reid, 'Coschogill writ', p. 132.
77. H. L. MacQueen and A. R. Borthwick, 'Cases', pp. 127–36.
78. *APS*, i, p. 706.
79. *Mort Reg*, ii, no 223.

80. H. L. MacQueen and A. R. Borthwick, 'Cases', pp. 136–48.
81. SRO, *Ailsa muniments*, GD 25/1/102; discussed in full in H. L. MacQueen, 'Kin of Kennedy', passim.
82. *ADA*, p. 12.
83. *APS*, ii, p. 101; discussed in H. L. MacQueen, 'Pleadable brieves', pp. 408–9.
84. *ADA*, p. 66.
85. *SHR*, xxix (1950), pp. 5–9.
86. *Mort Reg*, ii, no 70.
87. *Scots Peerage*, vi, pp. 341–3. See also W. D. H. Sellar, 'Courtesy', pp. 1–2; G. Neilson, *Trial by Combat*, pp. 216–17; and W. Fraser, *Douglas*, i, pp. 253 4.
88. *Statutes of the Realm*, i, pp. 71–2 (c. 1); A. W. B. Simpson, *Land Law*, p. 78.
89. S. F. C. Milsom, *Studies*, pp. 223–9, especially p. 226; P & M, ii, pp. 28–9.
90. See A. Grant, 'Thesis', pp. 207–9, 308–11; idem, 'Extinction of direct male lines among Scottish noble families in the fourteenth and fifteenth centuries', *Nobility Essays*, pp. 210–31. Cf. the review of the latter by W. D. H. Sellar, *SHR*, lxvi (1987), pp. 200–3.
91. See my discussion of this case in 'Kin of Kennedy', passim.
92. *Mort Reg*, ii, no 107; *AB Ill*, iii, p. 263.
93. For all this, see *RMS*, i, appendix 1, no 47; *RRS*, v, no 261, commented on in the introduction, pp. 66–9; *Scots Peerage*, vi, pp. 30–8. Note that John's son Robert, mentioned in the tailzie, must have predeceased his grandfather without male issue.
94. On the development of non-entry, principally by the Crown, see R. Nicholson, 'Feudal developments', pp. 19–20, and C. Madden, 'Royal treatment of feudal casualties in late medieval Scotland', *SHR*, lv (1976), pp. 181–4.
95. See above, pp. 113, 157.
96. *APS*, i, p. 575.
97. See H. L. MacQueen and A. R. Borthwick, 'Cases', pp. 139–48, for details.
98. *Panm Reg*, ii, p. 160.
99. For the details, see H. L. MacQueen, 'Kin of Kennedy', pp. 288–9.
100. *Reg Brieves*, p. 61 (no 96).
101. *Mort Reg*, ii, nos 100, 101, 130, 136, 141 and 142; *RRS*, vi, no 105.
102. *APS*, ii, p. 254 (c. 41). See above, pp. 161–2.
103. Cambridge University Library MS Ee.4.21, f. 273v; *St A Form*, i, p. 253.
104. Sir James Balfour, *Practicks*, ii, pp. 420–33; J. Skene, *DVS*, sv '*Breve de morte antecessoris*'; J. Skene, *RM (Latin)*, ff. 86v–89r.

7

The Brieve of Right

The first references to brieves of right (*de recto*) in the Scottish historical record are found towards the end of the thirteenth century. In 1290, Robert Bruce 'the Competitor', grandfather of the future King Robert I, made an agreement with Sir Nicholas Biggar that the latter would pursue a claim to the lands of Garioch by a *breve regium de recto*, as part of Bruce's complex manoeuvres against John Balliol in the Great Cause over the Scottish crown.[1] Bruce, Balliol and John Hastings jointly held Garioch as descendants of Earl David of Huntingdon, who had been granted Garioch between 1178 and 1182, so presumably Biggar's claim was based on some antecedent twelfth-century 'right'.[2] At about the same time, Master Roger Bartholomew '*recuperavit seysinam suam* by an assize following upon a brieve of right in Berwick burgh court.[3] It is clear even from these few references that by the end of the thirteenth century the brieve of right was in use as a remedy for the recovery of land and was not merely 'a writ to hear someone's claim or right to something'.[4]

Our earliest evidence for the style of the brieve of right (*breve de recto*) comes from the fourteenth-century 'registers' and *Quoniam*. The registers contain two styles, one addressed to the sheriff, the other to the provost (alderman) and bailies of a burgh, the latter being headed '*breve de recto in burgo*'. The forms are otherwise identical. The typical style runs as follows:[5]

> The king to the sheriff (or to the provost and baillies of a burgh): We command that you make N, the bearer of the presents, have full right of four carucates of land with the pertinents in the tenement of K in your bailiary which he claims to hold of us in heritage, rendering annually to us thereupon twenty silver shillings and performing for us as much forinsec service and aid as pertains to half the service of one knight; of which carucates of land with the pertinents R de B unjustly deforces him as he alleges. Act hereupon in such a way that we do not hear any further complaint for default of right.

That this was the form in early fourteenth-century practice is borne out by the text of an actual brieve of right sent to the burgh court of Aberdeen in 1317, which still survives, sewn to the court roll. It runs as follows:[6]

> Robert by the grace of God king of Scots to his faithful officers and baillies of Aberdeen, greetings: We command and ordain you that you cause John, son of Laurence, and Marjory, daughter of the late Brice de Cragy, his wife, to have full right by reason of their said marriage of a perticate of land with the pertinents lying in the said burgh of Aberdeen on the eastern side of the street known as Gallowgate, between the lands which belonged to the late William Fiechet on the southern side at one end, and the lands on the northern side which belonged to the late Reginald de Grendoun at the other, which perticate of land with the pertinents he claims to hold of us heritably by reason of his said wife, rendering annually therefor to us and our heirs six silver pennies in this way, three pennies at the feast of Whit and three pennies at Martinmas, also rendering to the brothers of the order of the Trinity in Aberdeen six shillings and eight silver pennies half-yearly, in this way at the above mentioned feast of Whit and the other half at the foresaid Martinmas, of which perticate of land with the pertinents Emma, daughter of the foresaid late Brice de Cragy, has unjustly deforced them, so they say, acting thereupon so that we do not hear any just complaint for want of full right therein.

This is distinct in a number of ways from the original English writ of right, which ran as follows:[7]

> The king to Earl William, greeting. I command you to do full right without delay to N in respect of ten carucates of land in Middleton which he claims to hold of you and which Robert son of William is withholding from him. If you do not do it the sheriff will, that I may hear no further complaint for default of right in this matter.

Some derivations from the English writ are plainly to be discerned, in the formula of 'full right' and the accusation of 'deforcement' against the defender, but the contrasts are more striking. The English writ was directed to the lord of whom the demandant claimed to hold the disputed lands, and commanded him to do full right in the matter or else the sheriff would. By contrast, the Scottish brieve was addressed straight to the sheriff and commanded him to cause the pursuer to have full right of lands of which he was being unjustly deforced by the defender. Moreover, the resulting litigation would go through entirely in the sheriff's court, whereas in England the sheriff only acted on the lord's default and, if the tenant opted to put himself on the grand assize, the case would be heard before the royal justices.

The most important distinction, however, is that in all the Scottish formularies the bearer of the brieve (that is, the pursuer) is said to be one who claims to hold not of a lord but of the king; in other words, to be a tenant-in-chief. It seems from *Regiam* that it was not in fact so limited by the fourteenth century, for the treatise gives a form for the statement of claim to be made on a brieve of right, and by this the pursuer is made to claim to hold 'heritably of the lord king or (in the alternative) of another lord'.[8] However, the form of the brieve must reflect an earlier situation in which only the tenant-in-chief could make use of it. It cannot therefore be modelled entirely on the English writ of right, which could not be used by such a party, since the claimant was claiming to hold the land of the lord to whom the writ was addressed.

The remedy for the English tenant-in-chief was the writ *precipe*.[9] The *precipe* had a complex history. In *Glanvill*, it is simply a writ of summons for 'when anyone complains to the lord king or his justices concerning his fee or free tenement, and the case is such that it ought to be, or the lord king is willing that it should be, tried in the king's court'.[10] The style makes no reference to 'right' in land as such:[11]

> The king to the sheriff, greeting. Command N to render to R, justly and without delay, one hide of land in such-and-such a vill, which the said R complains that the aforesaid R is withholding [*deforciat*] from him. If he does not do so, summon him by good summoners to be before me or my justices on the day after the octave of Easter, to show why he has not done so. And have there the summoners and this writ.

It appears that this writ was used by both tenants-in-chief and others to initiate litigation concerning the right to land up to 1215, when clause 34 of Magna Carta prohibited the issue of *precipe* writs to anybody to deprive lords of their courts – that is to say, to a party claiming land held of a lord other than the king, whose actions should be commenced in the appropriate lord's court.[12] After Magna Carta, the tenant-in-chief used a writ called the *precipe in capite*, so described because it made clear that no lord was being deprived of his court, by mentioning that the claim was to hold in chief. However, it also referred to the claim as being 'of right'. It ran as follows:[13]

> The king to the sheriff. Command B that justly and without delay he render to A ten acres of land with appurtenances in such a vill, which he claims to be his right and inheritance, and to hold of us in chief and whereof he complains that the aforesaid B deforces him; and if he does not do it, and the said A shall have given you security to prosecute his claim, then summon by good summoners the afore-said B that he be before our justices at Westminster to show why he has not done this, and have there the summoners and this writ.

Elements of the Scottish brieve of right can be seen to derive from this writ also, namely the statement mentioned above that the demandant holds in chief of the king, and that the claim arises out of heritable right. The interest of this lies in the fact that the *precipe in capite* was not originally described as a writ of right, even though it was a means of recovering full right in land. According to Maitland, 'in course of time the term "Writ of Right" gains a somewhat extended sense and is used so as to include the *precipe in capite*, because by both writs the demandant sought full proprietary right'.[14] Maitland did not supply references or a precise chronology for this development. In the first half of the thirteenth century, his statement seems to be substantiated mainly by *Bracton*'s description of the *precipe in capite* as the writ of right for one who ought to hold of the king in chief,[15] although in *Judiciorum Essoniorum*, a tract dating from the 1220s and 1230s, it was recognised that the substantive law underlying the writ of right and the *precipe* was the same.[16] However, Holt has written as follows:

> The *precipe* was the baron's [i.e. tenant-in-chief's] writ of right, or as near as he could get to it. It is as a writ of right that it is usually described in baronial actions recorded in the Plea Rolls of John's reign; and it is very likely that any reference to a *breve de recto* in such actions is in fact to the *precipe*. The matter is put beyond serious doubt by royal grants, which gave beneficiaries protection from legal challenge except by writ of right. Such a proviso cannot have envisaged *Glanvill*'s writ of right. It must therefore refer to the mandatory action initiated by the *precipe*.[17]

Nevertheless, in the *Early Registers of Writs* spanning the period 1227 (or earlier) to c. 1320, the writ of right and the *precipe in capite* are always distinguished from each other, first because only tenants-in-chief could use the *precipe*, and, second, because of the technicalities of sealing the writ in chancery. The *precipe* was sent out 'close' – that is, it was so folded and sealed that it could not be read without first breaking the seal – while the writ of right was a letter patent, readable without breaking the seal. In none of these early registers is the *precipe in capite* called a writ of right.[18] Nor is it so described in treatises such as *Brevia Placitata* and *Novae Narrationes*. When these works and others such as *Britton* refer to the writ of right, they appear to be concerned only with the writ addressed to the lord's court.[19] The earliest references to the *precipe in capite* as a writ of right in court records known to me are of date 1276 and 1277.[20] When we reach the Year Books at the end of the thirteenth and the beginning of the fourteenth centuries, we can find several examples of the *precipe in capite* being called a writ of right; but it is noticeable that this usage is found in the reports rather than in the official records.[21]

There are yet other writs in the registers which, although basically in the *precipe* form, are called writs of right. These do not appear in the very earliest registers; the first is in the Luffield register of the 1260s:[22]

> The king to the sheriff. Command B that justly and without delay
> he render to A ten acres of land which he claims to be his right and
> inheritance and whereof he complains that the said B unjustly
> deforces him. And if he does not do it then summon the said B to
> be before our justices at Westminster to show us why he has not
> done this; because the chief lord of that fee has remitted to us his
> court thereof.

Here again we have B commanded to render land to A which the latter
claims as his right, or else answer before the king's justices. However,
there is no statement that the land in question is held of the king; instead,
there is a clause tacked on at the end of the writ saying that the lord has
remitted his court to the king. Such a clause had been made necessary
by clause 34 of Magna Carta: *precipe* writs had always to be shown not
to be depriving a lord of his jurisdiction, and to say that lands were held
of the king or that the lord had remitted his court did just that.[23] The
only distinction between the two writs lay in these phrases, yet the *precipe
quia dominus remisit curiam suam* was known officially as a writ of right;
this, it is tentatively suggested, being because it was established as a writ
of course later than the *precipe in capite*, at a date when the wider use of
the term 'writ of right' had become customary among English lawyers.

It might therefore be suggested that this wide use of the term 'writ of
right' became established around the middle of the thirteenth century,
perhaps chiefly influenced by *Bracton* and the recognition that each of the
various writs related to the same body of substantive law. That the wider
usage was firmly established in the second half of the thirteenth century
seems clear from provisions in the Statute of Wales in 1284, which gave
a number of writs to be available thenceforth to the English king's Welsh
subjects. Although these included novel disseisin and *mort d'ancestor*,
there is no sign of writs of right in the narrow sense, or of the *precipe in
capite*. Instead, the Welsh were to have what the statute called the *breve
commune* or the general writ.[24] This took the form of *Glanvill*'s *precipe*, use
of which had been stopped by Magna Carta, which in turn had no
application to Wales. The point of interest here, however, is that the *breve
commune* of the Statute of Wales was referred to subsequently in the
courts as the *'breve de recto'* of the laws of Wales.[25]

What light does this analysis of rather technical English developments
throw on the Scottish brieve of right? The first point must be that the
Scottish brieve is not so obviously drawn from a particular English writ
as is the case with novel dissasine and mortancestry. Instead, the model
appears to be a group of writs, initially regarded as distinct from each
other but by the second half of the thirteenth century all categorised as
'writs of right'.[26] Where English lawyers had a free hand to produce a

rationalised model of their system in Wales, they replaced the various forms of writs of right with the single *breve commune*. The same spirit seems to inform the Scottish brieve of right, in particular once it became available to those claiming to hold of subject-superiors, as *Regiam* informs us. In many ways, however, the brieve seems to owe more to the *precipe in capite*: a significant point may be that the brieve of right was also sent out of the king's chapel as a letter close.[27] There can be no doubt that once again English law provided a model; the only question is whether the Scots anticipated or followed the trend of thought on this matter in England.

Some clues towards answering this question may be found by considering further the point that the Scottish brieve was, according to its own terms, a remedy for tenants-in-chief. What, then, was the position of a dispossessed person who claimed to hold of a subject-superior – that is, the party who would have used the classical writ of right in England – before the brieve was made available to them? Discussing the rule requiring brieves to compel a man to answer for his lands, Cooper commented that 'so far as has been noted there are no examples in the Scottish records of the period [i.e. the thirteenth century] of a brieve of right addressed to a baron'.[28] This would hardly be surprising if the brieve of right was, as the styles suggest, confined to cases involving tenants-in-chief, or, alternatively, supposing that the brieve was generally available from an early date, invariably heard before the sheriff. However, there are cases on record in which action to recover lands was begun by a royal brieve in a lord's court. In none of them, it is important to stress, are we told that the writ was a brieve of right, or that it commanded the lord in question to do right or else the sheriff would. On the other hand, there is some circumstantial evidence that what we are dealing with is a brieve functionally similar to the classical writ of right addressed to the lord's court in England.

All the cases come from the thirteenth century. The earliest of them is, to judge from the witness list to the document in which it is recorded, dateable to the 1230s. The document notes a quitclaim to the monks of Durham serving God at Coldingham made by Matthew of Howburn for certain lands in Coldingham 'of which he had impleaded the prior and convent of Coldingham by brieve of the lord king in the court of the same prior of Coldingham'. The witness list is headed by the sheriff of Berwick, William de Lindsay; was he there to do right had the prior refused to do so?[29] A second, less explicit case may be the quitclaim by Michael of Auchencrow to the prior and convent of Coldingham of half a carucate in Old Cambus 'which he claimed by brieve of the lord king'.[30] It is not stated in which court the original claim was made, but the witnesses to the quitclaim are the suitors of the prior's court in the 1240s. Yet another case from the prior's court is the one in which Bertram, son of Henry of Ulvestoun, impleaded his cousin Waldeve Kokes for two oxgangs of land in Nether Ayton 'by letters of the lord king'. Again, we are not told to which court these letters were addressed, but the eventual settlement was reached 'in the full court of the lord prior of Coldingham at Ayton'. The name of the sheriff of Berwick is second in the list of witnesses to the settlement.[31]

The final case is another stage in the great Monachkenneran dispute discussed in earlier chapters. It will be recalled that Paisley abbey had recovered lands pertaining to its church of Kilpatrick and held of the earl of Lennox which had been wrongfully alienated by Dougal, brother to the earl and rector of the church. Dougal was allowed to retain his position as rector for life despite his misdeeds. He died in 1270, and in the following year his three grand-nieces were served as his co-heirs. Thereafter these women, together with their husbands, raised actions by royal letters in the earl's court against Paisley abbey, claiming rights in some of the lands attached to the church of Kilpatrick. The abbey bought off these claims for substantial sums. What was the nature of the claim against the abbey? As already noted, the lands were held of the earl of Lennox, so that a dispute about them naturally fell within the jurisdiction of his court. Grand-nieces could not have used the brieve of mortancestry, since they were outwith the degrees of relationship for that form of action, and there could be no question of any dissaisine. It seems very possible that the royal letters were in the nature of a brieve of right, therefore, but addressed to the court of the lord of the lands in issue.

The implication of this is that, at any rate until late in the reign of Alexander III, there was a brieve dealing with questions of right to land, distinct from novel dissaisine and mortancestry, and addressed to the lord rather than to the sheriff. Two further propositions will now be argued: one that the brieve addressed to the lord was rather similar to the classical English writ of right in providing that if the lord did not do right, the king's officer would; the other that its history stretches back to the twelfth century. A particularly important sentence at the end of the mature brieve of the styles instructs the court officers to 'act hereupon in such a way that we do not hear any further complaint for default of right'. It has already been made clear that in the twelfth century one important function of royal justice was to make good defaults of justice (*defectu iusticie*) elsewhere. In a particularly interesting charter of William I c. 1166, it is provided that claims against the men of Holyrood abbey should be begun by a request to the abbot to do full right (*plenum rectum*), if he fails to do so, then the sheriff and the justice will do it instead.[32] Again the context is certainly criminal, but the idea of the lord being given the opportunity to do full right before the king's officer takes over is redolent of the writ of right. The charter also repeats an earlier grant to Holyrood by David I, prohibiting the taking of poinds from its lands unless the abbot had failed to do right (*facere rectum et ius*).[33] Similarly, at around the same time, the king forbade the officers of the church of Wedale to detain the men of the abbot of Kelso if he offered to do reason and justice (*rationem et iusticiam*).[34] These documents may be contrasted with a prohibition issued by William I in favour of Coldingham priory, forbidding his justices, sheriffs, officers and good men from unjustly maintaining the priory's tenants against it in refusal to do 'what ought of reason (*de ratione*) to be done'.[35] Here again, we see the idea of the king's officers acting against a lord in favour of wronged tenants, although this is only to be done when it is just so to do.

The phrase 'full right' was certainly familiar in twelfth-century Scottish royal documents, albeit almost entirely in respect of the lands which were held in England. In a grant which was re-enacted by his son Earl Henry and by Malcolm IV, King David commanded all his men justly to maintain the monks of St Andrews at Northampton in his earldom of Huntingdon, providing that if any of his tenants presumed to wrong them, they should receive 'full right' (*plenariam rectitudinem* in David's grant, *plenum rectum* in the later documents).[36] The Holyrood charter with its reference to *plenum rectum* confirms, however, that it was used in the Scottish chapel for Scottish grants as well. Another document of King William prohibits the taking of poinds from the abbot of Kelso until the abbot or his officers had been required to do right (*rectitudinem*) and had failed to do so.[37] As in England, this certainly provided part of the background out of which the brieve of right grew. At this early stage, however, 'right' did not mean 'right to lands' so much as the correction of some wrong or default of justice: a failure by a lord to do justice in a complaint against his men (the Holyrood and Kelso documents); failure by tenants to do what they ought to do for their lords (the Northampton grants and, perhaps, the Coldingham one); failure to pay teind; and wrongdoing by royal officers.

The development of this general concept of doing right into the brieve of right for the recovery of land cannot be traced in surviving evidence. It seems likely, however, as Harding has argued, that it must have included such cases from the beginning.[38] Harding finds the origins of the concept of doing right in the ancient idea of the king's peace and protection of his men, and demonstrates that it included the right to the peaceful enjoyment of property and the prohibition of interference therewith, on pain of the king's forfeiture. Bound in with this might be commands to the king's officers to protect a man's property as though it were the king's own, and the right of property owners to be impleaded only before the king or his justices. In this context, unjust interference with property was clearly a wrong and a default of justice which might be remedied by commands to do right, supported by the jurisdiction of the king and his officers.

The narrowing in scope of the brieve of right to such situations alone must have occurred as other brieves developed to enforce the king's protection in specific areas. It seems clear, as argued in an earlier chapter, that the pleadable brieves *de compulsione*, which were for the enforcement of debt and other obligations, were early examples of brieves fashioned to deal with specific types of breach of protection, since they too conclude with a sentence commanding the sheriff to act so that the king does not hear any just complaint of his default.[39] The arrival of novel dissasine and mortancestry on the scene in the thirteenth century would have helped complete the picture of the brieve of right as a remedy specifically for the recovery of land in particular circumstances. It may not be too far-fetched to see the formation of the two Scottish brieves which were hypothesised earlier for the thirteenth century as also creations of this period, being part of a process of borrowing of the main English writs as they stood after Magna Carta in 1215. The pre-existing brieve was general in scope and available to enforce all kinds of right, but there was a general systematisation in the first half of the thirteenth century which looked to England for precise models and included not only novel dissasine and mortancestry but also brieves of right. There were perhaps different styles depending on whether or not the claim was to hold of the king, but at some later date, probably still in the thirteenth century, they were consolidated into a single brieve heard before the sheriff, thereby short-circuiting the process whereby claims begun in lords' courts found their way into the king's.

EARLY PROCEDURE

The early origins of the brieve of right explain a good deal of what we know about the brieve in the later period. Both *Regiam* and *Quoniam* stress the minutiae of pleading and procedure on the brieve of right. The law appears to have been in no hurry to cause the defender to compear; he might be cited to appear up to four times before his absence would cost him possession, and he could tender three lawful essonzies for each non-appearance. When he does appear, he may claim a view of the debateable lands, which will then be held fifteen days later, subject to further lawful essonzies for non-appearance. *Regiam* and *Quoniam* also give a form for the statement of claim by the pursuer with which proceedings open, each providing that the claim is based on heritable right and alleging unjust deforcement by the defender; only in *Regiam*, however, does the pursuer claim an assize on the matter. Finally, each states that the defender may deny the wrong, '*de verbo in verbum*' in *Quoniam*'s phrase, before going out of court thereafter to seek advice on his defence.[40] This is, of course, the famous 'interpolation' from the 1318 legislation which shows us that *Regiam* must be of date later than that year.[41]

The last point apart, this is the procedural world of *Glanvill* and twelfth-century England, and one which contrasts sharply with novel dissasine and mortancestry. The books seem to be largely substantiated by the practice of the courts, although no evidence of either the view or the statement of claim has been found. The principal feature is the lengthy nature of proceedings. Thus for example, in 1317, the defender in a case begun by brieve of right in Aberdeen burgh court persistently failed to compear, exploiting to the full her right to give essonzies for non-appearance. At the point where the record breaks off, the court had given her fourteen days, not to compear, but to arrange a settlement with the pursuers; it was only if this failed that the brieve would be put to an assize of twelve.[42] Even after the defender had finally been brought into court, much time might elapse before a final decision was given. A case in the Aberdeen sheriff court which began in February 1457 was only concluded, after four separate court days, in April.[43] In another case, we have evidence to show that an action by Robert Spens against James Nory, begun before February 1462, was still going in 1471, although this was probably due to a number of appeals to council and parliament rather than to the process in the sheriff court on the brieve of right itself.[44] Nonetheless, the evidence of the records thus supports the conclusion to be drawn from *Regiam* and *Quoniam*, that Scots law shared the English reluctance to come to a final conclusion on the question of right. There is a sharp contrast with procedure on novel dissasine and mortancestry, where the emphasis was, at least initially, on speedy decision-making. If the mature brieve of right was a late borrowing from English law and a product of rationalisation of earlier, more cumbersome English forms, it might have been expected that procedure would also be dealt with more critically, and something more comparable to the streamlined procedures of the possessory brieves adopted. The picture we have suggests instead that there had been borrowing from England much earlier which included the package of dilatory procedure; when administrative rationalisation of the Scottish brieves into a single form took place, the procedure attached to them was too well entrenched to suffer alteration and so survived into later medieval law as a fossil from another age.

A not dissimilar story may underlie the use of trial by combat on the brieve. A striking contrast between *Glanvill's* treatment of the writs of right and the discussion of the brieve of right in *Regiam* is that, according to the latter, the issue contained in a brieve of right is always put to an assize. There is nothing to suggest that *Glanvill's* account of trial by combat on the writ of right was regarded as relevant by the compiler of *Regiam*. Nothing in the brieve itself compels the use of an assize, however, by contrast with novel dissasine and mortancestry. According to *Regiam*, the pursuer's statement of claim would ask for an assize if the defender denied his claim and, if the defender had no relevant exception to plead, the question would then be put to 'twelve lawful men of the neighbour-hood or of the court'.[45] A century ago, however, George Neilson argued that 'the proof for the judicial duel in a plea of land in Scotland is very indefinite, yet there is such a body of floating provisions on the subject that in spite of the poverty of testimony it is reasonable to believe that it had at least some short existence there'.[46] Neilson's evidence lay in some chapters from the legal manuscripts printed amongst the '*Fragmenta Collecta*' in the first volume of the *Acts of the Parliaments of Scotland*.[47] These chapters are in fact from the compilations known as the *Leges Portuum* and the *Liber de Judicibus*, although Neilson did not identify these texts as such.[48] The first relevant chapter opens thus:[49]

> Whomsoever has lost his land by default, not by judgment, may seek it by brieve of right against the holder, unless his default was after he had placed himself upon the assize or had waged duel. In either of these cases the brieve would not avail him, as he and his heirs have then lost their right for ever.

It then proceeds with substantially *Glanvill's* account of combat on the writ of right, but it contains one long interpolated section which, in Neilson's summary, 'describes the appearance of the champions in the field, their oaths, and the procedure at the battle'.[50] Neilson was unable to identify a source for this passage, and conjectured that 'it is difficult to account for this seemingly independent adaptation on any other footing than that of authenticity'.

In fact, the interpolation is in substance similar to the accounts of battle found in the thirteenth-century English works, *Brevia Placitata* and *Novae Narrationes* (both written in Anglo-French).[51] However, this need not undermine the argument that combat was used on the early brieve of right. Neilson himself also drew attention to a reference of 1208 x 1213 to '*Waldevo pugile*' (Waldev the champion), pointing out that prior to 1230 champions were not allowed in duels of felony, so that 'the existence of such an occupation as his in Scotland twenty years before . . . is, in view of English analogies and the floating fragments of Scots law, confirmation strong for the opinion that the judicial duel was still practised in Scotland in pleas of land in the opening decades of the 13th century'.[52] Another interesting champion noted but not discussed in any depth by Neilson is John, the swineherd of Coldingham, who in the mid-thirteenth century was granted lands in Reston as a reward for a duel which he had successfully undertaken for Roger, son of Adam of Reston.[53] It may be that this combat had been fought in the prior's court on a plea of land, possibly following a brieve of right addressed to the prior.

Recently, David Sellar has offered an example of a plea over land which was resolved by combat in the fourteenth century, and suggested that it may have been initiated by brieve of right.[54] The case was another to involve James Douglas of Dalkeith and arose out of his various claims by virtue of rights of inheritance in the lands of his cousin Mary Douglas, who had died in childbirth. Mary's husband, Thomas Erskine, claimed courtesy in the lands, and seems to have been in possession after her death by virtue of his marriage. Douglas had never had sasine, so had no claim by novel dissasine, while Mary was not related to him within any of the degrees relevant to the brieve of mortancestry; accordingly, if Douglas initiated his action by brieve (and of this we have no evidence), then it must have been by brieve of right. Before Erskine could claim courtesy, a child had to be born of his marriage to Mary and heard to cry, even if it subsequently died. With a child which died at birth, perhaps through miscarriage, it would be difficult if not impossible to prove the preconditions of courtesy, and this difficulty of proof may explain why combat was used in this case, since it was the method of proof when none other was available or usable.[55] No doubt, however, the infection of law by chivalry, as Neilson would have put it,[56] is also part of this particular story.

The essential point is that there are grounds for believing that combat was available under the brieve of right, albeit that by the end of the thirteenth century it must have been extremely rare (if indeed it was ever common in such cases). Again, in all probability this pushes the history of the brieve back into the twelfth century. If we ask why the compiler of *Regiam* chose to edit *Glanvill*'s discussion of combat out of his work, two concurrent explanations suggest themselves: one the extreme rarity of combats on the brieve of right, perhaps amounting to desuetude in his day, and the other the high probability that he was a churchman and canon lawyer who would have found the combat a sacrilegious temptation of God which deserved to be extirpated.

Some support for these arguments about the early brieve of right may also be found by looking at the position in burgh courts. As noted in previous chapters, neither novel dissasine nor mortancestry was used there; but the brieve of right was.[57] An important factor leading to the introduction of the brieves of novel dissasine and mortancestry may have been this ability of the defender in brieve of right cases to claim trial by combat; the new actions had always to be determined by an assize, and their appearance would have meant that in what were perhaps the commonest type of complaints about the possession and ownership of land a rational mode of trial could be insisted upon. However, already in the twelfth century, the burgess seems to have been considered as normally immune from combat, if we may generalise from William Fs grant of the privilege to the burgesses of Inverness in 1196 or 1197;[58] certainly he was regarded as exempt from combat under the *Leges Burgorum*.[59] Therefore there would have been no need to narrow the scope of the brieve of right in the burgh court with special actions in which only the assize could be used. Accordingly, the brieve of right could be left as the sole remedy for the recovery of land in the burgh. After all, its terms, alleging that the pursuer was being deforced by an intruder of lands which he claimed by a heritable title, were perfectly capable of application to the situation covered by the brieve of mortancestry, which simply restricted the class of ancestors from whose possession a title might be derived. Similarly, the brieve of right could be used to deal with complaints of ejection such as would otherwise have been the subject of a novel dissasine.

THE LATER MEDIEVAL PERIOD

The process of change and development which led to the mature brieve of right seems to have been essentially complete by the reign of Robert I. The 1318 legislation makes only minor adjustments to procedure on the brieve, which have already been touched upon.[60] In 1456, departures from the procedural rules for brieves of right led to nullification of the entire proceedings in a particular case. Reference was made to the books of the law, presumably texts such as *Regiam* and *Quoniam*, for authoritative guidance on the law, suggesting little change from the position at the beginning of the previous century.[61] In 1505, the sheriff-depute of Lanark was sued for wrongous and inordinate proceeding upon a brieve of right, having failed to allow a debate upon an exception proposed by the defenders, and put the brieve to the determination of an assize.[62] This looks very much like a point drawn from the *Regiam* passage, mentioned above, about putting the case to the assize if the defender had no relevant exception to make. The burgh court of Haddington in 1425 referred a brieve of right to an assize of seventeen men, who took 'the grete ath at thai suld without fraude or favor of ony part determane lely qwilk of the said parties has ful rycht in the sayde tenements', the language of the record here presumably echoing the *'plenum rectum'* of the brieve.[63]

Another point upon which practice remained constant in the fourteenth and fifteenth centuries was that of jurisdiction. The brieve of right appears to have been competent only in the sheriff and burgh courts, again showing the accuracy of the formularies and treatises. As already noted, the earliest case on a brieve of right for which record survives was in Berwick burgh court about 1290, when Master Roger Bartholomew recovered his sasine of certain lands by an assize;[64] and the 1317 Aberdeen burgh court case has been touched upon a number of times in the previous discussion.[65] In the same Aberdeen court in 1405, a pursuer named John led a brieve of right which instructed the baillies to cause him to have full right of a tenement in the burgh.[66] Actions by brieve of right in the Haddington burgh court are recorded in 1425 and again in 1426,[67] and several actions begun by brieve of right are found in the Aberdeen burgh records of the 1430s and 1440s,[68] suggesting that there would be more evidence for the use of brieves of right in burgh courts if their records had survived in greater quantity than is in fact the case.

The first record of a brieve of right in the sheriff court is found as late as 1330, although it can only be due to chance that there is nothing earlier.[68a] In 1456 Reginald Cheyne sued Henry Cheyne for the lands of Esslemont and Meikle Arnage before the sheriff depute of Aberdeenshire.[69] In 1457, the same sheriff court was confronted with another brieve of right,[70] while 'the process of the breif of richt. . . tuiching the landis of Kittidy' between Robert Spens and James Nory and his son, which was going on from before 1462 until after 1471, took place in the sheriff court of Fife.[71] That this remained the jurisdictional position at the beginning of the sixteenth century is confirmed by the 1504 statute on falsing the doom, which mentions that 'the breve of rycht' was pursued before 'the schireff, Stewart or balze'.[72] The 'balze' was presumably the baillie of the burgh court, to whom the brieve of right in burgh was addressed; 'stewarts' were royal officers with a jurisdiction equivalent to that of the sheriff in regalities which had been forfeited to the crown, such as Kirkcudbright, Annandale, Strathearn and Menteith.

Brief notice may be taken here again of the brieve which was addressed to Robert lord Erskine in 1445, commanding him to render *complementum iuris* to the widow Ada Crab in respect of lands which she claimed to hold in chief of him, and which Alexander Chalmer was withholding from her.[73] The structure of this brieve is very much along the lines of the classical English writ of right, but it is not in any sense like the standard Scottish brieve of right. In particular, it makes no reference to *plenum rectum*, and for this reason it cannot be a late example of a brieve of right addressed to a feudal lord. The best explanation of the brieve seems to be connected to the fact that it sprang from a hearing before the auditors of causes and complaints. In this tribunal, it was sought to exercise the king's special duty to ensure speedy justice for the poor and needy, in particular widows, such as Ada Crab.[74] It may be that Ada's remedy in ordinary circumstances would indeed have been the brieve of right, but it involved a lengthy procedure. Rather than subject the possibly elderly Ada to these uncertainties, perhaps the auditors sought to deal with the matter as speedily as possible through the superior of the lands in question.

The accumulation of information about jurisdiction also enables us to suggest that certain cases involving brieves may well have been ones touching 'full right' rather than novel dissaine or mortancestry. The mid-thirteenth-century case in the sheriff court at Traquair whereby Mariota claimed an apparently heritable right to the lands of Stobo *per litteras regias* against the bishop of Glasgow is the earliest example of this, but, given the possibility already discussed that mortancestry may also have been competent to the sheriff at this time, the fact that the case was heard in his court is inconclusive.[75] A case before the sheriff of Inverness in 1454 is more likely to have been begun by brieve of right. The pursuer established his rights to certain lands against a defender whom he 'lachfullie followyt be brevis of law of our soveran lordis the kingis chapell.[76] At this date, the only pleadable brieve by which land could have been recovered before the sheriff was the brieve of right, so it seems that this must have been such a case. Returning to the thirteenth century, there are a couple of other cases before the burgh court of Perth which may have been begun by brieve of right, since both involved settlements of claims for the recovery of land. In the first, Henry the clerk, son of Laurence son of Huyth of Perth, claimed lands in the town held of the bishop of Dunkeld from the monks of Balmerino, impleading them by brieve of the lord king; the result was a quitclaim by Henry.[77] The other case, raised by Walter the baker and his wife against the abbot and convent of Inchaffray 'by letters of our lord king', resulted in an amicable composition in which the pursuers gave up 'all right (*jus*) and claim' to lands apparently in the burgh.[78] In both cases, the pursuer's claim seems to have been based on hereditary right, and the brieves were almost certainly *de recto in burgo*.

Another interesting case is recorded in a document of 1354 which narrates the history of the lands of Esperston in Midlothian. Probably in the reign of Robert I, a man named William Cook used '*litteras regis in forma capelle*' to recover the lands, from which his mother had been forcibly expelled perhaps thirty years previously. The case was heard before the sheriff of Edinburgh with a jury, and it was found that William was the son and nearest heir of his mother and that she had been vest and saised of Esperston for many years before her expulsion. The document describes the brieve as being *super iure* rather than *de recto*, and makes no mention of any defender (although the estates may have been in the possession of the knights of the Hospital, successors in title to the Templars who had ejected William's mother).[79] It is therefore possible that the brieve was merely one of inquest; but if the Hospitallers were in possession, then it is certain that William's remedy would have been a brieve of right. He himself had not been dissaised, so a brieve of novel dissasine was of no use. The basis of his claim was heritable right. The ancestor from whom he derived that right was within the degrees of relationship which permitted action upon the brieve of mortancestry, but she unfortunately had not been in possession at the date of her death. Accordingly, only the brieve of right would have enabled William to regain the lands. The case neatly illustrates the way in which, outside the burghs at least, the choice of remedy was dictated by the facts and circumstances of one's claim, and how the scope of each brieve could be determined by the others available.

Most of the other cases of which the details can be worked out concerned parties who were closely related. Thus the lands claimed by brieve of right in Aberdeen burgh court in 1317 had belonged to a certain Brice Craigie. The defender was his daughter Emma, described as 'an orphan and girl under age' (i.e. not yet having attained her majority); the pursuers were Emma's sister Marjorie and her husband John, son of Laurence.[80] The story may be explained by the provision in the *Leges Burgorum* (c. 24) that where a burgess had two or more wives, lands obtained during his first marriage passed on his death to its children, while the acquisitions made during his second marriage went to its children.[81] The defender to the brieve of right raised by James Skene in 1457 was the niece of his cousin William Keith, the first earl marischal. James and Robert Nory, the defenders to the brieve of right raised by Robert Spens in Fife sheriff court before 1461, were respectively the husband and son of Spens's niece Christian.[82] Almost certainly, the Reginald and Henry Cheyne who were respectively pursuer and defender under a brieve of right in 1456 were brothers.[83] The lands in dispute, Esslemont and Meikle Arnage, both near Ellon, Aberdeenshire, had been granted to Henry by his father John Cheyne, lord of Straloch, in April 1441. In a document recording the grant, John stated that 'giff it hapenis of case me or any of myn ayris to make any clame or move any questioun or again calling of this infeftment, I oblyse me and myn ayris' to pay five hundred pounds to Henry.[84] From this, it seems that Henry was not his heir. In 1450, Henry entered a suitor for the lands at Aberdeen sheriff court despite a protest 'for the son and heir of Reginald Cheyne'.[85] A Reginald Cheyne is designed of Straloch in July 1475, and it was probably his son and heir, John Cheyne of Straloch, who sued the still-surviving Henry before council in 1493 in another dispute about Meikle Arnage.[86] These fragments suggest that the Reginald who sued in 1456 was the heir of Straloch, being most probably Henry's elder brother.

The closeness of these relationships shows that under a brieve of right parties were not necessarily examining competing titles from their origins at some remote date in the past; indeed, as we shall see, the pursuers in the cases mentioned in the previous paragraph probably went no further back than the titles of their fathers. Technical difficulties stood in the way of using mortancestry, which otherwise might seem the more appropriate form of action. This is obvious in the case of the Craigie sisters, where the question seems to have been which of them was entitled to inherit from father Brice. The brieve of right may have been used here because mortancestry was not available in burgh. In 1456, the origin of the title in dispute between Reginald and Henry Cheyne was the grant of Henry's father in 1441. The grant could only have been challenged by brieve of right: Reginald could not have used mortancestry because his ancestor had not died vest and saised of the lands in question. The case of *Spens v Nory* is less clear, but it seems that the pursuer, Robert Spens, was a younger son whose eldest brother had predeceased, and who claimed the lands in issue, Kittedie in Fife, under a tailzie in favour of heirs-male. His brother had left two daughters who, as heirs-general, also laid claim to Kittedie with the support of their husbands.[87] Spens's action by brieve of right was part of this contest. It seems to follow that he had not had possession of the lands previously, since then his action would have been one of novel dissasine; nor could he use mortancestry since, as a younger son, he was not the nearest lawful heir of line. Finally, as Spens derived his claim from a tailzie in favour of heirs-male, then his use of the brieve of right rather than mortancestry would also have been made necessary by the act of 1430 laying down that the latter action protected only heirs of line, and not those whose claim depended entirely upon such tailzies.[88]

Even where, as in the case of *Skene v Keith*, the parties were not so closely related, the pursuer went no further back than his father to establish his hereditary right. Sometime before the battle of Harlaw in 1411, it would seem that Adam Skene borrowed money from his father-in-law, William Keith the marischal, on the security of his lands of Easter Skene. Adam was killed at Harlaw and was succeeded by his son James, who was to be the pursuer of 1457. Easter Skene had still not been redeemed by the Skenes in 1446, by which time the deeds recording the impignoration had been lost. Accordingly, it was necessary for the Skenes to obtain the depositions of elderly witnesses who could recall the transaction and the subsequent acknowledgements of its nature by the Keiths. Ten years later, the Skene claim had still not been satisfied, for yet another witness's deposition had to be obtained. This was presumably a prelude to James Skene's action by brieve of right in the early months of 1457. The defender then, Janet Keith, had come to the lands by virtue of a grant from her uncle William, who himself would have inherited them through his father and grandfather (to the latter of whom the lands had been originally granted by Adam Skene). Again, therefore, the pursuer's claim was derived from his father, but because the father had not died vest and saised of the lands in question it was necessary to sue by brieve of right rather than by mortancestry.[89]

THE PROPRIETARY REMEDY

What, then, was the nature of the 'right' claimed by a pursuer under the brieve? In 1457, James Skene was held to have 'greater right' (*maius ius*) to the lands of Easter Skene than Janet Keith. The phrase recalls English ideas that ownership of land was a mystery lying beyond human cognition, and that litigation could only determine which of the parties had the better right. Yet, as discussed in an earlier chapter, in England an action in the right was regarded as a final determination of the issue, excluding any claim made by a third party unless it had come in before judgment was given. There is no evidence to suggest that the Scottish position was otherwise. Under the brieve, the pursuer claimed 'full right', and there can be little doubt that this meant as full a right of ownership as was possible in a tenurial structure of land law.

Reference has already been made elsewhere in this book to the *Regiam* passage which states that as mortancestry touches fee and freehold it exceeds novel dissasine, which touches only freehold. It goes on to say that the brieve of right exceeds both these forms of action, 'because it touches fee and freehold and just right', and that 'this is why one can recover lost land (*terram amissam*) by brieve of right and not by brieve of mortancestry or of novel dissasine'.[90] The direct inspiration of thirteenth-century English theories about the relationship of the real actions lies behind this passage. The writ of right represented the pinnacle of the various remedies open to a dispossessed landholder. He who was put out by another had novel disseisin; he who was prevented from taking up an inheritance from certain close relatives had *mort d'ancestor*. However, the intruder ejected by virtue of one of these writs was not thereby excluded forever from the lands, for the actions were merely possessory in nature. He could reopen the question by a writ of right, a proprietary as opposed to a possessory action which alone could settle the question of ownership permanently. Thus one could distinguish various types of interest in land, each protected by a different form of action. There was the status of possessor, guarded by novel disseisin; the entitlement to inherit from one's close relatives in possession, enforced by *mort d'ancestor*, and ultimately ownership, protected by the writ which went 'highest in the right'.[91] It is this pyramidic structure into which *Regiam* strives to fit the Scottish real actions.

The relationship of this juristic construct, the division of actions into categories of possessory and proprietary, to real life and the practice of lawyers has been challenged by modern English legal historians.[92] Already in this book, it has been argued that the brieves of novel dissasine and mortancestry cannot be characterised as possessory in any simple or straightforward way, certainly not in particular to contrast them with proprietary actions. It seems unlikely, even if it was theoretically possible, that a party losing an action begun by one or other of them could have reversed the result by raising a new action with a brieve of right. The main distinction between novel dissasine and mortancestry in practice seems indeed, as *Regiam* itself suggests, to have been the kind of interest in land which was the minimum that a pursuer had to show: in the case of novel dissasine, sasine of a freehold; in mortancestry, a right to inherit from one of a narrowly-defined group of relatives. They were possessory only in the sense that a former lawful possession, either of the pursuer or of his ancestor, had to be shown for an action to be successful. The brieve of right seems to have been used in cases where for some reason these two actions were not available, rather than because the parties were anxious for a final determination of where ownership lay; it was not a more proprietary action than mortancestry, and it could be used to recover what one had formerly held so long as that holding had been based on a heritable rather than a mere freehold title.

Chapter 19 of the 1318 legislation treats the brieves of novel dissasine, mortancestor and right together in laying down that the defender was to be afforded a full statement of the case against him;[93] surely this is because practical men of the time looked at them together as means of vindicating claims to land from which a prospective pursuer made his choice according to the facts from which his grievance sprang. If in 1433 the brieve of dissasine could reach back into history to a time seventy years previously,[94] then it explored the origins of a current title further back than was done in any of the cases on the brieve of right of which we know. Even before 1318 and the reforms that year relating to the brieve of novel dissasine, it must have seemed very similar to the brieve of right in its operation, for prior to that time, as we have seen, even if the current tenant had not been the original dissaisor, he might still be the sole defender named in the brieve.[95] In that state of affairs, all that can have differentiated actions of novel dissasine and right was that the former had to be brought during the lifetime of the original dissaisor, and some procedural rules.

Donald Sutherland has used the English sources for the fourteenth and fifteenth centuries to show how in that period the assize of novel disseisin became the principal vehicle by which title might be tried, before ultimately it was superseded by trespassory actions. By contrast, the assize of *mort d'ancestor* fell into obsolescence, along with the writs of right and entry. A plaintiff who had an unrealised right to enter land could bring novel disseisin once he had made an attempt – in practice often little more than a fiction – to enter, and had then been ejected by the holder.[96] The picture is very different in Scotland, where the brieve of novel dissasine coexisted not only with the brieve of mortancestry but also with the brieve of right, and may have been the first of these three brieves to fall out of use (since the last direct evidence of it is dateable to the 1450s while the others are still found in the early sixteenth century). Thus, a Scot who had a right to enter land without ever having had sasine was not forced into fictitious dissasines as his English counterpart was for lack of another remedy. He could use mortancestry if his right of entry was derived from a deceased relative within the relevant degrees who had died with heritable sasine, or the brieve of right if his claim was from a more remote ancestor. Alternatively, if the ancestor had been ejected before his death, or had surrendered the lands unjustly, so that it was not possible to say that he had died vest and saised, then again he would have resort to the brieve of right. It is probably safe to say that novel dissasine in Scotland remained a remedy for one who had had sasine properly speaking, that is, had been infeft on an ex facie valid title, and had been put out by someone still alive. If the dissasine had been committed by one who had since died, then presumably the ejected person would usually turn to the brieve of right.

THE BRIEVE OF RIGHT AND WRITS OF ENTRY

The scope of the later brieve of right can therefore be seen as largely determined by that of the brieves of novel dissasine and mortancestry. It was the general as opposed to the specific action for the recovery of lands, used where other forms of action would for some reason be inappropriate. There is no sign of any equivalent of writs of entry in Scottish practice, but we can see the brieve of right being used in situations where in England such a writ would have provided the remedy. The most striking example is James Skene's action against Janet Keith to recover lands which his father had granted away to her great-grandfather in security of a debt.[97] According to *Bracton*, this would have been a case for the *breve si heres petat quod antecessor dimisit ad terminum* in England; the case would however most likely have been decided by a recognition as to whether the tenant Janet held the lands in fee or gage.[98] Similarly, Reginald Cheyne raised a brieve of right to complain of his ancestor's grant to another;[99] as Maitland pointed out, most of the developed writs of entry were about 'alienations made by someone who, though he was occupying and rightfully occupying had no power to alienate'.[100] Here, he was echoing *Bracton*'s remark that the writs lay 'against all who have their entry through those who transfer without having a free tenement or the right to transfer'.[101] In Scotland, it is submitted, the brieve of right covered the whole field of the writs of entry to permit attacks on flaws in the titles of current tenants. It would certainly have been the remedy to meet a case of entry *sur disseisin* where the dissaisor or dissaisee had died before recovery could take place by the brieve of novel dissasine.[102]

This view of the brieve of right as comprehending what in England would have been matter for the writs of entry seems to gain some support from the provisions of the Statute of Wales enacted in 1284.[103] This imported the current English writ system into conquered Wales but, as already noted, with only a single writ, the *breve commune*, in place of the writ of right and, moreover, no writs of entry. It seems that it was the intention of the legislators that the *breve commune* should stand alone in their place.[104] The reason for the development of the writs of entry in England is controversial, as discussed in the first chapter.[105] The elements of the controversy may throw some light on their non-appearance in the Statute of Wales and in Scotland. Milsom has argued that writs of entry grew out of writs of right and writs *precipe*, to enable lords to challenge the entries of those whom they would otherwise be compelled to warrant as their tenants. Such writs became *de cursu* and proliferated, especially after 1215 and clause 34 of Magna Carta, prohibiting the use of *precipe* writs to deprive lords of their jurisdiction. The entry clause in *the precipe* indicated that the writ would not have this effect but would rather enable a lord to get rid of a tenant with no valid title to hold of him.[106] Palmer has at least shown that this interpretation cannot be accepted as it stands, especially in the light of the number of writs of entry which grew out of problems with the petty assizes well before Magna Carta.[107] *Bracton*'s discussion of the writs of entry shows nevertheless how closely some thirteenth-century English lawyers linked them with writs of right. He explains how the party suing by a writ of entry might be forced to shift to the procedure of a writ of right, 'because of a very distant entry which cannot be proved by a witness's own sight and hearing but that of another, as the sight and hearing of a father who instructed his son, in which case, because of necessity and the lack of other proof, the tenant must put himself on the grand assize or defend by the duel'.[108] Equally, a writ of right might become a writ of entry:[109]

> If, though, the writ of right begins to be a writ of entry by the *narratio* and the demandant puts forward his *intentio*, supports it and is prepared to prove it by the country, it is still in the election of the tenant whether he wishes to put himself on a jury with respect to such entry or not, since he has three remedies, namely, defending himself by the duel, or putting himself on the grand assize on the right, or on a jury as to the entry. Since it is in the tenant's discretion to elect whichever of these he wishes, the writ of right will not become a writ of entry until the tenant elects to defend himself by a jury against the entry.

The interchangeability of writs of right and entry in thirteenth-century England, depending on the course of pleading and procedure, is apparent from these passages of *Bracton*. Clearly, many technicalities of the law and procedure of the forms of action underlie the relationship of the remedies, technicalities which so far as can be told did not arise in Scotland. Nor is it possible to detect whether claims in the early brieve of right cases mentioned earlier in this chapter were either upward or downward looking in nature. All but one of those cases heard before lords' courts in the thirteenth century were upward claims by tenants to hold of lords; the nature of the remaining example is an inscrutable mystery.[110] Only one other case of a brieve of right is known before 1300, and this was heard in the burgh court, where feudal elements are unlikely to have been present.[111] Further, we have seen that the rule requiring brieves to make freeholders answer for their lands did not inhibit a lord's right to make his tenant 'show his holding', and it would seem from at least one case that he could use this action to reduce the title shown.[112] Thus one of Milsom's conditions for the development of writs of entry was not present in Scotland. Nor did Magna Carta apply in Scotland to make necessary the addition to brieves of right of explanatory clauses about jurisdiction. So superiors who wished to challenge the titles of their vassals and to proceed by way of brieve of right would not have been confronted with all the technical difficulties which may have led to some of the writs of entry in England.

Whatever the truth about the origins of the writs of entry, it seems clear that in Scotland their work could have been and probably always was done by the brieve of right. The brieve was in other words the remedy where the complaint was of a wrongful or exhausted alienation to the defender or his predecessor in title. We have also seen its importance in the recovery of burgage lands and tailzied holdings in circumstances where prima facie mortancestry or perhaps novel dissasine might have seemed more appropriate.[113] Unfortunately, it is not possible to say much about its significance in the feudal structure within which the operation of novel dissasine and mortancestry has been examined, save that probably an early form was addressed to lords' courts. Over the period of the later Middle Ages, however, there can be no doubt of its importance alongside the brieves of novel dissasine and mortancestry as a remedy to regain lands from intruders.

DECLINE OF THE BRIEVE OF RIGHT

The brieve of right remained a familiar form of action for the recovery of lands into the sixteenth century – so familiar, as David Sellar has pointed out, that it could be made the subject of allusion in contemporary poetry.[114] William Dunbar's 'Fasternis Evin in Hell', written c. 1507, contains the following lines:[115]

> Na menstrallis playit to thame but dowt,
> For glemen thair wer haldin owt
> Be day and eik by nicht –
> Except a menstrall that slew a man;
> Swa till his heretage he wan
> And entirt be breif of richt.

That the reference to the brieve of right in the 1504 act on falsing the doom[116] touched current practice is confirmed by the mention made in the acts of council for February 1503 of the brieve of right brought against the late William Baillie of Lamington by his namesake of Bagby to recover the lands of Hoprig and Panestone, as well as by the case of 1505 before the sheriff-depute of Lanark discussed earlier.[117] There is a style for the brieve of right in the St Andrews formulary identical to those in the fourteenth-century registers of brieves, and examples of its use within the city and regality of St Andrews may also be found in occasional references in the acts of council.[118] The early sixteenth-century Cambridge 'register' also contains styles for brieves of right *infra* and *extra burgo*.[119] Although there are no cases involving brieves of right in the earliest surviving sheriff court books, those for Fife from 1515 to 1522, this need not mean that the brieve had suddenly gone out of use. As late as 1541, land was being recovered by royal brieves before the sheriff of Renfrew.[120] Although the brieves are not identified, it is possible that they were *de recto*. Like mortancestry, however, the brieve of right clearly ceased to be of practical importance during the first half of the sixteenth century. The nonappearance of a brieve of right in the *Formulary E* 'register' may be significant. When the Lords of Council and Session asserted an exclusive jurisdiction in cases touching heritage in *Wemyss v Forbes* in 1543, it seems that they rejected an argument that such cases ought to be determined by brieve of right, and declared that 'the breif of rycht is nor hes nocht yit bene mony yeiris usit in this realme'.[121] By 1559, according to the *Discours Particulier d'Escosse*, the sheriff had ceased to have jurisdiction in matters of fee and heritage, and the brieve of right was so ill-remembered at the end of the sixteenth century that Sir John Skene thought that it pertained to the justiciar's court.[122] The pleadable brieves had disappeared, and Scots lawyers would soon forget that their law had once had its own forms of action.

NOTES

1. E. L. G. Stones and G. G. Simpson, *Edward I*, ii, pp. 342–3.
2. For comment on Biggar's claim, see G. W. S. Barrow, *Bruce*, pp. 43–4; K. J. Stringer, *Earl David*, pp. 84, 292 note 26.
3. J. Stevenson, *Documents*, i, pp. 384–6; G. W. S. Barrow, *Bruce*, pp. 51–2.
4. A. A. M. Duncan, *Kingdom*, p. 605.
5. *Reg Brieves*, pp. 39–40 (nos 18–19), 61 (no 91).
6. *Abdn Ct Bk*, pp. 7–8; *RRS*, v, no 121.
7. For this style, see *Glanvill*, XII, 3.
8. *RM (APS)*, I, 9; *RM (Cooper)*, I, 10.
9. Note that in Normandy there was no writ of right addressed to the lord's court, but only a writ *rectum faciendi in curia ducis*, which ordered the lord to see right done in the court of the Duke of Normandy (R. C. van Caenegem, *Birth*, p. 59); but it seems unlikely that this had any influence in Scotland.
10. *Glanvill*, I, 5.
11. *Glanvill*, I, 6.

12. On the background to and effect of Magna Carta, clause 34, see N. D. Hurnard, 'Magna Carta, clause 34', in *Studies in Medieval History presented to F. M. Powicke*, ed. R. W. Hunt, W. A. Pantin and R. W. Southern (Oxford, 1948), p. 157; M. T. Clanchy, 'Magna Carta, clause thirty-four', *EHR*, lxxix (1964), p. 542; S. F. C. Milsom, *LFEF*, pp. 68–71; J. C. Holt, *Magna Carta*, pp. 140–4, 173–8.
13. For this style, see *ERW*, p. 18.
14. F. W. Maitland, *The Forms of Action at Common Law* ed. A. H. Chaytor and W. J. Whittaker (Cambridge, 1936) p. 19. See also his 'History of the Register of Original Writs', *Harvard Law Review*, iii (1889–90), p. 110 note 1.
15. *Bracton*, f. 328b (iv, p. 49).
16. For *Judiciorum Essoniorum*, see *Four Thirteenth-Century Law Tracts*, ed. G. E. Woodbine (New Haven, 1910), pp. 116 and 132–3. For its date, see an unpublished paper delivered by P. A. Brand at the Tenth British Legal History Conference, Oxford, July 1991.
17. J. C. Holt, *Magna Carta*, pp. 142–3. The royal protections could still refer to *Glanvill's* writ of right, it seems to me. I am grateful to Professor Holt for discussing this point with me in correspondence, although I have not persuaded him.
18. *ERW*, pp. 1–2, 18, 33, 108, 113. For an argument that the earliest of the registers is dateable to 1210, not 1227, see P. A. Brand, 'Ireland and the literature of the early common law', *Irish Jurist*, xvi (1981), p. 95
19. *Brevia Placitata*, ed. G. J. Turner (Selden Society, vol. 66), pp. 11, 53, 86, 163; *Novae Narrationes*, p. 41 (B 38 A); *Britton*, ed. F. M. Nichols, 2 vols (Oxford, 1865), ii, pp. 326–44.
20. Cambridge University Library MS Dd.7.14, ff. 403b–404a; CP 40/19, m 20. I owe these references to the kindness of Dr P. A. Brand.
21. The earliest Year Book reference I have noted is *20 & 21 Edward I 1292–1293* (Rolls Series, 1866), pp. 378–9. For others, see, e.g. *6 Edward II 1313* (Selden Society, vol. 43), pp. 6–9; *8 Edward II 1314–15* (Selden Society, vol. 41), pp. 172–4; *10 Edward II 1316–17* (Selden Society, vol. 54), pp. 104–5; *12 Edward II 1318* (Selden Society, vol. 65), pp. 103–6 and 115–16. See also *The Eyre of Northamptonshire 1329–1330*, ed. D. W. Sutherland, 2 vols (Selden Society, vols 97, 98), ii, p. 523.
22. *ERW*, p. 36 (no 8). See also ibid., p. 113 (no 23).
23. M. T. Clanchy, 'Magna Carta clause thirty-four', pp. 543–4.
24. *Statutes of the Realm*, i, p. 60 (12 Edw I, c. 6).
25. L. B. Smith, 'The Statute of Wales 1284', *Welsh History Review*, x (1980–1) pp. 141–4.
26. For classification of writs as 'of right', and the consequences thereof, in thirteenth- and fourteenth-century English law, see D. J. Seipp, '*Bracton*, the Year Books, and the "transformation of elementary legal ideas" in the early common law', *LHR*, vii (1989), p. 175.
27. See *RRS*, v, pp. 108–9, 193–4 and 394 (note to no 121).
28. *RM (Cooper)*, p. 213.
29. *ND*, no 296.
30. Ibid., appendix, no 91.

31. W. Fraser, *Keir*, pp. 197–8.
32. *RRS*, ii, no 39.
33. *ESC*, no 153.
34. *RRS*, ii, no 68.
35. *RRS*, ii, no 294; *ND*, no 33.
36. *ESC*, nos 57, 115; *RRS*, i, no 144.
37. *RRS*, ii, no 95.
38. See A. Harding, 'Brieves', pp. 119, 126–7.
39. See above, pp. 124–9.
40. *RM* (*APS*), I, 5–10; *RM* (*Cooper*), I, 6–11; *QA* (*Fergus*), ch. 42; *QA* (*APS*), ch. 40; *QA* (*Cooper*), ch. 57.
41. The legislation is *RRS*, v, p. 412 (c. 19); *APS*, i, p. 470 (c. 19). For the interpolation point, see A. A. M. Duncan, '*Regiam Majestatem*', pp. 210–16.
42. *Abdn Ct Bk*, pp. 9, 10, 12, 14–15.
43. *AB Coll*, pp. 281, 284. See also *APS*, xii, p. 25 (no 46).
44. See SRO, *Spens of Lathallan writs*, GD 1/1042/5; *ADA*, p. 16.
45. *RM* (*APS* and *Cooper*), I, 10. Cf. *Glanvill*, II, 3.
46. G. Neilson, *Trial by Combat*, p. 87.
47. *APS*, i, p. 742 (c. 9); ibid., p. 746 (cc. 28–9); ibid., p. 747 (c. 30).
48. See the 'Table of Authorities' prefixed to *APS*, i, pp. 262–3.
49. *APS*, i, p. 742 (c. 9).
50. *APS*, i, p. 746 (c. 29); G. Neilson, *Trial by Combat*, p. 93.
51. I owe this observation to M. J. Russell, 'Trial by battle and the writ of right', *JLH*, i (1980), p. 129 note 12. Both works mentioned were published by the Selden Society (vols 66 and 80) only after Neilson's death. See G. Neilson, *Trial by Combat*, pp. 86–96; *Brevia Placitata*, pp. lxxxviii, 2–3, 42–3, 127, 191–2, 225; *Novae Narrationes*, pp. xxxiii–v, 26–9, 148–50. *Judicium Essoniorum* also contains the champions' oaths: *Four Thirteenth-Century Law Tracts*, pp. 120–4.
52. G. Neilson, *Trial by Combat*, p. 134. '*Waldevo pugile*' appears in the witness list of a charter of Robert of Lyne to the bishop of Glasgow (*Glas Reg*, p. 76).
53. *ND*, nos 397 and 398; G. Neilson, *Trial by Combat*, pp. 135–6.
54. W. D. H. Sellar, 'Courtesy', pp. 1–8.
55. R. Bartlett, *Trial by Fire and Water*, pp. 106–9, 114–16.
56. See G. Neilson, *Trial by Combat*, p. 145.
57. See further above, pp. 155–6, 176–7.
58. *RRS*, ii, no 388.
59. *Leges Burgorum*, cc. 12 and 13 (*APS*, i, p. 335). See also the interesting 1475 case in *Abdn Counc*, i, pp. 406–7, discussed in G. Neilson, *Trial by Combat*, pp. 281–2.
60. *RRS*, v, 412 (c. 19); *APS*, i, p. 470 (c. 19); and see above, pp. 152, 178.
61. *AB Ill*, iii, p. 8.
62. SRO, *Acta dominorum concilii*, CS 5/16, ff. 144v–145r.
63. SRO, *Haddington Court Book 1423–1514*, B 30/9/1, f. 1; printed *PSAS*, ii (1855), p. 386.
64. J. Stevenson, *Documents*, i, pp. 384–6.
65. See above, pp. 189, 197.
66. *Abdn Ct Bk*, p. 214.

67. SRO, *Haddington Burgh Court Book 1424–1514*, B 30/9/1, f. 1 (both cases).
68. Aberdeen City Archives, CR, iv, pp. 49, 213, 293, 295, 344, 363, 369; v (1), p. 61.
68a. SRO, *Bruce of Clackmannan cartulary*, GD 235/1/1. I owe this reference to Dr A. R. Borthwick.
69. *AB Ill*, iii, p. 8.
70. *AB Coll*, p. 281.
71. See SRO, *Spens of Lathallan writs*, GD 1/1042/5; *ADA*, p. 16.
72. *APS*, ii, p. 254 (c. 41).
73. SRO, *Mar and Kellie papers*, GD 124/6/4.
74. See further below, pp. 220–1.
75. *Glas Reg*, nos 130–1. See above, p. 171.
76. *Family of Rose*, p. 46.
77. *Balm Lib*, no 30. See also ibid., nos 25–7 for background.
78. *Inchaff Chrs*, no 110; T. M. Cooper, *Cases*, no 66. Cooper's note on this case is misleading in some respects but makes clear the difficulty in determining whether or not the case was heard before burgh or sheriff court, or, indeed, ecclesiastical authorities. It is suggested that the case began in the burgh court, but that others became involved for reasons now wholly obscure.
79. For the document, see *SHR*, v (1908), pp. 24–5; see further above, pp. 150, 152.
80. *Abdn Ct Bk*, p. 14.
81. *APS*, i, p. 337 (c. 24).
82. See W. D. H. Sellar, 'Spens family heraldry', *Notes and Queries of the Society of West Highland and Island Historical Research*, xxii (1983), p. 26.
83. See A. Y. Cheyne, *The Cheyne Family in Scotland* (Eastbourne, 1931), pp. 52–6.
84. *AB Ill*, iii, pp. 6–7.
85. *AB Ill*, iii, pp. 7–8.
86. *AB Ill*, iii, pp. 11; *ADC*, i, p. 281.
87. W. D. H. Sellar, 'Spens family heraldry', pp. 26–7; SRO, *Spens of Lathallan writs*, GD 1/1042/5, confirms existence of tailzie in favour of Spens.
88. *SHR*, xxix (1950), p. 5; see above, pp. 180–1.
89. For the story, see *AB Ill*, iii, pp. 318–23; also W. F. Skene, *Memorials of the Family of Skene of Skene* (New Spalding Club, 1887).
90. *RM (APS)*, IV, 40; *RM* (Cooper), p. 296 (Supplement, no 22).
91. See P & M, ii, pp. 74–5, and D. J. Seipp, '*Bracton*', for discussion of this analysis.
92. By e.g. S. F. C. Milsom, *HFCL*, pp. 122–4; but cf. D. J. Seipp, '*Bracton*', showing its deployment in the courts of the thirteenth and fourteenth centuries, albeit in a way that did not reproduce the Roman classification, and hinting at canonical influence.
93. *RRS*, v, p. 412 (c. 19); *APS*, i, p. 471 (c. 19).
94. As in *CA Chrs*, ii, no 128; above, p. 146.
95. See above, p. 148.
96. D. W. Sutherland, *Novel Disseisin*, chs 4 and 5.
97. See *AB Coll*, pp. 281, 284; *AB Ill*, iii, pp. 318–23; *APS*, xii, p. 25 (no 46).

98. *Bracton*, f. 321 (iv, p. 30). For the recognition as to whether lands were fee or gage, see *Glanvill*, XIII, 26–7.
99. *AB Ill*, iii, p. 8.
100. P&M, ii, p. 68.
101. *Bracton*, f. 318 (iv, p. 21).
102. On entry *sur disseisin*, see G. D. G. Hall, 'The early history of entry *sur disseisin*', *Tulane Law Review*, xlii (1968), p. 584.
103. *Statutes of the Realm*, i, p. 60.
104. L. B. Smith, 'Statute of Wales', pp. 141–4.
105. See above, pp. 18–19
106. S. F. C. Milsom, *LFEF*, pp. 92–102, and *HFCL*, pp. 143–9.
107. R. C. Palmer, 'Feudal framework', pp. 1154–61; 'Origins of property', pp. 24–47.
108. *Bracton*, f. 318 (iv, p. 23).
109. Ibid., f. 318 (iv, pp. 22–3).
110. The mysterious case is W. Fraser, *Keir*, pp. 197–8; the other cases are *ND*, nos 91 and 296, and *Pais Reg*, pp. 180, 192 and 198. See above, pp. 193–4.
111. J. Stevenson, *Documents*, i, pp. 384–6.
112. See above, pp. 120–2. The case is that of the bishop of Aberdeen against John Crab (*Abdn Reg*, i, pp. 143–55).
113. See above, pp. 155–6, 176–7, 180–1, 188–9, 200–1, 204.
114. W. D. H. Sellar, 'Courtesy', p. 6.
115. *The Poems of William Dunbar*, ed. J. Kinsley (Oxford, 1979), p. 153, lines 103–8. For the date, see ibid., pp. 335–6.
116. *APS*, ii, p. 254 (c. 41).
117. SRO, *Acta dominorum concilii*, CS 5/13, ff. 35r–36r; CS 5/16, ff. 144v–145r.
118. *St A Form*, i, p. 254; SRO, *Acta dominorum concilii*, CS 5/12, f. 129v (8 February 1503) and ff. 152r–153r (10 February 1503).
119. Cambridge University Library, MS Ee.4.21, f. 273r–v.
120. W. Fraser, *Lennox*, ii, no 149.
121. On the records of this case, see H. L. MacQueen, 'Jurisdiction in heritage', pp. 62–6, and further below, pp. 239–40.
122. P. G. B. McNeill, '*Discours Particulier d'Escosse*, 1559/60', *Stair Misc II*, p. 109; J. Skene, *DVS*, sv '*Breve de Recto*'. See further below, p. 239.

8

Council, Fee and Heritage

INTRODUCTION

Sometime in the fifteenth century William, Richard and Henry Graham were summoned before the king's council to show their charters and other documents by which they held the lands of Hutton. As already discussed, they invoked the rule by which a landholder could only be ejected through action begun by pleadable brieve; but they did not rest their resistance to the king's summons on the brieve rule alone. The document recording their pleadings continues as follows:[1]

> We understande that our soverayne lorde the kyngis counsale is na cowrte to plede fee na herytage na lyfe na lym. Quharfor we beseke our soverayne lord the kyng for the lufe of Gode that of his mychty majeste that he walde kepe us as we that ar his pure legis unwrangyt otherwayis [in] oure lyfis and in oure lande in ony other wayis bot as the course of commoune law wyll and at we may byde befor our jugegis ordynare as the ordur of law of Scotland wyll.

The plea is here making a clear reference to two well-attested limitations on the jurisdiction, not only of the king's council in its judicial capacity, but also of parliament's 'auditors of causes and complaints'. As their records make plain, when in the later fifteenth century a case before either body concerned serious crime ('lyfe na lym') or 'fee and heritage', jurisdiction would be declined and the case remitted to the 'judge ordinary'. The Grahams' pleading suggests a connection between the latter fee and heritage rule and the brieve rule. If so, then the brieve rule, and the forms of pleadable brieve associated with it, assume further significance in the general legal history of Scotland: they played an important role in defining the early jurisdiction of what was to become the Court of Session, and in the history of that court its eventual assumption of jurisdiction in heritage has to be connected with the decline of the brieve system.

The origins of the Court of Session lie in the development of the jurisdiction of council and auditors in the late fifteenth and early sixteenth centuries. By the middle of the sixteenth century, the jurisdictional picture described in the earlier chapters of this book, and in the previous paragraph, had been transformed: the Session, a central court sitting in Edinburgh, claimed exclusive jurisdiction in cases concerning heritage, excluding the sheriff, while the justiciary court had ceased to exercise much civil jurisdiction and was mostly concerned with crime. Two questions therefore arise. First, to what extent was the original limitation on jurisdiction a consequence of the structure of pleadable brieves used to recover disputed land? Second, what if any link is there between the decline of the pleadable brieve system, which the evidence of the last four chapters suggests was well advanced by the end of the fifteenth century, and the development by the evolving Session of a jurisdiction in heritage?

As a simple matter of practicalities, the second question is much harder to answer than the first. The crucial evidence is the substantially unpublished record of conciliar justice after 1503 and up to, say, 1550, by when we can be certain that the jurisdiction in fee and heritage causes was well established. Both in terms of bulk and the difficulty of the scripts in which the records were kept, a complete search would be a formidable task indeed. Moreover, as Athol Murray has been able to show, the treatment of the records over the centuries, and in particular in the nineteenth century, has rendered understanding of how they were originally made extremely difficult; as a result, interpretations based on the records' present form may well be unsustainable.[2] Knowledge of what was happening independently in the justiciary, sheriff, burgh and other local courts would obviously also be essential to the completion of the picture. The job lies beyond the scope of the present work. A preliminary analysis is possible, however, which may have the merit of suggesting some of the questions which could be asked in a more ambitious undertaking.

FEE, HERITAGE AND THE JUDGE ORDINARY

The origins of what became the Session lie in a problem which confronted Scottish royal government throughout the later medieval period, dealing with a mass of individual petitions for justice made to the king and his council, in and out of parliament. The evolution of various solutions, particularly in the fifteenth century, has been traced in many excellent studies, and there is no need to go over the ground in detail here.[3] It suffices for present purposes to note that petitions to parliament were dealt with at the time of parliament by a committee termed the auditors of causes and complaints. The king's council also dealt with petitions, often picking up the business left unfinished by the parliamentary auditors. There was enough business to require regular record-keeping by the mid-fifteenth century, and the records which survive from the reign of James

III onward show that both the auditors and members of the judicial council regularly included a number of persons, both ecclesiastical and lay, who can be regarded as professional judges. The number of petitions clearly caused difficulties in the fifteenth century, and from the time of James I there is evidence for the use of special 'sessions' to deal with them, perhaps deflecting some pressure from council in and out of parliament. However, there seems to be no direct connection between these and the judicial sessions or sittings of council which emerged in the last decade of the century, and from which progress to the Session reconstituted as the College of Justice in 1532 can fairly be traced.

As noted above, when the records of council and the parliamentary auditors become available in the second half of the fifteenth century, it is immediately apparent that when a case before either body concerned 'fee and heritage', jurisdiction would be declined and the case remitted to the 'judge ordinary'. This is also exactly what is sought by the Grahams of Hutton in their petition quoted at the beginning of this chapter. 'Fee and heritage' was already a phrase with a long pedigree in Scotland going back to twelfth-century charters. Well before the period with which we are now concerned, it had come to mean the title of a landholder which would pass on death to the heir or heirs. The jurisdictional limitation was therefore concerned with cases in which heritable title to land was under dispute. The concept of the 'judge ordinary', on the other hand, originated in the canon law, where it was used in contrast to the 'judge delegate'. The judge delegate was one assigned to a particular cause or causes by some higher authority, a practice very familar in medieval canonical practice, as we have seen. The phrase 'judge ordinary' appears never to have been defined independently in the canonical texts, but its implication seems to have been that of one who had jurisdiction by virtue of permanent office rather than through delegation from above. Within the church, for example, the bishop was the ordinary judge of his diocese, while Tancred could state that the pope was the judge ordinary of all Christendom. Within his diocese, however, the bishop might delegate his jurisdiction to archdeacons, commissaries and officials; similarly, papal judges delegate were familiar figures throughout medieval Europe.[4] *Bracton* appropriated the contrast between ordinary and delegated jurisdiction for use in the secular context, suggesting that the king was the ordinary of his realm, 'for he has in his hand all the rights belonging to the crown and the secular power and the material sword pertaining to the governance of the realm'.[5] The writer also commented that those whom the king appointed as his justices, sheriffs and other officials were his delegates, having no authority but that committed to them by the king.[6]

The distinction between ordinary and delegated jurisdiction was of course familiar in Scotland from ecclesiastical practice, and seems to have remained so throughout the medieval period.[7] Of its use to describe secular jurisdictions, nothing seems to have survived from before the fifteenth century, and then the earliest example is an act of 1458 concerning the sessions. Significantly, it lays down that certain causes 'salbe decydit and determyt before the ordinar jugis of the realme, the lordis of the sessione haifande na power to know apone thame'.[8] Another act of 1487 seeking to limit the business to be brought before the council speaks of the judge ordinary as one 'to quham the acciounis pertenis and efferis to be determyt and decidit',[9] recalling the words of another act in 1425 stating that bills of complaint which could not be dealt with by parliament should go to the judges 'to quham thai perten of law'.[10] It seems clear from the acts of 1458 and 1487 that neither the sessions nor the king and his council were regarded as judges ordinary. It is possible to derive a list of the 'ordinaries' from the fifteenth-century statutes referring to the subject, and all were officers whom *Bracton* would have regarded as royal 'delegates' rather than 'ordinaries'. The act of 1487 says that the ordinaries are 'the justice, chaumerlane, schireffis, barones, provostis and baillies of borowis and uther officiaris, jugis and ministeris of law'.[11] In 1500, a sheriff *in hac parte* – that is, appointed for a particular cause only – was described as '*judex delegatus*', while the sheriff principal of the sheriffdom was '*judex ordinarius*' within his bailiary.[12]

What we may be seeing here is a development somewhat analogous to one which took place in the church: the delegates of the ordinary exercise the ordinary's jurisdiction, and in course of time by the establishment of their offices are increasingly seen as exercising jurisdiction by virtue of their office rather than through the delegation constituted by appointment to the office.[13] So archdeacons and officials came to be ordinaries, having started as delegates of the bishop; similarly, it is suggested, justiciars and sheriffs in Scotland came to be seen as judges ordinary as the jurisdiction of their courts became a matter of custom and thereby law. The authority of the officers had ceased to be a matter of delegation from the king and was rather something which the law defined in relation to the office, no matter by whom or on whose appointment it was held.

ORIGINS OF THE FEE AND HERITAGE RULE

The object now is to place the development of this limitation of the jurisdiction of auditors and council in the context of the argument of the preceding pages. As noted in the first chapter, historians have usually explained the fee and heritage rule as the consequence of a 'feudal victory', the survival of the idea that pleas concerning landholding should be heard in the court of the lord of whom the land was held.[14] It is clear, however, that this explanation is unacceptable since, even if this 'feudal

theory' ever did apply in Scotland, it would appear to have been superseded by the brieves rule.[15] Even though on the two occasions in the
printed records when the judge ordinary to whom cases are remitted is
named he turns out to be a lord of regality, this is not inconsistent with
the argument just made, since, as observed elsewhere, the brieve rule
applied and the pleadable brieves were issued within regalities.[16]

A more subtle explanation of the exclusion of council from fee and
heritage cases has been advanced by A. A. M. Duncan.[17] Because council
could not call upon the men of the neighbourhood to give a verdict, it was
debarred from dealing with landownership. This he seems to link with the
fact that council, unlike parliament, was not fenced and had no dempster;
thus council, unlike parliament, was not a court. Although Duncan does
not make the point explicit, it might be thought to follow from this that
parliament, as a court, did have jurisdiction in fee and heritage.

The difficulty with such a view is the fact that parliament's auditors of
causes and complaints could not hear cases of fee and heritage, and there
is, it is submitted, no good reason for supposing that the auditors here
exercised a lesser jurisdiction than that which would ordinarily have been
available to the full parliament. It is true that parliament could appoint
an assize and pronounce a doom based on the verdict of that assize; it did
so constantly in cases of treason. We may also note that the auditors of
falsed dooms, the committee which sat on appeals from the lower courts,
reported back to parliament so that the verdict could be pronounced by
its dempster within the fenced full court.[18] If such a procedure was
conceivable for falsed dooms, it is difficult to see why it could not also
have been used by the auditors of causes and complaints in cases of fee
and heritage. The better view is that the auditors had no jurisdiction in
such cases because parliament generally did not exercise jurisdiction in
them either.

It should be stressed that this is not to say that parliament had no
jurisdiction in fee and heritage cases. It would be more accurate to say
that parliament was generally not concerned to deal with causes where
there was a remedy in the general common law. There are examples of
complainers in parliament being told to claim elsewhere at common law.
Thus in 1368, Robert Stewart, lord of Menteith, was told that the action
he had brought in parliament should be pursued and defended in another
court according to the order and form of the common law, the defender
having contended that, according to the custom of the realm, it should be
heard in the justiciar's court.[19] Similarly, in 1401, Marjorie Lindsay was
sent to the common law regarding certain matters not central to a
complaint for which parliament had given her a remedy.[20] There is a
parallel here with English parliamentary practice of the fourteenth century when, according to a document of 1309, the most important class of

petitions to parliament concerned grievances which it was claimed could not be redressed by the common law nor in any other manner save by special warrant. Where, however, parliament determined that a petitioner had an action at common law, he would be sent to that remedy rather than given one under his petition.[21]

Somewhat similar ideas underlay the restricted original jurisdiction of the king's council. As late as 1487, it was possible to say that only cases 'pertenyng in speciale to our soverane lord' fell within the proper jurisdiction of his council, these being 'accions and complaintis made be kirkmen, wedowis, orphanis and pupillis, accions of strangearis of uther realmis and complaintis made apone officiaris forfalt of execucioun of thair office'.[22] In other words, the king and council were to protect the specially vulnerable and needy, and to take responsibility for the misdeeds of royal administration. All these were cases where the common law might be in need of supplementation. This is very clear with regard to the jurisdiction over complaints about royal officers: as other fifteenth-century acts make clear, intervention was to occur if they failed to administer justice or were partial.[23] The idea that council should not intervene 'bot as the course of commoune law will' is also articulated in the petition of the Grahams of Hutton.

The argument that parliament and council generally excluded themselves from matters which could be dealt with at common law is reinforced by the observation that the application of the brieve rule would have had the effect of restricting the jurisdiction of both parliament and council, since none of the brieves described in *Regiam* or *Quoniam* as pleadable was addressed to these institutions. The little evidence that exists on how actions were brought before parliament and council suggests that a summons was issued in response to a bill of complaint and that in the early fifteenth century the summons took the form of a brieve 'under the testimony of the great seal'. This means that the document was written in Latin on parchment and was authenticated by the quarter seal – that is, one half of the king's great seal.[24] Since we only know definitely of the quarter seal from the reign of James I,[25] the position in the fourteenth century is uncertain, but it seems most likely that the brieve of summons, either under the great seal proper or the quarter seal, was the standard writ by which defenders were brought before parliament or council to answer complaints. It has been said that the privy seal was 'commonly used by the council from the later fourteenth century', but all the examples cited in support of that statement show this to have been in the execution of decrees rather than to summon defenders.[26] Sometime in the first half of the fifteenth century, summonses before council and the parliamentary auditors began to be issued under the king's signet seal. Signet letters were in the vernacular and written on paper, by contrast with the Latin and parchment of the quarter seal brieve; ultimately they were to oust the brieve as the principal writ of summons.[27] While, then, brieves were used to commence actions in parliament and council, they did not meet the requirements of the 1318 act, since they were not among the pleadable brieves; in any event, they were being used less and less frequently during the fifteenth century.

There is another critical point to be made here about the various seals under which the king's written will was communicated to his subjects. From the later fourteenth century on, there were regular legislative attempts to control the issue of royal letters under whatever seal which were not in the due form of the common law: as it was expressed in an act of 1430, the king was not to send out 'uncoursabyll letteris . . . agayne the cowrse of commoune law'.[28] The culmination of this was an act of 1491 providing that 'the forme of the chancellarie be keiped and observed without innovation or eiking of new termes, and gif ony beis gevin utherwaies that they be of na force na effect'.[29] It is clear that, whatever the purpose of these repeated statutes may have been, they did not in fact prevent a king from issuing letters to intervene in causes to which his attention had been directed.[30] His intervention might be justified by his obligations to protect the church, foreigners or those too weak to protect themselves; for example, in 1460 James II wrote to the aldermen and baillies of Aberdeen and Perth under his 'Signet of the Unicorn', explaining that 'it effeirs to the king of law to defend orphans and pupils being under age'.[31] These ideas may also explain the same king's brieve addressed to Robert lord Erskine following a decreet of the parliamentary auditors in 1445: he was to do *complementum iusticiam* to the widow Ada Crab, who claimed to hold lands of him which were being withheld by a third party. The brieve concluded with a statement redolent of the ancient concept of the king's protection: Erskine was to act so that the king heard no further complaint of default of justice.[32] What is visible here is a tension between the ordinary procedures of the common law and the king's duty to administer justice, made real by written statements of his will. The development of judicial business in council and parliament may well be at least partly explicable by the need to resolve such conflicts; hence, perhaps, the commitment of a cause to council by James I in 1424, and the reference in an act of 1469 to the king's 'emplesance' (pleasure) as a basis for council hearing cases.[33]

The point is that parliament and, more especially, council operated at least partly on a basis which was outside the structure or the course of the ordinary law. This must not be seen as a matter of lawlessness, although presumably the acts against the king's uncoursable interventions were aimed at abuse of the system. Rather, the king as the fount of justice was to remedy the law's mechanical defects. However, when it came to claims to land, even more caution had to be observed. Heritage was after all a fundamental interest and, as Robert III said in 1391, 'it suld nocht be his wil . . . oucht to do or to conferme that suld ryn ony man in preiudice of thair heritage attour the commoune lauch'.[34] Here, too, the common law compelled the use of coursable letters, or brieves *de cursu*: the pleadable brieves of right, mortancestry and novel dissasine.

However, it is clear that the connection between the brieve rule and the fee and heritage rule was not quite as simple as it may appear from the preceding paragraphs. There is a difficulty with the view that the brieves rule operated directly to deprive parliament and council of jurisdiction, and that is the difference, more than just one of words or of formulation, between saying that a court has no jurisdiction in fee and heritage and that a man cannot be put out of his freehold except by pleadable brieve. The difference between a freehold, an interest enduring for one man's lifetime, and the potentially perpetual interest of heritage, has been explained elsewhere in this book.[35] It means that, at any rate by the time records begin, the jurisdiction of parliament and council was wider than a strict application of the brieves rule would have permitted. An example will illustrate the point. A freeholder, or franktenementer, dispossesses a tercer. The tercer is forced to action by pleadable brieve because the franktenementer can claim to be vest and saised of a freehold. The tercer's only remedy is the brieve of dissasine, because under that brieve she need only show a freehold interest herself. However, by 1466 it would seem that such a case could be dealt with by parliament and council because no question of fee and heritage arose in it.

Differences between the two rules also emerge from consideration of the cases in which the fee and heritage exception was pleaded after 1466. It was usually raised by way of dilatory exception by the defender,[36] and in most cases it is apparent that he was in possession of the lands in issue. Thus the defender could also have pleaded the brieve rule. However, there were also cases where the lords remitted the action because in the course of the litigation it emerged that at the heart of the dispute there were claims on both sides to a heritable title; in such circumstances, the fee and heritage rule might protect a defender not in possession from action before the lords.

The cases in which it is most apparent that the defender is in possession are those where the complaint is of wrongful occupation. Wrongful occupation was most typically an action by owners against tenants holding on a lease which had expired. An act of 1458 also made provision for the problem, referring to 'maisterfull men that schapis thame to occupy maisterfully lordis landis', whom the sheriff was to make 'devoide the grounde' if he found 'na resone in the occupacioun of the grounde'.[37]

This was not the only situation in which the action of wrongful occupation might be brought, however. In 1473, William Ramsay unsuccessfully claimed wrongful occupation by the tenant of the lands of Newmill, who held by a tack from the prior of St Andrews. The action before the parliamentary auditors failed; other sources show that Ramsay was a former holder of the tack who had been evicted for failure to answer for it in the prior's court. The process of eviction had taken nearly two years.[38] In this case, therefore, it was the tenant who claimed wrongful occupation against the landlord and his new tenant. Nearly twenty years earlier, the abbey of Arbroath had complained to parliament that part of its barony of Tarves in Aberdeenshire had been wrongfully occupied by the lord of the neighbouring barony of Meldrum – a straight dispute as to the ownership of ground.[39] Unfortunately, we do not know whether in reply the lord of Meldrum invoked the fee and heritage exception.

Many of the cases in which the fee and heritage exception was pleaded were most probably disputes about whether the tenant held on a tack or by a heritable title. In 1483, William Ayton claimed that Duncan Toshack had wrongfully occupied his heritage of Petteny for eight years. Toshack replied that he held the lands heritably in feu-ferme by a grant of Ayton's father and excepted to the jurisdiction of the lords. Toshack having proved his lawful possession of the lands, the case was remitted to the judge ordinary as concerning fee and heritage.[40] Similarly, in another action for wrongful occupation in 1490, this time concerning the barony of Fordell in Fife, the defender produced a royal charter under the great seal and a sasine and claimed the lands as her heritage. When the pursuer produced his sasine, the defender argued that the case should be remitted to the judge ordinary. The lords duly declined jurisdiction 'because the disputaccioun thirof micht exclude ane of the said partiis perpetualy fra the heretage of the said landis and als because the disputaccioun of the saidis sesing concernis the fee and heretage of the saidis landis'.[41] A complaint in 1492 of wrongful occupation of the barony of Luss was referred to the judge ordinary after the defender had alleged the lands to be his fee and heritage 'and wochit [vouched] the samyn with the parell [parole oath] of law'.[42] In 1495, the defender answered a complaint of eighteen years' wrongful occupation of Lammelethin, Fife, by claiming it as his heritage and producing an instrument of sasine. The lords referred the action to the judge ordinary as it concerned fee and heritage.[43]

In these cases of wrongful occupation held to concern fee and heritage (of which there are other examples[44]), it is obvious that the defender is in possession since otherwise the action would be unnecessary, but it is also apparent that he had to prove some title to support his possession and his claim of heritage. If he failed in this, the action proceeded before the lords.

So, in 1502 when the abbot and convent of Jedburgh sued Andrew Ker of Ferniehurst for twenty years' wrongful occupation of Thornyhaugh in the forest of Jed, Ker produced his charter and sasine of Ferniehurst and claimed that Thornyhaugh was a pertinent of those lands. No proof of this was offered, and his argument that the dispute was one of fee and heritage and should be remitted to the judge ordinary was rejected.[45] The defender thus had to show lawful possession, possession of the kind which under the 1318 act would have compelled the pursuer to use a pleadable brieve to eject him. So, in these cases at least, we can see the fee and heritage rule operating in the same way as the 1318 act, protecting lawful possession, the only real difference being in the legal nature of the possession protected, heritage as distinct from freehold.

However, the exception to the jurisdiction was not pleaded only in cases of wrongful occupation. Probably the commonest types of case where it was pleaded were actions of error against inquests in the service of heirs and actions of spuilzie. In the former, the exception would be raised normally by the person served heir at the inquest, since it was his title, not that of the members of the inquest, which the action put in issue. Generally speaking, he would have been summoned as a defender to the action for his interest and might have sasine as a consequence of the service. So, again, such a defender would have had protection under the 1318 act.[46] However, none of the cases recorded in print shows clearly the nature of the defender's possession, if any, and so it is also possible that here the fee and heritage rule operated in a different way from the brieves rule, looking not for the defender's possession but simply for two competing claims to land. This need not mean that there was no relationship between the two rules; it would show rather that by the latter part of the fifteenth century the fee and heritage rule had by virtue of its separate formulation acquired an independent content and application. The question would then be to explain how this development came to take place.

Actions of spuilzie also raise difficult problems. Spuilzie was in essence an action to recover possession of goods, in which the dispossessed pursuer was to 'be restorit but [without] delay'.[47] So, in 1443, the goods of which David Scrymgeour had been 'spolyheit' were to be restored to him by the sheriff of Aberdeen.[48] An act of parliament in 1458 divided spuilzie cases into two classes: one 'nocht tuiching fee nor heretage', the other 'spoliacioun . . . done becaus of landis or possessionis debatable or grondyt apone fee or heretage'.[49] Only in the latter case, presumably, would the fee and heritage exception be a possible issue; and, as we shall see later, the 1458 act made special provision for how the lords of session were to deal with such cases.[50] In these cases, it would seem, the defender's justification for seizing the goods was his assertion of some right in land. In many of the cases of which we learn from other sources before the records of auditors and council become available, the claim of spuilzie in relation to lands seems to be connected with the uplifting of the rents of the land in question by the defender. Thus, in 1450, John Wallace, lord of Craigie, acknowledged that he '*spoliavit*' the monks of Paisley abbey of the '*firmis*' of the lands of Thornlie in the barony of Renfrew which Hugh Wallace, John's brother-german, had granted to the monks with the consent of his brother William and a royal confirmation.[51] Again, in 1456, Adam Hepburn's *querela spoliacionis* against Oswald Weir and others before the king's council concerned the *firmis* of Dunsyre in Lanarkshire as well as the breaking of his hereditary sasine.[52] Another type of case closely related to those of spuilzie of rents may be one before the parliamentary auditors in 1445 where William Carlisle and Herbert lord Maxwell disputed the right to certain fishings between Cummertrees and Lochar, and had apparently been guilty of mutual spoliations in the assertion of their claims; the latter issue was remitted to judges specially deputed by the king.[53]

In the records of auditors and council, the spuilzie cases in which the fee and heritage exception was pleaded may be further subdivided into two main types: either the spuilzie of rents of lands or the spuilzie of animals from lands. The basis for the defender's actions was of course either ownership or lordship of the lands and entitlement to take the rents and profits thereof. The pursuer would either be a rival claimant or a tenant. In one of the earliest cases of spuilzie of rents, it was alleged that the defenders had been uplifting the maills of Kimmerghame for the past three years.[54] The exception of fee and heritage was upheld and the case remitted to the judge ordinary. The facts are not completely clear, but the case appears to have arisen out of a dispute between the heir-male and the daughters of John Sinclair of Herdmanston. The daughters were the defenders in the spuilzie case and subsequently acquired ownership of Kimmerghame, presumably as heirs-general.[55] It seems very likely therefore that they were in possession for the three years during which they were taking the rents and that they were not mere interlopers. Accordingly, here again, the rule about fee and heritage operated as the 1318 act would have done; perhaps a similar situation lies behind two other near-contemporaneous cases of spuilzie of rents in which also the fee and heritage exception was upheld.[56]

The spuilzie of animals cases are less straightforward. In the action brought by Adam Blackadder against Thomas Edington in 1480, Edington claimed that he had taken the beast as a herezeld – that is, in exercise of the right of a superior to the best animal of his deceased tenant.[57] Acting as a superior is not of course quite the same thing as being vest and saised of the superiority on a formal title; it might rather be a way of laying claim to the title of superior as against another. Nevertheless, the record states somewhat ambiguously that 'the Lard of Dalwolsy, advocate for Thomas Edington, allegit that a part of the landis of Blakader pertenis to the said Thomas in heritage and that the resoun of the landis he tuke a herezelde and is in possessioun thirof'. It is not clear whether this means that Edington claimed to be in possession of the lands themselves, or whether he was merely explaining his possession of the herezeld by reference to his claim of a heritable title; but at all events the lords held that the case depended upon fee and heritage and remitted it to the judge ordinary. Legal possession does however appear to be important in the complex case of William lord Ruthven against Archibald Preston in 1495.[58] William alleged spuilzie of oxen from him and his tenants of Coustland by Archibald, who replied by claiming that the lands were his heritage, that he was in possession and that he had taken the beasts for the maills. William called Henry lord Sinclair for warrandice and the argument became one between Henry and Archibald as to who had right to uplift the maills of Coustland. Archibald argued that Henry only had right by virtue of an agreement with his sister, whose rights ended on her marriage. The lords fixed a proof of the manner of the parties' possession, presumably as a preliminary to determining whether to uphold Archibald's exception that as the case touched fee and heritage it should be referred to the judge ordinary. By contrast, nothing about the nature of the parties' possession emerges from the two other cases of spuilzie of cattle which were sent to be decided by the judge ordinary because, as all parties claimed heritable title to the lands in question, they concerned fee and heritage.[59]

Another interesting group of cases is those where the pursuer alleged that an annualrent due to him was being wrongfully withheld from him by the defender. In essence, these would have been actions for payment, but on a number of occasions in the printed records we find them being sent to the judge ordinary 'becaus it is fe and heretage and kan nocht be decidit but one of the partiis be hurt in the richt of thir heretage'.[60] An annualrent was a method of securing repayment of the loan of a capital sum without infringing the prohibition of usury. The sum lent was treated as purchasing the lender a right to receive a rent from the borrower's lands. The lender was formally infeft in his annualrent as a right in land and so acquired a heritable title. However, by contrast with the position under a wadset, the borrower was not divested of his own heritable title and possession.[61] It is significant that according to *Quoniam* the creditor's remedy in the case of the debtor's default was the brieve of right rather than the brieve of distress.[62] In the actions remitted to the judge ordinary by council, the problem appears to have arisen because the original holder of the annualrent right had assigned it to another and the validity of the transfer was denied by the borrower. So, in 1480, John Porterfield claimed that an annualrent in the lands of Schethum had been assigned to him by his father, but was met by an allegation that this had been without the consent of the owner of the lands, the defender, Thomas Schethum.[63] Thomas would be in possession and his argument would have been that John's invalid claim would put him out of the free enjoyment of his heritage. So the lords' decision to remit the case to the judge ordinary as one of fee and heritage can be seen as a recognition that the claim challenged the free title of a man in possession. Similarly, in 1478, Andrew Mowbray sued John Burton for an annualrent and called Alexander Knightson, presumably the original creditor of the rent, as his warrant; it seems probable that Barton, like Schethum, was denying the validity of an assignation to the pursuer, so making the case one of competing claims to heritable rights appropriate only to the judge ordinary.[64] Following *Quoniam*, it would appear that in both cases the creditors' remedy was the brieve of right.[65]

Finally, we may note two of the many cases which arose out of the complex question of the succession to the lands of Sir Thomas Wemyss of Rires and Leuchars in Fife.[66] Sir Thomas died in the winter of 1478–9. By virtue of a royal grant of 1477,[67] Rires should then have passed to Arthur Forbes, husband of Elizabeth Wemyss (the granddaughter and heir of Sir Thomas). However, when in March 1479 Forbes raised an action of spuilzie of thirty oxen and large quantities of crops 'out of the maynis of Reras' against John and Thomas Wemyss, 'sons to umquhile Schir Thomas of Wemis of Reras', the case was 'referrit and remittit be the lordis of counsale to be determit before the juge ordinare, because the landis that the said gudis was takin of is clamyt fee and heretage be baith the said parties and the questioun of the richt dependis apoun heretage'.[68] In the context of the present discussion, the main point of interest lies in the fact that the Wemyss brothers were protected by the fee and heritage rule although in 1479 they could show no ex facie valid title to justify any possession of Rires they may have had. Accordingly, they could not have claimed the protection of the 1318 act; but, as I have attempted to show in detail elsewhere, John Wemyss did have some claim to a better right than that of Arthur Forbes in Rires.[69] The remission of Forbes's action of spuilzie to the judge ordinary was therefore based on the existence of competing claims of heritable right only and not on the lawful possession of Wemyss, showing that by this time the fee and heritage exception was wider in scope than the brieves rule.

The case may be contrasted with another action of spuilzie, this time of the lands of Wester Cruivie in Fife, brought in 1480 against James Bonar by Baldred Blackadder.[70] Blackadder's title to Wester Cruivie was derived from the conjunct fee of his wife, Margaret Melville, who was the widow of Sir Thomas Wemyss.[71] Nevertheless, the case was remitted to the judge ordinary as a matter of heritage. Bonar had produced 'a letter of testimonials schewand that he was enterit as are to his fader ... be Arthur of Forbace as his oure lord'; in other words he was in apparently lawful possession and so protected not only by the fee and heritage rule but also by the 1318 act.

This examination of the cases in which the exception of fee and heritage was pleaded has shown that, while there was a substantial overlap with the brieve rule, there were situations where the lords declined jurisdiction even though the defender would have been unable to show that he held possession so that he could only be put out by pleadable brieve. It would seem therefore that there is no direct link between the two rules. Some other explanation for the fee and heritage rule must be found. In the remainder of this chapter, it will be argued that the true origin of the fee and heritage rule lies in the exclusion of the jurisdiction of parliament and council where there was an ordinary common-law remedy. The gradual abandonment of this position in the fifteenth century did not affect issues of landholding however, because in that area there was the additional hurdle of the brieves rule to be overcome. In this way, the brieves rule helped to define what became one of the few limitations on the jurisdiction of parliament and, in particular, council. It will also be shown that council always enjoyed a particular jurisdiction to determine certain questions about the possession of land, and from this the tentative suggestion will be made that the canonist distinction of proprietary and possessory actions may have led to some idea that council was excluded only from proprietary actions, that is, those about ownership of lands or, in the terminology of medieval Scots law, the fee and heritage.

THE EARLY RESTRICTIONS

Duncan states that, in the fourteenth and early fifteenth centuries, 'where an action concerned fee and heritage, the council had no jurisdiction'.[72] He bases this conclusion upon the evidence of a small number of cases, but in fact none of these gives direct support to the statement since, while all involved disputes over land, in none did the council decline jurisdiction. Thus Duncan refers to the decree of council general in March 1416 holding that the governor of the realm ought to recognosce the superiority of the barony of Cessford and to maintain William Cockburn and his wife as tenants there. Cockburn and his wife had alleged molestation by William Douglas of Old Roxburgh, who claimed to be the superior of the lands against the argument of the Cockburns that the lands were held of the king.[73] There is no hint of a declinature of jurisdiction here. Rather, council general acts to maintain the possession of the Cockburns, which was apparently justified by charters. A case of 1373 decided by the *presides* of parliament appears to be of a similar nature: the decreet is that David Graham ought to remain in possession of the lands of Old Montrose, and that the king ought to stand with him as warrantor, notwithstanding anything to the contrary by John Lindsay of Thurston.[74] Duncan speaks of the 'delivery of possession' and the 'giving of sasine' by council in connection with these cases, but that is not quite what happens; it looks more as though existing possession is protected by the decreets.

Duncan also mentions two cases of 1416 and 1423 recorded in two documents first printed by him.[75] Both involved the procedure of recognition, here meaning the process by which lands in dispute were taken into the hands of the superior of whom they were held in order to determine which of the competing parties had been the last lawful possessor thereof. The effect of the award was not to settle the whole question at issue between the parties but simply to define who should be pursuer and defender in the eventual litigation which would determine where the better title lay.[76] The person in possession as a result of the recognition could only be ejected by action against him begun by pleadable brieve. Thus, in the first of Duncan's cases, Sir John Ross of Hawkhead received lands which he claimed to hold of the king in fee and heritage, but only upon giving a pledge and subject to reservation of the rights of others. In the second case, the lands had been recognosced and the pursuer, having given documentary evidence of his title (and so established the lawfulness of his possession), received the lands in pledge.

These cases are not therefore evidence about council's lack of jurisdiction in fee and heritage. Instead, they are examples of what was a common form of process, not just before council but also before parliament, the justiciar and, as shown in an earlier chapter, private lords. Thus, in 1385, the lands of the earldom of Buchan were in dispute between Sir James Lindsay of Crawford and Alexander Stewart of Badenoch, and council general decided that the lands should be recognosced and not given to Alexander in *borgh*.[77] By contrast, in 1422, Herbert Maxwell, lord of Carlaverock, received the lands of Nether Dryppis, which had been recognosced by the governor, in pledge, having given evidence of his title to the superiority.[78] In 1427, the king recognosced lands disputed between 'the lorde Kambal' and Sir John Scrymgeour as the first step in what were to be lengthy proceedings to determine their ownership.[79] Acting in his capacity as abbot of Inchcolm before the chamberlain-depute's court in 1435, Walter Bower unsuccessfully sought the loosing of a recent recognition made in the justiciar's court of a tenement in the burgh of Kinghorn granted to the abbey by Hugh Scott, a burgess there.[80] The parliamentary auditors (who included Bower) held in 1445 that William Carlisle should remain in possession of certain fishings between

Cummertrees and Lochar, but that Herbert lord Maxwell might pursue his claim of right in form of law.[81] In 1459, recognosced lands were given in *borgh* (i.e. pledge) to Thomas Allardice by king and council;[82] similarly, in 1467, the king in presence of his council commanded the chancellor to relax a recognition over certain lands in favour of David Hay of Yester.[83] The lands of Wormit in Fife were 'debateable' between James Hay, lord of the barony of Naughton, and his sister Elizabeth in 1472, and were accordingly recognosced by the king in his council; but Hay still uplifted the rents for the Whit term, because the recognition was later.[84] The prolonged litigation between Robert Spens and James Nory by brieve of right over the lands of Kittedie (also in Fife), which took place between 1461 and 1471, involved a recognition of the lands before the king's council, which let the lands to Nory subject to a *borgh*. The document which tells of this proceeding also states that Spens had previously recovered the lands by brieve of right, and now proposed an appeal to parliament.[85] Something similar appears to have happened after James Skene had recovered lands from Janet Keith by brieve of right in Aberdeen sheriff court in 1457; Skene's procurator, his son Alexander, later made several protests about a subsequent recognition by the king in parliament which resulted in the return of possession to Janet.[86] That the procedure of recognition might be followed in parliament itself is confirmed by the dispute over the ownership of the barony of Rires between Arthur Forbes and John Wemyss of Pittencrieff. Forbes and Wemyss were unable to agree on who the judge should be and upon which of them should be pursuer or defender. In 1481, parliament decided that the lands of Rires should be recognosced by the king, 'for staynchin of debate betuix the saide partiis, but nocht lattin thaim to borgh to nowther of thame'.[87] In 1485, Forbes sued Wemyss before council 'anent the asking of the lands of Reris to borgh quhilkis ar recognist in our soverane lordis handis for the debatis betuix the said partiis'. It would seem that Wemyss had gained possession, for it was 'complenit be the said Arthur that the hous of Reras is takin fra him be uncoursable lettrez purchest be the said Johne of Wemis'.[88] Subsequently, the question of who had been the last lawful possessor was settled in favour of Forbes: in 1491, the records of the parliamentary auditors note 'That our soverane lordis faider quham god assolze let the said landis of Reres to borgh to the said Arthure Forbes efter congnitioun of the cause him self sittand in jugement'.[89]

This last example shows very well how contentious and difficult to resolve the issue of possession might be and that it was not merely a matter of preserving the status quo. What was critical was the lawfulness of the possession; that is to say, possession based upon some ex facie valid and regular title such as a charter and sasine. It is clear that in most cases the determination of this question was only a preliminary to further action; the successful party had to find a pledge, or *borgh*, as an acknowledgement that his possession was interim only and not that of an owner. Many further examples of the process can be found in the records of council and the parliamentary auditors once these become available in the second half of the fifteenth century, and these make the position quite clear.[90] However, it does not necessarily follow from this that council had no jurisdiction to hear questions of fee and heritage; all that can be said is that council (and parliament) had jurisdiction to maintain and, if required, to determine issues as to the most recent lawful possession of lands.

A more fruitful approach is to examine the small amount of evidence showing parliament and council declining jurisdiction in cases apparently concerned with the ownership of land. What is striking about them is that jurisdiction was declined, not on the grounds that the cases concerned fee and heritage, but on the grounds that the parties ought to use the common law. Two examples have been mentioned elsewhere in this book, the cases of Robert Stewart lord of Menteith in 1368 and Marjorie Lindsay in 1401.[91] Both raised complaints in parliament and were told that their remedy lay at common law. In another chapter, it was suggested that Robert Stewart's remedy for the recovery of terce lands belonging to his wife by reason of a former marriage would have been a brieve of dissasine.[92] The case is complex. The link between Stewart and the defender, Archibald Douglas, was most probably the earlier marriage of Stewart's wife, Margaret, countess of Menteith, to Sir John Murray of Bothwell. Murray had died in 1351, to be succeeded by Sir Thomas Murray, who in turn died in 1361. His widow, herself a Murray of Drumsargard, married Archibald Douglas in 1362, bringing with her a liferent of Bothwell as the conjunct fiar thereof with Sir Thomas.[93] It seems highly probable that in 1368 Stewart was seeking to regain the terce of Bothwell pertaining to his wife Margaret, while Douglas was asserting a freehold in the whole of the lands by virtue of the conjunct fee of his wife. Here, then, we have an actual example of the hypothetical situation discussed earlier, a dispute over lands, not involving any question of fee and heritage, which under the 1318 act should have been litigated by pleadable brieve. In declining jurisdiction, however, parliament did not mention the brieve rule; instead it was simply stated that Stewart must have resort to the common law in the court of the justiciar. Yet, a century later, the case could have been heard by parliament or council because it did not involve any dispute about fee and heritage.

This case is extremely important. It shows a dispute over land being remitted by parliament to another court and the common law. In other words, at common law, parliament was not a forum for such litigation even though it involved lands held in chief of the king. The declinature of

jurisdiction was not couched in terms of either the brieves rule or the fee
and heritage rule; indeed, if the latter had been the rule at the time, the
case would not have been sent away to another court. It seems clear that
the case was remitted on the basis that parliament was unwilling to deal
with complaints for which there existed remedies at common law – in this
instance, the brieve of dissasine in the justiciar's court.

Similarly, Marjorie Lindsay's case does not seem to have involved
any question of fee and heritage. Her complaint concerned dispossession
from her terce of the estates of her deceased husband, Henry Douglas
of Lochleven and Lugton,[94] as well as from the tutory of her son
William. The defender was Henry Douglas's brother, James Douglas
the elder (*patre*) of Dalkeith. As Marjorie had a conjunct fee of her
husband's principal lands of Lochleven, Lugton and Langnewton,[95]
her claim to terce must have been to the lands of Crossraguel,
Lanarkshire, which Henry held of his brother. We know that after Henry's
death James recognosced Crossraguel and that there was a dispute over
the tutory of Henry's heir William.[96] In his testament, Henry had
apparently provided that Marjorie should be the tutor,[97] but at common
law William's nearest agnate, his uncle James, would be entitled to the
office. Thus, at bottom, this dispute was really about the right to possess
and administer lands where the undoubted heir was not yet of full age.
No question of fee and heritage arose, yet parliament declined jurisdiction. If the recognition by James had put Marjorie out of her terce,
nevertheless his consequent possession was ex facie lawful and regular; it
could therefore be shown to be wrongful only by an action at common
law. It may be suggested that Marjorie's remedy was the brieve of novel
dissasine.

This case demonstrates again the concern of parliament and council
to protect the most recent lawful state of possession and its reluctance to
go further into land disputes. A similar rationale appears to underlie a
case of 1430 in which parliament overruled a plea in a dispute over lands
that, 'the cause ought not to be determined by parliament'.[98] The reasons
for advancing the plea are not known, but what is said of the facts of the
case suggests that they were connected with the jurisdiction of parliament
to determine questions of landholding where there was a common-law
remedy. The pursuer complained that the defenders had despoiled her of
the lands of Luchald in the barony of Dalmeny and now unjustly held
them. Accordingly, this looks like a situation in which once again a brieve
of novel dissasine would have provided an appropriate remedy, and it was
probably this which underlay the defender's contention that parliament
had no jurisdiction. Nevertheless, parliament restored the pursuer to the
lands. The reason for this seems to have been the inability of the defenders
to justify their possession of the lands once the pursuer had stated that she

held not of them but of the king. Thus hers was the last lawful possession, and that could only be challenged, in accordance with principle, by action at common law.

Finally, this protection of possession emerges clearly from another case in 1385 where die pursuer was sent to his common-law remedy, this time by council general rather than parliament." The case also shows that complaints might be remitted to the common law even though they did not concern landholding directly. William Fenton complained that he had been *exspoliatus* of his tenement, and obtained a decree of restoration. The facts were very special. Fenton had been ejected from his lands in the barony of Dirleton, East Lothian, by judgment of the baron court. He had falsed the doom in the sheriff court of Edinburgh and, pending the outcome of this appeal, had been restored to his former possession. The baron, however, had again put him out, and Fenton had sought a remedy for this abuse of process before king and council; a decree for his restoration had been pronounced and executed, but once more the baron moved to expel him from possession. It was this last action of which Fenton complained before council general and for which he received another decree of restoration until the discussion of the doom of the baron court. The complaint was thus of contempt of a decree of council, which doubtless explains why, exceptionally in this period, council general dealt with the matter. However, Fenton was sent to the common law 'concerning other articles contained in his complaint which do not depend from the falsing of the doom'. Fenton was in lawful possession, and that would be protected by council; all else would require procedure at common law.

In conclusion, therefore, it seems that the jurisdiction of parliament in the fourteenth and early fifteenth centuries was indeed limited in practice, but that limitation was not expressed as an exclusion from cases touching fee and heritage. Rather, it excluded cases where a remedy might be had through ordinary common-law procedure. Council general appears to have been subject to a similar limitation and, we must assume, so was council. However, parliament and council did protect, and determine questions concerning, the most recent state of lawful possession of lands. This can be seen as part of the jurisdiction to supplement the common law. At common law, the rule was that no-one vest and saised of lands could be ejected from them except by action begun by pleadable brieve. The last lawful possessor was entitled to the protection of the rule, but if his or her identity was disputed, how was the matter to be resolved? The capacity of council and parliament to deal with such questions should not however be misunderstood; this was undoubtedly a jurisdiction to estab-lish and maintain the most recent state of possession of lands, and thus to identify who should have the benefit of defending the subsequent action on the question of the right. It was not a covert substitute for a jurisdiction which belonged to other courts.

With this understanding of council's jurisdiction, we can make sense of an act passed in 1450, which Duncan suggests concerns spuilzie.[100] It dealt with defenders contumaciously not compearing in answer to summonses before council. In general, the defender was to be given three separate days to answer; if he continued contumacious throughout, then on the third day the action should proceed in his absence. There were, however, special provisions 'gif the cause be of fee and heritage'. The case should not be proceeded with; instead, the pursuer was to be put in possession of the lands where he was to remain until the defender paid the expenses and unlaws incurred through his contumacy. That done, 'he salbe herde in the principale cause movit agaynis hym nochtagaynstand- and the decrete of possessioune befor gevin'. Only if 'prescripcioune lauchful' ran against him by reason of the length of time for which his liabilities remained unsatisfied would he be prevented from answering the cause of fee and heritage. It seems clear that this statute is modifying the procedure not of spuilzie but of recognition before council. The pursuer is to be given possession without having either to establish that he was the last lawful possessor or to give a *borgh*. If the defender subsequently purges his contumacy, then the issue of last lawful possessor may be re-opened, unless prescription operates to prevent this. It is the reference to prescription which makes this interpretation particularly likely. Scots law has never known the possibility of acquiring ownership of land by prescription based on possession alone;[101] on the other hand, medieval canon law allowed the pursuer in an action where the defender was contumacious to be awarded interim possession of its subject matter which would become definitive after one year without challenge.[102] What the act of 1450 is saying here is that the possession awarded where the defender has persisted in contumacy cannot be challenged on the basis that the pursuer was not in fact the last lawful possessor: the pursuer's possession is now established, and it is for the defender to raise the action concerning the right to which the recognition was a preliminary. The references to 'causes of fee and heritage' obscure the meaning of the act from modern eyes; but the phrase was used because recognitions and determinations of possession by council were the opening stages of just such causes, not because council had then acquired a jurisdiction to decide them finally itself.

THE EMERGENCE OF THE FEE AND HERITAGE RULE

Earlier in this chapter, it was argued that in the course of the fifteenth century the idea that parliament and council could not act where there was a common-law remedy was gradually superseded. Perhaps the most likely explanation of this is that increasingly parties were allowed to raise actions before council by the king's 'emplesance' (this being perhaps linked with the development of the signet summons, a direct expression of the king's will). In 1458, the lords of session were given jurisdiction over most forms of civil action, it being indicated that in all these causes parties had 'ml fredome' to sue before either the session or the judge ordinary. The jurisdiction of the session included all 'accionis the quhilkis concernys nocht fee nor heretage', while there were also special provisions about spuilzie. In 'spoliacione of movabill gudis nocht tuiching fee nor heretage', the lords might proceed 'indifferentle'; but, in 'spoliacione . . . done becaus of landis or possessionis debatable or grondyt apone fee and heretage', then they were to call upon the sheriff to restore the ground 'without preiudice of any party tuichande thir fee and heretage'. This was to be done by the familiar processes of recognition: the lands were to be recognosced into the king's hands, the sheriff was to hold an inquest on who had been the last lawful possessor of the lands, and to him the king would give the lands on receipt of a *borgh*. Although the act does not say so expressly, this was presumably intended to be only the first step towards an action before the judge ordinary to determine where the ground right truly lay.[103] So, here again, the act is evidence of the limited competence of the sessions in cases of fee and heritage.

This act of 1458 is the first recorded use of the phrase 'fee and heritage' to define the limits of conciliar jurisdiction, and it is necessary to explain how that formulation of the rule emerged. The starting point is the idea that parliament and council had no jurisdiction where there was a common-law remedy. This idea survived the act of 1458; as was shown earlier, in 1469 and again in 1474 there were attempts to bring the jurisdiction of council back to its old limited scope.[104] More particularly, where an action related to some issue about landholding other than ownership, it remained the practice to remit the parties to some other remedy. Thus, as a number of cases demonstrate, where parties were 'grevit in exceding of marches and divise of land', a brieve of perambulation should be used, for 'the mater standis upon perambulacioun and redding of marchis'.[105] Similarly, brieves of division were appropriate for disputes between heirs-portioner or their representatives: for example, in 1498 council ordained that 'because thir partiis allegis thare portionaris of thir landis and for the contencione had ymangis thame thareof, that the chancellary be opin and that brevis of divisione be gevin thame efter the forme of the chancellary'.[106] In two other cases, the parliamentary auditors stated that the action should be begun by a brieve *de aqueductu*. Thus, in 1483, David Lauder of Popple and James Ogill agreed that their respective claims to the mill dam of

Popple should be determined by such a brieve,[107] while in 1491 James Mushet's action against John lord Drummond for the destruction of his mill and waterway of Tullygarth was remitted to the sheriff 'because thare is a breif of our soverane lordis chapell de aque ductu'.[108]

Another case of a different type came before the parliamentary auditors in 1479.[109] This concerned a land and tenement in Edinburgh to the ground right of which there were various claims. The matter having been often before both auditors and council previously, a final decision to set the matter before a 'great assize' was reached. Letters were to be addressed to the provost and bailies of Edinburgh to set a lawful day for the hearing, on forty days' notice to the parties. The assize was to be made up of the best and unsuspect persons of the burgh and, if required, of the other burghs round about. The purpose of the assize was to find who had right and was nearest and lawful heir to the lands, 'that thir may be a finale ende and the trew grund fundyn in the said mater, ande quhat beis fundin be the said gret assise to haf place and be kept in tyme tocum'. At first sight, it looks as though the letters to the provost and bailies would take the form of a brieve of right (in which, it will be recalled, the burgh court had jurisdiction), but from the language used it seems more likely that the procedure to be adopted was to be that known as 'the great assize of right'.[110] This action was one appropriate where, as in the 1479 case, there were several competing claims to a piece of land and it appears to have been common in, although not confined to, burghs.

In all these cases concerning land, the view of the court seems to have been that the parties should make use of an existing remedy available elsewhere to resolve their dispute. In none, it should be noted, had the fee and heritage exception been pleaded, and only in the example of the brieve *de aqueductu*[111] was the remedy suggested one involving a pleadable brieve. In actions relating to land, there was available a comprehensive range of remedies, and parties were expected to use them.

It is also this idea which lies behind the fee and heritage exception, where parties were told that their action should be taken before the 'judge ordinary', that is, the judge having jurisdiction at common law over the land in issue.[112] The availability of remedies in his court means that parliament or council ought not to act. So it is clear that the remit to the judge ordinary in the later fifteenth century is another way of expressing the idea, current in the fourteenth century, that the parties must resort to the common law. There is perhaps a change or development of vocabulary, but not in the basic idea. What is important, however, is that by the later fifteenth century this idea was operative only in cases relating to land and in particular in relation to disputes about ownership. What distinguished issues of landownership from other civil actions that they remained competent only in the courts of the ordinaries?

The answer must be the continuing force of the common-law rule that, when a pursuer sought to recover lands from the possession of another, he had to proceed by way of a pleadable brieve. This rule distinguished disputes over title to land from all others. No similar rule compelled the use of the brieves *de conventione* to enforce contracts or recover debts, or of the brieve *de proteccione regis infricta* to gain reparation for other personal wrongs. For this reason, it is submitted, issues of landownership remained distinct even in an era when the existence of other remedies was ceasing to exclude the jurisdiction of parliament and, more especially, council: the necessary forms of initial writ pertained to the sheriff, burgh or justiciary courts.

It remains to explain, however, why, if the fee and heritage restriction was thus connected with the brieve rule, it was expressed in terms not of freeholdings but of fee and heritage. This was not a direct result of the act of 1458. None of the subsequent fee and heritage cases refers to that act as might be expected if it were the immediate source of the rule. Moreover, the act referred only to the 'sessions'and not to parliament or the full council (although it is reasonable to suspect that by the 1470s council had inherited the jurisdiction of the sessions outlined in 1458.)[113] In the light of the earlier act of 1450, which refers to 'causes of fee and heritage',[114] it seems likely that the terminology had become established before 1458 as part of the development of which that act was itself the outcome.

The explanation to be advanced here is almost entirely speculative but not altogether without substance. It is based on the fact that, as shown earlier in this chapter, parliament and council enjoyed a jurisdiction over certain issues about the possession of land, in that the determination and maintenance of recent lawful possession was competent to them.[115] If, as seems possible, this led to talk of a possessory jurisdiction, then the familiar dichotomy of possessory and proprietary may have had some effect. In other chapters, it has been seen that medieval jurists saw the heritable title as the proprietary one, with all others being possessory.[116] Such an analysis was simplistic and misleading but, if and when made, it was capable of taking on a life of its own and effecting changes in the jurisdictional position. If issues about freeholdings were possessory, then a court with possessory jurisdiction could deal with them. So, the original limited nature of that possessory jurisdiction might be forgotten; the court would only be excluded from proprietary matters, that is, in the lawyers' vernacular, those touching the fee and heritage.

This in turn must have affected the brieve rule and the use of brieves. By contrast with the brieves of right and mortancestry where the pursuer had to show a heritable title, there is only one piece of indirect evidence for the 'possessory' brieve of novel dissasine after the 1450s (the act of 1504 referring to brieves pleadable before the justiciar). Was this because those dispossessed now had actions before parliament and council? Thus, for example, in 1459, Janet Borthwick successfully sued in parliament to recover the barony of Morton, Dumfriesshire, from which she claimed to have been *dejecta et expulsa* although she had a life interest as conjunct fiar with and widow of James Douglas, first lord of Dalkeith.[117] This certainly looks like a case where a brieve of novel dissasine would have been an appropriate remedy. An earlier case already mentioned, decided in 1430 when novel dissasine was certainly still in use, may have been of importance in changing the law and practice in cases of dispossession. This was the case about the possession of the lands of Luchald in the barony of Dalmeny, in which parliament overruled a plea that it should not hear the case, where the pursuer's complaint was of ejection from her property.[118] The petition of the Grahams of Hutton expressed the brieves rule in terms of fee and heritage rather than freeholding;[119] was this because at the time the petition was made the law had changed by virtue of the developing jurisdiction of parliament and council?

THE BRIEVE RULE AND FEE AND HERITAGE: CONCLUSIONS

The petition of the Grahams of Hutton mentions two rules which exclude the jurisdiction of the king's council, one concerning pleadable brieves, the other a statement about council and fee and heritage. There is no suggestion there that one rule follows from or is a consequence of the other. They appear independent and self-supporting. The picture thus given seems to be a true one, for the two rules did have a separate content and effect. Nevertheless, there was a link between them, the brieves rule being critical, it is suggested, in confining the jurisdiction of the central courts of parliament and council at a time when these bodies, and in particular the latter, were admitting an increasing number of actions before them as a matter of course. The procedure which the law required to be followed could not be used in courts other than those to which the appropriate pleadable brieves were addressed. The lack of record and of any contemporary accounts of the jurisdiction of parliament and council defeats any attempt to produce a definitive explanation of the shifts and changes which took place during the fourteenth and fifteenth centuries. The story is a complex one, involving many factors in Scottish legal history which are now beyond recovery. However, that there was connection between the two rules discussed in this book surely admits of little doubt. It is submitted that the emergence of the fee and heritage rule, whenever that took place, was linked with the brieves rule by virtue of the fact that the latter distinguished and marked off a category of disputes for uniquely restricted treatment under the procedures of the ordinary courts of the common law.

DEVELOPMENT OF THE SESSION'S JURISDICTION IN HERITAGE

Later sixteenth-century writers cited cases of the 1540s as authorities for the proposition that the Lords of Session enjoyed what had become an exclusive jurisdiction in heritage. Thus it is stated in Balfour's *Practicks*:[120]

> Item, the lordis of sessioun alanerlie, and na uther judge, ar jugeis competent to actiounis of reductioun of infeftmentis, evidentis, or sasines, and of all actiounis of heritage betwix all the liegis of this realme, spiritual or temporal, and to all obligatiounis and contractis followand as accessory thairupon, 20 Mart 1545, Sir James Caldwell contra Sir James Maisoun.

Sir John Skene also cites a case of the 1540s ('ult Februar 1542, Patrick Weems contrair Forbes of Reres') in his *De Verborum Significatione* for the proposition that the Lords of Council and Session were 'judges competent in all causes of heretage'. He points out that in earlier times questions of 'the ground richt and propertie of lands' had been determined before the justice-general by the brieve of right, but that in *Weems* the Lords had determined this process 'nocht to have bene nor yit to be thir mony yeires in use', so justifying their taking jurisdiction in such matters.[121] It is clear that Skene derived this decision from the practicks of John Sinclair, a collection of the decisions of the lords from 1540 to 1549 made by one of their number.[122] Under the heading, 'That reductioun of auld infeftmentis pertenis to the lordis of sessioun', appears the following passage:[123]

> The last of Februar anno eodem in causa Patricii Weymes contra dominum de Rires, the said lairdis procuratour allegit that the lordis of counsall wer na judges competent to the reductioun of his infeftment vi yeiris auld, becaus thairthrow vald cum in disputatioun of the rycht of his landis, quhilk ground rycht of lands aucht be act of parliament to be decydit be ane breif of rycht befoir the justice and nocht befoir the lordis of sessioun. The lordis of counsall nochtwithstanding decernit thame competent judges in this mater, sic as thai wer thir divers yeiris in use of calling sic materis befoir thame, and divers sic interlocutoris gevin, ut in causa domini de Sanquhair et in causa cuiusdam Pringill de Torsounis et aliis diversis, and als becaus the breif of rycht is nor hes nocht yit bene mony yeiris usit in this realme.

Although examination of the official record of this case in the Acts and Decreets reveals no reference to the desuetude of the brieve of right, it does show that the *prelocutor* for Forbes of Reres 'allegit the said mater was auld and that the lordis war na competent jugis thareto', and that the plea was repelled by a bench which probably did include John Sinclair.[124] It seems quite likely, therefore, that his report can be taken as evidence that in developing jurisdiction in heritage the Lords of Session were consciously departing from the old law requiring brieves. Indeed, it is possible that, when Forbes's *prelocutor* argued that the 'ground rycht of landis aucht be act of parliament to be decydit be ane breif of rycht', he was referring to the 1318 statute of Robert I providing that no man was to be ejected from his free holding except by pleadable brieve. No act of parliament other than one of 1504 refers to the brieve of right, and that act is concerned with procedure in doom-falsing rather than with the remedy provided by the brievet itself.[125] The 1318 act, on the other hand, is clear that a pleadable brieve is required in claims to land, and the *prelocutor* may only have been aware of the brieve of right as such a brieve still conceivably in use.

The desuetude of the pleadable brieves and so of the 1318 act must have been because parties seeking to recover lands were turning to other, less unsatisfactory remedies. The 1504 act on falsing the doom stated that 'thar has been grete abusioune of justice and grete expens to the partiis persewand thar land and heritage be the breve of rycht and other brevis pledabill be proponing of exceptiounis frivole, and borghis and recontraris and falsing of dumys, thro presumyng of delais.'[126] The act attempted to provide an accelerated procedure for falsing the doom. However, one attraction of going to council was that there was no appeal. By 1532, the year of the act for the erection of the College of Justice, it was being argued that the Lords were the most appropriate judges to try causes of heritage.[127] In one case, this was because sheriffs (that is, the officers to whose courts the brieve of right was directed) were 'small persounis of little knowledge and undirstanding to decid apoun auld hiritage'[128]; in another, because the sheriff and his deputes are 'oure simple of knowledge to decyde apoun auld heretage'.[129] There is a formulaic ring to this repetition which suggests that a well-known device for having cases heard by the Lords was being used. The remedy of advocation, by which the Lords took before themselves a cause begun in another court if reason to do so was shown, seems to have been taking shape in this period.[130] The formula of alleging the inadequacy of the lower court as a ground of transfer may have been used in the development of the remedy; if so, it would have been an important means of bringing causes of heritage before the Lords. Action before council may also have lessened the practical problems of suing in the local courts, where local prejudices and power structures, emerging not only through the presiding officer but also through the suitors and assizers, may often have been adverse to the interests of one of the parties to any litigation. In a number of cases, it appears that the parties to a dispute over heritage agreed to resort to the Lords rather than the judge ordinary.[131] It has also been suggested that use of possessory remedies such as wrongful occupation, spuilzie and molestation enabled the court to deal with questions truly affecting ownership and not just possession.[132] This thesis may gain support from looking back to the later fifteenth-century cases in which the fee and heritage exception was pleaded, which included actions of wrongful occupation, spuilzie of rents and animals, and withholding payment of annualrents.[133] It is at least possible that in some of these cases the pursuer was trying to invoke conciliar remedies while being perfectly aware of the risk that he would be forced to take action by brieve.

Another form of action before the Session which was of great importance in the development of its jurisdiction in heritage was the reduction of infeftments. In 1532 and 1533, it was still arguable that the Lords had no jurisdiction in such cases, presumably because, since a successful action would destroy a title to land, they touched heritage.[134] However, in *Duddingston v Duddingston* in 1533, the Lords declared themselves competent to reduce infeftments, while recognising that this meant acquiring jurisdiction in proceedings against heritage.[135] In 1539, it was decided that 'all summondis rasit for reductioun of infeftmentis be privilegiat, tablit and callit be the Monundayis table wolkly becaus the samin concernis tinsale of heritage'.[136] *Wemyss v Forbes* and *Caldwell v Mason* both fit into this development. *Wemyss* appears to be part of a reversal of a decision, made as recently as 1535, that the Lords could not reduce 'old' infeftments;[137] Sinclair's report of the case is headed 'That reductioun of auld infeftmentis pertenis to the lordis of sessioun'; and the exception pleaded on behalf of Forbes was that the lords were not competent judges on old infeftments. *Caldwell* asserts the exclusive nature of the jurisdiction. The record of the case, like the report in Balfour's *Practicks*, states that the Lords 'are in use to tak the decisioun of all actiounis of retretting [i.e. reduction] of infeftmentis, evidentis or seisingis to tharne selfis'[138] Here was a further important step: not only did the court have jurisdiction in heritage, but it would act to prevent other courts exercising such a jurisdiction. *Caldwell* is an example of the use of the remedy of advocation to enforce the court's will. The old position was being reversed: *Discours Particulier* confirms that the sheriff's jurisdiction was excluded before 1560.[139] It appears that neither *Wemyss* nor *Caldwell* was actually the first decision on the particular point for which each stood, however, or indeed on the general jurisdiction in heritage, which seems to have been accepted by the end of the 1530s.[140] Sinclair's report of *Wemyss* states that 'divers sic interlocutoris' had been given previously, while he also reports a case called *Wachtoun v Sinclair*, decided before *Caldwell* in 1543, to the effect that '*de iure et practica Scotie* thair is na juge spirituall nor temporall to reduce heretabill infeftment or cognitioun in materis of heretage bot the lordis of counsall alanerlie'.[141] Both *Wemyss* and *Caldwell* seem therefore to be links in a chain of decisions by which the court established its 'practick' and, in a piecemeal, step-by-step way, the meaning of its jurisdiction in heritage.

It therefore cannot be said categorically that the Lords expanded the jurisdiction of the court as a direct consequence of the act establishing the College of Justice in 1532, which expressly gave it competence over all civil actions.[142] Clearly, however, the statutory words could have provided an answer to any doubts about the power of the court to change its practice in this way. Murray's study of Sinclair's practicks suggests that the Lords were expanding their jurisdiction in a number of other fields as well in this period, and, although the erection of the College effected no change in the structure, personnel or record-keeping of the court, it does seem to have provided an impetus to its legal development.[143] The lawyers' tradition of the historic importance of events in 1532 may be mistaken as to specifics, but they do nonetheless mark some sort of divide between the law of medieval Scotland and the law which was now to evolve under the aegis of the increasingly powerful Lords of Session and the bar practising before them.

NOTES

1. *HMC Various Collections*, v, p. 77, amended from SRO, RH 4/124/ 1. See above p. 112.
2. See Dr Murray's introduction to *ADC*, iii, which he kindly allowed me to see in typescript in advance of publication in 1993.
3. The starting point is the works of R. K. Hannay, now gathered in *College of Justice*; see also A. A. M. Duncan, 'Central courts'; T. M. Chalmers, 'Thesis', chs 3 and 4; L. J. Macfarlane, *Elphinstone*, pp. 86–122, 420–4; A. R. Borthwick, 'Thesis', pp. 242–301.
4. For this discussion see O. J. Reichel, *A Complete Manual of Canon Law*, 2 vols (London, 1896), ii, pp. 210–21; F. W. Maitland, *Roman Canon Law in the Church of England* (London, 1898), p. 104; R. Naz, *Dictionnaire de Droit Canonique*, 7 vols (Paris, 1935), sv 'Ordinaire'; S. D. Ollivant, *Official*, pp. 19–22.
5. *Bracton*, f. 55b (ii, p. 166).
6. *Bracton*, f. 108 (ii, p. 306).
7. See *Dryb Lib*, pp. 77–8; S. D. Ollivant, *Official*, pp. 22–7.
8. *APS*, ii, p. 47 (c. 2).
9. *APS*, ii, p. 177 (c. 10).
10. *APS*, ii, p. 8 (c. 24).
11. *APS*, ii, p. 177 (c. 10); cf. ibid., pp. 8 (c. 24), 94 (c. 2).
12. *Cawdor Bk*, p. 104. On the distinction, reference is made to *Regiam*, but I have been unable to trace the passage.
13. S. D. Ollivant, *Official*, pp. 20–24.
14. See above, p. 25.
15. See above, pp. 105–13.
16. *ADA*, pp. 13, 15, 17 (regality of the earl of Angus); *ADC*, i, p. 188 (regality of archbishop of St Andrews). See above, pp. 112–13.
17. A. A. M. Duncan, 'Central courts', p. 328; Duncan, *James I*, p. 3.
18. A. A. M. Duncan, 'Central courts', pp. 337, 340.
19. *APS*, i, p. 505.
20. *APS*, i, p. 582; *Mort Reg*, i, appendix, no 12.

21. H. G. Richardson and G. O. Sayles, *Parliaments and Great Councils in Medieval England* (London, 1961) p. 37; A. Harding, 'Plaints', p. 80.
22. *APS*, ii, p. 177 (c. 10). See, for an example of a protected widow, the case of Ada Crab, discussed above, pp. 56–7, 201, 221.
23. See *APS*, ii, pp. 94 (c. 2) and 107 (c. 11), acts of 1469 and 1474 respectively.
24. See especially *Highland Papers*, ii, pp. 158–60. On the quarter seal, see J. M. Thomson, *Public Records*, pp. 75–6.
25. J. M. Thomson, *Public Records*, p. 75; cf. *RRS*, vi, p. 28.
26. A. A. M., Duncan, 'Central courts', p. 334 and sources there given.
27. R. K. Hannay, *College of Justice*, pp. 293–6.
28. See *APS*, i, pp. 498, 509, 535; R. K. Hannay, *College of Justice*, p. 280; *SHR*, xxix (1950), p. 3.
29. *APS*, ii, p. 224 (c. 5). See H. McKechnie, *Brieves*, pp. 23, 28: 'the death knell of brieves was probably the act of 1491'.
30. A. R. Borthwick, 'Thesis', pp. 340–4, 353–64.
31. W. C. Dickinson, '"Our Signet of the Unicom"', *SHR*, xxvi (1947), pp. 147–8.
32. SRO, *Mar and Kellie papers*, GD 124/6/4.
33. See *Pais Reg*, p. 70; *APS*, ii, p. 94 (c. 2).
34. *APS*, i, pp. 578–9.
35. See above, pp. 113–14, 156–8, 181–3.
36. See e.g. *ADA*, pp. 3, T23; *ADC*, i, pp. 161, 216; *ADC*, ii, p. 350; *ADC* (*Stair*), iii, pp. 44, 63, 139, 179.
37. *APS*, ii, p. 51 (c. 25).
38. R. K. Hannay, 'A fifteenth-century eviction', *SHR*, xxii (1925), p. 193.
39. *Arb Lib*, ii, no 123 (1456).
40. *ADA*, pp.' *123, 128*.
41. *ADC*, i, p. 161.
42. *ADC*, i, p. 216.
43. *ADC*, i, p. 419.
44. E.g. *ADA*, pp. 10, 48; *ADC*, ii, pp. 212, 258.
45. *ADC* (*Stair*), iii, p. 145.
46. E.g. *ADC*, i, pp. 5, 6–7, 25, 36, 57, 67–8, 223; *ADC*, ii, p. 175; *ADC* (*Stair*), iii, p. 139.
47. For this, see APS, ii, pp. 32 (c. 2) and 36 (c. 7). The name spuilzie, and the principle of immediate restoration of possession, recall the canonist *actio spolii*, and it is significant that the earlier of the two statutes just cited is primarily concerned with 'kyrk gudis'. See also the important case of 1369 recorded in *Moray Reg*, no 153, which is concerned with spoliation of multures claimed by the priory of Pluscarden and disputed by Robert Chisholm, lord of Quarrywood, who defies an ecclesiastical sentence on the matter, leading to the invocation of the secular arm and the rule that no-one is to be ejected from heritage without the king's pleadable brieve (this point in the case is discussed above, p. 111).
48. *AB Ill*, iv, p. 43.
49. *APS*, ii, p. 47 (c. 2).
50. See below, p. 235.
51. *Pais Reg*, pp. 82–4.

52. W. Fraser, *Douglas*, iii, no 87.
53. *HMC*, xv (8), p. 45 (no 84).
54. *ADA*, pp. 13, 15.
55. See *ADC*, ii, pp. 394, 396.
56. See *ADA*, pp. 9, 13.
57. *ADC*, i, p. 78.
58. *ADC*, i, p. 405.
59. *ADA*, p. 94; *ADC*, i, p. 33.
60. *ADC*, i, p. 63.
61. H. H. Monteath, 'Heritable rights', in *ISLH*, p. 187.
62. *QA (Fergus)*, ch. 42; *QA (APS)*, ch. 40; *QA (Cooper)*, ch. 57.
63. *ADC*, i, p. 58.
64. *ADC*, i, p. 18.
65. For another, more complex case concerning annualrents which was remitted to the judge ordinary as concerning fee and heritage, see *ADC*, i, p. 118. The precise nature of the dispute is unclear.
66. See generally H. L. MacQueen, 'Jurisdiction in heritage'.
67. *RMS*, ii, no 1305.
68. *ADC*, i, p. 22.
69. 'Jurisdiction in heritage', pp. 68–75.
70. *ADC*, i, pp. 65–6.
71. For Margaret's right to Wester Cruivie, see *RMS*, ii, no 1303. For all the issues arising, see 'Jurisdiction in heritage', pp. 72–4.
72. A. A. M. Duncan, 'Central courts', p. 328.
73. *HMC*, xiv (3), p. 15 (no 24).
74. *APS*, xii, p. 18 (no 32).
75. In 'Councils general 1404–1423', *SHR*, xxxv (1956), pp. 141–2.
76. On this form of recognition, see J. Skene, *DVS*, sv 'Recognition', no 5.
77. *APS*, i, pp. 551, 553.
78. W. Fraser, *Carlaverock*, ii, no 31.
79. *Highland Papers*, ii, pp. 152–75.
80. *HMC*, vi (1), p. 670.
81. *HMC*, xv (8), p. 45 (no 84). Note that it was also decreed that with reference to William's claim for five pounds he should pursue his right before the judge ordinary because he had failed to make proof at the term assigned.
82. *HMC*, v, appendix, pp. 629–30.
83. *Yester Writs*, no 137.
84. W. Fraser, *Grant*, iii, no 37
85. SRO, *Spens of Lathallan writs*, GD 1/1042/5.
86. *AB Ill*, iii, p. 323; *APS*, xii, p. 25 (no 46); *AB Ill*, iii, pp. 326–7; *AB Coll*, 284.
87. *APS*, ii, p. 134.
88. *ADC*, i, p. *107.
89. *ADA*, p. 159. See H. L. MacQueen, 'Jurisdiction in heritage', p. 74.
90. See *ADA* and *ADC*, i and ii, indices, sv 'Recognition'.
91. *APS*, i, pp. 505, 582. See above, pp. 52, 157, 219.
92. See above, p. 157.
93. *Scots Peerage*, iii, pp. 161–3; vi, pp. 138–40.
94. For Henry Douglas, see *Scots Peerage*, vi, pp. 364–5.
95. *MortReg*, ii, nos 190–2.

96. See *Mort Reg*, ii, nos 194 and 217. For Crossraguel, Lanarkshire (Glassford parish), see *RMS*, i, no 490 and *Mort Reg*, ii, no 106.

97. *Mort Reg*, ii, no 194.

98. *RMS*, ii, no 146; *APS*, ii, p. 28 (no 6).

99. *APS*, i, p. 552.

100. *APS*, ii, p. 37 (c. 18); A. A. M. Duncan, 'Central courts', p. 333.

101. Thomas Craig, *JF*, II, 1, viii; C. D'O. Farran, *Land Law*, p. 187.

102. O. J. Reichel, *Canon Law*, ii, p. 274 note 84.

103. *APS*, ii, p. 47 (c. 2). For different interpretations, see A. A. M. Duncan, 'Central courts', p. 332, and A. Grant, *Independence and Nationhood*, p. 160.

104. *APS*, ii, p. 94 (c. 2); *APS*, ii, p. 107 (c. 11); and see above, p. 220.

105. *ADA*, pp. 76, 78; *ADC*, i, pp. 29, 62, 71, 72, 394.

106. *ADC*, ii, p. 119; cf. *ADA*, p. 67.

107. *ADA*, p. *119.

108. *ADA*, p. 147.

109. *ADA*, p. 83. Other relevant references are *ADA*, p. 61; *ADC*, i, pp. 17, 43; *APS*, ii, p. 133.

110. For other examples, see *Melr Lib*, ii, no 526; W. Fraser, *Maxwell Inventories*, no 18 (misunderstood as a *brieve* of right in H. McKechnie, *Brieves*, p. 19); W. Fraser, *Carlaverock*, ii, no 35; *Dunf Recs*, no 46; and *ADC*, i, p. 21.

111. Although *aqueductu* is not among the pleadable brieves in the lists surviving from the medieval period, it was an offshoot of the brieve of novel dissasine: see above, pp. 156–61.

112. See above, pp. 217–18.

113. See above, p. 235.

114. *APS*, ii, p. 37 (c. 18).

115. See above, pp. 228–31.

116. See above, pp. 157–8, 204–7.

117. *APS*, ii, p. 79 (no 42); *RMS*, ii, no 224.

118. *RMS*, ii, no 146; *APS*, ii, p. 28, no 6.

119. *HMC Various Collections*, v, p. 77.

120. Sir James Balfour, *Practicks*, i, p. 269.

121. J. Skene, DVS, sv '*Breve de Recto*'.

122. On Sinclair's practicks, see A. L. Murray, 'Sinclair's practicks,' in *Lawmaking and Lawmakers in British History* (London, 1980), pp. 90–104.

123. For this text of Sinclair's report of *Wemyss v Forbes*, see H. L. MacQueen, 'Jurisdiction in heritage', p. 63.

124. SRO, *Acts and decreets*, CS 7/1/1, ff. 248v – 250r, printed in H. L. MacQueen, 'Jurisdiction in heritage', pp. 64–6. For Sinclair's presence, see also ibid., p. 66.

125. For the 1504 act, see *APS*, ii, p. 254 (c. 41), and above, pp. 161–2.

126. *APS*, ii, p. 254 (c. 41).

127. See *Acta Sessionis* (Stair), case nos 30, 33, 70.

128. *Acta Sessionis* (Stair), p. 46.

129. *Acta Sessionis* (Stair), p. 104.

130. H. L. MacQueen, 'Jurisdiction in heritage', pp. 83–4.

131. E.g. *Acta Sessionis* (Stair), case nos 30, 33, 70.

132. By Lord Clyde in *ADC* (Stair), iii, introduction, p. xli; and by W. C. Dickinson, 'Administration of justice', p. 350.

133. See above, pp. 222–8.
134. *Set Acta Sessionis (Stair)*, case nos 15 (also printed in *Wigt Chrs*, p. 143) and 89.
135. *Acta Sessionis (Stair)*, case no 89.
136. *Acts of Council (Public Affairs)*, p. 478. For 'privileged causes', see R. K. Hannay, *College of Justice*, pp. 28–34, 203–4, 207–8, 213, 296.
137. *Acts of Council (Public Affairs)*, p. 440.
138. SRO, *Acta dominorum concilii et sessionis*, CS 6/20, ff. 18r–v, printed in H. L. MacQueen, 'Jurisdiction in heritage', pp. 80–1.
139. P. G. B. McNeill, *'Discours Particulier'*, p. 109.
140. *Acts of Council (Public Affairs)*, pp. 484, 486.
141. Edinburgh University Library, Laing MS III 388a, c. 322.
142. *APS*, ii, p. 335 (c. 2).
143. A. L. Murray, 'Sinclair's practicks', p. 98; see also W. D. H. Sellar, 'Common Law', p. 94.

9

Conclusions

This study has shown that for most of the medieval period there existed in Scotland a structure of legal remedies for the recovery of land, i.e. the brieves of novel dissasine, mortancestry and right. In general, the brieves were issued in the king's name and were addressed to the king's officers; they can be seen as central in the general development of regularised royal justice in the thirteenth century, and hence of a Scottish common law. The law compelled the use of the remedies by means of the rule that no-one in possession could be put out of land except by legal action begun by pleadable brieve. The brieves led to action in royal rather than feudal courts, although this needs to be qualified by reference to the franchise enjoyed by many regalities, that of issuing pleadable brieves to commence litigation in courts held before the lord's officers rather than the king's. However, it is clear that this regalian jurisdiction was exercised not on the basis that the lord as such enjoyed the right to determine disputes about the ownership of land held of him, but by virtue of a royal grant of what would otherwise be royal privileges.

The ultimate origin of the brieve system lay in the exercise by the king of powers and duties which were derived from the concepts of the king's peace and the king's protection. Just how general was the king's peace and how comprehensive the king's protection in the twelfth century cannot be told, and most probably it varied greatly from time to time and from place to place. It is clear, however, that the king, or others under his command, could and did intervene in many situations, including disputes over land, debt and general wrongdoing, where there was a complaint of breach of his peace and protection, default of justice, or failure to do right. The king might also legislate, probably needing the consent of his great men, but nonetheless manifesting a power to make new law and change old custom. Royal authority was made effective through officers who held courts in which disputes could be determined. There is evident through the twelfth and thirteenth centuries a growing systematisation and regularisation of royal justice, achieved not at the expense of feudal justice but clearly subordinating it to that of the king.

It is in this context of growing regularisation of royal justice that the introduction of the brieves of novel dissasine, mortancestry and right must be set. The brieves were plainly developed in imitation of the equivalent writs found in late twelfth-century England, although the period of their introduction into Scotland, or, in the case of the brieve of right, of evolution into a final form, was appreciably later. Nonetheless, much of this study has shown the pertinence of the arguments of Milsom about the English writs to the explanation of the origins of the Scottish brieves. The lord-tenant relationship is clearly one of the keys to understanding the legal and social world in which the brieves took effect, and one of the aims of the brieves was to regulate that relationship. The lord's failure to infeft a deceased tenant's heir was probably the typical case of mortancestry in the beginning, while the act introducing novel dissasine in 1230 is explicit in its identification of lords as typical dissaisors, perhaps even as the prime category of dissaisor.[1] The complex origins of the brieve of right certainly included the idea of providing a remedy when a lord failed to do justice, or right, in a case concerning one of his men. The lord's court of the twelfth and thirteenth centuries was a forum in which disputes about lands held of the lord were discussed, settled and perhaps, where settlement was not achievable, adjudged. The evidence does not permit a conclusion as to whether in such matters the lord's court was immoveably biased in favour of the sitting tenant, although most probably there was a preference for the status quo so long as the lord was happy with it. This may provide one context for a lord failing to do justice in respect of his man, and hence for royal intervention by brieve addressed either to the lord commanding him to do right, or to the king's officer commanding him to act on the lord's default.

It is difficult to determine what norms applied to the lord-tenant relationship in the twelfth and early thirteenth centuries by which failure to do justice might be determined; but it does seem appropriate to say that there were norms, even if their content was not precisely defined. Our best evidence of these norms is the charters in which the relationship was formally expressed. It must be accepted that these charters do not tell the full story of any particular relationship. The striking point is that, from an early date in the twelfth century, the contents of charters settled along broadly standardised lines which were to remain common form for centuries. It is from these that we can tell that there was a common understanding that land was held of a lord for service to the lord, that there were expectations that land and lordship would pass on to heirs, and that there was a language and terminology in which such ideas could be expressed.[2] Were such norms 'law', in the absence of any regular external mechanism of control? It may be that this is an anachronistic question, and that the positivist assumptions of commentators in the debate on this question in England and France would not have been made in the Middle Ages. Paul Hyams has noted that the progress of the Scots charter towards regularity and standardisation occurred without anything comparable to the development of the common law in England, and has suggested that it is to be explained by increasing recognition of the value of a written record or proof of transactions.[3] This is certainly so, but it does not explain the formation of a consensus round a particular vocabulary and style to give written expression to the transaction and relationship between lord and tenant. At the same time, however, it must be acknowledged that charters are generally silent on points which are nevertheless mentioned on occasion – for example, warrandice, or on what is to happen when the tenant does not render his service. The interpretation of such general but not total silence is fraught with difficulty. In the end, therefore, while it is argued here that there were such things as 'norms' governing twelfth-century feudal society, it cannot be said that these were sufficiently clear-cut and certain to mean that the introduction of novel dissasine, mortancestry and right was simply to give them greater effect.

The desire to regulate feudal lordship in accordance with feudal norms cannot in any event be the whole story, at least in Scotland. The 1230 act which introduced novel dissasine makes the point with its reference to dissasine not just by a lord but also by any other man. The present study suggests at least two other settings in which the brieves were important: those provided by the church and the burghs. Ecclesiastical corporations clearly used the brieves in the protection of their own interests, as for example when Coldingham priory reclaimed the lands of Swinewood from Patrick, earl of Dunbar, in 1231,[4] and the protection of the church's property from the depredations of lay lords and neighbours may have been a motivating force behind the introduction of novel dissasine in particular. Protection of the church was less likely to lie behind the brieves of mortancestry and right, where in general the pursuer's claim was based on a heritable title. On the other hand, the existence of these remedies may have given laymen some protection against the claims of the church, whether based on lordship or some other right arising, for example, under canon law. In the twelfth and thirteenth centuries, ecclesiastical claims to land were often made in the church courts against laymen, who in turn invoked secular jurisdiction. This was clearly a contentious issue throughout the period, and may provide one possible explanation of the regularisation of royal justice in the field of claims to land.

The position in the burghs also raises complex questions. At first sight, it seems to support the theory that novel dissasine and mortancestry arose primarily in a feudal context, since neither brieve was found in the burghs. There, by and large, the king was lord, and the burgesses held their lands of him. Yet the brieve of right was used in the burgh courts, and this throws important light on the introduction of the other brieves elsewhere. A key feature of both novel dissasine and mortancestry is the employment of the assize or recognition as the invariable mode of proof. With the brieve of right outwith the burgh, though, there is evidence that one mode of proof – perhaps in the twelfth and early thirteenth centuries, the only mode of proof for this kind of case – was the duel. However, exemption from the duel was a vital burghal privilege, established in Scotland in the twelfth century and probably fairly general in all burghs by 1230 if not before. In the burghs, the mode of proof in land cases may already have been through the witness of neighbours, whether as compurgators or as assizers, and so there was no need for the special privilege conferred upon landward parties by the brieves of novel dissasine and mortancestry.

The suggestion that part of the impetus lying behind the introduction of novel dissasine and mortancestry was a move away from, or against, the duel takes on support from the general historical context in the reign of Alexander II. By prohibiting clerical participation in ordeals in 1215 (a prohibition to which Alexander gave some effect in his 1230 legislation[5]), the fourth Lateran council had forced new thought and action on modes of proof, and had undermined the credibility of the duel. The church disapproved of the duel on the grounds that it involved the shedding of Christian blood.[6] Clergy who participated in duels were subject to canonical penalties, and it may be that the use of the duel for property disputes in secular tribunals lay behind the church's regular resort to its own courts to defend its lands even against lay parties. Denunciations of the 'pestiferous custom' of the duel involving the clergy in Scotland were made to the bishop of Glasgow by Pope Innocent III and the archbishop of Lyons between 1200 and 1216, and these may have borne fruit in one of King Alexander's statutes of 1230 making provision for the clergy to have an alternative to the duel in cases of theft.[7] Another of the 1230 statutes shows concern to regulate the duel generally.[8] Such concerns were not confined to Scotland. In England, the Grand Assize had already been offered in 1179 as an alternative to battle for the resolution of disputes about land. In 1231, the Emperor Frederick II restricted the availability of the duel in Italy, and in 1258 Louis IX abolished it in the French royal demesne.[9] It was perfectly possible, therefore, for men to think of the need to provide alternatives to the duel in the thirteenth century, and the evidence suggests that this was a matter of concern to the lawmakers at Scone in 1230. The introduction of the recognition of novel dissasine in Scotland thus fits into a European pattern, consciously turning away from the old forms of proof and replacing them with new ones, in particular the sworn testimony of witnesses.

The argument so far suggests that in one way and another the church had a good deal to do with the development of the brieve system in the thirteenth century. If so, then the Romano-canonical distinction between proprietary and possessory remedies may have played some part in the way the brieves were conceptualised from the beginning. The distinction was well-developed in the canon law by the mid-thirteenth century, and had been used in Scotland by ecclesiastical judges delegate in 1226. The bishop of Moray was seeking to recover the lands of Rhynie from various laymen, and the judges delegate granted him possession while expressly reserving the question of property.[10] By the time novel dissasine was introduced in 1230, it was also familiar doctrine in England that novel disseisin and *mort d'ancestor* were possessory rather than proprietary. The effect of this was that, probably from the start, novel dissasine and mortancestry were thought of as possessory remedies, concerned with the most recent state of affairs, and the results of which could be reversed later by the proprietary claim under the brieve of right. This is not to say, however, that in every case of novel dissasine a later proprietary action was anticipated; often, and perhaps normally, the possessory remedy was all that was required, and was the means whereby the person with right in the fullest sense regained his property. The importance of the possible influence of the possessory/proprietary dichotomy is what it tells us about the overall policy lying behind the development of the brieves: a concern with preservation of the status quo by protecting security of tenure and orderly inheritance. These were matters with which the community as a whole was concerned, and of which it was the best witness; hence the appropriateness of using the recognition of neighbours in the community to determine what was the status quo.

It seems clear, however, that the development of the brieves is not to be explained by any general tenurial crisis comparable to that arising in twelfth-century England and underlying the rise of the common law under Henry II. There were no upheavals in twelfth- and early thirteenth-century Scotland which left a large class of disinherited set against another with seisin. As in any medieval society, there were many disputes over possession and inheritance, and the customs of inheritance may not have been uniform, consistent or completely worked out; but there is no evidence to suggest that this was a general political or social problem requiring sustained royal intervention on the scale undertaken by Henry II. If a political explanation for Scottish developments is to be found, it lies in the controversy between the church and secular jurisdiction.

What was the effect of the operation of the brieves, and the associated rule requiring their use in cases about free holdings? If lords once enjoyed a purely feudal jurisdiction to adjudicate on claims to hold land of them, or at least to have such actions begin in their courts – and they probably did so in the twelfth and thirteenth centuries – it seems to have been virtually, if not entirely, eliminated by the later medieval period. The rule that no man could be ejected from his land without the king's pleadable brieve may have meant initially that claims could still be made in the lord's court, with the initial brieve being addressed to the lord; but, by the fourteenth century, pleadable brieves were directed to the king's courts alone. The later medieval lord had one role in proprietary disputes, however: the power to determine which of the contending parties was the most recent lawful possessor, which gave the successful one the benefit of the brieve rule by compelling the other to determine which of the brieves he should use to make his claim in the king's court.

However, lords retained disciplinary powers over their tenants, the exercise of which could affect tenants' possession of their lands in appropriate cases. These disciplinary powers emphasised the point that the tenant's holding was conditional on the performance of obligations to the lord. This basic principle seems to have been unaffected by the rule requiring the use of brieves to eject somebody from his land. Perhaps one effect is to be detected, however, in that the lord who exercised disciplinary powers against land did not thereby deprive the tenant permanently of his property, but was instead bound simply to hold it, or to let the tenant retake possession on an interim basis, until the matter in issue was resolved. The tenant's position in law in relation to the land was therefore rather stronger than the lord's, since he had rights which survived his failure to fulfil the obligations owed to the lord.

How are we to understand the contrast that seems to emerge between the Scottish and English situation? Robert Burgess has written as follows on the matter:[11]

> the essential point must surely be that the object of the Scottish brieves was simply to provide a remedy: the background of transference of actions from local to national courts was just not there, if only because there were no national courts of the centralised type set up by Henry II in England. And it was this lack of transference that was the important point, for the existence of a powerful local jurisdiction under little or no central control could be and was an instrument of power and influence in the hands of its proprietor.

Yet this may miss the really important point. It is true that for most of the period with which we have been concerned there was no 'centralised national court'; and it may also be important that Scottish lordships retained a compact territorial character until well on in the later medieval period, a factor tending towards relative self-containment of disputes and their resolution within the lordship. There was also, however, a decentralised system of royal justice which made claims of superiority over other local courts through appellate mechanisms of various kinds, intervened in local courts' affairs when there was default of justice and commanded the use of royal remedies in particular cases. However, it was never intended to use this structure of royal justice to challenge local feudal jurisdictions; that would indeed have been, as Milsom put it, to cut across the grain and to depart from the framework of the medieval world. The brieves were certainly intended to work in a world where lords held courts for and of their tenants. As we have seen, some of the constrictions on these courts in England arose as a result of particular interpretations of the requirement of a writ in cases touching freehold. In *Glanvill*, however, these effects were not yet fully worked out, and in other circumstances different developments might have taken place. Later medieval Scots lawyers drew on *Glanvill* to provide a legal framework for the world in which they worked, and that view of the law certainly upheld the exercise of the disciplinary jurisdiction without writ. Perhaps *Glanvill* strengthened the lord's court by providing clear rules where hitherto there had been rather ill-defined and variable customs; perhaps it simply reflected what was already there. The same may even have been true of the *Libri Feudorum*. The essential point is that the brieves of novel dissaine, mortancestry and right were not fundamentally incompatible with strong feudal courts.

Another important point about Scottish royal justice is that, being decentralised, it never lost its connection with the local community. Unlike the English royal justices, the justiciars' courts were made up of the suitors of the sheriffdom, upon whom fell the responsibility of making judgment. Although no doubt the justiciar and his assessors from the king's council were dominant figures in the deliberations of the court, nonetheless the local community of barons and freeholders had a voice which could not have been ignored. Thus, where the English royal justices came into the local community and imposed their own view of the law and of the correct way to settle disputes, so to speak from above, in Scotland decision-making in court combined views from above with those from below who would be affected by it. This may even have encouraged compromise rather than adjudication, a practice to be discussed in more detail later in this chapter. Here, though, we may note an interesting example of 1348 which shows the suitors of the justiciar's court at Forfar supplicating the abbot of Arbroath to settle a dispute with the burgesses of Dundee over liability to pay toll, with the abbot being moved eventually not to exact damages but to accept simple restitution for the wrong done to him and his men.[12] Here, the interest of the community of Forfar in the existence of good neighbourhood between its most significant burgh and religious house outweighs what may have been strict legal right; and the presiding royal officer seems happy to accept the compromise thus achieved. Taken altogether, therefore, we can see that Scottish royal justice did not by its very existence as a regular and formal system necessarily challenge or undermine local jurisdictions.

The brieve system was in its heyday in the fourteenth and fifteenth centuries, and around each brieve there grew bodies of substantive and procedural law. This reinforces the argument that there was no break in the continuity of Scottish legal development as a result of the Wars of Independence. Indeed, there is some reason to think that use of and thinking about the brieves was stimulated in this period by something akin to the tenurial crisis following the Anarchy of Stephen in twelfth-century England. It was therefore entirely appropriate for contemporary Scots lawyers to look to *Glanvill* for statements of the principles on which the land law rested; his world, and the problems faced by the courts of his time, mirrored those in early fourteenth-century Scotland. The 1318 legislation of Robert I dealt with each of the brieves and expanded the scope of both novel dissasine and mortancestry in certain respects. Thus, from 1318, mortancestry could be brought in respect of claims derived from the title of grandparents, and this became a very common type of claim thereafter. In novel dissasine, the rule generally was that the action had to be brought in the lifetime of the dissaisor; but where a dissasine was by a group of people, the 1318 legislation allowed the action to be brought so long as any member of that group remained alive, and even though the principal dissaisor – presumably the lord or leader of the group – was dead. In both these instances, it is clear that the legislators were anxious to allow claimants to reach back as far as possible in time, perhaps to enable them to reach the settled conditions before the death of Alexander III in 1286. Certainly, such claimants might have made use of the brieve of right in both instances, but the procedure on that brieve was lengthy and slow; it was in the interests of stability and peace if all claims could be settled as speedily as possible. Exactly the same policy was given effect in other ways in 1318; thus most of the act on novel dissasine concentrates on protecting the position of the sitting tenant, while the act which reaffirmed, or removed doubts concerning, the rule that no man could be put out of his lands except by pleadable brieve reminded claimants that self-help was frowned upon. Like Henry II, therefore, Robert I sought a balance between the protection of existing sasines on the one hand and hereditary claims on the other. Inevitably, in this situation, claims became more complex, and the recognition of this fact surely lies behind the theme of the other 1318 provisions referring to the brieves of novel dissasine, mortancestry and right, which is that pursuers should state their claim fully rather than in set words, and that defenders should be given ample opportunity to consider their response before they are regarded as having entered their defences.

The choice of brieve depended on the nature of the interest in land being claimed, and on the facts which had led to the person claiming being out of possession. Their continuing relevance is to be explained primarily by the structure of land law, which might lead to several coexisting rights in land, and a consequent need to define the scope and limits of each of these. There was of course the concept of tenure, where land was held of another, and this remained fundamental to the whole of land law. However, there were many other possible rights. The widow's claim to terce was clearly a source of conflict between her and her deceased husband's heir or perhaps his lord. The situation would be exacerbated if the widow married again. Conjunct infeftments of a married couple raised similar problems, because the surviving spouse held the whole of the property for which the anxious heir was waiting. Again, grants of life interests in land, with the heritable fee becoming a merely reversionary interest while the grant lasted, had the potential to cause conflict, while grants which diverted heritage away from the heir often opened up disputes between that heir and the grantee. Tailzies in favour of heirs-male often also had a similar effect where the heir at common law was female. Again, land was used as a source of security for credit, leading to conflicts between the debtor and the creditor and, perhaps, the debtor's lord. Leasing was another form of exploitation of landed resources in which persons might come to occupy land in which others had rights, and was also productive of disputes – for example, whether possession was held under a lease or by a grant in feu-ferme, or whether it was heritable.

It was against this background that the brieves of novel dissasine, mortancestry and right functioned. What was their effect on the substantive land law? One important point may have been the idea of ownership within a tenurial framework of landholding. Although the lord retained certain rights in the land, and the power to deprive the tenant of his land for breach of duty, it is clear, as already noted, that by the fourteenth century the lord could not deprive the tenant of the land permanently. Indeed, the lord's seizure of the land for breach of duty was largely symbolic in the eyes of the law, since the tenant could regain possession pending a determination of his dispute with the lord. Similarly, it does not appear that on a tenant's death the lord had any right other than to claim the casualty of non-entry if the heir failed to claim the land immediately. The brieves of mortancestry and right had succeeded in eliminating any discretion that there might once have been. The idea that land held in demesne was 'owned', albeit that it was held of another, emerges clearly in the terminology of the fifteenth century, when such land was described as the holder's 'property' and contrasted with his 'tenandry', the land held of him by others on a feudal grant.[13] In turn, the tenants of the 'tenandry' also had 'property' if they held in demesne, whereas their lord did not. The survival of the proprietary remedy of the brieve of right must also have ensured the survival of a legal idea of ownership of land.

Novel dissasine also required some definition of sasine. Sasine was originally possession of land. When a person entered land, he would be given sasine symbolically by the lord or other grantor, but sasine was also continued enjoyment and exploitation, for example by sowing and harvesting crops, or by uplifting rents. One of the important changes which probably occurred in the fourteenth century was the introduction of a documentary element into the legal concept of sasine. This was the notarial instrument of sasine, in which a notary recorded the execution of the ceremony of symbolical delivery. The earliest example so far discovered is of 1385.[14] In part, this may have become necessary because, in the increasingly complicated structure of land law, reliance on what people had seen and heard as a basis for the protection of sasine was not enough. In other words, landholders needed the evidence which instruments of sasine provided to guard their interests adequately. By the fourteenth century, novel dissasine no longer dealt simply with cases where one person had recently put another out of visible possession and enjoyment of land; it could reach back a long way in time and could undo quite complex transactions. In this situation, where one's sasine might be challenged through the brieve, or where one might wish to be sure that the remedy provided by the brieve would be available in case of need, having notarial evidence of the giving of sasine made good sense.

The brieve system also affected the continuing development of the structures of royal justice in the later medieval period. The exclusion of conciliar justice from matters of fee and heritage in the fifteenth century is clearly to be explained by the background of continuing resort to action by pleadable brieves made necessary by the rule requiring their use. The decline of the brieve system as the principal means in law of resolving disputes over rights to land, which seems to have begun in the second half of the fifteenth century, was completed when the Session, which was the final product of the development of conciliar justice, assumed jurisdiction in fee and heritage in the first half of the sixteenth century. However, the king's council in its various guises had already long played a role in disputes about land, which was identical to the one played by lords and noted above, the power to recognosce disputed territory and to give interim possession to whoever was the last lawful possessor. This seems likely to have affected the brieve of novel dissasine in providing a means of restoring sasine to one who had been dispossessed, and it is significant that it was the first of the brieves to disappear. In addition, many other actions over which council had jurisdiction were related to the possession of land and the exercise of rights therein. Long before the end of the fifteenth century, therefore, disputes about land were part of council's staple diet of cases, albeit strictly speaking only as a means of supplementing the structure of remedies provided for by the common law. From this, and from litigants' perception of tactical advantages of various kinds to be gained from action before council, it was perhaps only a small step to the desuetude of the brieve system and to the assumption of a fee and heritage jurisdiction by the Session.

What were the disadvantages of the brieve system which led the fifteenth-century litigant to turn elsewhere? A variety of factors seem identifiable. In the 1530s, people claiming heritage before the Session argued that the sheriff was not sufficiently knowledgeable to deal with their cases. The lack of knowledge among those in the sheriff courts was also a cause of concern underlying the 'Education Act' of 1496, which commanded barons and freeholders to send their eldest sons to 'the sculis of art and jure' so that 'thai that ar schireffis or jugeis ordinaris may have knawlege to do justice that the pure pepill suld have na neid to seike oure soverane lordis principale auditouris for ilk small iniure'.[15] Such concerns must have extended beyond the sheriff to the suitors and assizers in his court, who would also be the suitors and assizers before the justiciar when he came into the sheriffdom. The brieve system was founded on the decision of the assize, which had begun as a group of witnesses – men who best knew the verity. That had worked when novel dissasine and mortancestry dealt with recent facts; but, by the fifteenth century, cases turned not on what the assizers had seen and heard themselves but on the interpretation of complicated technical documents (which might be forged) and the recollection of facts, sometimes many decades old, by witnesses whose credibility would have to be judged by the assizers. The difficulties which historians face today in reconstructing what led to particular cases from the surviving documents about them were probably no less for the courts which had to deal with them. It has already been suggested that the need for better evidence than what people had seen and heard led to the instrument of sasine in the fourteenth century. Sometimes the court can be seen going wrong. In 1455, for example, an assize of mortancestry at Dumfries held Margaret Mundell entitled to two quarters of certain lands in the sheriffdom which were in the possession of two of her sisters. The view of the assize seems to have been that the two sisters were illegitimate (thereby precluding them from the inheritance) while Margaret presumably was not. If so, the assize was mistaken, as there had been a papal decision on the legitimacy of Margaret's sisters before 1437. The ignorance of the assize may be understandable, however; the women's father did not spend much time on his Dumfriesshire lands, and the legitimation procedure eighteen years before may have been either ill-remembered or altogether unknown, since it had to be reaffirmed for other reasons in 1469. An assize drawing on local knowledge only was unlikely to be able to handle this complex situation with any reliability.[16]

Another difficulty was delay. This was inherent in the procedure associated with the brieve of right, with its four essonzies before the action even began, the possibility of warrandice claims and other aspects. In addition, the action could only be begun at the thrice-yearly head courts of the sheriff and the burgh. The brieves of novel dissasine and mortancestry were designed for greater despatch: no essonzies and, in the case of novel dissasine, no sisting of process for the calling of warrantors. Even with these brieves, however, the opportunity to raise them came at best twice a year with the arrival of the justice ayre. While it was possible to obtain a specially commissioned justiciar to deal with the case, this must have added to the expense involved. Once any of the brieves was in court, the time had arrived for the pleading of dilatory exceptions, dealing not with the substance of the claim but with objections to the manner in which it was brought. In particular, there might be exceptions to the brieve itself: that it was not in due form, or that it was 'rasit and blobit' (erased and blotted) in 'suspect placis', such as the names of the parties or the lands, the cause upon which the brieve had been purchased, or its date.[17] The pleading of such exceptions seems to have been a constant cause of concern to parliament in the fifteenth century, which legislated for their control at regular intervals. Only once all such matters were out of the way would the merits of the case begin to be considered, with further pleadings of law and of peremptory exceptions. On all or any of these pleadings the decision of the court could not be final, for there was still the possibility of appeal by way of falsing the doom. Thus, cases on the brieves could and did drag indecisively on for many years in various fora. The classic example is the mortancestry action brought by Andrew Bisset against John Dishington of Ardross, if only because during the case parliament upheld the need to 'pas ordourly furthwart fra excepcioun to excepcioun, how oft that ever the dome be falsit, on to the time that the brief be brocht to the recognicioun of an assise'.[18] This case first came before parliament in 1471 and was still going in 1478. A similar process probably lies behind the final decision in 1390 on the mortancestry case between Thomas Hay and William Keith, which we are told had been before the justiciar's court twice previously, with the dooms given on each occasion being subsequently falsed in parliament.[19] Most of the other long-drawn-out cases of which we know were on brieves of right: for example, the litigation between Robert Spens and James Nory over Kittedie, Fife began before 1462 and was still going in 1471, and the dispute between the Skene and Keith families over the lands of Skene was determined in the sheriff court in 1457 but was still going on in parliament in 1460.[20]

All this provides some explanation of why litigants may have preferred the peremptory procedures of council and parliamentary auditors, tribunals made up of men of considerable legal skills who were not subject to local pressures in their judgment, who exercised the direct and immediate authority of the king, and from whose decisions there was no appeal to a higher court. Yet this cannot be the whole story, if indeed it is part of the story at all. The records of council and auditors reveal many examples of long-drawn-out disputes, of which the most prominent example among the cases considered in this book is the litigations over the lands of Rires and Leuchars initiated amongst the descendants of Sir Thomas Wemyss after his death in 1478, which were still going on in 1543.[21] This was certainly not a dispute where procedure before council and parliament provided a speedy resolution. Indeed, if it is correct to surmise that there would also have been actions in the sheriff court of Fife which awaited the long-delayed outcome of recognition proceedings in parliament in this case, it might be that the jurisdiction of council was a further cause of delay in the system considered as a whole. Resort to council and parliament might also be deliberately undertaken as a means of engendering delay. There seems to be some abuse of process involving council and parliament in the brieve of right cases of *Skene v Keith* and *Spens v Nory*. In both cases, an initial verdict was given in the sheriff court but was followed by a recognition in council or parliament, seemingly a reversal of usual procedure. In both cases, the defender who had lost in the sheriff court regained possession of the lands in issue, forcing the pursuer into further action.[22] The delay inherent in the brieve of right procedure was thus aggravated by the role of council and parliament rather than circumvented.

Persistence in long-drawn-out disputes shows, however, the value which was placed upon land as the chief source not only of wealth but also of status and power, both local and national, in medieval society. Geoffrey Barrow has written:[23]

> The apparent mobility of the feudal and entrepreneurial classes in twelfth- and thirteenth-century Scotland should not hide from us the keen – one might almost say the fiercely passionate – attachment which land-owners at every level of society felt towards their land. Every ploughgate, oxgang, furlong, acre, rig and butt, each soum of pasture, each shieling and peatmoss, was minutely perambulated, measured, described, chartered, jealously guarded, carefully steered from one heir to the next, and at the same time enviously coveted by greedy neighbours. However illogical it may seem, men who would seize the chance of war to add to their estates were united in their determination not to be deprived of their inheritance and in their belief that at the end of a war the first duty of a ruler was to restore to his lieges whatever had been taken from them unjustly.

Barrow illustrates his point with the Esperston case, which has also been discussed in this book. This began with the dissasine of Christiana, lady of Esperston, by the Templars sometime in the reign of Alexander III, and continued through various dispossessions and recoveries until in 1354 Robert Symple, who could trace his right back to that of the lady Christiana, gained sasine from the Hospitallers, successors in title to the Templars.[24] The same determination to hold on to and make good claims to land over long periods of time can be amply demonstrated from other examples mentioned in this book. The family dispute amongst the Cheynes of Straloch over the lands of Esslemont and Meikle Arnage in Aberdeenshire began in the 1440s, and litigation was still going on in 1493.[25] The Douglases of Drumlanrig experienced many problems in their barony of Hawick between 1420 and 1465 as a result of the vicissitudes in the fortunes of their superiors, the earls of Douglas, during that period, but each generation of the Drumlanrig family set about repairing the damage to their heritage arising as a result, making full use of the law to do so.[26] The patrimony of tile Kennedys of Dunure was fragmented in the first half of the fifteenth century by homicide, family feuds and forfeiture, but from the mid-1440s Gilbert lord Kennedy set about its reconstruction, with legal action or the threat of it as a principal tool towards his goal.[27] In some cases, claims were apparently revived after many decades (although in some of these there may have been earlier actions of which no evidence now survives). Thus, in his action of mortancestry against William Keith in 1390, Thomas Hay of Errol relied on the sasine of Inverpeffer which his grandfather had had over sixty years before.[28] The monks of Coupar Angus brought a claim of dissasine against the thane of Glentilt some seventy years after the event in 1434,[29] while the claim made by James Skene against Janet Keith by brieve of right in 1457 related to his ancestor's loss of the lands in 1411.[30]

Litigation therefore formed an important part of the armoury by means of which landowners sought to protect their hold on lands, to recover it when lost, and to make good hereditary claims. The career of James Douglas of Dalkeith is another illustration of this point, for it shows how he used legal action to help him become one of the greatest landowners in early Stewart Scotland. The basis of his estates was derived by inheritance from his uncle William Douglas of Liddesdale, who died in 1353. Some of this was the result of a tailzie in favour of heirs-male, but for the rest James had to await the death in 1367 of William's daughter Mary. This, possibly coupled with the end of his minority, provided the starting point for a series of legal actions by James to make good his claims. First there was the duel in 1367 with Mary's husband, Thomas Erskine, over the latter's claim to courtesy in Mary's lands. The proceedings may have begun with a brieve of right raised by James.[31] Thomas having yielded up his claim, James moved on in 1368 to bring a brieve of mortancestry to recover the lands of Kilbucho and Newlands which he claimed under his uncle's tailzie.[32] In 1369, he was involved in a further dispute, this time over the lands of Roberton in Lanarkshire, which had been part of Mary's inheritance, and it was agreed that the matter should be settled by brieve of mortancestry.[33] In all these cases, James was clearly seeking sasine of his inheritance. Once he was in possession of these and other estates, he had to defend them against the claims of others. Thus, in 1372, he was confronted in the justiciar's court at Dumfries with a claim to the lands of Morton, which had been granted to him by his brother-in-law, the earl of March.[34] James then brought a brieve of warrandice of charter against the earl, who in the sheriff court of Edinburgh accepted his obligation to warrant the title.[35] In 1378, James received quitclaims of the lands of Flemington in the barony of Kilbucho and Newlands (which he had recovered by brieve of mortancestry ten years before) from both Thomas Hay of Errol and Robert de Normanville, who had presumably raised actions against him in respect of these properties, or were in possession against James's wishes.[36]

From all this, it seems clear that James's successful building-up of his landed property was achieved through aggressive assertion and defence of his legal rights in the forum of the courts, as well as by the other usual techniques of advantageous marriages and shrewd purchases.[37] A consciousness of legal rights and their value is evident not only in his possession of law books but also in the compilation of the Morton register, one of the earliest surviving lay cartularies, in which all his land dealings and details of the administration of his estates were carefully recorded. Grant has demonstrated that in buying, selling and granting land, James was always attentive to his feudal rights, ensuring that the casualties in lands held of him remained exigible while arranging that this was not so in respect of the lands which he acquired.[38] Even in his dealings with his family and their dependants, careful regard for his own legal rights is apparent: for example, the claim to terce of his brother's lands of Crossraguel made in 1401 by his sister-in-law, Marjorie Lindsay, was resisted all the way up to parliament, and did not end there. Meanwhile, James had recognosced the lands, and had ward of the heir; while his rights might be restricted in law, nonetheless he was in possession and the immediate profits of the lands would accrue to him.[39] Something of his generally tough approach may have passed on to his son, who in 1425 recognosced the lands of Carlops from his tenant David Menzies of Vogrie and infeft Alan Erskine in his place.[40]

Yet it would be wrong to draw a wholly one-sided picture of James Douglas of Dalkeith as a ruthless exploiter of his legal rights who acted without regard for other interests. Many of his litigations ended not in adjudication but in settlement. The 1367 duel with Thomas Erskine was not fought to a conclusion but was ended by negotiation, royal mediation and payment of certain sums of money to Thomas by James and the king. The dispute with William Cresswell over Roberton ended with a quitclaim by William, but he received in return a life grant of the lands from James.[41] It is difficult to believe, in the light of this, that James's action of warrandice against his brother-in-law in 1372 was anything other than a matter of form, perhaps even in collusion with the earl, the main purpose being to delay the process in the main action in the justiciar's court in Dumfries. Litigation and legal rights were part but not the whole of James's strategy in the advance of his interests; they were means to the end of driving the best possible bargain in the settlement of his disputes.

As a litigator who was prepared to compromise, James Douglas of Dalkeith can be seen as representative of the medieval landowning class in Scotland. From the twelfth century through to the sixteenth, litigation was a preliminary to settlement of dispute by agreement. Nearly all the examples of proprietary and disciplinary cases in twelfth- and thirteenth-century lords' courts which have been discussed in this book ended in quitclaims or some other form of settlement. The royal courts were no less willing to countenance settlement of cases brought before them by brieve. Often these settlements appear one-sided, in that the result is the apparently permanent exclusion of a party from the lands in issue; but we may suspect that frequently the quitclaim had been bought by the beneficiary 'for peace and quiet', as it was put by the bishop of Glasgow in narrating the settlement of his dispute with Mariota, daughter of Samuel, over the lands of Stobo in the mid-thirteenth century by giving her a grant of ten marks annually from the rents of his estate of Eddleston.[42] Patrick, son of the earl of Dunbar, was persuaded to give up his claim to the lands of Swinewood in 1231 when Thomas, prior of Coldingham, paid him 100 silver marks.[43] Again, in 1253, Emma of Smeaton abandoned her mortancestry claim to the lands of Smeaton when the defenders Dunfermline abbey offered her payment of twenty marks annually for her lifetime.[44] Another quitclaim for money was made in the king's court at Scone in 1262; after William Mortimer had impleaded his cousin Gilbert, lord of Ruthven in Strathearn, by brieve of the lord king, Gilbert resigned and quitclaimed all right which he had by descent from his grandmother Cecilia of Maule in return for payment of a certain sum of money given to him by William.[45] The merits of these cases are unclear, but the advantages of compromise obviously outweighed the value of establishing strict legal right for the parties. For example, Emma of Smeaton had a brother Nicholas, who might be expected to have had a better claim than she did to the lands unless he was a brother-uterine, while the basis of Dunfermline abbey's claim lay in the canon law rules against alienation of church property. Emma and her husband were impoverished, however, and were no doubt glad of the income which the settlement provided, while for its part the abbey obtained what it sought, control of Smeaton.[46]

This picture of litigation as an element in negotiating mutually acceptable settlements of disputes remains good in the fourteenth and fifteenth centuries. The example of James Douglas of Dalkeith has already been discussed. Other instances are not hard to find. The dispute between the Skenes and the Keiths over the lands of Skene seems to have been resolved by a grant of the lands to Alexander Skene by William Keith, earl marischal, in 1464, with Alexander to hold of William.[47] Most striking of all is the dispute between Gilbert lord Kennedy and Robert lord Fleming over lands which Kennedy claimed to hold of Fleming. Before this case was finally litigated in the justiciar's court at Dumbarton in 1466, the parties sought settlement through private negotiation, marriage contracts involving their offspring, bonds of manrent, arbitration, and action in Robert's court, the whole process being drawn out over at least a five-year period. Of course, in the end, the negotiations failed, and the matter was put to the determination of an assize; but even then there was still room for some sort of discussion, for, although the assize held for Kennedy, the lands ended up with the Flemings, apparently not through any formal process. We know that Fleming falsed the doom of the court, so the verdict of the assize did not preclude further manoeuvring by the parties, while the general political situation changed to Kennedy's disadvantage shortly after the hearing at Dumbarton.[48] Once again, whatever the merits of the dispute may have been, the parties were probably prepared to settle for what, on a realistic assessment of their own and the other party's situation, they could reasonably expect to get.

Just as it would be a mistake to think of medieval claimants to land as pursuing their legal rights to the exclusion of all other considerations, so it would be equally wrong to paint a picture in which the resolution of such claims was characterised by the omnipresence of sweet reason, consensus and harmony. Claims were pursued aggressively, and it was worthwhile to try to make them good in the real world, for example, by going along to uplift the rents from the inhabitants, throwing down a march-dyke or dam, or diverting a watercourse. Nevertheless, the material discussed so far surely shows that the traditional picture of can agitated and arid world . . . in which malefactors hurry about attacking people, ejecting them from their lands, hoping to get away with obvious wrongs',[49] must be set firmly on one side and forgotten. Rather, the brieves were used to deal with essentially civil questions which presuppose a relatively stable background of law and society, questions about the rights of lords, about entitlement to inherit and alienate, and the scope of holdings and the boundaries of lands. However, all available weapons were used alongside the brieves, for there must be no sign of weakness to suggest that the claimant did not believe his own case to the full. In such a world, not all were equally able to pursue or recognise their own interests, hence the gradual rise of advisers and assistants who were the forerunners of a secular legal profession.

What, finally, were the forces driving legal change in the society just outlined? To what extent was change imposed from above, by kings determined to stamp the kingdom with their authority and, perhaps, to increase their revenues? Or was change the product of factors welling up from below, compelling royal government to act to meet insistent demands for justice? Or was it the result of juristic accident, of litigants thinking only of winning their own cases and judges of doing justice, cumulatively and without thinking about it, transforming the law and with it the world? In the first chapter, reference was made to Alan Watson's theory of legal transplants, which can be summarised broadly as a view that a principal method of legal development is through one system 'transplanting' or 'borrowing' the law of another as a basis for its law.[50] It is obvious, as stated in the first chapter, that the Scottish brieves of novel dissasine, mortancestry and right were legal transplants, although it should be noted that the borrowing was not total or wholly uncritical. There is plenty of evidence that capable legal minds were at work adapting the English material. It also seems clear that medieval Scots law continued to develop by means of transplants. The 1318 legislation on novel dissasine shows that reference was still made to English law, and the use of *Glanvill* in composing *Regiam Majestatem* may have had the effect of introducing, or consolidating the place of, some doctrines of English origin in Scots land law. Reference might also be made to the burgh laws, which drew on English material, and possibly to the exclusion of council from causes of fee and heritage, which parallels the exclusion of the English council from freehold cases. In this latter instance, however, the explanation may simply be that in both systems there was a similar response to the basic legal rule found in each requiring the use of brieves and writs in such cases. What Watson calls 'transplant bias' – that is, one system consistently looking to another as a source for borrowing – is very evident here. However, transplant bias in Scotland was not confined to English law. The *Libri Feudorum* were evidently known and used, and may have had an important effect, for example, in the definition of the lord's right to control alienation. Most apparent of all is the influence of the canon law, which is particularly striking in the development of the possessory process of recognition as a preliminary to the determination of proprietary claims, but can also be seen in a number of other areas associated with terminology, procedure and substantive doctrines.

If legal transplants were an important mechanism of legal change in medieval Scotland, it becomes relevant to consider other aspects of Watson's thesis about the nature of legal change. Watson argues that the phenomenon of borrowing shows that the changing content of law is not necessarily determined by changes in society, and that transplant bias demonstrates the relative lack of interest which governments and ruling elites generally have in the substance of the law. If law is regularly borrowed from another system, that may show a lack of interest in its content; what is more important is that there should be some law, and that general order and peace are maintained as a result. The nature of the transplant bias is a product of the donee system's own legal culture, which determines the appropriate donor system and the rules to be borrowed. Even in customary systems, where the law is theoretically dependent on what people do in society rather than on the will of a sovereign, the law develops by borrowing, and is not necessarily dependent on social norms. Frequently in medieval customary systems – and again Scotland provides an excellent example, with especial reference to the reception of *Glanvill* in the form of *Regiam Majestatem* – there was uncertainty as to what the customs were; they were identified not by looking at what the people normally did, but by reference to the decisions of courts and to the customs of neighbouring regions.[51]

Watson does not deny, of course, that legal change can be caused by social, political and economic factors; the essence of his case is that there is no necessary connection between these factors and development in the law. In medieval Scotland, it is quite clear that social, political and economic factors did lie behind some major shifts in law and the administration of justice. Thus, for example, it seems certain that many of the innovations in judicial administration in the twelfth century were a response to the presence of new elements in Scottish society which could not be easily fitted into the existing ways of handling disputes. If the argument made earlier in this chapter is sound, the introduction of the pleadable brieves in the thirteenth century was at least partly a response to the political and perhaps moral pressures which the church was bringing to bear on secular authority in various ways. Again, the reforms of 1318 were clearly connected with an attempt at a political settlement in Scotland following the upheavals of the past thirty years. In both of the major developments in 1230 and 1318, there is evidence that the transplanting was partial rather than entire; the borrowing from English law was critical and selective. Scottish kings and their advisers were clearly interested in the law and its content; the legislative activity of the later Middle Ages bears continuing witness to that fact.

Does this level of royal interest unseat Watson's general arguments and suggest that the principal factor driving legal change in Scotland was active government from above? It is thought not, in both cases. First, as already noted, Watson's view encompasses the possibility of external factors playing a role in legal development. His argument is that, even when these factors do operate, they generally operate within the legal culture of the system, which is the principal determinant of the nature of the change. That there was a legal culture in medieval Scotland, and that it was a very complex one, cannot now be denied. From the twelfth century, it was heavily influenced by the English model and also, increasingly, by the canon law. Ultimately, these facts must be explained by the close social and political connections with England, and the general preeminence of the church in society, but the law which evolved under these influences clearly took on a life of its own which did dictate the pattern of change to a large degree. When in 1318 the king and his advisers looked to the legal system as a means to achieve their political settlement, they had to work with the system as it was, and the accessible source for possible change was the law of England. In the fifteenth century, there was clearly criticism of the law and dissatisfaction with its uncertainty and lack of clarity which led parliament to consider wholesale revision and reform. Yet the basis of this was always to be *Regiam* and the existing written law, statutory and otherwise,[52] and reform was generally partial and interstitial in nature, rather than a new beginning. Government never succeeded in removing the discontent, even if it was interested in doing so.

A similar lack of concern with the detailed problems of the law may be evident in the complex history of the arrangements to deal with the judicial business of council and parliament. The main characteristic of governmental response to the amount of business needing to be done was to ensure that it did not interfere with the ability of council and parliament to deal with the important affairs of state; hence the delegation to committees, sessions and other devices. Here, pressure can be seen coming from below, as litigants persisted in bringing matters before council even when, as in 1487, a positive effort had been made to turn them away; within six months, the command to litigants to seek out the judges ordinary instead had to be rescinded, 'becaus the kingis hienes undirstandis that it wer deferring of justice to mony partiis'. This of course shows royal government responding to pressure, but once again it was not by any fundamental change; parties were to be free to raise actions before the council 'like as thai wer wont in tymes bigane'.[53] When finally the judicial sessions of council were reconstituted as the College of Justice in 1532, it 'was no more than an excuse to mulct the Church',[54] rather than the erection of a central court to solve some of the problems in the administration of justice. And when the court assumed jurisdiction in fee and heritage, overturning the medieval law on the recovery of land, it was not the result of any clear legislative act but rather a decision of the judges following arguments at the bar, and was the outcome of years of litigation and decisions about how to conduct it which had never directly considered change in the law itself.

In conclusion, law was an important element in medieval Scotland, developing as the result of a variety of factors which operated upon it at different times and in different ways. It was important for good government at all levels, and the branches of it considered in this book were also of great importance to the landowning classes in protecting their possessions and furthering their claims to others, so advancing their interests and position in society. To suggest that change in this law was not necessarily the result of any particular social change is not to deny the role which law played in society, or that we can tell a good deal about society from the law and the evidence left behind by its operations. The extent to which law penetrated the society and institutions of medieval Scotland, and the strength of its legal culture, can in the end perhaps be gauged best by noting the survival down to the present day of sheriff courts, the justiciary court as the High Court of Justiciary, the Court of Session and, above all, of the feudal land law. All of these legal institutions have of course changed considerably since the end of the medieval period, but they remain vital parts of the Scottish legal system, bearing silent witness to the durability and resilience of the medieval law. As these pages were being written, the Scottish Law Commission, a government law reform body, published a document entitled *Abolition of the Feudal System.*[55] The survival of feudalism as a form of land law, long after it had ceased to be related in any sense to the actual organisation of society, is an excellent illustration of the divergence of law and society. Moreover, the system has been seen as socially inappropriate since the mid-eighteenth century, when military tenures and heritable private jurisdictions were abolished. There have been numerous partial reforms of the land law since then, but so deep-rooted are the feudal principles that outright abolition is still required to bring the land law into conformity with present perceptions of what would be consonant with social needs and values. Medieval law has left a legacy which is testimony to its vigour and importance in the society which lived under its rules and institutions.

NOTES

1. *APS*, i, p. 400 (c. 7).
2. See G. W. S. Barrow, The Scots charter', in *Studies in Medieval History presented to R. H. C. Davis*, ed. H. Mayr-Harting and R. I. Moore (London, 1985), pp. 149–64.
3. P. R. Hyams, 'The charter as a source for the early common law', *JLH*, xii (1991), pp. 179–80.
4. *ND*, no 126.
5. *APS*, i, p. 400 (c. 6). On the interpretation of this statute, see G.

Neilson, *Trial by Combat*, p. 113; I. D. Willock, *Jury*, pp 23–8; A. A. M. Duncan, *Kingdom*, p. 540; R. Bartlett, *Trial by Fire and Water*, p. 132.

6. R. Bartlett, *Trial by Fire and Water*, p. 117–19.
7. *APS*, i, p. 399 (c. 5).
8. *APS*, i, p. 400 (c. 8).
9. R. C. van Caenegem, 'Methods of proof in Western medieval law', in *Legal History: A European Perspective* (London, 1991) pp. 89–92; R. Bartlett, *Trial by Fire and Water*, pp. 120–6.
10. *Moray Reg*, nos 73–4; T. M. Cooper, *Cases*, no 19.
11. R. Burgess, *Perpetuities in Scots Law*, p. 55.
12. *Panm Reg*, ii, pp. 169–70.
13. The distinction will be found in any collection of later medieval charters.
14. SRO, *Spens of Lathallan papers*, GD 1/1042/1.
15. *APS*, ii, p. 238 (c. 3).
16. H. L. MacQueen and A. R. Borthwick, 'Cases', pp. 132–3.
17. *APS*, ii, pp. 10 (c. 10), 17–18 (cc. 1–7).
18. *APS*, ii, p. 101
19. *Spalding Misc*, ii, p. 319.
20. See above, pp. 197, 201, 203, 204, 230.
21. See H. L. MacQueen, 'Jurisdiction in heritage', pp. 64–80; above, pp. 227–8, 239.
22. See *AB Ill*, iii, pp. 326–7 and *AB Coll*, p. 284; SRO, *Spens of Lathallan writs*, GD 1/1042/5.
23. G. W. S. Barrow, 'Aftermath of war', p. 112.
24. See above, pp. 56, 150, 152, 202; G. W. S. Barrow, 'Aftermath of war', pp. 112–15.
25. See above, p. 203.
26. H. L. MacQueen and A. R. Borthwick, 'Cases', pp. 140–5; above, p. 182.
27. H. L. MacQueen, 'Kin of Kennedy', passim; above, pp. 51, 75–6, 96–8, 178–9, 182–3.
28. *Spalding Misc*, ii, p. 319.
29. *CA Chrs*, ii, no 128.
30. See above, p. 204.
31. Sellar, 'Courtesy', pp. 1–8; above p. 199.
32. *RRS*, vi, no 417.
33. *Mort Reg*, ii, no 107.
34. For the grant, see *Mort Reg*, ii, nos 100, 101 (*RRS*, vi, no 508).
35. *Mort Reg*, ii, no 130.
36. *Mort Reg*, ii, nos 159–61.
37. On Douglas's strategies in building up his estates, see A. Grant, 'Thesis', pp. 240–5.
38. A. Grant, 'Thesis', pp. 195–6, 245–55.
39. See above, pp. 52, 219; and for Douglas's attitude to his family, see A. Grant, 'Thesis', pp. 247–9.
40. See above, p. 117.
41. *Mort Reg*, ii, nos 123, 126.
42. *Glas Reg*, i, no 172.
43. *ND*, no 119.
44. *Dunf Reg*, no 82.

45. *Panmure Reg*, ii, p. 82.
46. For the details, see *Dunf Reg*, nos 82, 180, 185, 194, 195.
47. *Memorials of the Family of Skene of Skene*, ed. W. F. Skiene (New Spalding Club, 1887), p. 22.
48. See H. L. MacQueen, 'Kin of Kennedy', for full discussion.
49. S. F. C. Milsom, *LFEF*, p. 5.
50. For Watson's summaries of his own views with references to numerous previous works, see *Slave Law in the Americas* (Athens, Georgia, 1989), pp. 1–21; also 'Legal change: sources of law and legal culture', *University of Pennsylvania Law Review*, cxxxi (1983), p. 1121.
51. For Watson's views on custom, see *The Evolution of Law* (Edinburgh, 1985), pp. 43–65; also 'The evolution of law: continued', *LHR*, v (1987), pp. 545–9.
52. See above, pp. 91–3.
53. *APS*, ii, p. 183 (c. 17). For the earlier act, see *APS*, ii, p. 177 (c. 10).
54. A. A. M. Duncan, 'Central courts', p. 336.
55. Scottish Law Commission Working Paper No 93 (1991).

Bibliography

The bibliography consists of sources actually cited in the book. In abbreviations, I have generally followed the conventions laid down in *Scottish Historical Review*, xlii (1963), supplement.

I. PRIMARY SOURCES

(*a*) *Published*

Abbotsford Misc – *Miscellany of the Abbotsford Club* (Abbotsford Club, 1837).

AB Coll – *Collections for a History of the Shires of Aberdeen and Banff* (Spalding Club, 1843).

Abdn Counc – *Extracts from the Council Register of the Burgh of Aberdeen* (Spalding Club, 1844–8).

Abdn Ct Bk – *Early Records of the Burgh of Aberdeen 1317; 1398–1407*, ed. W. C. Dickinson (Scottish History Society, 3rd series, vol. 49, 1957).

Abdn Reg – *Registrum Episcopatus Aberdonensis* (Spalding and Maitland Clubs, 1845).

AB Ill – *Illustrations of the Topography and Antiquities of the Shires of Aberdeen and Banff* (Spalding Club, 1847–69).

Aboyne Recs – *Records of Aboyne 1230–1681*, ed. Charles Gordon, 11th marquis of Huntly (New Spalding Club, 1894).

Acta Sessionis (Stair) – *Acta Dominorum Concilii et Sessionis 1532–1533*, ed. I. H. Shearer (Stair Society, vol 14, 1956).

Acts of Council (Public Affairs) – *Acts of the Lords of Council in Public Affairs 1501–1554*, ed. R. K. Hannay (Edinburgh, 1932).

Acts of the Lords of the Isles 1336–1493, ed. J. and R. W. Munro (SHS, 1986).

ADA – *The Acts of the Lords Auditors of Causes and Complaints*, ed. T. Thomson (Edinburgh, 1839).

ADC, i – *Acts of the Lords of Council in Civil Causes*, ed. T. Thomson (Edinburgh, 1839).

ADC, ii – *Acts of the Lords of Council 1496–1501*, ed. G. Neilson and H. M. Paton (Edinburgh, 1918).

ADC (Stair) – *Acta Dominorum Concilii 1501–1503*, ed. J. A. Clyde (Stair Society, 1943).

Anderson, *Early Sources* – Anderson, A. O., *Early Sources of Scottish History 500 to 1286* (Edinburgh, 1922).

APS – *The Acts of the Parliaments of Scotland*, ed. T. Thomson and C. Innes (12 vols, Edinburgh 1814–75).

Arb Lib – *Liber Sancte Thome de Aberbrothoc* (2 vols, Bannatyne Club, 1848–56).

Balfour, *Practicks* – *The Practicks of Sir James Balfour of Pittendreich*, ed. P. G. B. McNeill (2 vols, Stair Society, 1962–3).

Balm Lib – *Liber Sancte Marie de Balmorinach* (Abbotsford Club, 1841).

Beauly Chrs – *The Charters of the Priory of Beauly* (Grampian Club, 1877).

Borough Customs – *Borough Customs*, ed. M. Bateson (2 vols, Selden Society, 1904–6).

Bracton – *Bracton's De Legibus et Consuetudinibus Angliae*, ed. G. E. Woodbine, trans, with revisions and notes by S. E. Thorne (Harvard, 1968–77).

Brechin Reg – *Registrum Episcopatus Brechinensis* (Bannatyne Club, 1856).

Brevia Placitata, ed. G. J. Turner (Selden Society, 1947).

Britton – *Britton*, ed. F. M. Nichols (Oxford, 1865).

CA Chrs – *Charters of the Abbey of Coupar Angus*, ed. D. E. Easson (2 vols, SHS, 1947).

CA Rent – *Rental Book of the Cistercian Abbey of Coupar Angus* (Grampian Club, 1879–80).

Carn Ct Bk – *Court Book of the Barony of Carnwath 1523–1542*, ed. W. C. Dickinson (SHS, 1937).

Cawdor Bk – *The Book of the Thanes of Cawdor* (Spalding Club, 1859).

CDS – *Calendar of Documents relating to Scotland*, ed. J. Bain and others (5 vols, Edinburgh and London, 1881–1989).

Chron Bower – Walter Bower, *Scotichronicon*, ed. D. E. R. Watt and others (8 vols, Aberdeen, 1987 to date).

Chron Fordun – Johannis de Fordun, *Chronica Gentis Scotorum*, ed. W. F. Skene (Edinburgh, 1871–2).

Chron Holyrood – *A Scottish Chronicle known as the Chronicle of Holyrood*, ed. M. O. Anderson (SHS, 1938).

Chron Lanercost – *Chronicon de Lanercost* (Maitland Club, 1839).

Chron Majora – Matthew Paris, *Chronica Majora*, ed. H. R. Luard (7 vols, Rolls Series, 1872–3).

Chron Melrose – *The Chronicle of Melrose* (Facsimile Edition), ed. A. O. Anderson and others (London, 1936).

Chron Wyntoun – Andrew of Wyntoun, *The Orygynale Cronykil of Scotland*, ed. D. Laing (Edinburgh, 1872–9).

Cold Corr – *The Correspondence, etc., of the Priory of Coldingham*, ed. J. Raine (Surtees Society, 1841).

Coldstream Chrs – *Chartulary of the Cistercian Priory of Coldstream* (Grampian Club, 1879).

Cooper, *Cases* – Cooper, T. M. (Lord), *Select Scottish Cases of the Thirteenth Century* (Edinburgh, 1944).

Craig, *JF* – Thomas Craig, *Jus Feudale* (Edinburgh and London, 1655; Leipzig, 1716; Edinburgh, 1732), translation by J. A. Clyde (Edinburgh, 1934).

Dryb Lib – *Liber Sancte Marie de Dryburgh* (Bannatyne Club, 1847).

Dunf Burgh Recs – *The Burgh Records of Dunfermline*, ed. J. E. Beveridge (Edinburgh, 1917).

Dunf Ct Bk – *Regality of Dunfermline Court Book 1531–1538*, ed. J. M. Webster and A. A. M. Duncan (Dunfermline, 1953).

Dunf Reg – *Registrum de Dunfermlyn* (Bannatyne Club, 1842).

English Law Suits from William I to Richard I, ed. R. C. van Caenegem (2 vols, Selden Society, 1990–1).

Erskine, *Institute* – Erskine, J., *An Institute of the Law of Scotland*, 5th ed. by J. B. Nicholson (Edinburgh, 1871).

ER – The Exchequer Rolls of Scotland, ed. J. Stuart and others (Edinburgh, 1878–1908).

ERW – Early Registers of Writs, ed. E. de Haas and G. D. G. Hall (Selden Society, 1970).

ESC – Early Scottish Charters prior to 1153, ed. A. C. Lawrie (Glasgow, 1905).

Eyre of Northamptonshire 1329–1330, ed. D. W. Sutherland, 2 vols (Selden Society, 1981–2).

Familie of Innes – Ane Account of the Familie of Innes (Spalding Club, 1864).

Family of Rose – A Genealogical Deduction of the Family of Rose of Kilravock (Spalding Club, 1848).

Fife Ct Bk – Sheriff Court Book of Fife 1515–1522, ed. W. C. Dickinson (SHS, 1928).

Form E – Formulary E: Scottish Letters and Brieves 1286–1424, ed. A. A. M. Duncan (University of Glasgow, Scottish History Department Occasional Paper, 1976).

Four Thirteenth-Century Law Tracts, ed. G. E. Woodbine (New Haven, 1910).

Fraser, *Buccleuch* – W. Fraser, *The Scotts of Buccleuch* (Edinburgh, 1878).

Fraser, *Carlaverock* – W. Fraser, *The Book of Carlaverock* (Edinburgh, 1873).

Fraser, *Douglas* – W. Fraser, *The Douglas Book* (Edinburgh, 1885).

Fraser, *Eglinton* – W. Fraser, *Memorials of the Montgomeries Earls of Eglinton* (Edinburgh, 1859).

Fraser, *Grandtully* – W. Fraser, *The Red Book of Grandtully* (Edinburgh, 1868).

Fraser, *Grant* – W. Fraser, *The Chiefs of Grant* (Edinburgh, 1883).

Fraser, *Keir* – W. Fraser, *The Stirlings of Keir* (Edinburgh, 1858).

Fraser, *Lennox* – W. Fraser, *The Lennox* (Edinburgh, 1874).

Fraser, *Maxwell Inventories* – W. Fraser, *Inventories of the Families of Maxwell, Herries and Nithsdale* (Edinburgh, 1865).

Fraser, *Melville* – W. Fraser, *The Melvilles Earls of Melville and the Leslies Earls of Leven* (Edinburgh, 1890).

Fraser, *Menteith* – W. Fraser, *The Red Book of Menteith* (Edinburgh, 1880).

Fraser, *Pollok* – W. Fraser, *Memoirs of the Maxwells of Pollok* (Edinburgh, 1863).

Frasers of Philorth – The Frasers of Philorth, ed. A. Fraser, Lord Saltoun (Edinburgh, 1879).

Fraser, *Southesk* – W. Fraser, *History of the Carnegies Earls of Southesk and of their Kindred* (Edinburgh, 1867).

Fraser, *Wemyss* – W. Fraser, *Memorials of the Family of Wemyss of Wemyss* (Edinburgh, 1888).

Gild Court Book of Dunfermline 1433–1597, ed. E. P. D. Torrie (SRS, new series, vol. 12).

Glanvill – Tractatus de Legibus et Consuetudinibus Angliae qui Glanvilla vocatur, ed. G. D. G. Hall (London, 1965).

Glas Reg – Registrum Episcopatus Glasguensis (Bannatyne and Maitland Clubs, 1843).

Herlihy, *Feudalism* – D. Herlihy, *The History of Feudalism* (New York, 1970).

Highland Papers, ed. J. R. N. Macphail (4 vols, SHS, 1914–34).

HMC – Reports of the Royal Commission on Historical Manuscripts (London, 1870 to date).

Inchaff Chrs – Charters, Bulls and other Documents relating to the Abbey of Inchaffray (SHS, 1908).

Inchcolm Chrs – Charters of the Abbey of Inchcolm, ed. D. E. Easson and A. Macdonald (SHS, 1938).

Irvine Muniments – Muniments of the Royal Burgh of Irvine (Archaeological and Historical Collections relating to Ayrshire and Galloway, 1890–1).

Kel Lib – Liber Sancte Marie de Calchou (Bannatyne Club, 1846).

Laing Chrs – Calendar of the Laing Charters 854–1837, ed. J. Anderson (Edinburgh, 1899).

Lawrie, *Annals – Annals of the Reigns of Malcolm and William, Kings of Scotland*, ed. A. C. Lawrie (Glasgow, 1910).

Leges Henrici Primi, ed. L. J. Downer (Oxford, 1972).

Libri Feudorum – Many editions. See Craig, *JF* (above).

Lind (Abbotsford) – Liber Sancte Marie de Lundoris (Abbotsford Club, 1841).

Lind Chrs – Chartulary of the Abbey of Lindores (SHS, 1903).

May Recs – Records of the Priory of the Isle of May, ed. J. Stuart (Edinburgh, 1868).

Melr Lib – Liber Sancte Marie de Melros (Bannatyne Club, 1837).

Moncreiffs – The Moncreiffs and the Moncreiffes, ed. F. Moncreiff and W. Moncreiffe (Edinburgh, 1929).

Monro's Western Isles of Scotland, ed. R. W. Munro (Edinburgh, 1961).

Moray Reg – Registrum Episcopatus Moraviensis (Bannatyne Club, 1837).

Mort Reg – Registrum Honoris de Morton (Bannatyne Club, 1853).

Munro of Foulis Writs – Calendar of Writs of Munro of Foulis 1299–1823, ed. C. T. McInnes (SRS, 1940).

Nat MSS Scot – Facsimiles of the National Manuscripts of Scotland (London, 1867–71).

ND – J. Raine, *The History and Antiquities of North Durham* (Appendix) (London, 1852).

Newb Reg – Registrum Sancte Marie de Neubotle (Bannatyne Club, 1849).

Novae Narrationes, ed. E. Shanks and S. F. C. Milsom (Selden Society, 1963).

Pais Reg – Registrum Monasterii de Passelet (Maitland Club, 1832; New Club, 1877).

Panm Reg – Registrum de Panmure, ed. J. Stuart (Edinburgh, 1874).

Peebles Chrs – Charters and Documents relating to the Burgh of Peebles (Scottish Burgh Records Society, 1872).

Pitfirrane Writs – Inventory of Pitfirrane Writs 1230–1794, ed. W. Angus (SRS, 1932).

Prot Bk Young – Protocol Book of James Young 1485–1515, ed. G. Donaldson (SRS, 1952).

QA (Fergus/APS/Cooper) – see prefatory Note on Editions of Texts.

Radulphi de Hengham Summae, ed. W. H. Dunham (Cambridge, 1932).

Records and Register of Holm Cultram Abbey, ed. F. Grainger and W. G. Collingwood (Cumberland and Westmorland AAS Records Series, 1929).

Reg Brieves – The Register of Brieves 1286–1386, ed. T. M. Cooper (Stair Society, 1946).

RM (APS/Cooper) – see prefatory Note on Editions of Texts

RMS – Registrum Magni Sigilli Regum Scottorum, ed. J. M. Thomson and others (Edinburgh, 1882–1914).

Robertson, *Concilia – Concilia Scotiae* (half-title: *Statuta Ecclesiae Scoticanae*), ed. J. Robertson (Bannatyne Club, 1866).

Ross, *Lectures* – Ross, W., *Lectures on the Law of Scotland*, 2nd ed. (2 vols, Edinburgh, 1819).

RRS – Regesta Regum Scottorum, ed. G. W. S. Barrow and others (Edinburgh, 1959 to date).

RSS – *Registrum Secreti Sigilli Regum Scottorum*, ed. M. Livingstone and others (Edinburgh, 1908 to date).

Scone Lib – Liber Ecclesie de Scon (Bannatyne and Maitland Clubs, 1843).

Select Cases before the King's Council 1243–1482, ed. I. S. Leadam and J F Baldwin (Selden Society, 1919).

Select Cases of Trespass from the King's Courts 1307–1399, ed. M. S. Arnold (2 vols, Selden Society, 1985–7).

Shropshire Roll – Roll of the Shropshire Eyre of 1256, ed. A. Harding (Selden Society, 1980).

SHS – Scottish History Society.

SHS Misc – The Miscellany of the Scottish History Society (SHS, 1893–1965).

Skene, *DVS* – J. Skene, *De Verborum Significatione* (Edinburgh, 1597).

Skene, *RM* (*Latin*) – see prefatory Note on Editions of Texts.

Soutra – Charters of the Collegiate Churches of Midlothian: Registrum Domus de Soltre (Bannatyne Club, 1861).

Spalding Misc – The Miscellany of the Spalding Club (Spalding Club, 1841–52).

SRS – Scottish Record Society.

St A Form – St Andrews Formulare 1514–1546, ed. G. Donaldson and C. Macrae (2 vols, Stair Society, 1942–4).

St A Lib – Liber Cartarum Prioratus Sancti Andree in Scotia (Bannatyne Club, 1841).

Statutes of the Realm (Record Commission, London, 1810).

Stair Misc – The Miscellany of the Stair Society (2 vols, Stair Society, 1970–84).

Stevenson, *Documents – Documents Illustrative of the History of Scotland 1286–1306*, ed. J. Stevenson (Edinburgh, 1870).

Stones, *Relations – Anglo-Scottish Relations 1174–1328: Some Selected Documents*, ed. E. L. G. Stones (London, 1965)

Stones and Simpson, *Edward I – Edward I and the Throne of Scotland 1290–1296*, ed. E. L. G. Stones and G. G. Simpson (2 vols, Oxford, 1979).

Stubbs' Select Charters – Stubbs' Select Charters from the beginning to 1307, 9th edn, ed. H. W. C. Davis (Oxford, 1913).

TA – Accounts of the Lord High Treasurer of Scotland, ed. T. Dickson and J. B. Paul (Edinburgh, 1877–1916).

Watt, *Fasti* – D. E. R. Watt, *Fasti Ecclesiae Scoticanae Medii Aevi ad annum 1638* (SRS, 1969).

Welsh Assize Roll 1277–1284, ed. J. Conway Davies (Cardiff, 1940).

Wigt Chr Chest – Charter Chest of the Earldom of Wigtown (SRS, 1910).

Wigt Chrs – Wigtownshire Charters, ed. R. C. Reid (SHS, 1960).

Year Books:

20 & 21 Edward I 1292–1293 (Rolls Series, 1866).

6 & 7 Edward II 1313 (Selden Society, 1918).

8 Edward II 1314–15 (Selden Society, 1924).

10 Edward II 1316–17 (Selden Society, 1934).

12 Edward II 1318 (Selden Society, 1946).

Yester Writs – Calendar of Writs preserved at Yester House 1166–1503 (SRS, 1930)

(b) Unpublished National Library of Scotland

Auchinleck MS, Adv MS 25.4.15.

Bute MS, MS 21,246.

Cromertie MS, Adv MS 25.5.10

Adv MS 25.4.13

Fleming of Wigtown papers
Foulis MS, Adv MS 25.4.10.

Scottish Record Office

Acta dominorum concilii, CS 5.
Acta dominorum concilii et sessionis, CS 6.
Acts and decreets, CS 7.
Ailsa muniments, GD 25.
Ayr MS, PA 5/2.
Berne MS, PA 5/1.
Bruce of Clackmannan cartulary, GD 235/1/1.
Crown Office writs, AD 1.
Forglen muniments, GD 185.
Glencairn muniments, GD 39.
Haddington Burgh Court Book 1423–1514, B 30/9/1.
Mar and Kellie papers, GD 124.
Peebles Burgh Records, B 58/17.
Rollo of Duncub muniments, GD 56.
Society of Antiquaries writs, GD 103.
Spens of Lathallan writs, GD 1/1042.
Swinton charters, GD 12.

British Library

Arbroath abbey cartulary, Addit MS 33,245.
Regiam Majestatem, Addit MS 18,111.

Edinburgh University Library

Sinclair's practicks, Laing MS 388a.

Cambridge University Library.

Dd.7.14.
Liber quem vulgus Regiam Majestatem vocat, Ee.4.21.

Others

Aberdeen City Archives: Council Records.
Aberdeen University Library: *Gordon of Buthlaw papers*
Durham Cathedral, Dean and Chapter Muniments, Miscellaneous.
Kyle and Carrick District Council, Carnegie Library, Ayr: *Ayr Burgh Court Book 1428–1478*
Public Record Office, London: *Ancient correspondence* and *Common Pleas.*

II. SECONDARY SOURCES

(a) Works of reference

British Chronology – Handbook of British Chronology, ed. F. M. Powicke and E. B. Fryde (London, 1961).
du Cange, C, *Glossarium Mediae et Infimae Latinitatis* (nouveau tirage, Paris, 1937).
Naz, R., *Dictionnaire de Droit Canonique* (7 vols, Paris, 1935).
OS – Ordnance Survey, Landranger Series of Great Britain Maps, scale 1:50,000.
Scots Peerage – The Scots Peerage, ed. J. B. Paul (Edinburgh, 1904–14)

(b) Monographs

Anderson, M. O., *Kings and Kingship in Early Scotland* (Edinburgh, 1973).

Baker, *IELH* – Baker, J. H., *Introduction to English Legal History*, 3rd ed. (London, 1990).

Baldwin, J. F., *The King's Council in England during the Middle Ages* (Oxford, 1913).

Barrow, *ANE* – Barrow, G. W. S., *The Anglo-Norman Era in Scottish History* (Oxford, 1980).

Barrow, *Bruce* – Barrow, G. W. S., *Robert Bruce and the Community of the Realm of Scotland*, 3rd ed. (Edinburgh, 1988).

Barrow, *Kingdom* – Barrow, G. W. S., *The Kingdom of the Scots* (London, 1973).

Bartlett, R., *Trial by Fire and Water: The Medieval Judicial Ordeal* (Oxford, 1986).

Bloch, M., *Feudal Society* (2 vols, London, 1962).

Brand, P. A., *The Origins of the English Legal Profession* (Oxford, 1992).

Brown, A. L., *The Governance of Later Medieval England 1272–1461* (London, 1989).

Brown, J. M. (ed.), *Scottish Society in the Fifteenth Century* (London, 1977).

Burgess, R., *Perpetuities in Scots Law* (Stair Society, 1979).

Campbell, J., *Essays in Anglo-Saxon History* (London and Ronceverte, 1986).

Cheyne, A. Y., *The Cheyne Family in Scotland* (Eastbourne, 1931).

Chibnall, M., *Anglo-Norman England 1066–1166* (Oxford, 1986).

Clanchy, M. T., *From Memory to Written Record: England 1066–1272* (London, 1979).

Clanchy, M. T., *England and Its Rulers 1066–1272* (London, 1983).

Cooper, *Papers* – Cooper, T. M. (Lord), *Selected Papers 1922–1954* (Edinburgh, 1957).

Crouch, D., *The Beaumont Twins* (Cambridge, 1986).

Davis, R. H. C, *King Stephen 1135–1154*, 3rd ed. (London, 1990).

Dickinson/Duncan, *Scotland* – Dickinson, W. C, *Scotland from the Earliest Times to 1603*, 3rd ed. by A. A. M. Duncan (Oxford, 1978).

Duncan, *Kingdom* – Duncan, A. A. M., *Scotland: The Making of the Kingdom* (Edinburgh, 1975).

Dunlop, A. I., *The Life and Times of James Kennedy Bishop of St Andrews* (St Andrews, 1950).

Ewan, E. L., *Townlife in Fourteenth-Century Scotland* (Edinburgh, 1990).

Farran, *Land Law* – Farran, C. D'O., *Principles of Scots and English Land Law* (Edinburgh, 1958).

Frame, R., *The British Isles 1100–1400* (Oxford, 1990).

Ganshof, F. L., *Feudalism* (London, 1964).

Gilbert, J. M., *Hunting and Hunting Reserves in Medieval Scotland* (Edinburgh, 1979).

Gimpel, J., *The Medieval Machine* (London, 1979).

Gordon, W. M., *Studies in the Transfer of Property by Traditio* (Aberdeen, 1970).

Grant, A., *Independence and Nationhood: Scotland 1306–1469* (London, 1984).

Grant, A. and Stringer, K. J. (eds), *Medieval Scotland: Crown, Lordship and Community* (Edinburgh, 1993).

Green, J. A., *The Government of England under Henry I* (Cambridge, 1986).

Hannay, R. K., *The College of Justice and other essays*, ed. H. L. MacQueen (Stair Society supplementary series, 1991).

Harding, A., *The Law Courts of Medieval England* (London, 1973).

Harding, A. (ed.), *Lawmaking and Lawmakers in British History* (RHS, 1980).

Holdsworth, W. S., *A History of English Law* (London, 1903–65).

Holt, J. C, *Magna Carta*, 2nd ed. (Cambridge, 1992).

Hudson, J., *Land, Law and Lordship in Anglo-Norman England* (Oxford, 1993).

Hume, D., *Commentaries on the Law of Scotland respecting Crimes*, 2nd ed. (Edinburgh, 1819).

Hyams, P. R., *Kings, Lords and Peasants in Medieval England* (Oxford, 1980).

ISLH – Paton, G. C. H. (ed.), *An Introduction to Scottish Legal History* (Stair Society, 1958).

Kames, *HLT* – Kames, Henry Home (Lord), *Historical Law Tracts*, 1st ed. (Edinburgh, 1757).

Kinsley, J. (ed.), *The Poems of William Dunbar* (Oxford, 1979).

Kolbert, C. F., and Mackay, N. M., *History of Scots and English Land Law* (Berkhamsted, 1977).

Le Patourel, J., *The Norman Empire* (Oxford, 1976).

Macdougall, *James III* – Macdougall, N. A. T., *James III: A Political Study* (Edinburgh, 1982).

Macfarlane, *Elphinstone* – Macfarlane, L. J., *William Elphinstone and the Kingdom of Scotland 1431–1514* (Aberdeen, 1985).

Maclean, I., *Interpretation and Meaning in the Renaissance: The Context of Law* (Cambridge, 1992).

McFarlane, K. B., *The Nobility of Later Medieval England* (Oxford, 1973).

Maitland, F. W., *Roman Canon Law in the Church of England* (London, 1898).

Maitland, F. W., *The Forms of Action at Common Law*, ed. A. H. Chaytor and W. J. Whittaker (Cambridge, 1936).

Milsom, *HFCL* – Milsom, S. F. C, *Historical Foundations of the Common Law*, 2nd ed. (London, 1981).

Milsom, *LFEF* – Milsom, S. F. C, *The Legal Framework of English Feudalism* (Cambridge, 1976).

Milsom, *Studies* – Milsom, S. F. C, *Studies in the History of the Common Law* (London and Ronceverte, 1985).

Napier, M., '*The Lanox of Auld*': *An Epistolary Review of 'The Lennox' by Sir William Fraser* (Edinburgh, 1880).

Neilson, G., *Trial by Combat* (Glasgow, 1890).

Nicholson, *LMA* – Nicholson, R., *Scotland: The Later Middle Ages* (Edinburgh, 1974).

Nobility Essays – *Essays on the Nobility of Medieval Scotland*, ed. K. J. Stringer (Edinburgh, 1985).

Ollivant, *Official* – Ollivant, S. D., *The Court of the Official in Pre-Reformation Scotland* (Stair Society, 1982).

Palmer, *County Courts* – Palmer, R. C, *The County Courts of Medieval England 1150–1350* (Princeton, 1982).

Palmer, R. C, *The Whilton Dispute 1264–1380* (Princeton, 1984).

Plucknett, T. F. T., *The Legislation of Edward I* (Oxford, 1949).

Plucknett, T. F. T., *A Concise History of the Common Law*, 5th ed. (London, 1956).

Plucknett, T. F. T., *Early English Legal Literature* (Cambridge, 1958).

P & M – Pollock, F., and Maitland, F. W., *The History of English Law before Edward I*, 2nd ed. (2 vols, Cambridge, 1896, reprinted with an introduction by S. F. C. Milsom, Cambridge, 1968).

Reichel, O. J., *A Complete Manual of Canon Law*, 2 vols (London, 1896).

Richardson, H. G., and Sayles, G. O., *Parliaments and Great Councils in Medieval England* (London, 1961).

Richardson, H. G., and Sayles, G. O., *Law and Legislation from Ethelbert to Magna Carta* (Edinburgh, 1966).

Richardson, H. G., and Sayles, G. O., *The English Parliament in the Middle Ages* (London, 1981).

Robinson et al., *IELH* – Robinson, O. F., Gordon, W. M., and Fergus, T. D., *An Introduction to European Legal History* (Milton Keynes, 1985).

Scottish Law Commission Working Paper No 93, *Abolition of the Feudal System* (1991).

Shaw, J., *Water Power in Scotland 1550–1870* (Edinburgh, 1984).

Simpson, *Land Law* – Simpson, A. W. B., *An Introduction to the History of the Land Law*, 2nd ed. (Oxford, 1986).

Skene, W. F., *Memorials of the Family of Skene of Skene* (New Spalding Club, 1887).

Smith, T. B., *A Short Commentary on the Law of Scotland* (Edinburgh, 1962).

Stenton, *English Justice* – Stenton, D. M., *English Justice between the Norman Conquest and the Great Charter 1066–1215* (London, 1965).

Stenton, *English Feudalism* – Stenton, F. M., *The First Century of English Feudalism 1066–1166*, 2nd ed. (Oxford, 1961).

Stenton, F. M., *Anglo-Saxon England*, 3rd ed. (Oxford, 1971).

Stringer, *Earl David* – Stringer, K. J., *Earl David of Huntingdon 1151–1219: A Study in Anglo-Scottish History* (Edinburgh, 1985).

Sutherland, *Novel Disseisin* – Sutherland, D. W., *The Assize of Novel Disseisin* (Oxford, 1973).

Tabuteau, E. Z., *Transfers of Property in Eleventh-Century Norman Law* (Chapel Hill, North Carolina, 1988).

Thomson, J. M., *The Public Records of Scotland* (Glasgow, 1922).

van Caenegem, *Birth* – van Caenegem, R. C, *The Birth of the English Common Law*, 2nd ed. (Cambridge, 1989).

Vaughan, R., *Matthew Paris* (Cambridge, 1958).

Walker, *Legal History* – Walker, D. M., *A Legal History of Scotland* (Edinburgh, 1988 to date).

Warren, W. L., *The Governance of Norman and Angevin England 1086–1272* (London, 1987).

Watson, A., *Legal Transplants* (Edinburgh, 1974).

Watson, A., *The Evolution of Law* (Edinburgh, 1985).

Watson, A., *Slave Law in the Americas* (Athens, Georgia, 1989).

Watson, W. J., *The History of the Celtic Place-Names of Scotland* (Edinburgh, 1926).

White, S. D., *Custom, Kinship and Gifts to Saints: The Laudatio Parentum in Western France 1050–1150* (Chapel Hill, North Carolina, 1988).

Willock, *Jury* – Willock, I. D., *The Origins and Development of the Jury in Scotland* (Stair Society, 1966).

Wormald, J. M., *Court, Kirk and Community: Scotland 1470–1625* (London, 1981).

Wormald, J. M., *Lords and Men in Scotland: Bonds of Manrent 1442–1603* (Edinburgh, 1985).

(c) *Periodical and other articles*

Abbreviations: *AJLH – American Journal of Legal History*
EHR – *English Historical Review*
JLH – *Journal of Legal History*
JR – *Juridical Review*
LHR – *Law and History Review*
LQR – *Law Quarterly Review*
SHR – *Scottish Historical Review*
TvR – *Tijdschrift voor Rechtsgeschedienis*
TRHS – *Transactions of the Royal Historical Society*

Ash, M., 'The Church in the reign of Alexander III', in *Scotland in the Reign of Alexander III*, ed. N. H. Reid (Edinburgh, 1990).

Bailey, S. J., 'Warranties of land in the reign of Richard I', *Cambridge Law Journal*, ix (1945–7) p. 192.

Baird Smith, D., 'A note on *juramentum calumniae*', *JR* li (1939), p. 7.

Bannerman, J. M. W., 'The Scots language and the kin-based society', in *Gaelic and Scots in Harmony: Proceedings of the Second International Conference on the Languages of Scotland*, ed. D. S. Thomson (Glasgow, 1990).

Bannerman, J. M. W., 'Macduff of Fife', in *Medieval Scotland: Crown, Lordship and Community*, ed. A. Grant and K. J. Stringer Edinburgh, 1992).

Barrow, G. W. S., "The reign of William the Lion king of Scots', *Historical Studies*, vii (Dublin, 1969), p. 19.

Barrow, G. W. S., 'The pattern of lordship and the feudal settlement in medieval Cumbria', *Journal of Medieval History*, i (1975), p. 1.

Barrow, G. W. S., 'The aftermath of war: Scotland and England in the late thirteenth and early fourteenth centuries', *TRHS*, xxviii (1978), p. 103.

Barrow, G. W. S., 'Popular courts in early medieval Scotland: some suggested place-name evidence', *Scottish Studies*, xxv (1981), p. 1.

Barrow, G. W. S., 'The early Scots charter', in *Studies in Medieval History presented to R. H C. Davis*, ed. H. Mayr-Harting and R. I. Moore (London, 1985).

Barrow, G. W. S., 'Badenoch and Strathspey, 1130–1312', *Northern Scotland* viii (1988,), p. 1.

Bates, D., 'The earliest Norman writs', *EHR*, c (1985), p. 266.

Bates, D., 'Normandy and England after 1066', *EHR* civ (1989), p. 851.

Biancalana, 'Want of justice' – Biancalana, J., 'For want of justice: legal reforms of Henry II', *Columbia Law Review* lxxxviii (1988), p. 433.

Black, R., 'A historical survey of delictual liability in Scotland for personal injuries and death', *Comparative and International Law Journal of Southern Africa*, viii (1975), p. 53.

Brand, P. A., 'Formedon in the remainder before *De Donis*', *Irish Jurist*, x (1975), p. 318.

Brand, P. A., Review I, *Irish Jurist* x (1975), p. 363.

Brand, P. A., '*Hengham Magna*: a thirteenth-century English common law treatise and its composition', *Irish Jurist*, xi (1976), p. 147.

Brand, P. A., 'Ireland and the literature of the early common law', *Irish Jurist*, xvi (1981), p. 95.

Brand, P. A., 'The origins of the English legal profession', *LHR*, v (1987), p. 31.

Brand, P. A., Review II, *LHR*, vi (1988), p. 197.

Brand, 'Henry II' – Brand, P. A., '*Multis invigilis excogitatam et inventam:* Henry II and the creation of the English common law', *Journal of the Haskins Society*, i (1990), p. 197.

Brand, 'Lordship and distraint' – Brand, P. A., 'Lordship and distraint in thirteenth-century England', *Thirteenth-Century England*, iii (1991), p. 1.

Brown, A. L., 'The Scottish "establishment" in the later fifteenth century', *JR*, xxiii (1978), p. 89.

Brown, E. A. R., 'The tyranny of a construct: feudalism and the historians of medieval Europe', *American Historical Review*, lxxix (1974), p. 1063.

Brown, J. M. (now Wormald), 'The exercise of power', in *Scottish Society in the Fifteenth Century*, ed. J. M. Brown (London, 1977).

Brundage, J. A., 'Legal aid for the poor and the professionalization of the law in the Middle Ages', *JLH*, ix (1988), p. 169.

Cairns, J. W., 'Craig, Cujas and the definition of a *feudum:* is a feu a usufruct?', in *New Perspectives in the Roman Law of Property*, ed. P. Birks (Oxford, 1989).

Cam, H. M., 'An East Anglian shire-moot of Stephen's reign', *EHR*, xxxix (1924), 570.

Chandler, V., 'Ada de Warenne, queen mother of Scotland (c.1123–1178)', *SHR*, lx(1981), p. 119.

Cheney, M., 'The litigation between John Marshal and Archbishop Thomas Becket in 1164: a pointer to the origins of novel disseisin?', in *Law and Social Change in British History* ed. J. A. Guy and H. G. Beale (Royal Historical Society, 1984).

Cheney, M., 'A decree of Henry II on defect of justice', in *Tradition and Change*, ed. D. Greenway et al. (Cambridge, 1985).

Cheney, M., 'Inalienability in mid-twelfth century England', *Proceedings of the Sixth International Congress of Medieval Canon Law 1980: Monumenta Iuris Canonici Series C* (Vatican, 1985), vii, p. 467.

Clanchy, M. T., 'Magna Carta, clause thirty-four', *EHR*, lxxix (1964), p. 542.

Clanchy, M. T., 'Law and love in the Middle Ages', in *Disputes and Settlements*, ed. J. Bossy (Cambridge, 1983).

Clancy, M. P., 'A further note on *juramentum calumniae*', *JR*, xxxi (1986), p. 170.

Cooper, T. M. (Lord), 'Freehold in Scots law', *JR*, lvii (1945), p. 1.

Crawford, B. E., 'The earldom of Caithness and the kingdom of Scotland 1150–1266', in *Nobility Essays*.

Dickinson, W. C., 'Freehold in Scots law', *JR*, lvii (1945), p. 135

Dickinson, W. C., '"Our Signet of the Unicorn"', *SHR*, xxvi (1947), p. 147.

Dickinson, W. C., 'The acts of the parliament at Perth 6 March 1429/30', *SHR*, xxix (1950), p. 1.

Dickinson, 'Administration of justice' – Dickinson, W. C, 'The administration of justice in medieval Scotland', *Aberdeen University Review*, xxxiv (1951–2), p. 338.

Dickinson, W. C., 'The High Court of Justiciary', in *ISLH*.

Donaldson, G., 'The legal profession in Scottish society in the sixteenth and seventeenth centuries', *JR*, xxi (1976), p. 1.

Donaldson, G., 'Problems of sovereignty and law in Orkney and Shetland', in *Stair Misc*, ii.

Donaldson, G., 'Early Scottish conveyancing', supplementary to *Formulary of Old Scots Legal Documents*, ed. P. Gouldesbrough (Stair Society, 1985).

Duncan, A. A. M., 'Councils general 1404–1423', *SHR*, xxxv (1956), p. 132.

Duncan, A. A. M., 'An interim list of the heads of some Scottish monastic houses before c.1300', *The Bibliotheck*, ii (1959), p. 4.

Duncan, 'Central courts' – Duncan, A. A. M., 'The central courts before 1532', in *ISLH*.

Duncan, A. A. M., '*Regiam Majestatem:* a reconsideration', *JR*, vi (1961), p. 199.

Duncan, A. A. M., 'The Laws of Malcolm MacKenneth', in *Medieval Scotland: Crown, Lordship and Community*, ed. A. Grant and K. J. Stringer (Edinburgh, 1993).

Duncan, A. A. M., and Dunbar, J. G., 'Tarbert castle', *SHR*, p. i (1971), p. 1.

Durkan, J., 'The early Scottish notary', in *The Renaissance and Reformation in Scotland*, ed. I. B. Cowan and D. Shaw (Edinburgh, 1983).

Edwards, J., 'The Templars in Scotland', *SHR*, v (1908), p. 13.

Flett, I., and Cripps, J., 'Documentary sources', in *The Scottish Medieval Town*, ed. M. Lynch et al. (Edinburgh, 1988).

Forte, A. D. M., 'The horse that kills', *TvR*, lviii (1990), p. 95.

Gane, C. H. W., 'The effect of a pardon in Scots *law*', *JR*, xxv (1980), p. 18.

Grant, A., 'Extinction of direct male lines among Scottish noble families in the fourteenth and fifteenth centuries', in *Nobility Essays*.

Grant, A., 'Crown and nobility in late medieval Britain', in *Scotland and England 1286–1815*, ed. R. Mason (Edinburgh, 1987).

Grant, A., 'Scotland's "Celtic fringe" in the late Middle Ages: the Macdonald Lords of the Isles and the kingdom of Scotland', in *The British Isles 1100–1500*, ed. R. R. Davies (Edinburgh, 1988).

Grant, A., 'The Wolf of Badenoch', in *Moray: Province and People*, ed. W. D. H. Sellar (Scottish Society for Northern Studies, 1993).

Gretton, G. L., 'The feudal system', *Stair Memorial Encyclopedia of the Laws of Scotland*, vol. 18, 1993, paras 41–113.

Hackney, J., Review, *JLH*, v (1984), p. 79.

Hall, G. D. G., 'The early history of entry *sur disseisin*', *Tulane Law Review*, xlii (1968), p. 584.

Hamilton Grierson, P. J., 'Falsing the doom', *SHR*, xxiv (1927), p. 1.

Hannay, R. K., 'A fifteenth-century eviction', *SHR*, xxii (1925), p. 193.

Harding, A., 'The medieval brieves of protection and the development of the common law', *JR*, xi (1966), p. 115.

Harding, A., '*Regiam Majestatem* amongst medieval law books', *JR*, xxix (1984), p. 97.

Henderson, E. G., 'Legal rights to land in the early chancery', *AJLH*, xxvi (1982), p. 97.

Holt, J. C., 'Politics and property in early medieval England', *Past and Present*, no 57 (1972), p. 3.

Holt, J. C., 'Feudal society and the family in early medieval England I: the revolution of 1066', *TRHS*, xxxii (1982), p. 193.

Holt, J. C., 'Feudal society and the family in early medieval England II: notions of patrimony' *TRHS*, xxxiii (1983), p. 193.

Holt, J. C., 'Feudal society and the family in early medieval England III: patronage and polities', *TRHS*, xxxiv (1984), p. 1.

Holt, J. C., 'Feudal society and the family in early medieval England IV: the heiress and the alien', *TRHS*, xxxv (1985), p. 1.

Holt, J. C., 'Magna Carta 1215–1217: the legal and social context', in *Law in Medieval Life and Thought*, ed. E. B. King and S. Ridyard (Press of the University of The South, USA, 1990).

Hudson, J., 'Life grants of land and the development of inheritance in Anglo-Norman England', *Anglo-Norman Studies*, xii (1989), p. 67.

Hudson, 'Milsom's legal structure' – Hudson, J., 'Milsom's legal structure: interpreting twelfth-century law', *TvR*, lix (1991), p. 47.

Hurnard, N. D., 'Magna Carta, clause 34', in *Studies in Medieval History presented to F. M. Powicke*, ed. R. W. Hunt, W. A. Pantin and R. W. Southern (Oxford, 1948).

Hyams, P. R., Review, *EHR*, xciii (1978), p. 856.

Hyams, P. R., 'The common law and the French connection', *Anglo-Norman Studies*, iv(1981), p. 77.

Hyams, P. R., 'Henry II and Ganelon', *Syracuse Scholar*, iv (1983), p. 24.

Hyams, P. R., '"No register of title": the Domesday inquest and land adjudication', *Anglo-Norman Studies*, ix (1986), p. 127.

Hyams, P. R., 'The charter as a source for the early common law', *JLH*, xii (1991), p. 173.

Hyams, 'Warranty' – Hyams, P. R., 'Warranty and good lordship in twelfth-century England', *LHR* (1987), p. v.

Hyams, P. R., and Brand, P. A., 'Seigneurial control of women's marriage', *Past and Present*, ic (1983), p. 124.

Irvine Smith, J., 'Criminal law', in *ISLH*.

King, E., 'The Anarchy of Stephen's reign', *TRHS*, xxxiv (1984), p. 133.

Loengard, J. S., 'The assize of nuisance: origins of an action at common law', *Cambridge Law Journal*, xxxvii (1978), p. 144.

Lyall, R. J., 'Scottish students and masters at the universities of Cologne and Louvain in the fifteenth century', *Innes Review*, xxxvi (1985), p. 55.

Lyall, R. J., 'Vernacular prose before the Reformation', in *The History of Scottish Literature: Origins to 1660*, ed. R. D. S. Jack (Aberdeen, 1988).

Lyall, R. J., 'Books and book owners in fifteenth-century Scotland', in *Book Production and Publishing in Britain 1375–1475*, ed. J. Griffiths and D. Pearsall (Cambridge, 1989).

MacQueen, H. L., 'Dissasine and mortancestor in Scots law', *JLH*, iv (1983), p. 21.

MacQueen, 'Jurisdiction in heritage' – MacQueen, H. L., 'Jurisdiction in heritage and the Lords of Council and Session after 1532', in *Stair Misc*, ii.

MacQueen, H. L., 'Pleadable brieves, pleading and the development of Scots law', *LHR* iv (1986), p. 403.

MacQueen, 'Alexander III' – MacQueen, H. L., 'Scots law under Alexander III', in *Scotland in the Reign of Alexander III*, ed. N. H. Reid (Edinburgh, 1990).

MacQueen, 'Laws of Galloway' – MacQueen, H. L., 'The laws of Galloway: a preliminary survey', in *Galloway: Land and Lordship*, ed. G. Stell and R. Oram (Scottish Society for Northern Studies, 1991).

MacQueen, H. L., 'Kin of Kennedy' – MacQueen, H. L., 'The kin of Kennedy, kenkynnol and the common law', in *Medieval Scotland: Crown, Lordship and Community*, ed. A. Grant and K. J. Stringer (Edinburgh, 1993).

MacQueen, H. L., '*Glanvill* resarcinate: Sir John Skene and *Regiam Majestatem*', in *The Renaissance in Scotland*, ed. A. A. MacDonald *et al.* (Leiden, 1994).

MacQueen and Borthwick, 'Cases' – MacQueen, H. L., and Borthwick, A. R., 'Three fifteenth-century cases', *JR*, xxxi (1986) pp. 123–51.

MacQueen and Windram, 'Burghs' – MacQueen, H. L., and Windram, W. J., 'Laws and courts in the burghs', in *The Scottish Medieval Town*, ed. M. Lynch et al. (Edinburgh, 1988).

McNeill, P. G. B., '*Discours Particulier d'Escosse* 1559/60', in *Stair Misc* ii.

Madden, C, 'Royal treatment of feudal casualties in late medieval Scotland', *SHR*, lv (1976), p. 172.

Maitland, F. W., 'History of the Register of Original Writs', *Harvard Law Review, in* (1889–90).

Maxtone-Graham, R. M., 'Showing the holding', *JR*, ii (1957), p. 251.

Milne, I. A., 'Heritable rights: the early feudal tenures', in *ISLH*.

Monteath, H. H., Heritable rights', in *ISLH*.

Mortimer, R., 'Land and service: the tenants of the Honour of Clare', *Anglo-Norman Studies*, viii (1985), p. 177.

Murray, A. L., 'The lord clerk register', *SHR*, liii (1974), p. 124.

Murray, A. L., 'Sinclair's practicks', in *Lawmaking and Lawmakers in British History*, ed. A. Harding (Royal Historical Society, 1980).

Nicholson, 'Feudal developments' – Nicholson, R., 'Feudal developments in late medieval Scotland', *JR*, xviii (1973), p. 1.

Palmer, 'Feudal framework' – Palmer, R. C., 'The feudal framework of English law', *Michigan Law Review*, lxxix (1981), p. 1130.

Palmer, 'Origins of property' – Palmer, R. C., 'The origins of property in England', *LHR*, iii (1985), p. 1.

Palmer, R. C., 'The economic and cultural impact of the origins of property: 1180–1220', *LHR*, iii (1985), p. 375.

Post, J. B., 'Courts, councils and arbitrators in the Ladbroke manor dispute', in *Medieval Legal Records in Memory of C. A. F. Meekings*, ed. R. F. Hunnisett and J. B. Post (London, 1978).

Postles, D., 'Securing the gift in Oxfordshire charters in the twelfth and early thirteenth centuries', *Archives*, lxxxiv (1990), p. 1.

Postles, D., 'Gifts in frankalmoign, warranty of land, and feudal society', *Cambridge Law Journal*, 1 (1991), p. 330.

Powell, E., 'Arbitration and the law in England in the later Middle Ages', *TRHS*, xxxiii (1983), p. 49.

Powell, E., 'Settlement of disputes by arbitration in fifteenth-century England', *LHR*, ii(1984), p. 21.

Rawcliffe, C., 'The great lord as peacekeeper: arbitration by English noblemen and their councils in the later middle ages', in *Law and Social Change in British History*, ed. J. A. Guy and H. G. Beale (Royal Historical Society, 1984).

Reid, 'Coschogill writ' – Reid, R. C., 'An early Coschogill writ', *Transactions of the Dumfriesshire and Galloway Natural History and Antiquarian Society*, xxx (1951–2), p. 132.

Robertson, J. J., '*De Composicione Cartarum*', in *Stair Misc*, i.

Round, J. H., 'The date of the Grand Assize', *EHR*, xxxi (1916), p. 268.

Russell, M. J., 'Trial by battle and the writ of right', *JLH*, i (1980), p. 111.

Seipp, D. J., '*Bracton*, the Year Books, and the "transformation of elementary legal ideas" in the early common law', *LHR*, vii (1989), p. 175.

Sellar, 'Courtesy' – Sellar, W. D. H., 'Courtesy, battle and the brieve of right 1368 – a story continued', in *Stair Misc*, ii.

Sellar, W. D. H., 'Spens family heraldry', *Notes and Queries of the Society of West Highland and Island Historical Research*, xxii (1983), p. 21.

Sellar, W. D. H., Review, *SHR*, lxvi (1987), p. 200.

Sellar, 'Common law' – Sellar, W. D. H., 'The common law of Scotland and the common law of England', in *The British Isles 1100–1500*, ed. R. R. Davies (Edinburgh, 1988).

Sellar, 'Celtic law' – Sellar, W. D. H., 'Celtic law and Scots law: survival and integration', *Scottish Studies*, xxix (1989), p. 1.

Sellar, W. D. H., 'Forethocht felony, malice aforethought and the classification of homicide', in *Legal History in the Making*, ed. W. M. Gordon and T. D. Fergus (London and Ronceverte, 1991).

Smith, L. B., 'The Statute of Wales 1284', *Welsh History Review*, x (1980–81) p. 127.

Stein, 'Roman law' – Stein, P. G., 'Roman law in Scotland', *Ius Romanum Medii Aevi*, paras v, 13b (Milan, 1968).

Stein, P. G., 'The source of the Romano-canonical part of *Regiam Majestatem*', *SHR*, xlviii (1969), p. 107.

Stevenson, W., 'The monastic presence in Scottish burghs in the twelfth and thirteenth centuries', *SHR*, lx (1981), p. 97.

Stoddart, C. N., 'A short history of legal aid in Scotland', *JR*, xxiv (1979), p. 170.

Strayer, J. R., 'The writ of novel disseisin in Normandy at the end of the thirteenth century', in *Medieval Statecraft and the Perspectives of History* (Princeton, 1971).

Stringer, K. J., 'The charters of David, earl of Huntingdon and lord of Garioch: a study in Anglo-Scottish diplomatic', in *Nobility Essays*.

Stringer, K. J., 'Periphery and core in thirteenth-century Scotland: Alan son of Roland, Lord of Galloway and Constable of Scotland', in *Medieval Scotland: Crown, Lordship and Community*, ed. A. Grant and K. J. Stringer (Edinburgh, 1993).

Thomson, J. M., 'A roll of the Scottish parliament 13445, *SHR*, ix (1912), p. 235.

Thorne, S. E., 'Livery of seisin', *LQR*, lii (1936), p. 345.

Thorne, S. E., 'English feudalism and estates in land', *Cambridge Law Journal*, xvii (1959), p. 193.

van Caenegem, R. C, 'Methods of proof in Western medieval law', in *Legal History: A European Perspective* (London, 1991).

Watson, A., 'Legal change: sources of law and legal culture', *University of Pennsylvania Law Review*, cxxxi (1983) p. 1121.

Watson, A., 'The evolution of law: continued', *LHR*, v (1987), p. 537.

Watt, D. E. R., 'Scottish university men in the thirteenth and fourteenth centuries', in *Scotland and Europe 1200–1850*, ed. T. C. Smout (Edinburgh, 1986).

Webster, B., 'David II and the government of fourteenth-century Scotland', *TRHS*, xvi (1966), p. 115.

White, 'Inheritances' – White, S. D., 'Inheritances and legal arguments in western France, 1050–1150', *Traditio*, xliii (1987), p. 55.

Windram, W. J., 'What is the *Liber de Judicibus*?', *JLH*, v (1984), p. 176.

Wormald, J. M., 'Bloodfeud, kindred and government in early modern Scotland', *Past and Present*, no 87 (1980), p. 54.

Wormald, J. M., 'Taming the magnates?', in *Nobility Essays*.

Wormald, J. M., 'The Sandlaw dispute', in *The Settlement of Disputes in Early Medieval Europe*, ed. W. Davies and P. Fouracre (Cambridge, 1986).

Yver, J., 'Le bref Anglo-Normand', *TvR*, xxix (1961), p. 313.

(*d*) *Pamphlets*

Duncan, A. A. M., *James I King of Scots 1424–1437*, 2nd ed. (University of Glasgow, Scottish History Department Occasional Papers, 1984).

McKechnie, *Brieves* – McKechnie, H., *Judicial Process upon Brieves 1219–1532*, 23rd David Murray Lecture (Glasgow, 1956).

(*e*) *Theses*

Borthwick, A. R., 'The king, council and councillors in Scotland, c. 1430–1460' (Edinburgh, 1989).

Chalmers, T. M., 'The king's council, patronage and the governance of Scotland 1460–1513' (Aberdeen, 1982).

Fergus, T. D. ,'Quoniam Attachiamenta' (Glasgow, 1988).

Grant, A., 'The higher nobility in Scotland and their estates c. 1371–1424' (Oxford, 1975).

MacQueen, H. L., 'Pleadable brieves and jurisdiction in heritage in later medieval Scotland' (Edinburgh, 1985).

O'Brien, I. E. 'The Scottish parliament in the fifteenth and sixteenth centuries' (Glasgow, 1980).

Index of Persons

Index of Places

Index of Subjects

EU Authorised Representative: Easy Access System Europe Mustamäe tee 5

0, 10621 Tallinn, Estonia gpsr.requests@easproject.com

Printed and bound by CPI Group (UK) Ltd, Croydon, CR0 4YY

05/05/2025

01860497-0001